... morning. Finally
...en we were back at th...
...e if I had dreamed ... ...able
...told him I had ... and ... asked me if
...ere good or bad, I said ... bad.
Was it about the Happy Hunting. I'
He grunted, we were all a little
...also that Miss Mary had seen the
...goni ... and no one else had seen
...the exact place of the other
...t, also it had not looked like
... place of the other hunt and I ha...
...r seen the big tree at all. But
...i had picked up one of my solids.
...ds were scarce and very valuable
... were your only protection when
...e out with the light rifle.
...ther Ngui nor I made a practice
...pping them ...

UNDER KILIMANJARO

Under Kilimanjaro

By ERNEST HEMINGWAY

Edited by Robert W. Lewis and Robert E. Fleming

The Kent State University Press ⊠ Kent, Ohio

Map and drawings by Nina Smart.

© 2005 by The Ernest Hemingway Foundation
ALL RIGHTS RESERVED
Library of Congress Cataloging-in-Publication Number 2005006235
ISBN-10: 0-87338-845-3
ISBN-13: 978-0-87338-845-0
Manufactured in the United States of America

10 09 08 07 06 05   5 4 3 2 1

LIBRARY OF CONGRESS CATALOGING-IN-PUBLICATION DATA
Hemingway, Ernest, 1899–1961.
Under Kilimanjaro / by Ernest Hemingway ;
edited by Robert W. Lewis and Robert E. Fleming.
p. cm.
Includes bibliographical references.
ISBN-13: 978-0-87338-845-0 (alk. paper)
ISBN-10: 0-87338-845-3 (alk. paper)
1. Americans—Kenya—Kilimanjaro, Mount, Region—Fiction.
2. Kilimanjaro, Mount, Region (Kenya)—Fiction.
3. Americans—Africa—Fiction.   4. Big game hunting—Fiction.
5. Safaris—Fiction.   6. Africa—Fiction.
I. Lewis, Robert W. (Robert William), 1930–
II. Fleming, Robert E. (Robert Edward), 1936–   III. Title.
PS3515.E37U53 2005
813'.52—dc22
2005006235

CONTENTS

Lake Rudolf

ITALIAN
SOMALILAND

KENYA

Lake Victoria

Chisimaio

Nairobi

Mt. Kilimanjaro

Moshi

Mombasa

TANGANYIKA

ZANZIBAR

Dar es Salaam

INDIAN
OCEAN

INTRODUCTION

On January 23 and 24, 1954, Ernest Hemingway's dream safari ended in the nightmare of two plane crashes. With his wife Mary, Hemingway had hoped to recreate the joyous experiences of the 1933–34 safari chronicled in *Green Hills of Africa* (1935), a two-month sojourn that also resulted in two of his best stories, "The Short Happy Life of Francis Macomber" and "The Snows of Kilimanjaro." But a crash during their aircraft tour of the Belgian Congo and Uganda, intended as a Christmas gift to Mary, left the Hemingways and their pilot, Roy Marsh, aground near Murchison Falls. Rescued from their makeshift camp near the falls, the Hemingways were taken by boat to Butiaba, Uganda, where they suffered a second major accident when their plane bound for Entebbe crashed on takeoff. Newspapers worldwide carried their obituaries on January 25. While these dramatic notices were premature, the second mishap left Ernest in very bad shape from a concussion and internal injuries. His immediate response to the crashes was a wry and chatty two-part report published in *Look* magazine just three months after the incident. But after he returned to Cuba, Hemingway began to write about the safari itself.

From late October 1954 to the spring of 1956, Hemingway worked hard on a book that was distinctly different from anything he had written before. As he had done with the narrative of his earlier safari, he embroidered some events imaginatively, but the manuscript of *Under Kilimanjaro* differed radically from *Green Hills of Africa* in the voice of the narrator and the nature of his persona as well as in his attitudes toward Africans, big-game hunting, and many other topics. *Green Hills of Africa* was written when Hemingway was still relatively young (in his midthirties) and still fighting to keep the literary reputation he had won during the previous decade. *Under Kilimanjaro*, however, was written by a master who had just experienced two major triumphs, the overwhelmingly positive reception of *The Old Man and the*

Sea (1952) and the award of the Nobel Prize for Literature (1954). The result is a lively, good-humored book in which the author Hemingway is completely comfortable depicting his persona with self-deprecating humor. In place of the always-supportive Poor Old Mama, the *Green Hills of Africa* character based on Pauline Pfeiffer Hemingway, Ernest's second wife, *Under Kilimanjaro* features Mary Welsh Hemingway, his fourth wife, who feels no hesitation in puncturing the ego of her husband. Hemingway always complained that he was not given sufficient credit for his humorous writing. In this remarkable book, he shows his talent as a humorist in this most lighthearted yet unconventionally serious book. As had been said about another Nobel Prize winner, George Bernard Shaw, Hemingway fused "high seriousness with comedy." Anticipating the tensions of racism, feminism, and the Cold War, Hemingway here neither explains nor argues. He narrates, showing rather than telling, and in so doing once more demonstrates the superiority of narrative to exposition.

Hemingway's progress on the book was rapid and steady. Working at his usual disciplined pace of two pages per day, on January 16, 1955, he recorded the date in the margin of page 186 of his manuscript. By December 29 of that year, he was on page 748. He last noted a date on page 843, February 27, 1956. He then set aside the long manuscript.

In his later years, Hemingway sometimes referred to the manuscripts he had deposited in his Cuban safe-deposit box as his "life insurance," the implication being that his widow, Mary Hemingway, would merely have to take them to Scribner's for publication and profit. As scholars who have worked with the manuscripts of *A Moveable Feast, Islands in the Stream,* and *The Garden of Eden* know, such was not the case. "The African book," as Hemingway informally referred to this manuscript in his letters, is 850 pages of part-handwritten, part-typed text, much of it heavily edited in Hemingway's hand. It contains some marginal notes (to himself) to rewrite some passages, expand others, check facts, and resolve linguistic problems associated with his use of Swahili, Kamba, and Masai words. Finally, the narrative remains inconclusive: we cannot know what Hemingway might have added, subtracted, or revised or how he might have titled the book. Its last paragraph ends with an incomplete sentence.

Lacking conclusive directions from Hemingway to his publishers, editors, or heirs as to his intentions or desires concerning his unpublished writing (apart from his letters, which he did not want published), his heirs faced a range of options. Knowing of his care and devotion to his writing craft, some critics and fellow artists argue that without Hemingway's explicit approval, no work of his should be posthumously published. Mixed or negative reviews of such work might seem to offer proof of that belief.

Yet given Hemingway's implicit approval of this manuscript as his legacy and given the work's considerable and original merit and the uncontestable value of the author's previous work, we believe that this book deserves as complete and faithful a publication as possible without editorial distortion, speculation, or textually unsupported attempts at improvement.

Our intent has been to produce a complete reading text of Ernest Hemingway's manuscript based on his second East African safari (1953–54), a text that contains as few distracting elements as possible. In so doing, we have avoided footnotes but have attached appendixes to identify the principal characters, define some possibly unfamiliar words, reproduce significant marginalia, and explain changes to Hemingway's manuscript that went beyond mere copy editors' corrections of spelling, grammar, and punctuation. The resulting text is more complete than the previously published versions of this work: three excerpts edited by Ray Cave and printed as "African Journal" in *Sports Illustrated* (1971–72) and Patrick Hemingway's abridged version of the work published as *True at First Light* (1999). *Under Kilimanjaro* is as close as we could come to what we think its author might have hoped to publish. Working on it was both a great privilege and a grave responsibility.

We were guided in our editing of the text by two principles. First, although Hemingway often strenuously objected to substantive changes by editors, he obviously expected and relied on copy editors to correct errors in spelling, punctuation, grammar, and factual errors of quotations or geography and the like. We addressed all such matters, but regarding Hemingway's marginal notes, we were extremely conservative. Where it was necessary to make substantive corrections, we used the example of a fine edition whose editors faced some of the same problems we did (a deceased author and a manuscript that contained certain inconsistencies): Harrison Hayford and Merton M. Sealts Jr.'s edition of Herman Melville's *Billy Budd, Sailor* (1962). Adapting Hayford and Sealts's principles in light of our own problems, we arrived at the following standards:

- We excluded from the text (though we reproduced them in appendixes) all substantive marginal notes and queries.
- We supplied chapter numbers. (Hemingway simply noted chapter breaks with the heading "new chapter.")
- We corrected minor errors such as repetitions and missing words. When Hemingway left blanks to be filled in later, we filled them in when we were able to do so with some certainty. For example, he mentions using a recently published book on African birds, and we identified one published in 1952. (Patrick Hemingway came to the

same conclusion in his edition.) In a few cases Hemingway left blanks that we were unable to fill. If we were not able to do so by consulting other sources, such as Mary Hemingway's autobiography *How It Was* (1976), Patrick Hemingway's edition *True at First Light*, or sources such as the *Rough Guide to Kenya*, we simply retained the spaces rather than speculate on what Hemingway might have added if he had been able to check the facts.

- We corrected a few quotations.
- We occasionally supplied an omitted word when it was necessary for the sense of a sentence.

  If a correction was clearly intended, we followed Hemingway's direction. For example, he frequently deleted single words or phrases by overtyping or by crossing out in pencil. On two occasions large blocks of text are crossed out with a large X. We omitted such passages but included them in an appendix. If no correction was marked, although one might have been contemplated, however, we reproduced the text as Hemingway left it. For example, there are two versions of a conversation between the Hemingway persona and his headman Keiti concerning Hemingway's relationship with the Kamba girl Debba. Separated by roughly twenty-five pages, the two passages cover the same ground and employ some of the same language. Hemingway would possibly have canceled one passage, but without knowing which, we have left both intact, choosing to err on the side of conservative editing.

- We declined to speculate on how Hemingway might have revised and concluded the book. In *True at First Light* Patrick Hemingway omitted passages from and shortened the last chapter to end the book conveniently at the end of a safari day. Unlike other editors of Hemingway's posthumously published works, Patrick wisely did not claim to know how his father might have changed or edited the manuscript. Had the book been published as "African Journal," as the three excerpts in *Sports Illustrated* were titled (though not by Hemingway), one might have expected it to encompass the whole of Hemingway's African sojourn. But such was not the range of his earlier book on Africa, which also begins in medias res and concludes before the actual safari ended.

Hemingway introduced *Green Hills of Africa* with the statement that he had "attempted to write an absolutely true book to see whether the shape of a country and the pattern of a month's action can, if truly presented, compete with a work of the imagination." Much the same might be said of *Under Kilimanjaro.* In dealing with his experience during late 1953 and early 1954, Hemingway, as he had done in the 1930s, based his narrative for the most part on actual events, as Mary Hemingway testified to in her autobiography. But as in his earlier "true" book, Hemingway also introduced fictional elements to improve and shape the story of day-to-day life in Africa into a pastoral romance recalling that of Virgil's *Georgics,* which both Mary and Ernest were reading in C. Day Lewis's translation (Chapter 19). Another similarity to *Green Hills of Africa* is the author's tendency to digress from his narrative to interesting asides set in Europe and America (a strategy also reminiscent of *Death in the Afternoon* and "The Snows of Kilimanjaro").

As he had done in *Green Hills of Africa,* Hemingway subtly formed his story. In spite of the title Ray Cave supplied for the *Sports Illustrated* segments of the work, *Under Kilimanjaro* is no more a mere journal covering a leisurely African safari than Henry David Thoreau's *A Week on the Concord and Merrimack Rivers* is a boating story. *Green Hills of Africa* had been shaped by a "plot" treating the competitive hunting of big game by two men (one of whom is unaware that he is in a competition). And in spite of the fact that it was left suspended and set aside, *Under Kilimanjaro* is a rounded narrative about two hunting stories, a half-serious December–May romance of the narrator and a young Wakamba woman, and a chronicling of the daily doings of a safari camp, often enhanced by humorous dialogue and by a sense of two impending disasters. The narrative is certainly based on actual people, places, and events (as confirmed by wife Mary and son Patrick Hemingway, who were also present for, if not always witness to, the events Ernest eventually related in the account that biographer Carlos Baker described as "slightly fictionized").

The central hunting stories are less complicated than the "pursuits" that unify *Green Hills of Africa.* Two hunters, not in competition in the later book, are determined to kill certain animals, each for reasons of his or her own. Mary Hemingway is in search of one particular great lion that she had failed to kill before the beginning of the narrative. Challenged by her height, which makes it impossible for her to see over the tall vegetation, and by her erratic marksmanship, Mary is alternately depressed and excited as her chances to kill her lion come and go without success. Hemingway faces a different challenge. Earl Theisen, a photographer for *Look* magazine, had photographed him with a dead leopard that was not his to claim. (Although he helped to kill the animal, it had been first hit by Hemingway's Cuban friend Mayito Menocal. By the rules of the hunt, the game belonged to the first hunter to wound it.) Now, to retain his self-respect and also to rid the region of a leopard that has been raiding the Africans' livestock, Hemingway must actually kill this leopard himself before the photo appears in January 1954. Both hunters are successful, concluding two of the chief subplots that drive the action of the book.

The first of two sources of tension that cast a shadow over the pastoral narrative is the danger posed by the Mau Mau uprisings that troubled Kenya during the 1950s. The Mau Mau was a secret society of Africans (largely Kikuyus) whose goal was to expel white colonizers from Kenya. Beginning in 1952 the movement rebelled against whites and black Africans who supported the colonial government. When the Hemingway safari began on September 1, 1953, there was still danger of attacks by the Mau Mau. Hemingway highlighted this theme by beginning his narrative in medias res, plunging into a discussion between Hemingway and his headman about a possible attack by a group of Mau Mau who have recently escaped from government custody. While the Mau Mau are never far from the minds of the Hemingways, and the camp is kept in a state of readiness, no attack materializes.

A second source of tension emerges toward the end of the manuscript as the danger from the Mau Mau diminishes. As her Christmas gift, Mary proposes a flight to the Belgian Congo in a light aircraft, a flight that Hemingway opposes. The topic is anticipated earlier in brief discussions of low-level flying and Hemingway's observation that he and Willie, their pilot, have led Mary to underestimate the danger of flying "on the deck," as one does on a sightseeing flight. Because the Hemingways' two crashes in Uganda in January 1954 had been world news, and because Hemingway had quickly written and published "The Christmas Gift" in *Look* magazine in the three months that followed the crashes, by the time he began to write his African narrative, readers could be expected to sense that Hemingway's reservations about the trip represent an ominous note—the underwater portion of the iceberg that he always felt was essential to his best writing.

Another major similarity to *Green Hills of Africa* is the author's use of frequent digressions during lulls in the hunts to allow him to comment on the writing of fiction, its reception by readers and critics, the character and practice of fellow writers, politics, war, racial and ethnic differences, and a number of other topics about which he had strong or at least interesting opinions and ideas. Loosely united by his major plots and themes are campfire discussions, treated with humor in most cases, that range from Hemingway's disappointment over having been denied the Nobel Prize (lightly treated, since he was to win the prize in 1954), to attacks on critics (such as the man who wrote that Hemingway was "crazy," obviously a reference to Philip Young's trauma theory in *Ernest Hemingway* [1952]), then to the ridicule of uncomprehending readers (illustrated by a naïve letter from an Iowa matron). As he did in *Green Hills of Africa*, Hemingway sometimes makes fun of other writers, for example, telling stories about George Orwell and Ford Madox Ford and minimizing the literary career of his own brother, Leicester, who had recently published a book on World War II. But not all of the memories of other writers are negative. Hemingway anticipates *A Moveable Feast* (1964) with fond memories of his Paris years and his relationship with Ezra Pound, even foreshadowing that other posthumous work with "love . . . is a moveable feast" (351).

Most of these imbedded observations are treated comically, for this is the most humorous and easygoing of Hemingway's works. But occasionally potential tragedy shows through the lighthearted surface. On one occasion Mary criticizes Hemingway for his approach to learning languages. He refuses to study Swahili as she does, preferring to pick it up informally. For that matter, she says, although he speaks and reads French, he can't write the language accurately. When he jokingly scoffs at her criticism, she tells him he's "hopeless." Hemingway's reply is chilling in view of the manner of his death: "I'm not hopeless because I still have hope. The day I haven't you'll know it bloody quick" (241).

In some digressions Hemingway reflects on the changes in Africa since his 1933–34 safari and more particularly on his own changed attitudes toward Africa and its people. Although in the thirties Hemingway had befriended one member of the African safari crew, M'Cola, he singled out another member, whom he calls Garrick because of his theatrical manner, for sometimes bitter criticism, and he largely ignored the individuality of most of his white hunter's staff. In contrast, in *Under Kilimanjaro*, while again having one special "brother," Ngui, and only half-jokingly falling in love with Debba, his African "fiancée," Hemingway also makes the reader constantly aware of the individuality of most of the staff members: Keiti, the elderly major-domo of the camp and a wise adviser to Hemingway; Charo, Mary's gunbearer and special hunting mentor; Arap Meina, a former member of the King's African Rifles who serves as an askari during these troubled times; and even Nguili, a mess attendant who aspires to become a full-fledged hunting guide. Of his relationship to Ngui, his spiritual brother, Hemingway says that he envies his black skin and his African roots and that he thinks of himself as an adoptive Kamba. Even an equivalent of Garrick, the Informer, a renegade Masai warrior turned police informer, is treated with a gentle humor that acknowledges his humanity. On this trip

Hemingway makes an effort to learn not only Swahili but also some Masai and, most notably, Kamba as a way of better understanding black Africans.

Hemingway's attitude toward hunting also changed during the intervening twenty years. While Mary, a first-timer in Africa, is allowed to shoot her lion for his trophy hide, Hemingway as hunter has no desire to kill trophy game, and he vows never again to kill certain animals, such as the cheetah. Instead, he shoots meat for the camp and takes greater pleasure in merely watching the wildlife. His greatest moment of pleasure during the hunt for Mary's lion is not the spectacular long-range shot that drops the lion Mary has wounded but an earlier view of that same great cat lying on a mound one evening, surveying his kingdom. On another occasion he carefully stalks a massive old buffalo bull but merely dry-fires on it. The stalk was enough; killing the bull would have poisoned the pleasure of the hunt. Whenever possible his party avoids contact with rhinos, and Hemingway is relieved when a herd of elephants bypasses a nearby Kamba village without damaging it, for if it had, as an Honorary Game Ranger, he would have been forced to take action against the herd.

Readers of *Under Kilimanjaro* will encounter a Hemingway they have seldom experienced in previously published works. The author's sense of humor, which is not widely appreciated, comes into play, particularly joke-making at his own expense. For instance, discussing Winston Churchill's 1953 Nobel Prize, Hemingway suggests that since Churchill is known to be a heavy drinker, perhaps stepping up his own consumption of alcohol would finally result in his winning the prize. Or he could, one of his English companions suggests, win it for his bragging, since Churchill won at least partly for his oratory. Hemingway allows Mary the last word when she suggests that if he wrote something occasionally, he might actually win the prize for his writing.

Readers of this remarkable work will experience the mingled pleasure of revisiting the familiar and discovering the new. They will find links to Hemingway's other works, from the raucous humor of *The Torrents of Spring* and the sardonic comedy of *The Sun Also Rises* and *A Farewell to Arms* to the philosophic calm of *The Old Man and the Sea*. But this work does not merely look backward. Like all of Hemingway's posthumous books—from *A Moveable Feast* to *Islands in the Stream* (1970) and *The Garden of Eden* (1986)—*Under Kilimanjaro* shows Hemingway experimenting formally and stylistically. The flexible, humorous voice Hemingway finds in this late work is simply too full of intrinsic merit to be confined to a small audience of scholars with access to the manuscript. And although the book ends as it began, in medias res, omitting the anticlimax of the two nearly fatal airplane crashes, its major conflicts are resolved, its themes fully explored. In that sense it is not incomplete or flawed. It is perhaps the last gift left to us by a literary master.

This edition of the manuscript of Hemingway's African book was made possible with the cooperation of the Hemingway Estate, represented by Ernest Hemingway's son Patrick; the Ernest Hemingway Foundation; and the Kent State University Press. The editors are especially grateful to Patrick Hemingway and to Scott Donaldson, Linda Wagner-Martin, and Linda Patterson Miller of the Hemingway Foundation and to Joanna Hildebrand Craig and her colleagues at the Kent State University Press for their aid in bringing this posthumous work to print in its entirety. Our workers in the vineyard gave us cheerfully and well the help any such project needs: Ursula Hovet (our major-domo); the reference librarians of the University of North Dakota libraries; Nina Smart for her artwork; and Albert Bickford, Carl Eby, Kristin Ellwanger, Esther Fleming, Jeremiah Kitunda, Petter Løvås, John Rogers, Nile Spicer, and Susan Wrynn for their kind assistance. Asante sana.

ROBERT W. LEWIS
ROBERT E. FLEMING

CHAPTER 1

"No. They will not do that," the old man said. "They would not do anything so stupid. These are the Wakamba Mau Mau."

The old man had no idea how old he was but he must be over seventy years. He was the head man of this outfit and he had kind, smiling eyes and a handsome face with a mouth that was cut across his face like a slash. But the slash turned up at the corners when he smiled. He was a Wakamba and had served throughout the First World War as a rifleman and then as a scout. He had been the personal boy of a very great white hunter for forty-three years and had served with his master in the first war and again in the last war in which his master was too old. He loved his master and his master loved him.

This old man wore a semimilitary tunic, long trousers, and a turban because he was a converted and devout Mohammedan. He had a great knowledge of the logistics of a safari and of the art of making people comfortable and keeping them healthy. He was simple and cunning and very skillful. He was, like all Wakamba, very humorous and he was very cynical. He had five wives and the youngest wife had borne him a child almost nine months to the day after his second major heart attack. He was now expecting another child and he had experienced no further heart attacks. He was as fussy as an old woman and as severe as a noncommissioned officer of thirty-years' service. His religion was absolute but I never knew how much of it was snobbishness and a desire for a special ritual and how much was true belief. There were very many things I did not know. There were more every day. This old man had nursed his master when his master had ordinary fever, blackwater fever, ordinary and amoebic dysentery, a ruptured spleen, and, lately, a tick fever much like the spotted fever of the Rocky Mountains which would have been deadly in the days before antibiotics and was still fairly deadly. He had also seen him through spinal injuries, chronic sciatica, various pneumonias, and piles. His master depended on him very much and in the evening you could hear them talking in the tent while he stood and watched his master taking his bath in the canvas tub. It would have been impossible for him to sit in his master's presence yet, standing, he made fun of him and scolded him as though his master were an irresponsible child. They knew each other so well and, having fought together well many times, admired each other and respected each other so much that it would be difficult to define their relationship at the evening time of the bath. They always seemed to me like two accomplices. They had known and served and protected royalty, spoiled rich American children, great and serious collectors of dead animals, various Americans so rich and old and convinced of their importance and power that they made reigning princes seem like well-mannered schoolboys, and many people who had hoped to come to East Africa during most of their lives and who devoted themselves diligently to killing the necessary beasts that represented, in big-game hunting, so many academic degrees. These were the easiest people to handle. They were sensible and reasonable and devoted themselves to enjoying and savoring every minute, hour, and day of their expensive pleasure. When they were not too rich they tipped well, they studied Swahili, and they made a point of learning the names of those who served them instead of shouting, "Boy." The headman's name was Keiti and no one who called him by it knew that it was a very noble name in Kamba. Keiti knew it and he also knew he had no noble lineage but that at his unknown age he could track and hunt as well as any except the talented bad boys who would almost certainly come to no good end. That is he knew he could do this until the time when he would precipitate another heart attack.

Things were not too simple in this safari because things had changed very much in East Africa. The white hunter had been a close friend of mine for many years. I respected him as I had never respected my father and he trusted me which was more than I deserved. It was, however, something to try to merit. He had taught me by putting me on my own and correcting me when I made mistakes. When I made a mistake he would explain it. Then if I did not make the same mistake again he would trust me a little more. He was a very complicated man compounded of absolute courage, all the good human weaknesses, and a strangely subtle and very critical understanding of people. He was completely dedicated to his family and his home and he loved much more to live away from them. He loved his home and his wife and his children. But he was nomadic. When he was finally leaving us because it was necessary for him to be at his farm, which is what they call a twenty-thousand-acre cattle ranch in Kenya, he told me in the morning before daylight, "Pop, I won't say anything about the Memsahib. I've trusted her to you for a long time now. Only that bloody Magadi." He drew on his pipe and blew the smoke out. "You cannot trust anybody with anything there. You could get killed there with either of us backing up each other. I didn't like you being there."

"I was careful."

"There are places where you can't be careful. It isn't the poor bloody animal's fault either."

"I know. I was spooked most of the time."

"It's a big-gun country. But you had a big gun."

"I really loved it and so did the Memsahib."

"I know," he said. "But the boys didn't. There are none of them that I know that were spooky. But they didn't like it."

"I'm sorry," I said. "I didn't know and I should have. I suppose it was those bloody tunnels."

"Those and the animals that made them. It's too thick a country."

"I'm sorry I didn't know," I said. "That was stupid. I was afraid of those huge branches falling in a wind."

"No," he drank some tea. "You didn't make any mistakes there. You inherited some."

"Did you notice how every zebra had lion claw marks on his haunches?"

"Did I not."

"Pop, give me some gen about handling the safari. You know how worthless my Swahili is."

"Keiti will handle the safari. He understands whatever that language is you talk. The Memsahib has learned a lot of Swahili."

"I'm studying Kamba."

"Look who's here," he said.

"What about Keiti? Does he trust me?"

"He trusts you very much but he thinks you are a little bit bad."

"So is he."

"Of course he is. But that's how he can recognize it."

"What should I do?"

"Try and not be bad."

"What's bad?"

"You know."

"You know things are changed. I can't go around being a pukka sahib and hold my bads nor hold anybody."

"You do all right on that. Only don't be too bad and take Keiti's judgment on everything tactical unless you have a fight. I don't think you'll have to fight but you might. Then make sure he understands. Remember how many Mohammedans and mzees you have and take care of them on their proper meat and have birds for Keiti. They're good for him and they're legal to eat and he loves them. Get them the posho that they like and the right snuff. That's very important. Pop, don't try to be too good and have fun."

"I will."

"Do you have any problems?"

"I don't want to make a fool of myself with elephants."

"You'll learn."

"Anything else?"

"Know everybody knows more than you do but you have to make the decisions and make them stick. Leave the camp and all that to Keiti. Be as good as you can."

There are people who love command and in their eagerness to assume it they are impatient at the formalities of taking over from someone else. I love command since it is the ideal welding of freedom and slavery. You can be happy with your freedom and when it becomes too dangerous you take refuge in your duty. For several years I had exercised no command except over myself and I was bored with this since I knew myself and my defects and strengths too well and they permitted me little freedom and much duty. Lately I had read with distaste various books written about myself by people who knew all about my inner life, aims, and motives. Reading them was like reading an account of a battle where you had fought written by someone who had not only not been present but, in some cases, had not even been born when the battle had taken place. All these people who wrote of my life both inner and outer wrote with an absolute assurance that I had never felt.

On this morning I wished that my great friend and teacher Mr. Philip Percival did not have to communicate in that odd shorthand of understatement which was our legal tongue. I wished that there were things that I could ask him that it was impossible to ask. I wished more than anything that I could be instructed fully and competently as the British instruct their airmen. But I knew that the customary law which prevailed between Philip Percival and myself was as rigid as the customary law of the Kamba. My ignorance, it had been decided long ago, was to be lessened only through learning by myself. But I knew that from now on I had no one to correct my mistakes and, with all the happiness one has in assuming command, it made the morning a very lonely one.

For a long time we had called each other Pop. At first, more than twenty years before, when I had called him Pop, Mr. Percival had not minded as long as this violation of good manners was not made in public. But after I had reached the age of fifty, which made me an elder or mzee, he

4

had taken, happily, to calling me Pop which was in a way a compliment, lightly bestowed and deadly if it were withdrawn. I cannot imagine a situation or, rather, I would not wish to survive a situation in which I called him, in private, Mr. Percival or he addressed me by my proper name.

So on this morning there were many questions I wished to ask and many things I had wondered about. But we were, by custom, mute on these subjects. I felt very lonely and he knew it of course.

"Ngui is staunch," he said. "He's the only boy I've had any trouble with though. Are you and he all right together?"

"We are brothers now. But why didn't you tell me he was M'Cola's son?"

"I thought you'd find out."

"Why didn't you tell me Molo was M'Cola's son?"

"By a different wife," Pop said. "Everyone is related. Don't start to worry about lineage."

"The young kids are all good."

"Yes," Pop said. "It's very rare. Cheer up a little. You'll never inherit better on a small scale."

"I'm not gloomy," I said. "I'm only lonesome because you're going."

"I never thought you were the sentimental type," Pop said. "You won't be lonesome. You'll have your problems to keep you from being lonely."

I did not say anything because I was looking into the coals of the small early fire where dead branches had been laid on the ashes of the dead big fire and it was quite true that I had problems.

"If you did not have problems it would not be fun," Pop said. "You're not a mechanic and what they call white hunters now are mostly mechanics who speak the language and follow other people's tracks. Your command of the language is limited. But you and your disreputable companions made what tracks there are and you can make a few new ones. If you can't come up with the proper word in your new idiom, Kamba, just speak Spanish. Everyone loves that. Or let the Memsahib talk. She is slightly more articulate than you."

"Oh go to hell."

"I shall go to prepare a place for thee," Pop said.

"And elephants?"

"Never give them a thought," Pop said. "Enormous silly beasts. Harmless everyone says. Just remember how deadly you are with all other beasts. After all they are not the woolly mastodon. I've never seen one with a tusk that made two curves."

"Who told you about that?"

"Keiti," Pop said. "He told me you bag thousands of them in the off-season. Those and your saber-toothed tigers and your brontosauruses."

"The son of a bitch," I said.

"No. He more than half believes it. He has a copy of the magazine and they look very convincing. I think he believes it some days and some days not. It depends on whether you bring him any guinea fowl and how you're shooting in general."

"It was a pretty well-illustrated article on prehistoric animals."

"Yes. Very. Most lovely pictures. And you made a very rapid advance as a white hunter when you told him you had only come to Africa because your mastodon license was filled at home and you had shot over your limit on saber-toothed tiger."

"What did you tell him? True."

"I told him it was God's truth and that you were a sort of escaped ivory poacher from Rawlins, Wyoming, which was rather like the Lado Enclave in the old days, and that you had come out here to pay reverence to me who had started you in as a boy, barefoot of course, and to try to keep your hand in for when they would let you go home and take out a new mastodon license."

"Pop, please tell me one sound thing about elephants. You know I have to do away with them if they are behaving badly and if they ask me to."

"Just remember your old mastodon technique," Pop said. "Try and get your first barrel in between that second ring of the tusk. On frontals the seventh wrinkle on the nose counting down from the first wrinkle on the high forehead. Extraordinary high foreheads they have. Most abrupt. If you are nervous stick it in his ear. You will find it's simply a pastime."

"Thank you," I said.

"You're most welcome. Now could you give me any new gen on the saber-toothed tiger? Keiti says you had 115 before those dastards picked up your license."

"You get very close," I said. "You should be able to touch the beast for best results. You then give an abrupt whistle."

"Then do you let him have it?"

"You take the words out of my mouth," I said.

"I trust they were in Kamba," he said. "Pop, please try to be a good boy. I'd much rather be proud of you than read about you in the comic papers. I've never worried ever about you taking care of the Memsahib. But take care of yourself a little bit and try to be as good a boy as you can."

"You try too."

"I've tried for many years," he said. Then in the classic formula he said, "Now it is all yours."

So it was. It was all mine on a windless morning of the last day of the month of the next to the last month of the year. I looked at the dining tent and at our own tent. Then back to the small tents and the men moving around the cooking fire and then at the trucks and the hunting car, the vehicles seeming frosted in the heavy dew. Then I looked through the trees at the mountain showing very big and near this morning with the new snow shining in the first sunlight.

"The mountain's lovely now," Pop said. "I don't think I've ever seen her more beautiful. Have you noticed the difference in her size and in her height on different mornings?"

"She has much more snow today."

"That's from that bloody great storm that went around us last evening," Pop said. "It didn't touch us. But above 12,000 feet that must have been a true blizzard."

"All we had of it was the wind."

"Didn't it blow though?" Pop said. "You might tell Mwindi to check all your pegs and have them ditch a little more. You'll catch the next one of those storms perhaps. Or one after that. They should be coming every day now."

"They seem to come in over the Chyulus and then work up that ridge and onto the mountain."

"They will drive in through you sooner or later," Pop said. He was being very generous now in imparting knowledge. "You know the boys have all been soldiers. Nearly all. I'd tighten up just a bit when I'm gone. A little more ditching. Be quite severe about the weapons. Feed a little better than when I was here. I think you'd be wise to have me ask Keiti in your name who wants to send allotments to Machakos. It hasn't rained there yet and that is all that worries them. I'll tell them you're worried about this. I'll send you word when it rains too and you can tell them."

"That was kind. I'll go and break out the shilingi for the allotments."

"I'm kind," Pop said. "I've just had to bring you up. If you were a mechanic and spoke the language it would be no work at all."

"Did you tell them that we were Cheyenne?"

"Did I not," Pop said. "Mayito too. They think that long cut he has where someone hit him with a bottle is a tribal scar."

"They asked me if Memsahib was the same tribe as me. I told them no and they said they had figured that she was not because she had different tribal scars."

"Yes," Pop said. "They're a little more delicate than yours. Remember they really love her and they loved Mayito. That's two things in your favor. Now go and get the shilingi while I make wise and thoughtful and knowledgeable inquiries in your name."

"Tell them about breakfast, please."

7

"You give the orders," Pop said. "There's no hurry for once. There's one stretch of road I'd like to have dry a little."

"Will you be all right in the truck?"

"Quite. It's a good road, you know, when it's dry."

"You take the hunting car. I won't need it."

"You're not that good," Pop said. "I want to turn this truck in and send you one that is sound. They don't trust this truck."

It was always "they." They were the people, the watu. Once they had been the boys. They still were to Pop. But he had either known them all when they were boys in age or had known their fathers when their fathers were children. Twenty years ago I had called them boys too and neither they nor I had any thought that I had no right to. Now no one would have minded if I had used the word. But the way things were now you did not do it. Everyone had his duties and everyone had a name. Not to know a name was both impolite and a sign of sloppiness. There were special names too of all sorts and shortening of names and friendly and unfriendly nicknames. Pop still cursed them in English or in Swahili and they loved it. I had no right to curse them and I never did. We also all, since the Magadi expedition, had certain secrets and certain things privately shared. Now there were many things that were secrets and there were things that went beyond secrets and were understandings. Some of the secrets were not at all gentle and some were so comic that you would see one of the three gunbearers suddenly laughing and look toward him and know what it was and you would both be laughing so hard that trying to hold in the laughter your diaphragm would ache.

"What are you crazies laughing about?" my wife would ask.

"Strange and funny things," I'd say. "Some very horrible."

"Will you tell me sometime?"

"Sure."

She had studied Swahili diligently and spoke it grammatically and better each day and I always deferred to her knowledge of the language and had her interpret for me in all routine matters. The people enjoyed her Swahili and sometimes I would see laughter start in the corner of the eyes or at the edge of the mouth. But it was always rigidly swallowed. They really loved Miss Mary and when I rejected something that all of us, the bad ones, wanted to do on the grounds that it would hurt Miss Mary it was a valid excuse. We had split into the goods and the bads a long time before this morning when Pop was leaving and he knew about this. Actually there was a third group, the anake or wmanake the young unspoiled boys that he had trained who according to Kamba law were not yet entitled to drink beer. This element were allies of ours. This was especially so in the matter of my fiancée.

The matter, or as it would be in French the question or the affair of my fiancée, was not yet a serious one. She was very beautiful and quite young and more than perfectly developed. She was the best dancer at the ngomas and both Ngui and I were deeply moved by her. One of the goods had told us, innocently, that he was thinking seriously of taking her as his second wife. This was one of the things which, when we thought of them while out on our duties, made us suddenly happy.

I went into the mess tent and sat down at the breakfast table and drank another cup of the early morning tea. Pop had dressed and I could see his people striking his tent. Miss Mary was brushing her hair and I called over to ask if she wanted breakfast yet. I did not want to hurry her as on so many mornings we had to hurry each other and it was bad for home life.

"I'm coming right over," she called. "Don't hurry me."

"Nguili," I called. "Lete chakula."

"Ndio," he answered. Nguili was one of the wmanake, clean, handsome, well mannered, and cheerful.

Miss Mary came over and into the dining tent which had been swept clean of bugs, beetles, and moths, the bottles put away, the table neatly set.

"Why don't you say please to him?" she said and put her arms around me. I pushed my hands hard against the side of her safari jacket. "No. Give me a good one." I held her hard and close and she said, "That's good. How did you sleep, darling?"

"Very well, and you?"

"Wonderfully."

"Why don't you say please to Nguili?"

"You always say it. He doesn't expect it from me."

"It would be nice if you said it."

"He'd think I was making fun of you. I'm a mzee. I don't say please to an anake."

"Wmanake," she corrected.

Pop came in and we all sat down. Nguili and Msembi came in with the breakfast. They were immaculate in their long green gowns and their black faces shone with affection and courtesy.

"Jambo, Bwana," they said to Pop.

"Jambo yourself you lazy dirty rascals," Pop answered.

"Jambo, Bwana," they said to me.

"Jambo indeed."

"Jambo, Memsahib."

"Jambo, Nguili. Jambo, Msembi," Miss Mary said sweetly.

They put down the plates of bacon and eggs and Pop's dish of prunes. Pop attacked the prunes.

"Supposed to save my life," Pop said. "Prunes every morning. Can't say I believe it's worth it."

"I don't know what we'll do without you," Miss Mary said.

"I don't know either," Pop said trying to get the prunes down. "Damn prunes," he said. "It isn't worth it. Only one thing. You run him and the home life and all and hold as tight a rein as you wish. Pull his head off and break his jaw for all I care. Keiti will run his end. I've told him the old man will see him each morning and I've told him to come to your worthless consort about anything as though he were me. Now you, Miss Memsahib, I want only one thing out of you. When you are out with guns or if you ever have to use guns here I want you to do whatever he tells you to and do it fast whether it seems to make sense or not."

"Haven't I always?"

"Yes. But you might get sick of it or you might be justifiably angry at him."

"I'll obey as though it were you. Not quite," she said. "But I'll obey."

"And fast."

"And fast," she repeated.

"We won't have any problems," I said.

"Of course not," Pop said. "You have no problems at all. I see that or I would never leave you here with him. But who were the last American husband and wife you know who were hunting difficult and problem lions tracking on foot without a white hunter and being entrusted and trusted on elephant control and mixed up in Mickey Mouse trouble? Sorry about the speech. It's probably the prunes."

"Anything else about the outfit?"

"No. You know the problems. Work them out. If you want to make me happy don't do anything that right or wrong can get you sucked into that tall papyrus in the swamp."

"I promise."

"One of your damned informers and some people from the Wakamba shamba are hanging around the edge of camp. You'd better deal with them."

"I will."

"He used to work for me. He's no good."

"He is a Masai now fallen to protecting a widow in a renegade Kamba shamba and informing for sixty-three shilingi a month."

"He's not a fool at all," Pop said. "But don't you trust him."

"I haven't and I won't."

"Keiti hates him."

"I know."

Pop had finished the bacon and eggs now and he said, "I'd best get along. I'll get the truck back to you or a better one and the list of things and all the papers I can buy. I'll send you the gen about the rains in the district. That's most important to them and the driver will bring any personal messages for the boys. They like this camp you know. God knows they should."

"We'll be fine, Pop. Really."

"I know you would or I wouldn't leave you. I'd have thought up some way to get you back in."

After Pop left I had to see the Informer. He was a tall dignified man who wore full-length trousers, a clean dark blue sport shirt with thin white lateral stripes, a shawl around his shoulders, and a porkpie hat. All of these articles of clothing looked as though they had been gifts. The shawl I had recognized as being made from trade goods sold in one of the Hindu general stores at Loitokitok. His dark brown face was distinguished and must once have been handsome. He spoke accurate English slowly and with a mixture of accents.

"Good morning, my brother," he said and removed his hat. "Good morning, my lady."

"Good morning, Reginald," I said. Miss Mary got up from the chair where she had been sitting and left the mess tent. She did not care for the Informer.

"Is the Memsahib displeased with me?" Reginald asked.

"No more than usual."

"I must bring her a suitable present," Reginald said. "I have important news. The man who calls himself Michael is an important agent of the Mau Mau."

"Really," I said. "How did you obtain this information?"

"I overheard a conversation outside the Masai Stores. It was an important conversation. Two chiefs agreed."

"A very rare thing," I said. "What else?"

"There is drunkenness at the three shambas."

"What about the other two?"

"I am unwelcome there."

"Why? Drunkenness?"

"My brother knows that I am not a drunkard. I am denied welcome through prejudice. The old prejudice against me."

"How is the widow?"

"She has been away for three days. There is no morality in the shamba now. She left for Loitokitok and she has not returned. My brother, do you have any of that medicine which was mentioned in the article in *The Reader's Digest* which makes a man as strong as he was in his youth?"

11

"There is such a medicine. But I do not have it."

"With that medicine here, first to use a little for myself, and then to learn to compound it and sell it, I could be a rich man."

"What about rhino horn?"

"First you must detach it from the rhino which is difficult and dangerous. As a loyal informer of the Game Department I could never participate in such a thing. The rhino must be killed and that is illegal. Then it is very expensive. Then as I have sadly proved it is worthless."

"I didn't know that. The Chinese buy it."

"They must have some hidden secret," he said. "They are a very secretive people. All I can tell you truly as your most loyal informer is that it is worthless."

"A great pity."

"Yes, my brother. It is tragic."

"Papa, aren't we ever going to get started?" Miss Mary called from our tent. "Everybody is ready and waiting for you."

"I'm coming now," I called.

"I wish we could get off," she said. "We're wasting the morning."

"Get everything in the car."

"My brother, since there is no such medicine and you must be off could you offer me anything to drink?"

"For medicinal purpose and in the line of duty?"

"Of course. I could not accept it otherwise."

"Nor could I give it," I said. "Pour it yourself."

Reginald poured it and drank it. His shoulders straightened and he was a younger man.

"I will have more information tomorrow, my brother," he said. "Make my respects to my lady."

He walked out of the tent bowing formally and I watched him walking away toward the trees of the safari lines as I went over to the hunting car.

That morning our inspection was almost routine. It was a clear and beautiful morning and we drove out across the plain with the mountain and the trees of the camp behind us. There were many Thomson gazelle ahead on the green plain switching their tails as they fed. There were herds of wildebeest and Grant's gazelle feeding close to the patches of bush. We reached the airstrip we had made in a long open meadow by running the car and the truck up and down through the new short grass and grubbing out the stumps and roots of a patch of brush at one end. The tall pole of a cut sapling drooped from the heavy wind of the night before and the wind sock, homemade from a flour sack, hung limp. We stopped the car and I got out and felt of the pole. It was solid although bent and the sock would fly once the breeze rose. There were wind clouds high in the sky and it was beautiful looking across the green meadow at the mountain looking so huge and wide from here.

"Do you want to shoot any color of it and the airstrip?" I asked my wife.

"We have that even better than it is this morning. Let's go and see the bat-eared foxes and check on the lion."

"He won't be out now. It's too late."

"He might be."

So we drove along our old wheel tracks that led to the salt flat. On the left there was open plain and the broken line of tall green-foliaged yellow-trunked trees that marked the edge of the forest where the buffalo herd might be. There was old dry grass growing high along the edge and there were many fallen trees that had been pulled down by elephants or up-rooted by storms. Ahead there was plain with new short green grass and to the right there were broken glades with islands of thick green bush and occasional tall flat-topped thorn trees. Everywhere there was game feeding. They moved away as we came close moving sometimes in quick bursts of galloping, sometimes at a steady trot, sometimes only feeding off away from the car. But they always stopped and fed again. When we were on this routine patrol or when Miss Mary was photographing they paid no more attention to us than they do to the lion when he is not hunting. They keep out of his way but they are not frightened.

I was leaning out of the car watching for tracks in the road as Ngui, who sat in the outside position behind me, was doing. Mthuka, who was driving, watched all the country ahead and on both sides. He had the best and quickest eyes of any of us. His face was ascetic, thin, and intelligent and he had the arrowhead tribal cuts of the Wakamba on both cheeks. He was quite deaf and he was Keiti's son and he was a year older than I was. He was not a Mohammedan as his father was. He loved to hunt and he was a beautiful driver. He would never do a careless or irresponsible thing but he, Ngui, and myself were the three principal bads.

We had been very close friends for a long time and one time I asked him when he had gotten the big formal tribal cuts which no one else had. Those who did have them had very lightly traced scars.

He laughed and said, "At a very big ngoma. You know. To please a girl."

Now we were going closer to the forest as the tracks swung and both Ngui and I had seen the tracks of everything that had crossed or used the trail. The tracks of a single lioness had crossed the trail from the forest and we had checked the trail on foot for some distance after that. Her tracks had not touched the trail again but as we had walked on ahead of the

13

hunting car we had seen where a large bull elephant and a smaller bull had crossed the trail and gone on through the high grass and into the forest. Ngui looked at me.

"No," I said. "We know them. That same bull and his askari."

We walked on for a way until we were in sight of the gray mud flat with the papyrus swamp behind it and the rocky lava hills on the right. There were no tracks of the buffalo herd that used this trail when they came from the lower forest to the salt flat.

"Where do you think the buff have gone?"

"We can find out."

"Where do you think?"

"In the good feed toward the Chyulus where we saw them from the ndege. That is where the rain falls every day now. When we have real rain here they will be back."

"I agree," I said. "Call up the car."

When the car came up Miss Mary said, "That was a big bull, wasn't he? I wish we could see him."

"We could track him, honey," I said. "But the breeze has started and it's right at our backs. We might just keep him moving and it is awfully thick in there. We'll get him in the open sometime. He uses all the time back and forth between here and that country past the old manyatta."

"I never saw him," she said. "Every time I have to stay home you see him."

"Sometime we'll find him in the open."

"Should we go on and check the salt flat?" she said.

"That's what we figured to do."

"Mthuka spotted the lioness."

"Good. Where was she?"

"Over there on the right about four hundred yards back. She was by herself under that small tree. You remember?"

"Yes. We don't want to bother her. Should we move up to the end of the trees and then leave the car and go over and glass that flat?"

We left the car under the shade of a tree and using the trees ahead of us for cover walked up to where, still in the shadow of the tall yellowish-barked trees, we could look off across the gray flat. There was a pool in the center and beyond that were some large gray rocks. At the far end of the flat was the tall green and yellow line of the papyrus swamp and to the right as I looked with my field glasses the red lava boulders of the small hill showed clear. At the base of the hill the glasses showed the black shapes to be wildebeest grazing. Further to the right there were many zebra and a few Tommy gazelle feeding with them.

"No buff," said Ngui the gunbearer.

I looked carefully from right to left along the edge of the papyrus but the glasses showed nothing but a solitary wildebeest standing with his heavy head slumped forward. He looked old and tired. Then I saw the handsome waterbuck bull and his eleven cows. They were moving across the flat from the water toward the forest. I handed the glasses to Miss Mary. But she said, "I see them quite well. Isn't he lovely? And he takes such good care of them."

"I hope no one ever shoots him."

"They couldn't," she said. "Not if they had seen how noble and lovely he is. Not if they had ever seen him trot."

"I've never shot one," I said. "Once a long time ago I nearly shot a really wonderful one and I stopped myself just in time."

"I remember when I wouldn't shoot an impala," Miss Mary said.

"But that's different. They're one of the best things we have to eat and there are plenty of them. Nobody can eat waterbuck."

"Would you eat waterbuck?" Miss Mary asked Ngui.

"Hapana," and shook his head. "Not even Bwana would eat kuru."

Ngui and Charo, Miss Mary's gunbearer, both laughed. Now that we had seen the buff were not on the flat or at the edges of the swamp we were not serious any more. It was an old joke that I would not kill anything that I would not eat and they were glad to be joking again. A long time ago I had explained that it was against my religion to kill anything except vermin that I would not eat. Ngui had looked a little doubtful at this but Charo had told him it was true. Charo was a truly devout Mohammedan and was also known to be very truthful. He did not know how old he was, of course, but Pop thought he must be over seventy. With his turban on he was about two inches shorter than Miss Mary and watching them standing together looking across the gray flat at where the waterbuck that were now going carefully, upwind, into the forest, the big buck with his beautiful horns looking back and to either side as he entered last in line, I thought what a strange pair Miss Mary and Charo must look to the animals. No animals had any visual fear of them. We had seen this proven many times. Rather than fearing them, the small blonde one in the forest-green coat and the even smaller black one in the blue jacket, the animals appeared interested in them. It was as though they had been permitted to see a circus or at least something extremely odd and the predatory animals seemed to be definitely attracted by them.

On this morning we were all relaxed. Something, or something awful or something wonderful, was certain to happen on every day in this part of Africa. Every morning when you woke it was as exciting as though you were going to compete in a downhill ski race or drive a bobsled on a fast run. Something, you knew, would happen and usually before eleven o'clock. I never knew of a morning in Africa when I woke that I was not happy at least until I remembered unfinished business. But on this morning we were relaxed in the momentary irresponsibility of command and I was happy that the buffalo, which were our basic problem, were evidently some place where we could not reach them. For what we hoped to do it was necessary for them to come to us rather than for us to go to them. It was also necessary, periodically, to go to them without them seeing us and without frightening them so that we might keep track of their movements and take advantage of them for our ends. In the meantime I was happy that the buffalo were probably where Ngui and I believed them to be. It was necessary to make a check though since they might be in the forest on our left or in the thick, lush, and boggy area that bordered the swamp.

"Ngui," I said. "Go get the car and we will check."

"Ndio," he said. "It is better."

Charo nodded too. None of us wished to work but it was necessary before relaxing into straight pleasure.

"What are you going to do?" Miss Mary asked.

"Bring the car up and make a quick swing to check for tracks at the big water and then go into that place in the forest where it borders the swamp and check and then get out. We'll be downwind of the elephant and you might see him. Probably not."

"Can we go back through the gerenuk country?"

"Of course. I'm sorry we started late. But with Pop going away and everything."

"And you with your pimp informer."

"He's sort of sad," I said. "I'll tell you about him sometime."

"I like to go in there in that bad place. I can study what we need for a Christmas tree. Do you think my lion is in there?"

"Probably. But we won't see him in that kind of country."

"He's such a smart bastard lion. Why didn't they let me shoot that easy beautiful lion under the tree that time? That's the way women shoot lions."

"They shoot them that way and the finest black-maned lion ever shot by a woman had maybe forty shots fired into him. Afterwards they have the beautiful pictures and then they have to live with the goddamn lion and lie about him to all their friends and themselves the rest of their lives."

"I'm sorry I missed the wonder lion at Magadi."

"Don't you be sorry. You be proud."

"I don't know what made me this way. I have to get him and he has to be the real one."

16

"We overhunted him, honey. He's too smart. I have to let him get confidence now and make a mistake."

"He doesn't make mistakes. He's smarter than you and Pop both."

"Honey, Pop wanted you to get him or lose him straight. If he didn't love you, you could have shot any sort of lion."

"Let's not talk about him," she said. "I want to think about the Christmas tree. We're going to have a wonderful Christmas."

Mthuka had seen Ngui start down the trail for him and brought up the car. We got in and I motioned Mthuka toward the far water at the corner across the swamp. Ngui and I both hung out over the side watching for tracks. There were the old wheel tracks and the game trails to and from the papyrus swamp. There were fresh wildebeest tracks and the tracks of zebra and Tommy. Then we saw the tracks of a man. Then of another man wearing boots. These tracks had been rained on lightly.

"You and me," I said to Ngui.

"Yes," he grinned. "One of them has big feet and walks as though he is tired."

"One is barefooted and walks as though the rifle were too heavy for him. Stop the car," I said to Mthuka. We got out.

"Look," said Ngui. "One walks as though he were very old and can hardly see. The one with shoes."

"Look," I said. "The barefoot one walks as though he has five wives and twenty cows. He has spent a fortune on beer."

"They will get nowhere," Ngui said. "Look, the one with shoes walks as though he might die at any time. He staggers under the weight of the rifle."

"What do you think they are doing here?"

"How would I know? Look, the one with shoes is stronger now."

"He is thinking about the shamba," Ngui said.

"Kwenda na shamba."

"Ndio," Ngui said. "How old would you say the old one with the shoes is?"

"None of your damn business," I said. "Let us hunt beasts and find the Christmas tree."

"Better," said Ngui.

We motioned for the car and when it got up we got in and I motioned Mthuka toward the entrance to the forest. The driver was laughing and shaking his head.

"What were you two doing tracking yourselves?" Miss Mary said. "I know it's funny because everybody was laughing. But it looked quite silly."

"We were having fun."

"Do you and he really understand each other?"

"Too well."

"What do you speak?

"Ngui," Miss Mary said. "Can Bwana really speak Kamba?"

"Ndio," Ngui lied fiercely. "Mingi Kamba."

We were going into the forest now on our old track. It was a narrow track between high trees and now we were at the turn where the elephants had pulled the trees down. This was a sharp turn and there were branches on each side that slapped into the car. I looked at Ngui and made the motion of swinging with a panga and he nodded his head. There was a rhino with her calf that was often in this part of the forest and if it were ever wet that would not be a good place to meet her. The hunting car could stall there on that turn if the track was slick. We would have to open it up the first chance we had.

Now we passed through a part of the forest where the big herd of elephants had pulled almost all of the trees down. It looked as though it had been hit by a tornado except that the trees had fallen in all directions. There had been more than a hundred elephants in the herd and they had stayed there in the heavy forest close to the water of the stream that fed the swamp during the worst part of the drought. They had wrecked the most edible part of the forest and then migrated on east to where there was another permanent source of water and more edible trees.

I was always depressed by this part of the forest. The elephants had to eat something and it was proper that they should eat trees rather than destroy the native farms. But the destruction was so great in proportion to the amount they ate from the trees they pulled down that it was depressing to see it. Elephants were the only animal that were increasing steadily throughout their present range in Africa. They increased until they became such a problem to the natives that they had to be slaughtered. Then they were killed off indiscriminately. There were men who did this and enjoyed it. They killed old bulls, young bulls, cows, and calves and many liked their work. There had to be some sort of elephant control. Seeing this damage to the forest and the way the trees were pulled down and stripped and knowing what they could do in a native shamba in a night I started to think about the problems of control. But all the time I was watching for the tracks of the two elephants we had seen leading into this part of the forest. I knew those two elephants and where they would probably go for the day but until I had seen their tracks and was sure they were past us I must be careful about Miss Mary wandering around looking for a suitable Christmas tree.

We had come out of the torn-down forest into a glade and ahead was the bare patch where G.C. had killed the spitting cobra. The cobra had looked like a big stick ahead of the Land Rover. Then G.C. had seen it was a cobra and turned to run it down and it had risen up and drenched the windshield in front of G.C.'s eyes with venom. G.C. had shot it and the place of the spitting cobra marked where you turned to the right for the glade next to the border of high trees along the big swamp where the biggest buffalo herd usually lived. It was in this glade that Miss Mary had located the finest of the Christmas trees.

We stopped the car and I took the big gun and helped Miss Mary out of the car.

"I don't need any help," she said.

"Look, honey," I started to explain. "I have to stay with you with the big gun."

"I'm just going to pick out a Christmas tree."

"I know. But there could be every kind of stuff in here. There has been too."

"Let Ngui stay with me then."

"Charo's here."

"Honey, I'm responsible for you."

"You can be an awful bore about it too."

"I know it." Then I said, "Ngui."

"Bwana?"

The joking was all suspended.

"Go and see if the two elephants went into the far forest. Go as far as the rocks."

"Ndio."

He went off across the open space carrying my Springfield in his right hand and watching ahead for tracks in the grass.

"I only want to pick one out," Miss Mary said. "Then we can come out some morning and dig it up and get it back to camp and plant it while it is still cool."

"Go ahead," I said. I was watching Ngui. He had stopped once and listened. Then he went on walking very carefully. I followed Miss Mary who was looking at the different silvery thorn shrubs trying to find one with the best size and shape but I kept looking back at Ngui over my shoulder. He stopped again and listened then waved toward the deep forest with his left arm. He looked around at me and I waved him back to us. He came in fast, as fast as he could walk without running.

"Where are they?" I asked.

"They crossed and went into the forest. I could hear them. The old bull and his askari."

"Good," I said.

"Listen," he whispered. "Faru." He pointed toward the thick forest on the right. I had heard nothing. "Mzuri motocah," he said meaning, in short hand, "Better get into the car."

"Get Miss Mary."

I turned toward where Ngui had pointed. I could see only the silvery shrubs, the green grass, and the line of tall trees with vines and creepers hanging from them. Then I heard the noise like a sharp deep purr. It was the noise you would make if you held your tongue against the roof of your mouth and blew out strongly so your tongue vibrated as a reed. It came from where Ngui had pointed. But I could see nothing. I slipped the safety catch forward on the .577 and turned my head to the left. Miss Mary was coming at an angle to get behind where I stood. Ngui was holding her by the arm to guide her and she was walking as though she were treading on eggs. Charo was following her. Then I heard the sharp rough purr again and I saw Ngui fall back with the Springfield ready and Charo move forward and take Miss Mary's arm. They were even with me now and were working toward where the car must be. I knew the driver, Mthuka, was deaf and would not hear the rhino. But when he saw them he would know what was happening. I did not want to look around. But I did and saw Charo urging Miss Mary toward the hunting car. Ngui was moving fast with them carrying the Springfield and watching over his shoulder. It was my duty not to kill the rhino. But I would have to if he or she charged and there was no way out. I planned to shoot the first barrel into the ground to turn the rhino. If it did not turn I would kill it with the second barrel. Thank you very much, I said to myself. It is easy.

Just then I heard the motor of the hunting car start and heard the car coming fast in low gear. I started to fall back figuring a yard was a yard and feeling better with each yard gained. The hunting car swung alongside in a tight turn and I pushed the safety on and jumped for the hand hold by the front seat as the rhino came smashing out through the vines and creepers. It was the big cow and she came galloping. From the car she looked ridiculous with her small calf galloping behind her.

She gained on us for a moment but the car pulled away. There was a good open space ahead and at the place where the cobra had been killed Mthuka swung the car sharply to the left. The rhino went straight on galloping then slowed to a trot and the calf trotted too.

"Did you get any pictures?" I asked Miss Mary.

"I couldn't. She was right behind us."

"Didn't you get her when she came out?"

"No."

"I don't blame you."

"I picked out the Christmas tree though."

"You see why I wanted to cover you," I said unnecessarily and stupidly.

"You didn't know she was in there."

"She lives around here and she goes to the stream at the edge of the swamp for water."

"Everybody was so serious," Miss Mary said. "I never saw all of you joke people get so serious."

"Honey, it would have been awful if I had had to kill her. And I was worried about you."

"Everybody so serious," she said. "And everybody holding onto my arm. I knew how to get back to the car. Nobody had to hold onto my arm."

We were back to the bad turn now and I motioned to Mthuka to go on through. We would cut the brush another day.

"Honey," I said. "They were only holding your arm so that you wouldn't step in a hole or trip on something. They were watching the ground all the time. The rhino was very close and might charge any time and we're not allowed to kill her."

"How did you know it was a female with a calf?"

"It stood to reason. She's been around here for four months."

"I wish she wasn't right in the place where the Christmas trees grow."

"We'll get the tree all right."

"You always promise things," she said. "But things are much simpler and better when Mr. P. is here."

"They certainly are," I said. "And they are much easier when G.C. is here. But there is nobody here but us now and please let's not fight in Africa. Please not."

"I don't want to fight," she said. "I'm not fighting. I simply don't like to see all you private joke people get so serious and so righteous."

"Have you ever seen anybody killed by a rhino?"

"No," she said. "And neither have you."

"That's right," I said. "And I don't intend to. Pop's never seen it either."

"I didn't like it when you all got so serious."

"It was because I couldn't kill the rhino. If you can kill it there's no problem. Then I had to think about you."

"Well stop thinking about me," she said. "Think about us getting the Christmas tree."

I was beginning to feel somewhat righteous and I wished that Pop was with us to make a diversion. But Pop was not with us anymore.

"We are going back through the gerenuk country at least, aren't we?"

"Yes," I said, "we turn to the right at those big stones up ahead across the mud flat at the edge of the high tree bush those baboons are crossing into now and we proceed across the flat to the east until we come to that other rhino drop. Then we go southeast to the old manyatta and we are in the gerenuk country."

"It will be nice to be there," she said. "But I certainly miss Pop."

"So do I," I said.

CHAPTER 2

There are always mystical countries that are a part of one's childhood. Those we remember and visit sometimes when we are asleep and dreaming. They are as lovely at night as they were when we were children. If you ever go back to see them they are not there. But they are as fine in the night as they ever were if you have the luck to dream of them.

In Africa when we lived on the small plain in the shade of the big thorn trees at the edge of the swamp at the foot of the great mountain we had such countries. We were no longer, technically, children although in many ways I am quite sure that we were. "Childish" has become a term of contempt.

"Don't be childish, darling."

"I hope the Christ I am. Don't be childish yourself."

It is possible to be grateful that no one that you would willingly associate with would say, "Be mature. Be well balanced, be well adjusted."

Africa, being as old as it is, makes all people except the professional invaders and spoilers into children. No one says to anyone in Africa, "Why don't you grow up?" All men and animals acquire a year more of age each year and some acquire a year more of knowledge. The animals that die the soonest learn the fastest. A young gazelle is mature, well balanced, and well adjusted at the age of two years. He is well balanced and well adjusted at the age of four weeks. Men know that they are children in relation to the country and as in armies seniority and senility ride close together. But to have the heart of a child is not a disgrace. It is an honor. A man must comport himself as a man. He must fight always preferably and soundly with the odds in his favor but on necessity against any sort of odds and with no thought of the outcome. He should follow his tribal laws and customs insofar as he can and accept the tribal discipline when he cannot. But it is never a reproach that he has kept a child's heart, a child's honesty, and a child's freshness and nobility. The elders, who govern, are presumably those that govern in cold blood and legal procedure because they no longer have the hot blood that would sway a warrior's thinking. They are respected, but not loved, unless they can also think as a child, in his nobility, or as a young warrior would think in his quick hate, his pride, and his blindness.

At this time the great mystical country that Mary and I shared was the Chyulu Hills. This was always referred to by G.C., when he was with us, as "The country no white woman has ever set foot in including Miss Mary."

We saw the Chyulus each day distant, blue, classically broken in the way that hills are broken to break your heart and we had made several half-disastrous and half-comic attempts to reach them. Due to an impassable, proved swamp and a profusion of lava boulders blocking all detours, they had become one of those countries which you could not enter without an effort which was beyond us at the time. As substitute countries Mary had taken the gerenuk country which was a strange enough choice and I had taken the village of Loitokitok which was fourteen miles up the slope of Mount Kilimanjaro close to the border of the colony and the territory. Mary thought this was a strange enough choice too until she also became involved in it.

On this day after checking on the buffalo herd, the Christmas tree plantation, and encountering the cow rhino, we were now entering Mary's gerenuk country. I could see the Chyulu Hills with a storm gathering over them and high to the left and this side of the far blue hills I could see Lion Hill which was the jumping-off place for the Chyulus. You could always get to the rocky palm-crowned top of Lion Hill. It was from there on you had a choice of mistaken routes. Then I turned my back on this, having figured the storm would not possibly reach us before the afternoon, and we went into the broken bush toward the gerenuk country.

It was a country of dry bush and you drove along the game trails. One patch of dry bush was like another and you could not see a hundred yards in any direction. It was a country to hunt on foot in the early morning as there was much game in it and, moving quietly and working upwind, you would be close to any of the animals before they saw you. I could not let Mary hunt it alone with Charo because there were both rhino and elephant in the country. And three people made too much noise. In the morning, too, we had our duties.

No one knew why Mary needed to kill a gerenuk. They were a strange long-necked gazelle and the bucks had heavy short curved horns set far forward on their heads. They were excellent to eat in this particular country. But Tommy and impala were better to eat. The boys thought that it had something to do with Mary's religion. Her religion had been a fascinating topic of discussion for a long time. It started when she had eaten a raw slice of the heart of the first lion I had killed. I had handed her the triangular-shaped slice as a joke but she had taken it and eaten it and no one had laughed. Then as the lion was skinned out I had shown her the wonderful muscles. She had watched the skinning and when the four paws and the tail were finished and the skinner and Ngui started skinning up the back she had seen the tenderloin and asked to have it cut out. She smelled it and it smelled very good and was a really beautiful piece of meat.

She had spoken with the cook about it and that night we had it served in breaded cutlets. It tasted like the best of veal. G.C. was horrified and said so. Pop was rather subdued about it but tried it. I thought it was very good and Mary loved it. After that we always ate lion and I think G.C. ate it finally but I am not sure and would have to ask him. He had a career at stake and he staked it each day when he was with us and if he did eat lion and it was bad for his career I would lie and deny it.

Everyone understood why Mary must kill her lion. It was hard for some of the elders who had been on many hundreds of safaris to understand why she must kill it in the old straight way. But all of the bad element were sure it had something to do with her religion like the necessity to kill the gerenuk at approximately high noon. It evidently meant nothing to Miss Mary to kill the gerenuk in an ordinary and simple way.

At the end of the morning's hunt, or patrol, the gerenuk would be in the thick bush. If we sighted any by unlucky chance Mary and Charo would get out of the car and make their stalk. The gerenuk would sneak, run, or bound away. Ngui and I would follow the two stalkers from duty and our presence would insure the gerenuk would keep on moving. Finally it would be too hot to keep on moving the gerenuk about and Charo and Mary would come back to the car. As far as I know no shot was ever fired in this type of gerenuk hunting.

"Damn those gerenuk," Mary said. "I saw the buck looking directly at me. But all I could see was his face and his horns. Then he was behind another bush and I couldn't tell he was not a doe. Then he kept moving off out of sight. I could have shot him but I might have wounded him."

"You'll get him another day. I thought you hunted him very well."

"If you and your friend didn't have to come."

"We have to, honey."

"I'm sick of it. Now I suppose you all want to go to the shamba."

"No. I think we'll cut straight home to camp and have a cool drink."

"I don't know why I like this crazy part of the country," she said. "I don't have anything against the gerenuk either."

"It's a sort of an island of desert here. It's like the big desert we have to cross to get here. Any desert is fine."

"I wish I could shoot well and fast and as quick as I see to shoot. I wish I wasn't short. I couldn't see the lion that time when you could see him and everybody else could see him."

"He was in an awful place."

"I know where he was and it wasn't so far from here either."

"No," I said and to the driver, "Kwenda na campi."

"Thank you for not going to the shamba," Mary said. "You're good about the shamba sometimes."

"You're who is good about it."

"No, I'm not. I like you to go there and I like you to learn everything you should learn."

"I'm not going there now until they send for me about something."

"They'll send for you all right," she said. "Don't worry about that."

When we did not go to the shamba the drive back to camp was very beautiful. There was one long open glade after another. They were linked together like lakes and the green trees and the brush made their shores. There were always the square white rumps of the Grant's gazelle and their brown and white bodies as they trotted, the does moving fast and lightly and the bucks with their proud heavy horns swung back. Then we would round a long curve of green bushy trees and there would be the green tents of the camp with the yellow trees and the mountain behind them.

This was the first day we had been alone in this camp and as I sat under the flap of the dining tent in the shade of a big tree and waited for Mary to come from washing up so we could have our drink together before lunch I hoped that there would be no problems and that it would be an easy day. Bad news came in quickly enough but I had seen no harbingers waiting around the cooking fires. The wood truck was still out. They would be bringing water too and when they came in they would probably bring news of the shamba. I had washed and changed my shirt and changed into shorts and a pair of moccasins and felt cool and comfortable in the shade. The rear of the tent was open and a breeze blew through off the mountain that was cool with the freshness of the snow.

Mary came into the tent and said, "Why, you haven't had a drink. I'll make one for us both."

She was fresh looking in her freshly ironed, faded safari slacks and shirt and beautiful and as she poured the Campari and gin into the tall glasses and looked for a cold siphon in the canvas water bucket she said, "I'm so glad we're alone really. It will be just like Magadi but nicer." She made the drinks and gave me mine and we touched glasses. "I love Mr. P. so much and I love to have him. But with you and me alone it's wonderful. I won't

be bad about you taking care of me and I won't be irascible. I'll do everything but like the Informer."

"You're awfully good," I said. "We always do have the most fun alone
together too. But you be patient with me when I'm stupid."

"You're not stupid and we're going to have a lovely time. This is so
much nicer a place than Magadi and we live here and have it all to our
own. It is going to be lovely. You'll see."

There was a cough outside the tent. I recognized it and thought something that I had better not write down.

"All right," I said. "Come in." It was the Informer. His face was sweating and happy and he held his hat in his hand and bowed to Miss Mary.

"Sir," he said. "I am happy to report that I have captured a murderer."

"What kind of murderer?"

"A Masai murderer. He is badly wounded and his father and uncle are
with him."

"Who did he murder?"

"His cousin. Don't you remember? You dressed his wounds."

"That man's not dead. He's in the hospital."

"Then he is only an attempted murderer. But I captured him. You will
mention it in your report, brother, I know. Please, sir, the attempted murderer is feeling very bad and he would like you to dress his wounds."

"OK," I said. "I'll go out and see him. I'm sorry, honey."

"It doesn't matter," Mary said. "It doesn't matter at all."

"May I have a drink, brother?" the Informer asked. "I am tired from the
struggle."

"Bullshit," I said. "I'm sorry, honey."

"It's all right," Miss Mary said. "I don't know any better word for it."

"I did not mean an alcoholic drink," the Informer said nobly. "I meant
only a sip of water."

"We'll get some," I said.

The attempted murderer, his father, and his uncle all looked very depressed. I greeted them and we all shook hands. The attempted murderer
was a young moran, or warrior, and he and another moran had been playing together making mock fighting with their spears. It had not been about
anything, his father explained. They were only playing and he had wounded the other young man accidentally. His friend had thrust back at him
and he had received a wound. Then they had lost their heads and fought
but never seriously, never to kill. But when he saw his friend's wounds he
was frightened that he might have killed him and had gone off into the
brush and hidden. Now he had come back with his father and his uncle

and he wished to surrender. The father explained all this and the boy nod-ded his assent.

I told the father through the interpreter that the other boy was in the hospital and was doing well and that I had heard neither he nor his male relatives had made any charges against this boy. The father said he had heard the same thing.

The medical chest had been brought from the dining tent and I dressed the boy's wounds. They were in the neck, the chest, and the upper arm and back and were all suppurating badly. I cleaned them out, poured peroxide into them for the magic bubbling effect and to kill any grubs, cleaned them again, especially the neck wound, painted the edges with Mercurochrome which gave a much admired and serious color effect, and then sifted them full of sulfa and put a gauze dressing and plaster across each wound.

Through the Informer, who was acting as interpreter, I told the elders that as far as I was concerned it was better for the young men to exercise at the use of their spears than to drink Golden Jeep sherry in Loitokitok. But that I was not the law and the father must take his son and present him to the police in that village. He should also have the wounds checked there and should be given penicillin.

After receiving this message the two elders spoke together and then to me and I grunted knowingly throughout their speech with that peculiar rising inflection grunt that means you are giving the matter your deepest attention.

"They say, sir, that they wish you to give a judgment on the case and they will abide by your judgment. They say all that they say is true and that you have already spoken with the other mzees."

"Tell them that they must present the warrior to the police. It is possible that the police will do nothing since no complaint has been made. They must go to the police boma and the wound must be checked and the boy receive penicillin. It must be done."

"Sir, how will they go? They say they have walked far."

"They will go in the wood truck after we have eaten. You will go with them and see that this is done as I have said and you will not say to the police that you have captured them. I will check on this."

After the Informer had told them that they would ride in the truck and that they were not prisoners but were to report themselves I shook hands with the two elders and with the young warrior. He was a good-looking boy, thin and very straight, but he was tired and his wounds hurt him although he had never flinched when they were cleaned out.

The Informer followed me to the front of our sleeping tent where I washed up carefully with blue soap.

"Listen," I said to him. "I want you to tell the police exactly what I said and what the mzee said to me. If you try anything fancy you know what will happen."

"How can my brother think I would not be faithful and do my duty? How can my brother doubt me? Will my brother loan me ten shillings? I will pay it back the first of the month."

"Ten shillings will never get you out of the trouble you are in."

"I know it. But it is ten shillings."

"Here is ten."

"Do you not want to send any presents to the shamba?"

"I will do that myself."

"You are quite right, brother. You are always right and doubly generous."

"Bullshit to you. Go along now and wait with the Masai to go in the truck. I hope you find the widow and don't get drunk."

I went in the tent and Mary was waiting. She was reading the last *New Yorker* and was sipping at her gin and Campari.

"Was he badly hurt?"

"No. But the wounds were infected. One pretty badly."

"I don't wonder after being in the manyatta that day. The flies were really something awful."

"They say the blowflies keep a wound clean," I said. "But the maggots always give me the creeps. I think while they keep it clean they enlarge the wound greatly. This kid has one in the neck that can't stand much enlarging."

"The other boy was hurt worse though, wasn't he?"

"Yes. But he had prompt treatment."

"You're getting quite a lot of practice as an amateur doctor. Do you think you can cure yourself?"

"Of what?"

"Of whatever you get sometimes. I don't mean just physical things."

"Like what?"

"I couldn't help hearing you and that Informer talking about the shamba. I wasn't overhearing. But you were right outside the tent and because he is a little deaf you talk a little loud."

"I'm sorry," I said. "Did I say anything bad?"

"No. Just about presents. Do you send her many presents?"

"No. Mafuta always for the family and sugar and things they need. Medicines and soap. I buy her good chocolate."

"The same as you buy me?"

"I don't know. Probably. There's only about three kinds and they are all good."

"Don't you give her any big presents?"

"No. The dress."

"It's a pretty dress."

"Do we have to do this, honey?"

"No," she said. "I'll stop it. But it interests me."

"If you say so I'll never see her."

"I don't want that," she said. "I think it's wonderful that you have a girl that can't read or write so you can't get letters from her. I think it's wonderful that she doesn't know that you are a writer or even that there are such things as writers. But you don't love her, do you?"

"I like her because she has such a lovely impudence."

"I have too," said Mary. "Maybe you like her because she's like me. It could be possible."

"I like you more and I love you."

"What does she think of me?"

"She respects you very much and she is very much afraid of you."

"Why?"

"I asked her. She said because you have a gun."

"So I have," said Miss Mary. "What does she give you for presents?"

"Mealies, mostly. Ceremonial beer. You know everything is based on exchanges of beer."

"What do you have in common, really?"

"Africa, I guess, and a sort of not too simple trust and something else. It's hard to say it."

"You're sort of nice together," she said. "I think I'd better call for lunch. Do you eat better here or there?"

"Here. Much better."

"But you eat better than here up at Mr. Singh's in Loitokitok."

"Much better. But you're never there. You're always busy."

"I have my friends there too. But I like to come into the back room and see you sitting there happily with Mr. Singh eating in the back room and reading the paper and listening to the sawmill."

I loved it at Mr. Singh's too and I was fond of all the Singh children and of Mrs. Singh who was said to be a Turkana woman. She was beautiful and very kind and understanding and extremely clean and neat. Arap Meina, who was my closest friend and associate after Ngui and Mthuka, was a great admirer of Mrs. Singh. He had reached the age when his principal enjoyment of women was in looking at them and he told me many times that Mrs. Singh was probably the most beautiful woman in the world after Miss Mary. Arap Meina, who for many months I had called Arab Minor by mistake thinking it was an English public school type name, was a Lumbwa which is a tribe related to the Masai or perhaps a branch tribe of the Masai and they are great hunters and poachers. Meina, which was his intimate name, was said to have been a very successful ivory poacher, or at least a widely traveled and little arrested ivory poacher, before he had become a Game Scout. Neither he nor I had any idea of his age but it was probably between sixty-five and seventy. He was a very brave and skillful elephant hunter and when G.C. his commanding officer was away he did the elephant control in this district. Everyone loved him very much and when he was sober or unusually drunk, he had an extremely sharp military bearing. I have rarely been saluted with such violence as Arab Minor could put into a salute when he would announce that he loved both Miss Mary and myself and no one else and too much for him to stand it. But before he had reached this state of alcoholic consumption with its attendant declarations of undying heterosexual devotion he used to like to sit with me in the back room of Mr. Singh's bar and look at Mrs. Singh waiting on the customers and going about her household duties. He preferred to observe Mrs. Singh in profile.

I was quite happy observing Arab Minor observing Mrs. Singh and with studying the oleographs and paintings on the wall of the original Singh who was usually depicted in the act of strangling a lion and a lioness, one in each hand. I pointed out to Arab Minor one time that the original Singh always strangled the lion with his right hand and I asked Mr. Singh if the original could not deal with a single male lion with his left hand as well. Mr. Singh explained that the feat had been performed before his time but that he believed it was more formal to take the male lion with the right hand.

I explained this to Arab Minor who looked cautiously away from Mrs. Singh and said that we, he and I, used either hand.

At Mr. Singh's, when it was necessary to employ an interpreter, we used a mission boy. These unhappy creatures were plentiful about Loitokitok but lived in a dread that they might be seen by a local missionary or be reported by a tale bearer if they entered Mr. Singh's. So if there was anything we needed to make absolutely clear with Mr. or Mrs. Singh or if I had any formal talks with local Masai elders we would use a mission-educated boy who would stand in the doorway to interpret holding a bottle of Coca-Cola prominently in his hand. Usually I tried to use the services of the mission boys as little as possible since they were officially saved and contact with our group could only corrupt them. Arab Minor was, allegedly, a Mohammedan, but I had long ago noticed that our devout Mohammedans would eat nothing that he, Arab Minor, halalled, that is, made the ceremonial throat cut that made the meat legal to eat if the cut was made by a practicing Moslem.

Arab Minor, one time when he had drunk quite a lot, told several people that he and I had been to Mecca together in the old days. The devout Mohammedans knew this was not true certainly insofar as Arab Minor was concerned and also that I had never known him in the old days, whenever they were, but there was some doubt as to whether I had been to Mecca. Charo had wished to convert me to Islam some twenty years before and I had gone all through Ramadan with him observing the fast. He had given me up as a possible convert many years ago. But nobody knew whether I had actually ever been to Mecca except myself. The Informer, who believed the best and worst of everyone, was convinced that I had been to Mecca many times. Willie, a half-caste driver who I had hired on his story that he was the son of a very famous old gunbearer who, I found, had not sired him told everyone in the strictest confidence that we were going to Mecca together.

Finally I had been cornered by Ngui in a theological argument and while he did not ask the question direct I told him for his own information that I had never been to Mecca and had no intention of going. This relieved him greatly.

CHAPTER 3

I was thinking of all these things when Mary mentioned Mr. Singh's and especially about how this part of Africa had changed for all of us since Pop had shown it to me for the first time. Mary and I had eaten an excellent lunch of cold meat, some tomatoes, and roasting ears from the shamba. The corn was tough and not like sweet corn but had a wonderful flavor and a good texture. It was not fashionable to eat it and when we had first come to Africa I hardly ever had it to eat except when I was alone with M'Cola. Now I had it at almost every meal and I knew who raised it and where it grew and where the gaps in the fences were and how the crop was doing every day.

Mary had gone to take a nap in the tent and I sat in the shade of the dining tent and read and thought about the shamba and Loitokitok. I knew I mustn't think about the shamba too much or I would find some excuse to go there. Debba and I never spoke to each other in front of the others except for me to say "Jambo, tú," and she would bow her head very gravely if there were others than Ngui and Mthuka present. If there were just the three of us she would laugh and they would laugh too and then the others would stay in the car or walk in another direction and she and I would walk a little way together. The thing she liked best about public society was to ride in the front seat of the hunting car between Mthuka, who was driving, and me. She would always sit very straight and look at everyone else as though she had never seen them before. Sometimes she would bow politely to her father and her mother but sometimes she would not see them. Her dress, which we had bought in Loitokitok, was pretty well worn out now in the front by sitting so straight and the color was not resisting the daily washing she gave it. We had agreed about a new dress. This was to be for Christmas or when we got the leopard. There were various leopards but this was one which had a special importance. He, for reasons, was as important to me as the dress was to her.

"With another dress I would not have to wash this one so much," she had explained.

"You wash it so much because you like to play with soap," I told her.

"Perhaps," she said. "But when can we go to Loitokitok together?"

"Soon."

"Soon is no good," she said.

"It's all I have."

"When will you come to drink beer in the evening?"

"Soon."

"I hate soon. You and soon are lying brothers."

"Then neither of us will come."

"You come and bring soon too."

"I will."

When we rode together in the front seat she liked to feel the embossing on the old leather holster of the pistol. It was a flowered design and very old and worn and she would trace the design very carefully with her fingers and then take her hand away and press the pistol and its holster close against her thigh. Then she would sit up straighter than ever. I would stroke one finger very lightly across her lips and she would laugh and Mthuka would say something in Kamba and she would sit very straight and press her thigh hard against the holster. A long time after this had first started I found that what she wanted, then, was to impress the carving of the holster into her thigh.

At first I spoke to her in Spanish. She learned it very quickly and it is simple if you start with the parts of the body and the things one can do and then food and the different relationships and the names of animals and of birds. I never spoke a word of English to her and we retained some Swahili words but the rest was a new language made up of Spanish and Kamba. Messages were brought by the Informer. Neither she nor I liked this because the Informer felt it his duty to tell me exactly her feelings in regard to me which he learned at second hand from her sister the widow. This third-party communication was difficult, sometimes embarrassing but often interesting and, at times, rewarding.

The Informer would say, "Brother, it is my duty to inform you that your girl loves you very much, truly very much, too much. When can you see her?"

"Tell her not to love an ugly old man and not to confide in you."

"I am serious, brother. You do not know. She wishes you to marry her by your tribe or by hers. There are no costs. There is no wife price. She wishes only one thing to be a wife if Memsahib, my lady, will accept her.

She understands that Memsahib is the principal wife. She is also afraid of Memsahib as you know. You do not know how serious this is. All of it."

"I have a faint idea," I said.

"Since yesterday you cannot conceive how things have been. She asks me only that you will show a certain politeness and formality to her father and her mother. The case has been reduced to that. There is no question of payment. Only of a certain formality. There are certain ceremonial beers."

"She should not care for a man of my age and habits."

"Brother, the case is that she cares. I could tell you many things. This is a serious thing."

"What can she care for?" I said, making a mistake.

"Yesterday there was the matter of you catching the roosters of the village and then putting them to sleep by some form of magic and laying them asleep in front of her family's lodge." (Neither of us could say hut.) "This has never been seen and I do not ask you what magic was employed. But she says you sprung at them with a movement that could not be seen, almost like a leopard. Since then she has not been the same. Then she has on the walls of the lodge the pictures from *Life* magazine of the great beasts of America and of the washing machine, the cooking machines and miraculous ranges, and the stirring machines."

"I am sorry about that. It was a mistake."

"It is because of that she washes her dress so much. She is trying to be like the washing machine to please you. She is afraid that you will become lonely for the washing machine and go away. Brother, sir, there is tragedy. Can you do nothing positive for her?"

"I will do what I can," I said. "But remember that putting the roosters to sleep was not magic. It is a trick. Catching them is only a trick too."

"Brother, she loves you very much."

"Tell her there is no such word as love. Just as there is no word for sorry."

"That is true. But there is the thing although there is no word for it."

"You and I are the same age. It is not necessary to explain so much."

"I tell you this only because it is serious."

"I cannot break the law if we are here to enforce the law."

"Brother, you do not understand. There is no law. This shamba is here illegally. It is not in Wakamba country. For thirty-five years it has been ordered removed and it has never happened. There is not even customary law. There are only variations."

"Go on," I said.

"Thank you, brother. Let me tell you that for the people of this shamba you and Bwana Game are the law. You are a bigger law than Bwana Game because you are older. Also he is away and his askaris are with him. Here you have your young men and warriors such as Ngui. You have Arap Meina. Everyone knows you are Arap Meina's father."

"I'm not."

"Brother, please try not to misunderstand me. You know the sense in which I say 'father.' Arap Meina says you are his father. Also you brought him to life after he died in the airplane. You brought him back to life after he lay dead in Bwana Mouse's tent. It is known. Many things are known."

"Too many things are improperly known."

"Brother, may I have a drink?"

"If I do not see you take it."

"Chin-chin," the Informer said. He had taken the Canadian gin instead of the Gordon's and my heart went out to him. "You must forgive me," he said. "I have lived all my life with the bwanas. May I tell you more or are you tired of the subject?"

"I am tired of part of it but other parts interest me. Tell me more about the history of the shamba."

"I do not know it exactly because they are Kamba and I am Masai. That shows there is something wrong with the shamba or I would not be living there. There is something wrong with the men. You have seen them. For some reason they came here originally. This is a long way from Wakamba country. Neither true tribal law nor any other law runs here. You have also seen the condition of the Masai."

"We have to talk about that another day."

"Willingly. Brother, things are not well. It is a long story. But let me tell you about the shamba. When you went there in the early morning and spoke through me about the all-night ngoma of the great drunkenness with such severity the people said afterwards that they could see the gallows in your eyes. The man who was still so drunk that he could not understand was taken to the river and washed in the water from the mountain until he understood and he entered the neighboring province the same day climbing the mountain on foot. You do not know what serious law you are."

"It is a small shamba. But very beautiful. Who sold them the sugar for the beer of that ngoma?"

"I do not know. But I could find out."

"I know," I said and told him. I knew that he knew. But he was an informer and he had lost out in life long ago and it was the bwanas who had ruined him although he gave full credit for that process to a Somali wife. But it was a bwana, a great Lord, who was the greatest friend the Masai ever had but who liked, he said, to do things backwards who, if what he said was true, had ruined him. No one knows how much is true that an informer says but his description of this great man had been done with such a mixture of admiration and remorse that it seemed to explain many things that I had never understood. I had never heard of any backward tendency on the part of this great man until I came to know the Informer. I always expressed disbelief at some of these surprising tales.

"You will hear, of course," the Informer said to me now that his zeal for informing had been heightened by the Canadian gin, "that I am an agent of the Mau Mau and you may believe it because I have said such things about this backwardness. But, brother, it is not true. I truly love and believe in the bwanas. True, all but one or two of the great bwanas are dead."

We sat and recalled the truly great bwanas who were dead and I brought him up to date on the manner of the death of various great bwanas who had died outside the country during the past ten years.

"I should have led a far different life," the Informer said. "Thinking of these great dead bwanas fills me with the resolution to lead a better and finer life. Is it permitted?"

"The last one," I said. "And only as a medicine."

At the word medicine the Informer brightened. He had a very nice and rather noble large face covered with the lines and wrinkles of good temper and uncomplaining dissipation and debauchery. It was not an ascetic face nor was there any depravity in it. It was the face of a dignified man who being a Masai and ruined by the bwanas and by a Somali wife now lived in an outlaw Wakamba village with the status of protector of a widow and earned eighty-six shillings a month betraying anyone betrayable. Yet it was a handsome face, ravaged and cheerful, and I was very fond of the Informer although I disapproved of him completely and had several times told him that it might be my duty to see him hanged.

"Brother," he said, "there must be those medicines. How would the great doctor with the Dutch name have written about them in such a serious review as *The Reader's Digest* if they did not exist?"

"They exist," I said. "But I do not have them. I can send them to you."

"Brother, you know that we are of the same age group. So you know that it is not a discourtesy when I say that always when the bwanas say I will send it to you never has anything come."

"Never?"

"In my case never. Others have had different experiences."

"I'm sorry," I said. "I may fail you too."

"Listen to me truly, brother. When I spoke of the bwanas I was not speaking of you. You are a bwana with the bwanas. But here you are a mzee. Not as a joke. Truly."

"It is not a great title."

"Brother, do not pretend to be ignorant. Bwana Game is respected and he is very well liked."

"He is brave, has a good heart, and is just. He *should* be respected and well liked."

"He *is* as I told you. I will not try to explain if you are not in a mood for understanding."

"I am in no such mood. Also Bwana Game is your superior officer and I am not yet such a fool as to discuss him with you."

"Yes, brother. Do you want me to call you Bwana?"

"In front of other people when it is the correct address."

"Brother, only one thing more. The girl is a very serious thing."

"If you ever say that again I will know you are a fool. Like all people when they drink you repeat yourself."

"I will excuse myself."

"Go, brother. I will try, truly, to send you the medicine and other good medicines. When I see you next be prepared to bring me more of the history of the shamba."

"Do you have any messages?"

"No messages."

CHAPTER 4

It always shocked me to realize that the Informer and I were the same age. We were not exactly the same age but were of the same age group which was near enough and bad enough. And here I was with a wife that I loved and who loved me and tolerated my errors and referred to this girl as my fiancée, tolerating because I was in some ways a good husband and for other reasons of generosity and kindness and detachment and wanting me to know more about this country than I had any right to know. We were happy at least a good part of each day and nearly always at night and this night, in bed together, under the mosquito netting with the flaps of the tent open so that we could see the long burned-through logs of the big fire and the wonderful darkness that receded jaggedly as the night wind struck the fire and then closed in quickly as the wind dropped, we were very happy.

"We're too lucky," Mary said. "I love Africa so. I don't know how we can ever leave it."

It was a cold night with the breeze off the snows of the mountain and we were snug under the blankets. The night noises were starting and we had heard the first hyena and then the others. Mary loved to hear them at night. They make a pleasant noise if you love Africa and we laughed together as they moved around the camp and out past the cook's tent where the meat was hung in a tree. They could not reach the meat but they kept talking about it.

"You know, if you are ever dead and I'm not lucky so we die together if anyone asks me what I remember best about you I'll tell them about how much room you could give your wife in a canvas cot. Where do you put yourself, really?"

"Sort of sideways on the edge. I've lots of room."

"We can sleep comfortably in a bed one person couldn't be comfortable in if it's cold enough."

"That's the thing. It has to be cold."

"Can we stay longer in Africa and not go home until spring?"

"Sure. Let's stay until we're broke."

Then we heard the thud of a lion's cough as he came hunting across the long meadow up from the river.

"Listen," Mary said. "Hold me close and tight and listen."

"He's come back," Mary whispered.

"You can't tell it's him."

"I'm sure it is him," Mary said. "I've heard him enough nights. He's come down from the manyatta where he killed the two cows. Arab Minor said he would come back."

We could hear his coughing grunt as he moved across the meadow toward where we had made the airstrip for the small plane.

"We'll know if it's him in the morning," I said. "Ngui and I know his tracks."

"So do I."

"OK. You track him."

"No. I only meant that I do know his tracks."

"They're awfully big." I was sleepy and I thought if we are going to hunt lion with Miss Mary in the morning I should get some sleep. For a long time we had known, in some things, what the other one of us was going to say or, often, to think and Mary said, "I'd better get in my own bed so you'll be comfortable and sleep well."

"Go to sleep here. I'm fine."

"No. It wouldn't be good."

"Sleep here."

"No. Before a lion I ought to sleep in my own bed."

"Don't be such a bloody warrior."

"I am a warrior. I'm your wife and your lover and your small warrior brother."

"All right," I said. "Good night, warrior brother."

"Kiss your warrior brother."

"You get in your own bed or stay here."

"Maybe I'll do both," she said.

In the night I heard the lion speak several times as he was hunting. Miss Mary was sleeping soundly and breathing softly. I lay awake and thought about too many things but mostly about the lion and my obligations to Pop and to Bwana Game and to others. I did not think about Miss Mary except about her height, which was five feet two inches, in relation to tall grass and bush and that, no matter how cold the morning was she must not wear too much clothing as the stock on the 6.5 Mannlicher was too long for her if her shoulder was padded and she might let the rifle off as she raised it to shoot. I lay awake thinking about this and about the lion and the way Pop would handle it and how wrong he had been the last time and how right he had been more times than I had ever seen a lion.

Then before it was daylight when the coals of the fire were covered by the gray ashes that sifted in the early morning breeze I put on my high soft boots and an old dressing gown and went to wake Ngui in his pup tent.

He woke sullen and not at all my blood brother and I remembered that he never smiled before the sun was up and sometimes it took him longer to get rid of wherever he had been when he was asleep.

We talked at the dead ashes of the cook fire.

"You heard the lion?"

"Ndio, Bwana."

This, a politeness, was also a rudeness as we both knew for we had discussed the phrase, "Ndio, Bwana," which is what the African says always to the White Man to get rid of him through agreement.

"How many lions did you hear?"

"One."

"Mzuri," I said meaning that was better and he was correct and had heard the lion. He spat and took snuff and then offered it to me and I took some and put it under my upper lip.

"Was it the big lion of Memsahib?" I asked feeling the lovely quick bite of the snuff against the gums and the pocket of the upper lip.

"Hapana," he said. This was the absolute negative.

"Are you sure?" I asked.

"Sure," he said in English.

"Where did he go?"

"You know."

The cook was awake now hearing us talk and so were the older men who were the lightest sleepers.

"Take tea for us," I said to Mwindi and gave good morning to him and all who were awake.

"You and I will go to look at the track where he crossed the motor car tracks," I said to Ngui.

"I will go," Ngui said. "You can get dressed."

"Take chai first."

"There is no need. Chai afterwards. It is a young lion."

"Send breakfast," I said to the cook. He woke cheerfully and now he winked at me. "Piga simba," he said. "We'll eat him for supper."

Keiti was standing by the cooking fire now with his slashed-flat doubting smile. He had wound his turban in the dark and there was an end that should have been tucked in. His eyes were doubting too. There was nothing of the feeling of a serious lion hunt.

"Hapana simba kubwa sana," Keiti said to me his eyes mocking but apologetic and absolutely confident. He knew it was not the big lion that we had heard so many times. "N'anyake," he said to make an early morning joke. This meant, in Kamba, a lion old enough to be a warrior and marry and have children but not old enough to drink beer. His saying it and making the joke in Kamba was a sign of friendliness, made at daylight when friendliness has a low boiling point, to show, gently, that he knew I was trying to learn Kamba with the non-Moslem and alleged bad element and that he approved or tolerated.

Ngui had started down the track the hunting car had worn in the new grass. He was walking in his contemptuous imitation of the way he had been trained to march in the King's African Rifles. It was not contemptuous toward anyone nor toward the K.A.R. It was how he felt in the too early morning on a fruitless errand. I should have called him back but he was carrying one of the killing spears and there was a definite report I must make to Mary and if I simply gave her opinions rather than evidence it would not make good feeling around home. No one could gauge nor measure how deeply she felt about the lion nor how many things were involved. I had functioned on this lion business almost as long as I could remember anything that had happened. In Africa you could remember around a month at a time if the pace was fast. The pace had been almost excessive and there had been the allegedly criminal lions of Salengai, the lions of Magadi, the lions of here, against whom allegations had now been repeated four times, and this new intruding lion who had, as yet, no fiche nor dossier. This was a lion who had coughed a few times and gone about hunting the game that he was entitled to. But it was necessary to prove that to Miss Mary and to prove that he was not the lion she had hunted for so long who was charged with many offenses and whose huge pug marks, the left hind one scarred, we had followed so many times only, finally, to see him going away into tall grass that led to the heavy timber of the swamp or to the thick bush of the gerenuk country up by the old manyatta on the way to the Chyulu Hills. He was so dark that with his heavy black mane he looked almost black and he had a huge head that swung low when he moved off into country where it was impossible for Mary to follow him. He had been hunted for many years and he was very definitely not a picture lion. Arap Meina said he was the father of the great dark-maned lion Mayito had killed when we had been in this country some months before.

Now I was dressed drinking tea in the early morning light by the built-up fire and waiting for Ngui. I saw him coming across the field with the spear on his shoulder stepping out smartly through the grass still wet with dew. He saw me and came toward the fire leaving a trail behind him through the wet grass.

"Simba dume kidogo," he said telling me he was a small male lion. "N'anyake," he said making the same joke Keiti had made. "Hapana mzuri for Memsahib."

"Thank you," I said. "I'll let Memsahib sleep."

"Mzuri," he said and went off to the cooking fire.

We both knew how hard Mary had hunted for so many days and it would be good for her to sleep as long as she could and wake of her own accord. She was more tired than she knew. Arab Minor would be in with the report on the big black-maned lion who had been reported by the Masai from a manyatta up in the western hills to have killed two cows and dragged one away with him. The Masai had suffered under him for a long time. He traveled restlessly and he did not return to his kills as a lion would be expected to. Arab Minor had the theory that this lion had once returned and fed on a kill that had been poisoned by a former Game Ranger and that he had been made terribly sick by it and had learned, or decided, never to return to a kill. That would account for his moving about so much but not for the haphazard way he visited the various Masai villages or manyattas. Now the plain, the salt licks, and the bush country were heavy with game since the good grass had come with the violent spot rains of November and Arab Minor, Ngui, and I all expected the big lion to leave the hills and come down to the plain where he could hunt out of the edge of the swamp. This was his customary way of hunting in this district.

The Masai can be very sarcastic and their cattle are not only their wealth but something much more to them and the Informer had told me that one chief has spoken very badly about the fact that I had two chances to kill this lion and instead had waited to let a woman do it. I had sent word to the chief that if his young men were not women who spent all their time in Loitokitok drinking Golden Jeep sherry he would have no need to ask for me to kill his lion but that I would see he was killed the next time he came into the area where we were. If he cared to bring his young men I would take a spear with them and we would kill him that way. I asked him to come into camp and we would talk it over.

He had turned up at camp one morning with three other elders and I had sent for the Informer to interpret. We had a good talk. The chief explained that the Informer had misquoted him. Bwana Game, G.C., had always killed the lions that it was necessary to kill and was a very brave and skillful man and they had great confidence in him and affection for him. He remembered too that when we had been here last in the time of the dryness Bwana Game had killed a lion and Bwana Game and I had killed a lioness with the young men. This lioness had done much damage.

I answered that these facts were known and that it was the duty of Bwana Game and, for this time myself, to kill any lions that molested cattle, donkeys, sheep, goats, or people. This we would always do. It was necessary for the religion of the Memsahib that she kill this particular lion before the Birthday of the Baby Jesus. We came from a far country and were of a tribe of that country and this was necessary. They would be shown the skin of this lion before the Birthday of the Baby Jesus.

We had all shaken hands and they had gone. I was a little worried about the time element as Christmas was getting close. But the lion would certainly come down to the plain with this amount of game that was here now and you always had to take some chances. To be a successful prophet you had to prophesy. I wondered how many of the Masai would know him by that old scar on his foot. Probably plenty would know him. There was an answer to that. Mary could always shoot him in one foot.

As always I was a little appalled by my oratory after it was over and had the usual sinking feeling about commitments made. Miss Mary must, I thought, belong to a fairly warlike tribe if she, a woman, had to kill a long-time marauding lion before the Birthday of the Baby Jesus. But at least I had not said she had to do it every year. That might have been better though and might have given them more confidence. But we did have a slight advantage, though, in the way their young men had behaved in the surrounding and spearing of the last previous marauding lion incident. At the moment of getting out off the trucks to advance and close the circle on the patch of heavy bush where the lion and the lioness were laying up, spears were to be had for the asking. One young warrior had remained in the truck, on the floor, and G.C., who was Bwana Game, had taken his spear and his place in the hunt. One warrior had hysterics and threw himself into a thorn bush foaming at the mouth. This produced hysterics in another previously untried warrior who threw himself into another thorn bush. Since the lions were actually the marauding type of lion they did not wait for the encircling movement to be completed when they heard these hysterical manifestations and they took off. The wildest type of rat race, or lion race, then ensued and when it was over the lioness, who had been the killer, was dead but no spear went into her until she had been certified dead by Bwana Game. I had hit her and was tracking the blood spoor very carefully as she might be crouched under any bush and there were many isolated bushes. Then I saw G.C. (Bwana Game) on my right and saw him shoot and she was dead. So we did have this small incident in our favor. But the Birthday of the Baby Jesus was coming very close.

44

Keiti took the Birthday of the Baby Jesus very seriously since he had been on so many safaris with churchgoing and even devout bwanas. Most of these bwanas since they were paying so much for their safari and since the time was short did not let the birthday interfere with their shooting. But there was always a special dinner with wine and, if possible, champagne and it was always a special occasion. This year it was even more special since we were in a permanent camp and with Miss Mary taking it so seriously and it being so obviously such an important part of her religion and attended by so many ceremonials, especially that of the tree, that Keiti, loving order and ceremony, gave it a great importance. The ceremony of the tree appealed to him since in his old religion, before he had become a Moslem, a grove of trees had been of the highest importance.

The rougher pagan element of the camp thought that Miss Mary's tribal religion was one of the sterner branches of religion since it involved the slaying of a gerenuk under impossible conditions, the slaughter of a bad lion, and the worship of a tree which fortunately Miss Mary did not know produced the concoction which excited and maddened the Masai for war and lion hunting. I am not sure that Keiti knew this was one of the properties of the particular Christmas tree that Miss Mary had selected but about five of us knew it and it was a very carefully kept secret.

They did not believe that the lion was a part of Miss Mary's Christmas duty because they had been with her while she had sought a big lion now for several months. But Ngui had put forth a theory that perhaps Miss Mary had to kill a large black-maned lion in the year sometime before Christmas and being too short to see in the high grass she had started early. She had started in September to kill the lion before the end of the year or whenever the Birthday of the Baby Jesus was. Ngui was not sure. But it came before that other great holiday the Birth of the Year which was a payday.

Charo did not believe any of this because he had seen too many memsahibs shoot too many lions. But he was unsteadied because nobody helped Miss Mary. He had seen me help Miss Pauline years before and he was puzzled by the whole thing. He had been very fond of Miss Pauline but nothing to what he felt for Miss Mary who was obviously a wife from another tribe. Her tribal scars showed it. They were very fine delicately cut scars across one cheek and horizontal light traces of cuts on the forehead. They were the work of the best plastic surgeon in Cuba after a motor car accident and nobody could see them who did not know how to look for almost invisible tribal scars as Ngui did.

Ngui had asked me one day very brusquely if Miss Mary was from the same tribe that I came from.

"No," I said. "She is from a Northern Frontier tribe in our country. From Minnesota."

"We have seen the tribal marks."

Then afterwards one time when we were talking tribes and religion he asked me if we were going to brew and drink the Baby Jesus tree. I told him I did not think so and he said, "Mzuri."

"Why?"

"Gin for you. Beer for us. Nobody thinks Miss Mary should drink it unless her religion requires it."

"I know if she kills the lion she will not have to drink it."

"Mzuri," he said. "Mzuri sana."

Now on this morning I was waiting for Miss Mary to wake up of her own accord so she would be rested and have a good backlog of normal sleep behind her. I was not worried about the lion but I thought of him quite a lot and always in connection with Miss Mary. She had been hunting him a long time and always under adverse circumstances and the last big lion she had hunted before him had been under very adverse circumstances.

There is as much difference between a wild lion and a marauding lion and the type of lion tourists take pictures of in the national parks as there is between the old grizzly that will follow your trap line and ruin it and tear the roofs off your cabins and eat the supplies and yet never be seen and the bears that come up alongside the road to be photographed in Yellowstone Park. True, the bears in the park injure people every year and if the tourists do not stay in their cars they will get in trouble. They even get in trouble in their cars sometimes and some bears get bad and have to be destroyed.

Picture lions that are accustomed to being fed and photographed sometimes wander away from the area where they are protected and having learned not to fear human beings are easily killed by alleged sportsmen and their wives always, of course, backed up by a professional hunter. But our problem was not to criticize how other people had killed lions or would kill lions but to find and have Miss Mary find and kill an intelligent, destructive, and much hunted lion in a way that had been defined, if not by our religion, by certain ethical standards. Miss Mary had hunted by these standards for a long time now. They were very severe standards and Charo, who loved Miss Mary, was impatient with them. He had been mauled three times by leopards when things had gone wrong and he thought I was holding Mary to a standard of ethics which was too rigid and slightly murderous. But I had not invented them. I had learned them from Pop and Pop, on his last lion hunt and taking out his last safari, wanted things to be as they were in the old days before the hunting of dangerous game had been corrupted and made easy by what he always called "these bloody cars."

46

This lion had beaten us twice and both times I had easy chances at him which I had not taken because he was Mary's. The last time Pop had made a mistake because he was so anxious for Mary to get the lion before he had to leave us that he made an error, as anyone can who is trying too hard.

Afterwards we had sat by the fire in the evening, Pop smoking his pipe while Mary wrote in her diary where she put in all the things she did not wish to say to us and her heartaches and disappointments and her new knowledge that she did not wish to parade in conversation and her triumphs that she did not wish to tarnish by talking of them. She was writing by the gaslight in the dining tent and Pop and I were sitting by the fire in our pajamas, dressing gowns, and mosquito boots.

"He's a damned smart lion," Pop said. "We should have had him today if Mary had been a little taller. But it was my fault."

We avoided talking of the error which we both knew about.

"Mary will get him. But keep this in mind. I don't think he's too brave, mind you. He's too smart. But when he's hit he'll be brave enough when the time comes. Don't you let the time come."

"I'm shooting all right now."

Pop ignored that. He was thinking. Then he said, "Better than all right, actually. Don't get overconfident but stay as confident as you are. He'll make a mistake and you'll get him. If only some lioness would come into heat. Then he'd be money from home. But they're about ready to pup now."

"What sort of a mistake will he make?"

"Oh he'll make one. You'll know. I wish I didn't have to go before Mary gets him. Take really good care of her. See she gets some sleep. She's been at this now for a long time. Rest her and rest the damn lion. Don't hunt him too hard. Let him get some confidence."

"Anything else?"

"Keep her shooting the meat and get her confident if you can."

"I thought of having her stalk until fifty yards and then maybe to twenty."

"Might work," said Pop. "We've tried everything else."

"I think it will work. Then she can take them longer."

"She makes the damnedest shots," Pop said. "Then for two days who knows where it's going?"

"I think I have it figured out."

"So did I. But don't take her to any twenty yards on lion."

"I won't," I said. "Unless that's where we find him."

"I won't worry," Pop said. "But please think properly."

"I'll do it as you taught me."

"I'm not sure that's too bloody wonderful," Pop said. "Let's talk about something besides shop. Just see she's rested and try to get her shooting confidently."

It was more than twenty years before that Pop and I had first sat together by a fire or the ashes of a fire and talked about the theory and practice of shooting dangerous game. He disliked and distrusted the target-range or woodchuck-hunter type.

"Hit a golf ball off the caddie's head at a mile," he said. "Wooden or steel caddy of course. Not a live caddy. Never miss until they have to shoot a really great kudu at twenty yards. Then couldn't hit the mountainside. Bloody gun waving around and the great shooter shaking until I was shaking myself." He drew on his pipe. "Never trust any man, Pop, until you've seen him shoot at something dangerous or that he wants really badly at fifty yards or under. Never buy him until you've seen him shoot at twenty. The short distance uncovers what's inside of them. The worthless ones will always miss or gut shoot at the range we get to so we can't miss."

"Don't say 'we.'"

"I say it. Don't forget I brought you up."

"I'm your pup," I said. "But you're not responsible for all my bad points."

"No fear," he said. "I haven't taken any."

"Who's the best shot you've ever had?"

"That damned Mayito. He hasn't any nerves at all. And you may have noticed that he doesn't drink."

"He doesn't need to."

"Neither do we to shoot. But we have had fun with it."

We were calling each other Pop now and thinking about times a long way away.

"Do you remember when you had the amoebic and parts of you used to come out and the Memsahib decided that you had the piles?" Pop remembered. "We were walking along that donga to where we would shoot sand grouse at that little water. Do you remember that bloody great lion put his head up out of the donga and then his neck and shoulders and looked at you as though you had the piles? You were behind making heavy going of it and the Memsahib and I were ahead and we had walked right past the lion."

"And you looked backward sort of coldly and said, 'Can you hit him in the head, Pop?' And I heard your safety click and I was surprised you would have a safety that clicked."

"What an observant type," Pop said. "I don't think it did click, actually, I think you made that up."

"It clicked."

"Possibly," Pop said. "Then you said very softly, very softly and look-

48

ing like a man with a most awful attack of piles, 'I don't know about his head but I can break his fucking neck.' I remember thinking what long speeches you made with you and the lion looking at each other on such an intimate basis. But sure enough you broke his neck."

"Do you remember the odd noise it made?"

"Do I not. That was the day M'Cola started to get fond of you. You know he didn't think so much of you until then. But he never got over that noise."

"We were friends before then."

"I was only teasing you. When did you and Ngui get so mixed up with each other?"

"Magadi, I guess."

"He's the only boy in this lot I've ever had trouble with."

"He'd soldiered a lot in the K.A.R., Pop. Abyssinia and Burma both. He's a rough boy. But he isn't bad."

"You're both bad," Pop said.

I was thinking about this and happily about the old days and how fine this whole trip had been and how awful it would be if Pop and I would never be out together again when Arab Minor came up to the fire and saluted. He always saluted very solemnly but his smile started to come out as his hand came down.

"Good morning, Meina," I said.

"Jambo, Bwana. The big lion killed as they said at the manyatta. He dragged the cow a long way into thick brush. He did not return to the kill after he had eaten but went in the direction of the swamp for water."

"The lion with the scarred paw?"

"Yes, Bwana. He should come down now."

"Good. Is there other news?"

"They say that the Mau Mau who were imprisoned at Machakos have broken out of jail and are coming this way."

"When?"

"Yesterday."

"Who says?"

"A Masai I met on the road. He had ridden in the lorry of a Hindu trader. He did not know which duka."

"Get something to eat. I will need to speak to you later."

"Ndio, Bwana," he said and saluted. His rifle shone in the morning sunlight. He had changed to fresh uniform at the shamba and he looked very smart and he looked very pleased. He had two happy pieces of news. He was a hunter and now we would have hunting.

I thought I better go over to the tent and see if Miss Mary was awake. If she was still sleeping all the better.

49

CHAPTER 5

Miss Mary was awake but not all the way awake. If she had left a definite call to be wakened at a half past four or five she woke fast and efficiently and impatient with all delay. But this morning she woke slowly.

"What's the matter?" she asked sleepily. "Why didn't anybody call me? The sun's up. What's the matter?"

"It wasn't the big lion, honey. So I let you sleep."

"How do you know it wasn't the big lion?"

"Ngui checked."

"What about the big lion?"

"He isn't down yet."

"How do you know that?"

"Arab Minor came in."

"Are you going out to check on the buff?"

"No. I'm going to leave everything alone. We've got a little trouble of some sort."

"Can I help you?"

"No, honey. You sleep some more."

"I think I will for a little while if you don't need me. I've been having the most wonderful dreams."

"See if you can get back into them. You call for chakula when you're ready."

"I'll sleep just a little more," she said. "They're really wonderful dreams."

I reached under my blanket and found my pistol on the belt with the sling strap hanging from the holster. I washed in the bowl, rinsed my eyes with boric acid solution, combed my hair with a towel, it was now clipped so short that neither brush nor comb was needed, and dressed and shoved my right foot through the leg strap on the pistol, pulled it up and buckled the pistol belt. In the old days we never carried pistols and it would have been very bad form in the days when we were pukka sahibs. But now you put the pistol on as naturally as you buttoned the flap of your trousers. The strap around the leg was from an old Afrika Korps pair of binoculars and it was not to show off. It made the pistol much more practical. It was a very practical pistol anyway. It was a Colt Match Woodsman .22 caliber shooting high-speed hollow-point ammunition. It was very deadly and you could hit what you shot at and there were ten rounds in each clip. I carried two extra clips in a small plastic bag in the right-hand pocket of my bush jacket and carried the extra ammunition in a screw-top, wide-mouthed medicine bottle which had held liver capsules. This bottle had held fifty red and white capsules and now held sixty-five rounds of hollow points. Ngui carried one and I another.

Everyone loved the pistol because it could hit guinea fowl, lesser bustard, jackals, which carried rabies, and it could kill hyenas. Ngui and Mthuka loved it because it would make little sharp barks like a dog yapping and puffs of dust would appear ahead of the squat-running hyena then there would be the plunk, plunk, plunk, and the hyena would slow his gallop and start to circle. Ngui would hand me a full clip he had taken from my pocket and I would shove it in and then there would be another dust puff, then a plunk, plunk, and the hyena would roll over with his legs in the air.

"Do you want to go over and halal?" I would ask Charo.

"Hapana, Bwana." He would grin his old man's grin and Ngui would smile his love smile for pistol. It was never "the pistol." It was "pistol" as though pistol were a man or an animal or death or beer or supper. Pistol was our prodigy and our unbelievable champion. But what they loved best was to see pistol shoot fast.

"Shoot him fast," Ngui urged. "We have mingi, many, mingi cartridges."

"You shoot him fast."

"No, you. Shoot him fast for practice."

Then I would shoot him so fast at the dead hyena that the little barks chopped up almost into a blur.

"Seven," Ngui would say. "Three misses. Two chini, one juu."

"Pistol mzuri," Mthuka would say.

"Mzuri sana, Bwana," Charo said. "Mzuri sana."

Miss Mary was very patient about pistol. She shot pistol very well herself and I always thought that she was saving her demonstration of this for some time when it would be properly impressive. Maybe for the Birthday of the Baby Jesus. The spear was what she hated. But the spear came along much later.

Anyway I buckled on pistol and walked out to the lines to speak to Keiti about the developments. I asked him to come where we could speak alone and he stood at ease looking old and wise and cynical and partly doubting and partly amused.

"I do not believe they would come here," he said. "They are Wakamba Mau Mau. They are not so stupid. They will hear that we are here."

"My only problem is if they come here. If they come here where will they go?"

"They will not come here."

"Why not?"

"I think what I would do if I were Mau Mau. I would not come here."

"But you are a mzee and an intelligent man. These are Mau Mau."

"All Mau Mau are not stupid," he said. "And these are Kamba."

"I agree," I said. "But these were all caught when they went to the reserve as missionaries for Mau Mau. Why were they caught?"

"Because they got drunk and bragged how great they were."

"Yes. And if they come here where there is a Kamba shamba they will want drink. They will need food and they will need more than anything drink if they are the same people who were taken prisoner from drinking."

"They will not be the same now. They have escaped from prison."

"They will go where there is drink."

"Probably. But they will not come here. They are Wakamba."

"I must take measures."

"Yes."

"I will let you know my decision. Is everything in order in the camp? Is there any sickness? Have you any problems?"

"Everything is in order. I have no problems. The camp is happy."

"What about meat?"

"We will need meat tonight."

"Wildebeest?"

He shook his head slowly and smiled the cleft smile.

"Many cannot eat it."

"How many can eat it?"

"Nine."

"What can the others eat?"

"Impala mzuri."

"There are too many impala here and I have two more," I said. "I will have the meat for tonight. But I wish it killed when the sun is going down so it will chill in the cold from the mountain in the night. I wish the meat wrapped in cheesecloth so that the flies will not spoil it. We are guests here and I am responsible. We must waste nothing. How long would it take them to come from Machakos?"

"Three days. But they will not come here."

"Ask the cook please to make me breakfast."

I walked back to the dining tent and sat at the table and took a book from one of the improvised book shelves made from empty wooden boxes. It was the year there were so many books about people who had escaped from prison camps in Germany and this book was an escape book. I put it back and drew another one. This was called *The Last Resorts*, and I thought it would be more diverting.

As I opened the book to the chapter on Bar Harbor I heard a motorcar coming very fast, and then looking out through the open back of the tent I saw it was the police Land Rover coming at full speed through the lines, raising a cloud of dust that blew over everything including the laundry before the open motorcar pulled up to a dirt-track racing stop alongside the tent. The young police officer came in, saluted smartly, and put out his hand. He was a tall fair boy with an unpromising face.

"Good morning, Bwana," he said and removed his uniform cap.

"Have some breakfast?"

"No time, Bwana."

"What's the matter?"

"The balloon's gone up, Bwana. We're for it now. Fourteen of them, Bwana. Fourteen of the most desperate type."

"Armed?"

"To the teeth, Bwana."

"These the lot that escaped from Machakos?"

"Yes. How did you hear about that?"

"Game Scout brought the word in this morning."

"Governor," he said, this was a fatherly term that he employed and had no relation to the title of one who governs a colony. "We must coordinate our effort again."

"I am at your service."

"How would you go about it, Governor? The combined operation."

"It's your shauri. I'm only Acting Game here."

"Be a good chap, Governor. Help a bloke out. You and Bwana Game helped me out before. In these times we must all play the game together. Play it up to the hilt."

"Quite," I said. "But I'm not a policeman."

"You're Acting-bloody-Game though. We cooperate. What would you do, Governor? I'll cooperate to the hilt."

"I'll make a screen," I said.

"Could I have a glass of beer?" he asked.

"Pour a bottle and I'll split it with you."

"My throat's dry from the dust."

"Next time don't get it all over our fucking laundry," I said.

"Sorry, Governor. Couldn't be sorrier. But I was preoccupied with our problem and I thought it had rained."

"Day before yesterday. Dry now."

"Go ahead, Governor. So you'll put out a screen."

"Yes," I said. "There's a Wakamba shamba here."

"I had no idea of that. Does the D.C. know?"

"Yes," I said. "There are in all four shambas where beer is made."

"That's illegal."

"Yes, but you'll find they frequently do it in Africa. I propose to put a man in each of these shambas. If any of these characters show up he'll let me know and I'll close in on the shamba and we'll take them."

"Dead or alive," he said.

"You're sure about that?"

"Absolutely, Governor. These are desperate types."

"We ought to check on it."

"No need, Governor. Word of honor. But how will you get word from the shamba to you here?"

"In anticipation of this type of thing we've organized a form of Women's Auxiliary Corps. They're frightfully efficient."

"Good show. I'm glad you laid that on. Is it widely extended?"

"Quite. Frightfully keen girl at the head of it. True underground type."

"Could I meet her sometime?"

"Be a bit tricky with you in uniform. I'll think about it though."

"Underground," he said. "I always thought that might have been just my dish. The underground."

"Could be," I said. "We can get some old parachutes down and practice after this show is over."

"Can you gen it out just a little more, Governor? We have the screen now. The screen sounds like the thing. But there's more."

"I keep the balance of my force here in hand but absolutely mobile to move on any sensitive parts of the screen. You go back to the boma now and put yourself in a state of defense. Then I suggest that you lay on a roadblock in daylight on the turn of the road at about mile ten from here. Take it off on your speedometer. I suggest you move this roadblock at night down to where the road comes out of the swamp. Do you remember where we went after the baboons?"

"Never forget it, Bwana."

"There if you have any trouble I will be in touch with you. Be awfully careful about shooting people up at night. There's a lot of traffic comes through there."

54

"There's supposed to be none."

"There is though. If I were you I would post three signs outside the three dukas that the curfew is to be enforced absolutely on the roads. It could save you some trouble."

"Can you give me any people, Bwana?"

"Not unless the situation deteriorates. Remember I'm screening for you. Tell you what I'll do. I'll send a chit by you that you can telephone through Ngong and I'll get the plane down. I need her for something else anyway."

"Right, Bwana. Would there be any chance I could fly with you?"

"I think not," I said. "You're needed on the ground."

I wrote the chit asking for the plane any time after lunch tomorrow to bring mail and papers from Nairobi and put in two hours flying here.

"You'd better get along up to the boma," I said. "And please, kid, never come into camp in that cowboy style. It puts the dust on the food, in the men's tents, and on the laundry."

"Couldn't be sorrier, Governor. It'll never happen again. And thanks for helping me staff things out."

"Maybe I'll see you in town this afternoon."

"Good show."

He drained his beer, saluted, and went out and commenced to shout for his driver.

After he had left, driving gently, Keiti came in with Msembi who brought breakfast.

"Was there news from the police?" he asked smiling.

"The child of the police brought the news we know."

"I do not believe they will come. But there are four of our safari who know some of these who have escaped by sight. These Mau Mau are boys who went to work in Nairobi and have become no good. They are drunkards as you said."

I told him what the plan was.

"It is a good plan. But with this plan you and Memsahib Mary cannot hunt."

"It will give her a rest and it will give the lion a rest. I am getting the ndege to make patrol."

"Mzuri sana," he said. "Mzuri sana."

Since the Abyssinian war he had been a great believer in the aircraft.

"We can get the tree for Memsahib Mary," he said.

"She has selected the tree. It is better to wait so that the tree will not die. Maybe she would like to go to fish with the skinner and perhaps see the hippopotamus. Is the skinner one of those who does not know these Mau Mau?"

55

"He says he is," Keiti said. "I will go with him and Memsahib to the fishing pool if you wish. There are no rhino nor anything to fear there."

"Mthuka can drive you. Arap Meina can go with you with his rifle."

"I do not need Arap Meina to take care of Memsahib there."

"If he were there you might learn something from the road. Many people travel the road."

"Ndio," Keiti said. "But it is not a road where you will learn much."

Mary came into the tent looking morning fresh and shining. Keiti said, "Jambo, Memsahib." She smiled at him and answered his greeting and he left.

"Wasn't that the boy from the police? What kind of trouble is it?"

I told her about the gang breaking out of the jail in Machakos and the rest of it. She was properly unimpressed.

As we ate breakfast she asked, "Don't you think it is awfully expensive to get the plane down now?"

"I have to have that mail from Nairobi and any cables. We need to check on the buff to get those pictures. They're definitely not in the swamp now. We ought to know what's going on toward the Chyulus and I can make good use of her on this nonsense."

"I can't go back with her to Nairobi now to get the things for Christmas because I haven't got the lion."

"I've a hunch we are going to get the lion if we take it easy and rest him and rest you. Arab Minor said he was coming down this way."

"I don't need any rest," she said. "That's not fair to say."

"OK. I want to let him get confident and make a mistake."

"I wish he would."

"He will if we don't keep forcing him, if he doesn't think he's being hunted. Would you like to go fishing today with the skinner and Keiti and maybe get some pictures of the hippo?"

"No I wouldn't. If we're not going to hunt the lion or look for the buff I'm going to stay in camp and put things in order and have time to bring my diary up to date and write it properly. I have to write some letters too to go on the plane."

"Do you want to go with me up to Loitokitok?"

"I do not."

"I thought I'd go after lunch to be back in time to take you out to get the meat."

"That will be lovely. Where will we hunt?"

"Where it won't bother the lion if he comes in the way we think he will."

"I'll take a small nap and then write the letters. You'll really be back in time, won't you?"

"I have to be."

"But you'd be back anyway, wouldn't you?"

"Yes. You know that."

"All right," she said. "I know that."

CHAPTER 6

After lunch I realized it would be stupid to go to Loitokitok. If the police boy put up the notices Mr. Singh would be warned to keep off the road at night. They all had been warned and they all had orders if they broke down on the road to make a fire and camp for the night. They were supposed to carry supplies for such an emergency and the excuse that they were running at night because they were broken down on the way from Nairobi or Kajiado was not valid. I did not want Mr. Singh to get in trouble and I especially did not want him to get killed. By then I knew that keeping Mr. Singh out of trouble indefinitely was a career in itself. But I had some plans about that although I would have to wait to talk them over with G.C.

If without ever having read the law of a colony you are, due to an emergency, privileged to assist in the enforcing of any number of unknown statutes and emergency decrees, certain incongruities may arise. For instance, for more than twenty years I had been under the impression that it was illegal to give natives any form of drink but it had never been clarified for me whether it was legal for them to make beer or alcoholic drinks themselves. I knew from experience that they brewed many kinds of beer and also made some quite strong alcoholic drinks. I also knew about four different kinds of home-brewed heroic drugs which were habitually used to make men insanely brave and indifferent to pain. But I was very shaky about the law on these brews and concoctions although I was pursuing my researches. One thing I had learned was that all of these brews produced, after a few hours, a feeling of what the Spanish call malestar which is the opposite of well-being or euphoria.

Over a long time I had learned that for small gifts or rewards Wakamba preferred sugar to money. In my more innocent period in Africa I had supposed that this was because they had what is called a sweet tooth and I naively believed that they might even use this sugar to make some sort of native candy. This is not the case.

We were in another man's country and in such a country you feel no more impelled to denounce a brewery or a still than if you were traveling through Tennessee or Arkansas. As far as I knew all of the different beers had been in use long before any white man had ever come to Africa and they were a part of native custom and in no sense a parallel to the introduction of whiskey to the American Indians by unscrupulous traders. Certainly the white men had not introduced the various things the Masai used to make themselves brave. But it was not Africans who were sending north from South Africa that horrible, sweet, degrading concoction called Golden Jeep sherry which made so many Masai into drunkards. All rummies are ignoble but a sweet South African–made sherry rummy is as bad as they are made.

When I would lie awake in the night when there were no tactical things to think about I would wonder who it was who stood to profit the most if the white people were driven out of East Africa. Certainly it would not be the Africans. They were not yet ready to administer nor to govern. But other people were; or thought they were. Not as a people. There are no sins of a people or a race. But there were individual people who worried you and there was a movement that you saw the tracks and traces of as before you followed an animal into high grass you could half close your eyes and see, as delicately as though it had been made by the wind blowing, the way that the animal had moved.

I liked most of the Indians I knew in East Africa and some were very good friends. But some I neither liked nor trusted at all and this distrust had nothing to do with their race nor their religion. Until I had been asked to help in a certain department in an honorary capacity I had looked on certain things as comic. They still were comic. But now you had to order them stopped.

One of them was the manufacture of arrow shafts. These were cut, trimmed, seasoned, and bundled almost under the eyes of my great friend G.C. if he had been interested in the ax and knife work that went on and happened to look into the woodworking that went on in camp. The obvious work was on hoe and mattock handles. The arrow shaft production center was a little withdrawn into the bush. It seemed comic that this should go on and that then after the arrow shafts had been disposed of and finally fitted with heads, properly poisoned, and wrapped by the game poachers who bought them, G.C., tipped off by an informer, should raid the village and seize them. This seemed comic while I was an observer and was no part of my business. It was all between Wakambas and I was almost a Wakamba then. But when I became G.C.'s colleague as well as his friend and guest I went to the arrow manufacturers and told them there were to be no more

59

arrow shafts made. Now that I was working for Bwana Game I could not close my eyes to the production of arrow shafts. They understood.

I should have told G.C. when I first found out about arrow shaft making but he was not there and besides it had been told me in confidence. Ngui and I were coming back late after hunting leopard and we were coming into the back of the camp on the little stream in the heavy forest under the escarpment. We were trying, in the dusk, to come into camp so noiselessly that no one would hear us. We had twice on other evenings gone through the outer camp seeing what everyone was doing without being seen and we were trying it again. We could both walk so close to noiselessly that in some ways it was not funny and I was thinking of this and enjoying the smell of the smoke from the fires when I saw the two men by the fire scraping the pile of slender shafts. We got through without being seen and as we came up to the light of the big campfire I said to Ngui, "What the hell were those?"

"Mshale, tu."

This meant that they were arrows and that it was a matter of confidence. Anyway G.C. was away and it was only when he told me about seizing a certain arrow supply that I remembered. It did seem comic then but I did not want to bring it up since it was a Wakamba business. It was simpler to issue a no-arrow order. Besides there was no good arrow wood where we were camped now.

After lunch, while Mary was taking her siesta the Informer came in.

"There is much news, brother," he said. He was confident and happy and I could see he had been drinking.

I got up from the chair where I had been sitting with my feet on the bookcase and shook the Informer's hand.

"You have been drinking, Herr Informer," I said.

"A little wine, brother. I walked here down the mountain. After the exercise I took a little wine. It is my chest as always."

"What news have you?"

"The escape of the prisoners from Machakos. This you undoubtedly know. I saw the police jeep on the road."

"Yes."

"Singh is a dangerous man."

"Why? Did he sell you the wine?"

"Yes. It would be simple to make a case against him."

"Did you find the widow?"

"She had already returned to the shamba."

"What about that Masai boy who was wounded?"

"Everything was done as you ordered but the police were too busy to be bothered with him. He has gone on by road to the hospital."

"You are sure about this?"

"Absolutely. Listen, brother. There are Mau Mau who drink at Singh's. There are Mau Mau who drink next door to Singh. There are Mau Mau at the Tea Room."

"Good," I said. "Now you keep out of Loitokitok for a while. Don't you go there until I tell you to."

"Yes, brother. Mama thanks you for the presents."

"Don't call her mama."

"No, brother. But she thanks you."

"Drink the rest of your medicinal wine tonight and cure your chest cold. I want you to be sober and intelligent tomorrow. Did Singh send any message to me?"

"He said he wished to see you."

"I will be seeing him. Do you remember any other news?"

"A mission boy made some talk about elephants."

"Had there been damage?"

"Not yet. He was apprehensive. There is a movement of elephants."

"There should be," I said. "Is the widow well?"

"She is well. There is someone at the shamba who feels bad that you do not come there."

"Tell this person that I have many duties. If she comes here late this afternoon I will have a piece of meat for her. The truck or the hunting car will take her home."

"She and the widow will come. I will send them now as I return."

"Is the little boy all right?"

"You shall see. He will come with them. Have you nothing for me to drink, brother?"

"Nothing," I said.

CHAPTER 7

About four o'clock I called for Ngui and when he came told him to get Charo and the rifles and a shotgun and tell Mthuka to bring up the hunting car.

"Bring someone extra for lifting," I said. "Can you eat wildebeest?"

"Yes. But I'd rather eat pof."

"So would I. But there aren't any eland. I haven't seen one for two weeks."

"Pala?"

"An impala or a Tommy and a wildebeest."

"Mzuri."

Mary was writing letters and I told her I had asked for the car and then Charo and Ngui came and pulled the guns in their full-length cases out from under the cots and Ngui assembled the big .577. They were finding shells and counting them and checking on solids for the Springfield and the Mannlicher. It was the first of the fine moments of the hunt.

"Why didn't you go to Loitokitok?"

"It was too complicated and it wasn't necessary. Did you write some good letters?"

"Not really. The family mostly."

"I thought you wrote that on Sunday."

"Well we might have the lion on Sunday and we know we have the plane tomorrow. It's better to have it written."

"Sure. Are you through? We can wait."

"No. I'm just finished. What are we going to hunt?"

"We have to get the meat. We'll try an experiment Pop and I were talking about for practice for the lion. I want you to kill the wildebeest at twenty yards. You and Charo stalk him."

"I don't know if we can ever get that close."

"You'll get up close. Don't wear your sweater. Take it and put it on if it gets cool coming home. And roll up your sleeves now if you're going to roll them up. Please, honey."

Miss Mary had a habit, just before she was going to shoot, of rolling up the right sleeve of her bush jacket. Maybe it was only turning back the cuff. But it would frighten an animal at a hundred yards and over.

"You know I don't do that anymore."

"Good. The reason I mentioned the sweater is because it might make the rifle stock too long for you."

"All right. But what if it's cold in the morning when we find the lion?"

"I only want to see how you shoot without it. To see what difference it makes."

"Everybody's always experimenting with me. Why can't I just go out and shoot and kill cleanly?"

"You can, honey. You're going to now."

We rode out past the airstrip. The sun was on our left and the wind was blowing strongly from our right flattening the grass. There were big dark clouds but they were working between the Chyulu Hills and the mass of the mountain. There was cloud over the top of the mountain and in the afternoon light the trees and bush were a darker green. The grass was green with white flowers in it that made sections of the fields look moonlit. It was a very strange light and I thought it might be from the wind raising dust to the west where no rain had fallen.

Ahead on our right was the broken park country and in one meadow I saw two groups of wildebeest feeding and an old bull lying down not far from a clump of trees. I nodded at him to Mthuka, who had already seen him, and motioned with my hand for us to circle widely to the left and then back where we could not be seen behind the trees.

About four hundred yards from the trees I signaled to Mthuka to stop the car and Mary got out and Charo after her carrying a pair of field glasses. Mary had her 6.5 Mannlicher and when she was on the ground she lifted the bolt, pulled it back, shoved it forward, and saw that the cartridge went into the chamber, turned it down, and then moved the safety lever over.

"Now what am I to do?"

"You saw the old bull lying down?"

"Yes. I saw two other bulls in the bunches."

"You and Charo see how close you can get to that old bull. The wind is right and you ought to be able to get up to the trees. Do you see the patch?"

"Yes."

"If he's moved off shoot the closest bull. Charo will point him out to you."

I spoke to Charo and he nodded and said, "Ndio," and they moved off. None of us spoke and I signaled to Mthuka to make the turn back the way we had come so we could watch the stalk. If we were in sight I knew the wildebeest would be inclined to watch us rather than to watch for anything coming out of the trees. They knew there was nothing to fear in those trees or the old bull would not be lying down so close to them. They had, most probably, passed through those trees while they were feeding. They may have lain there in the shade at noon. When we could see the old bull still lying on the ground I pressed Mthuka's thigh to stop the car and we all watched Charo and Mary walking toward the trees. It was a thick island of trees and it gave them good cover. Charo in his turban and his old blue jacket was walking half bent over and Mary was walking just behind him and imitating him. Charo looked ahead as he walked and Mary looked at Charo's heels.

The old bull wildebeest lay there, black and strange-looking with his huge head, downcurved, widespread horns, and savage-looking mane. Charo and Mary were getting closer to the clump of trees now and the wildebeest stood up. He looked even stranger now and in the light he looked very black. He had not seen Mary and Charo and he stood broadside to them and looking toward us. I thought what a fine and strange-looking animal he was and that we took them too much for granted because we saw them every day. He was not a noble-looking animal but he was a most extraordinary-looking beast and I was delighted to watch him and watch the slow, bent double approach of Charo and Mary.

"He's fat," Ngui said. "Old but fat."

I watched the shine of his hide in the sun and the strange, proud, ugly head as he looked across the flowered meadow. His horns were very big and with the downcurve of the boss over his forehead they were impressive in their width. He seemed, at first, to be looking toward us but I saw he was looking across the meadow and the plain beyond us. I took the glasses and looked where he was looking and saw the yellow of a lioness crossing the plain between us and the swamp. She was long and yellow, swaying as she walked, and her head was down.

"Simba manamouki," Ngui said.

"Ndio," I said. "They better shoot and we get out of here."

"Manamouki kubwa sana," Ngui whispered.

"Heavy with cubs."

"Ndio."

Charo and Mary had reached the clump of trees and bush and were working sideways leeward of the bull so that Mary would have her shot with the sun behind her. The lioness was going away, diagonally to the northeast, and I saw the wildebeest still watching her. Then I saw another lioness following her at a distance of about two hundred yards. She was long and yellow too but not as heavy. All the wildebeest were watching them now and I knew that they might bolt at any minute.

Mary was at the edge of the trees where she could shoot now and we watched Charo kneel and Mary raise her rifle and lower her head. We heard the shot and the sound of the bullet striking bone almost at the same time and saw the black form of the old bull rise up in the air and fall heavily on his side. The other wildebeest burst into a bounding gallop and we roared toward Mary and Charo and the black hump in the meadow. The two lionesses had turned their heads at the shot and then kept on their way speeding up their gait but not running.

Mary and Charo were standing close to the wildebeest when we all piled out of the hunting car. Charo was very happy and had his knife out. Everyone was saying, "Piga mzuri. Piga mzuri sana, Memsahib. Mzuri, mzuri sana."

I put my arm around her and said, "It was a beautiful shot, Kitten, and a fine stalk. Now shoot him just at the base of the left ear for kindness."

"Shouldn't I shoot him in the forehead?"

"No, please. Just at the base of the ear."

She waved everyone back, turned the safety bolt over, raised the rifle, cheeked it properly, took a deep breath, expelled it, put her weight on her left front foot, and fired a shot that made a small hole at the exact juncture of the base of the left ear and the skull. The wildebeest's front legs relaxed slowly and his head turned very gently. He had a certain dignity in death and I put my arm around Mary and turned her away so she would not see Charo slip the knife into the sticking place which would make the old bull legal meat for all Mohammedans.

"Aren't you happy I got so close to him and killed him clean and good and just how I was supposed to? Aren't you a little bit proud of your Kitten?"

"You were wonderful. You got up to him beautifully and you killed him dead with one shot and he never knew what happened nor suffered at all."

"I must say he looked awfully big and, honey, he even looked fierce."

"He looked big and he looked very imposing from where we were. Did you see the two lionesses?"

"No. Were there?"

"They went off. Kittner, you go and sit in the car and have a drink from the Jinny flask. I'll help them load him in the back."

"Come and have a drink with me. I've just fed eighteen people with my rifle and I love you and I want to have a drink. Didn't Charo and I get up close?"

"You got up beautifully. You couldn't have done better."

The Jinny flask was in one pocket of the old Spanish double-cartridge pouches. It was a pint bottle of Gordon's we had bought at Sultan Hamud and it was named after another old famous silver flask that had finally opened its seams at too many thousand feet during the war and had caused me to believe for a moment that I had been hit in the buttocks. The old Jinny flask had never repaired properly but we had named this squat pint bottle for the old tall hip-fitting flask that bore the name of a girl on its silver screw top and bore no names of the fights where it had been present nor any names of those who had drunk from it and now were dead. The battles and the names would have covered both sides of the old Jinny flask if they had been engraved in modest size. But this new and unspectacular Jinny flask had close to tribal status.

Mary drank from it and I drank from it and Mary said, "You know Africa is the only place where straight gin doesn't taste any stronger than water."

"A little bit."

"Oh, I meant it figuratively. I'll take another one if I may."

The gin did taste very good and clean and pleasantly warming and happy making and to me not like water at all. I handed the water bag to Mary and she took a long drink and said, "Water's lovely too. It isn't fair to compare them."

I left her holding the Jinny flask and went to the back of the car where the tailgate was down to help hoist the wildebeest in. We hoisted him in entire to save time and so that those that liked tripe could take their pieces when he would be dressed out at camp. Hoisted and pushed in he had no dignity and lay there glassy-eyed and big bellied, his head at an absurd angle, his gray tongue protruding, like a hanged man. Ngui who, with Mthuka, had done the heaviest lifting put his finger in the bullet hole which was just above the shoulder. I nodded and we pushed the tailgate up and made it fast and I borrowed the water bag from Mary to wash my hands.

"Please take a drink, Papa," she said. "What are you looking gloomy about?"

"I'm not gloomy. But let me have a drink. Do you want to shoot next? We have to get a Tommy or an impala for Keiti, Charo, Mwindi, you, and me."

"I'd like to get an impala. But I don't want to shoot anymore today. Please I'd rather not. I don't want to spoil it. I'm shooting just where I want to now."

"Where did you hold on him, Kittner?" I said, hating to ask the question. I was taking a drink while I asked it to make it very easy and not too casual.

"Right on the center of his shoulder. Dead in the center. You saw the hole."

There had been a big drop of blood that had rolled down from the tiny hole high in the spine to the center of the shoulder and stopped there. I had seen it when the strange, black antelope lay there in the grass with the front part of him still alive, but quiet, and the after part quite dead.

"Good, Kitten," I said. "Are you sure you don't want to take the other one?"

"No. I want you to shoot. You ought to keep in practice too."

Yes, I thought. Maybe I should. I took another drink of the gin.

"I'll take the Jinny flask," Mary said. "I don't have to shoot any more. I'm so happy that I shot him so that it pleased you. I wish Pop had been here too."

But Pop was not here and, at pointblank range, she had shot fourteen inches higher than she had aimed, killing the beast with a perfect high spinal shot. So a certain problem still existed.

I pointed out to Mthuka how we would go and said, "Tommy."

"Hapana pala?" Ngui asked.

"Hapana. Memsahib shoots pala later."

We were going up through the park country now straight into the wind and the sun at our back. Ahead I saw the square white patches on the buttocks of the Grant's gazelles and the flicking tails of the Thomson gazelles as they grazed ahead of us bounding off as the car came close.

Ngui knew what it was all about and so did Charo. Ngui turned back to Charo and said, "Jinny flask."

Charo handed it over the seat back between the upended big gun and the shotgun in their clamps. Ngui unscrewed the top and handed it to me. I took a drink and it tasted nothing like water. I could never drink when we hunted lion with Mary because of the responsibility but the gin would loosen me up and we had all tightened up after the wildebeest except the porter who was happy and proud. Miss Mary was happy and proud too.

"He wants you to show off," she said. "Show off, Papa. Please show off."

"OK," I said. "One more to show off."

I reached for the Jinny flask and Ngui shook his head. "Hapana," he said. "Mzuri."

Ahead, in the next glade, two Tommy rams were feeding. They both had good heads, exceptionally long and symmetrical and their tails were switching as they fed quickly and eagerly. Mthuka nodded that he had seen them and turned the car so that when he stopped it my approach would be covered. I ejected two shells from the Springfield and put in two solids, lowered the bolt, and got down and started to walk toward the heavy clump of bush as though I took no interest in it. I did not stoop over because the bush was sufficient cover and I had come to the conclusion that in stalking, when there was much game around, it was better to walk upright and in a disinterested way. Otherwise you risked alarming other animals that could see you and they might alarm the animal you were after. Remembering that Miss Mary had asked me to show off I raised my left hand carefully and slapped it against the side of my neck. This was calling the location of the shot I would try for and anything else was worthless. No one can call their shot that way on a small animal like a Tommy when he may run. But if I should hit him there it was good for morale and if I did not it was an obvious impossibility.

It was pleasant walking through the grass with the white flowers in it and I slouched along with the rifle held behind me close to my right leg the muzzle pointing down. As I walked forward I did not think about anything at all except that it was a lovely early evening and that I was lucky to be in Africa. Before I got to the edge of the heavy clump of bush I absentmindedly lifted my left hand, very slowly, and clasped my neck. They would certainly be watching through the glasses and I might as well continue to clown. When I got to the bush I saw it was useless to try to get into it or work around to get a rest so I decided to go to the right end of the clump as I thought from the way the bucks were feeding they would break to the left and I knew I could swing better to the left than to the right.

Now I was at the far right edge of the clump and I should have crouched and crawled but there was too much grass and too many flowers and I wore glasses and I was too old to crawl. So I pulled the bolt back, holding my finger on the trigger so there was no snick, took my finger off the trigger and lowered it into place silently, checked the aperture in the rear sight, and then stepped out past the right end of the clump.

The two Tommy rams broke into full speed as I raised the rifle. The farthest one had his head turned toward me as I came out. They dug in with their small hooves into a bounding gallop. I picked up the second one in the sights, lowered my weight onto my left front foot, held with him and passed him smoothly with the sights, and squeezed when the rifle had gone ahead of him. There was the report of the rifle, the dry *whunck*, and as I shucked in the second shell I could see his four legs stiff in the air and his white belly and then the legs lowered slowly. I walked out to him hoping I had not shot him in the behind and raked him or given him the high spinal by mistake or hit him in the head, and I heard the car coming. Charo dropped out from it with his knife out and ran to the Tommy and then stood there.

I came up and said, "Halal."

"Hapana," Charo said and touched the poor dead eyes with the point of his knife.

"Halal anyway."

"Hapana," Charo said. I had never seen him cry and he was very close to it. This was a religious crisis and he was an old and devout man.

"OK," I said. "Stick him, Ngui."

Everybody had been very quiet on account of Charo. He went back to the hunting car and there were only us unbelievers. Mthuka shook hands with me and bit his lips. He was thinking of his father being deprived of the Tommy meat. Ngui was laughing but trying not to show it. Pop's gun-bearer that he had left with us had a face like a round, very brown elf. He put his hand up to his head in sorrow. Then slapped his neck. The porter looked on happy, cheerful and stupid and happy to be out with hunters.

"Where did you hit him?" Mary asked.

"In the neck, I'm afraid."

Ngui showed her the hole and he and Mthuka and the porter picked the ram up and swung him into the back of the car.

"It's a little too much like witchcraft," Mary said. "When I said to show off I didn't mean that far off."

"Charo," I said and put my arm around his shoulder. "Piga kanga." I knew he and Keiti and Mwindi loved guinea fowl.

"Good," he said. There is no word for sorry in Swahili or in Kamba. "I understand," I said.

"Hapana halal," he said. "Kufa." Then he slapped his neck too and started to laugh. Everyone then slapped their necks. I slapped mine and it felt very good.

"Buona notte," Ngui said. "Buona notte kubwa sana."

"You son of a bitch," I said. "I didn't know you talk Italian."

"Abyssinia," he said. "Mingi buona notte. Adesso piga kanga."

"Good," I said. Mthuka started toward the thicker bush country where we would find guineas.

Ngui said to Charo, "Leti Sten gun," meaning to hand him my old pump.

"Molto grazie," he said when the gun was passed forward.

He handed me the Jinny flask. I handed it to Mary.

"I see you crazies are all functioning again," she said.

Morale was very good.

Mthuka knew where the guineas were and in the last of the sunset we saw them scuttling ahead around a big tree. I hit the ground with the shot-gun and heard Ngui and Charo behind me. I ran to the right and as the flock started to cross the open space running with heads hunched down, I picked one in the line and fired and as they rose dropped two more. They were flopping, turning end over end, and Pop's boy was catching them and Charo was halalling. Ngui and I ran to the right and as a single bird rose clattering like a helicopter I hit him and hit him again as he fell. Charo came up and looked at the dead bird. He really looked dead.

"Kick him, Ngui," I said and the bird started to flop and Charo slit his throat and tossed him to Pop's gunbearer. I never could remember his name and he was one of my best friends and a member of our bad group. He grinned, both arms heavy with legal Islam kosher-killed guineas, and I fed shells into the magazine of the old Winchester pump.

"Let's try the trees," I said to Ngui.

"Maybe," he said and the four of us started to hunt into the sunset.

"Hiko," Charo said. "Hiko hapa."

He pointed where the guinea lay flattened down on the high jutting branch of a tree. The bird looked like a bulge on the branch. I aimed carefully, held my breath, and squeezed off as though the old shotgun were a rifle. As I shot guineas burst out from the heavy-topped trees. I shot four times fast and heard two thumping. Pop's gunbearer had left his in a pile and he, Ngui, and Charo were picking up.

The sun was down now and Mthuka was bringing the car up.

"Seven?" I said to Ngui.

"Ndio. Saba."

He was laughing. One guinea had scratched him and lined his forearm with a bloody crease from the inner side of the forearm to the wrist as he had carried it, protesting, to Charo for the ceremonial throat slitting. After its throat was slit it had scratched Ngui several times more and he tossed it into the back of the car without ceremony or sympathy.

"Kwisha," I said meaning that it was over.

We all got into the car and headed for camp in the dusk. Everyone was relaxed and happy and the country was beautiful.

"Jinny flask?" Ngui asked.

"Why not?" I said.

"Buona notte, kanga," he said.

"Goodnight, kanga, my darling, my sweetheart," I sang softly. "Goodnight, kanga, goodnight."

Mthuka could not hear nor understand the words, but he laughed at the part of the tune that came through his deafness. He knew it was a death song and a joke.

We did not say anything more until we came into camp pulling around carefully to drop off Miss Mary and raise no dust.

"It was a lovely afternoon," she said. "Thank you, everybody, so much."

70

She went toward her tent where Mwindi would have the hot bathwater ready to pour into the canvas tub and I was happy that she was happy about her shot and I was sure, aided by the Jinny flask, that we would work out all the problems and the hell with a small variation of fourteen inches vertical at twenty-five yards on a lion. Sure, the hell with that. And to back it up a Tommy ram hit by a showoff fancy fluke shot and a murder exercise on guinea fowl. We couldn't be in better shape, gentlemen, and I was glad Pop was not here. Then I thought a moment and I was not glad at all.

The car drove out, gently, to the grounds where we butchered and skinned out. Keiti came out with the others following and I got down and said, "Memsahib shot a wildebeest beautifully. There is a Tommy that was too dead to halal. There are seven Mohammedan kanga."

"Mzuri," Keiti said.

We left the lights of the car on for the game to be dressed out. Ngui had my best knife out and was joining the skinner who was squatting by the wildebeest and had started work. The Tommy ram lay alongside looking stiff and tired and the guineas were in a disorderly heap. I went over and tapped Ngui on the shoulder and drew him out of the light. He was intent at the butchering but he understood and came fast out of the light.

"Take a good big cut high on the back for the shamba," I said. I marked it with my finger on his own back.

"Ndio," he said.

"Wrap it in a part of the belly when the belly is clean. Put in the heart and the kidneys of the Tommy."

"Good."

"Give them a good piece of ordinary meat."

"Ndio."

I wanted to give away more meat but I knew it was not my right to do so and I covered my conscience with the fact that it was necessary for the next two days' operations and remembering this I said to Ngui, "Put in plenty of stew meat too for the shamba."

Then I walked away from the lights of the car to the tree just beyond the light of the cooking fire to where the widow, her little boy, and Debba were waiting. They wore their bright, now faded, dresses and they leaned against the tree. The little boy came out and bumped his head hard against my belly and I kissed the top of his head.

"How are you, Widow?" I asked. She shook her head.

"Jambo, tú," I said to Debba. I kissed her on the top of the head too and she laughed and I raised my hand up over her neck and her head feeling the close, stiff loveliness and she butted me twice against my heart and I kissed her head again.

The widow turned away and I heard the voice of the Informer saying, "Everyone is glad to see you, brother." He loomed in the dark like a blanketed statue of some historic American Indian. "Everyone has been waiting. There is meat for all."

"There is some of the neck for you," I said. "To remind you when you will hang. Go and get it."

He moved away in the darkness and into the light with his porkpie hat and his shawl over his shoulders. No one butchering paid any attention to him.

The widow was very tense and she said, "Kwenda na shamba," which meant let's go to the village. Debba said nothing. She had lost her lovely Wakamba impudence and I stroked her bowed head, which felt lovely, and touched the secret places behind her ears and she put her hand up, stealthily, and touched my worst scars.

"Mthuka will take you now in the car," I said. "There is meat for the family. I cannot go. Jambo, tú," I said which is the roughest and the most loving you can talk and ends things quickest.

"When will you come?" the widow asked.

"Any day. When it is my duty."

"Will we go to Loitokitok before the Birthday of the Baby Jesus?"

"Surely," I said.

Debba walked away until we were out of any light and then raised her face to be kissed.

"Kwenda na shamba," she said.

"Mthuka will take you."

"You come."

"No hay remedio," I said. It was one of the first things I had taught her to say in Spanish and she said it now very carefully. It was the saddest thing I knew in Spanish and I thought it was probably best for her to learn it early. She thought that it was part of my religion which she was learning since I had not explained to her what it meant, but only that it was a phrase that she must know.

"No hay remedio," she said very proudly.

"You have beautiful hard hands," I told her in Spanish. This was one of our first jokes and I had translated it very carefully. "You are the queen of the ngomas."

"No hay remedio," she said modestly. Then in the dark she said very fast, "No hay remedio. No hay remedio. No hay remedio."

"No hay remedio, tú," I said. "Get the meat and go."

That night in the night while I woke listening to the hyenas talking and disputing over the refuse from the butchering and watching the firelight through the door of the tent I thought about Mary sleeping soundly now and happy about her good stalk and clean kill on the wildebeest and wondered where the big lion was and what he was doing now in the dark. I figured he would kill again on his way down to the swamp. Then I thought about the shamba and how there was no remedy nor any solution. I was full of remorse that I had ever become involved with the shamba but no hay remedio now and maybe there never was a time. I did not start it. It started by itself. Then I thought some more about the lion and about tactics and about the Wakamba Mau Mau and that we would have to expect them from tomorrow afternoon on. No, if they had hitched any rides, all day tomorrow on. Now, I did not believe in them coming anymore than Keiti believed in it. But we would have to be just as careful as if we did believe.

Then for a moment there were no night noises at all. Everyone had stopped and I thought, shit, this is probably the Wakamba Mau Mau and I have been sloppy and I took the Winchester pump that I had loaded with buckshot and that I had been sleeping with under my right leg and listened with my mouth open to hear better while I could feel my heart pounding. Then the night noises started again and I heard a leopard cough down by the stream. It was a noise like the C string on a bass viol being stroked by a farrier's rasp. He coughed again, hunting, and all the night began to speak about him and I put the shotgun under my leg again and checked where pistol was and started to go to sleep feeling proud of Miss Mary and loving her and being proud of Debba and caring about her very much.

CHAPTER 8

In the morning there were many things to do. I got up at daylight and went out to the cook fire and the lines where the men's tents were. Neither Mary nor I ever called a man a boy. That was all right for Pop to do and for G.C. to do because they both loved Wakamba and G.C. loved the Masai as well. Mary and I both got along very well with Masai but I was a Wakamba if there were no Europeans or Masai around and that made things different for us. Mary called them "the boys" to me when we were alone and sometimes I would say "the boys" to her. She had learned it from Pop as I had and we always said "boys" in front of Pop. But she always knew people's proper names and called them by them.

Keiti was very conservative and this morning a little more so but we inspected the camp in a very military manner and I could see he was not upset about anything. Our meat was hung wrapped in cheesecloth and there was plenty of meat for three days for the men. Some of it was being roasted on sticks by the early risers.

"Keiti, why can't you eat wildebeest?" I asked. "It was halalled."

He shook his head and smiled and I knew the question was a mistake.

"Hapana wildebeest," he said. I knew I should have asked someone else and we went over the plans for intercepting the Mau Mau if they should come to any of the four shambas.

"The plan is good but they will not come," he said.

"Did you hear the quiet before the leopard last night?"

"Yes," he said and smiled. "But it was a leopard."

"Didn't you think it might be those people?"

"Yes. But it was not."

"All right," I said. "Please send Mwindi to me at the fire."

At the fire that had been built up by pushing the unburned ends of the logs together and putting a little brush on top of the ashes I sat down and drank my tea. It was cold by now and Mwindi brought another pot of tea with him. He was as formal and as conservative as Keiti and he had the same sense of humor except that his was rougher than Keiti's. Mwindi spoke English and understood it better than he spoke it. He was an old man and looked like a very black, narrow-faced Chinese. He kept all my keys and was in charge of the tent, making the beds, bringing the baths, doing laundry and boots, bringing early morning tea, and also keeping my money and all the money I carried to run the safari. This money was locked in the tin trunk and he kept the keys. He liked being trusted as people were trusted in the old days. He was teaching me Kamba but not the same Kamba I was learning from Ngui. He thought Ngui and I were bad influences on each other but he was too old and too cynical to be disturbed by anything except interruptions in the order of his work. He liked to work and he loved responsibility and he had made an orderly and pleasant pattern of safari life.

"Bwana wants something?" he asked standing looking solemn and dejected.

"We have too many guns and too much ammunition in this camp," I said. "If anyone knew it would be a big temptation to attack the camp."

"Nobody knows," he said. "You bring hidden from Nairobi. Nobody sees anything at Kitanga. We always carry hidden. Nobody sees. Nobody knows. You always sleep with pistol by your leg."

"I know. But if I were Mau Mau I would attack this camp at night."

"If you were Mau Mau many things would happen. But you are not Mau Mau."

"Good. But if you are not in the tent someone must be in the tent armed and responsible. The gunbearers and the ex-K.A.R. can take the watches in turn. I have decided on this and Keiti will give you the schedule. But I wished to tell you first because you are the boss of the tent."

"Have them stand the watch outside please, Bwana. I do not want anyone in the tent. The tent I am responsible."

"They will be outside."

"Bwana, they have to cross an open plain to come to this camp. Everybody would see them."

"Ngui and I came through the camp from end to end three times at Fig Tree and no one saw us."

"I saw you."

"Truly?"

"Twice."

"Why did you not say so?"

"I do not have to say everything I see that you and Ngui do."

"Thank you. Now you know about the guard. If Memsahib and I are gone and you leave the tent call the guard. If Memsahib is here alone and you are not here call the guard."

"Ndio," he said. "You don't drink the tea? It gets cold."

"Tonight I make some booby traps around the tent and we will leave a lantern on that tree."

"Mzuri. We will make a very big fire too. Keiti is sending out for wood now so the lorry driver can be free. He goes to one of the shambas. But these people that they say come here will not come here."

"Why do you say that so surely?"

"Because it is stupid to come here into a trap and they are not stupid. These are Wakamba Mau Mau."

"But I have to make the precautions. Please bring Ngui here. No. Call him."

Ngui came up with his swinging walk and said, "Jambo, Bwana."

"Ngui, why will not the people from Machakos come this way?"

"Bwana, it is not the first time Wakamba have had to leave the reservation. It is not the first time anyone has been in jail. There are three ways that they would go. This is not one of them."

"Will you tell me the three routes?"

"If you order me to. But it is a very old thing and concerns many people other than these ten who will all be caught. These routes were not made for Mau Mau."

"Good," I said. "We will set the trap here as agreed."

"Mzuri," Ngui said.

He and Mwindi went back to the lines and I sat by the fire with the new pot of tea and drank it slowly. I remembered about the arrow shafts and about how one of G.C.'s jobs as Game Ranger was to catch the Wakamba that poached south of the railway into the Game Reserve. I remembered how he said you spotted them. You glassed the country from the top of a high hill and you knew a poaching band from the dark shine of the red dried meat in the sun. I remembered how the railway was the boundary between the Wakamba country and the Masai country that lay to the south. In the old days both tribes had raided across the boundary for cattle long before the railway was built and many times since. The Masai were a pastoral and war-making people. They were not hunters. The Wakamba were hunters, the best hunters and trackers I had ever known. And now their game had been killed off by the white men and by themselves on their reserve, and the only place they could hunt was in the Masai reserves. Their own reserve was overcrowded and overfarmed, and when the rains failed there was no pasture for the cattle and the crops were lost.

As I sat and drank the tea I thought that the cleavage, a friendly cleavage in the camp but a cleavage in spirit and in outlook, was not between the devout and the unbelievers, nor the good and the bad, nor the old and the new, but basically between the active hunters and warriors and the others. Keiti had been a fighting man, a soldier, a great hunter and tracker, and it was he that held everything together by his great experience, knowledge, and authority. But Keiti was a man of considerable wealth and property and a conservative and in the changing times we had now the conservatives had a difficult role. The young men who had been too young for the war and who had never learned to hunt because there was no longer any game in their country and they were too good and inexperienced boys to be poachers and not trained to be cattle thieves looked up to Ngui and the bad boys who had fought their way through Abyssinia and again through Burma. They were on our side in everything but their loyalty to Keiti, to Pop, and to their work. We made no attempt to recruit them or to convert them or to corrupt them. They were all volunteers.

If Pop had been here now Keiti would have told him everything. Keiti would not tell it to me. He told me the truth but not the why of it and no tribal secrets. But Ngui had told me the whole thing and trusted me and put it on a straight base of tribal loyalty. I knew we, the hunting Wakamba, had gone a long way together. But sitting there, drinking the tea, and watching the yellow and green trees change in color as the sun hit them I thought about how far we had gone. It was a very long way. I finished the tea and walked over to the tent and looked in. Mary had drunk her early cup of tea, and the empty cup lay on the saucer where the mosquito netting now hung to the canvas ground sheet by the side of the cot. She was sleeping again and her lightly tanned face and her lovely rumpled blonde hair were against the pillow. Her lips were turned toward me and as I watched her sleeping, touched deeply as always by her beautiful face, she smiled lightly in her sleep. I wondered what she was dreaming about. Then I picked up the shotgun from underneath the blankets on my bed and took it outside the tent to take the shell out of the barrel. This morning was another morning that Mary could get her proper sleep.

I went over to the dining tent and told Nguili who was tidying it up what I wanted for breakfast. It was an egg sandwich with the egg fried firm with either ham or bacon and sliced raw onion. If there was any fruit I would have some and I would have a bottle of Tusker beer. G.C. and I nearly always drank beer for breakfast unless we were hunting lion. Beer before or at breakfast was a fine thing but it slowed you up, possibly a thousandth of a second. On the other hand it made things seem better sometimes when they were not too good and it was very good for you if you had stayed up too late and had gastric remorse.

Nguili opened the bottle of beer and poured a glass. He loved to pour beer and see that the foam rose just at the very last and topped the glass without spilling. He was very good looking, almost as good looking as a girl without being at all effeminate, and G.C. used to tease him and ask him if he plucked his eyebrows. He may very well have since one of the great amusements of primitive people is to arrange and rearrange their appearance and it has nothing to do with homosexuality. But G.C. used to tease him too much, I thought, and because he was a shy, friendly, and very devoted boy who was an excellent mess attendant and worshiped the hunters and the fighters we used to take him hunting with us sometimes. Everyone made fun of him a little for his wonderful surprise at and ignorance of animals. But he learned every time he was out and we all teased him lovingly. We all regarded any form of wound or disaster to one of us which was not crippling nor fatal as extremely comic and this was hard on this boy who was delicate and gentle and loving. He wanted to be a warrior and a hunter but instead he was an apprentice cook and a mess attendant. In the meantime that we lived in and were all so happy in that year one of his great pleasures, since he was not yet allowed by tribal law to drink, was to pour beer for those who were allowed to drink it.

"Did you hear the leopard?" I asked him.

"No, Bwana, I sleep too hard."

He went off to get the sandwich which he had called out to the cook to make and he hurried back to pour more beer and to watch the onions eaten. These onions, so strong that you could hardly get them down, were very strong magic. I had told him that I ate them as a tribal thing to give me courage and he had tried them. But they made him cry and he loved to pour the beer that was so fresh and cold from the night and watch the magic of the morning eating of the onion. The onions and the Jinny flask were part of the same magic and he loved to fill the Jinny flask almost as much as to pour beer and he always filled it as though he were serving the Mass.

Msembi the other mess attendant was a tall, handsome, rough boy who had been gentled down by Pop and by Keiti. He was very good at his job and very cheerful. He always wore his green mess attendant's gown very respectfully but still with the air of participating in a masquerade. He achieved this by the angle he wore his green skullcap and he had ways of manipulating the gown which showed that while he respected it for his service he realized it was a little comic. With Mary and me alone we did not need two men for the mess but the cook was going back to see his family shortly and take allotments to the families of the men and Nguili would cook while he was away. While we were waiting for the cook to go everyone had plenty of time off from their duty and we used to take Msembi out hunting and on patrols. He was no hunter nor had he served as a soldier. But he was a member of the wild bunch by adoption.

Like everyone but me he hated the Informer and this morning when the Informer appeared outside the mess tent and coughed discreetly he looked at Nguili meaningly, bowed at me, closing his eyes slightly, and they both went out.

"Come in, Informer," I said. "What is the word?"

"Jambo, my brother," the Informer said. He was closely muffled in his shawl and he removed his porkpie hat. "There are strange things happening."

"Yes?"

"Some of your men are drinking in the shambas. They go furtively and stay in the shambas drinking."

"In what shambas?"

He named them.

"Do you know their names?"

"Yes, I have them here."

I took the list and ran down it. It was quite correct. The screen was functioning.

"Is anyone drinking in your shamba too?"

"Yes," he said. "I hated to name him."

"Name him."

He did and I knew that the screen, such as it was, now was complete.

"You are a diligent and faithful informer," I said. "What news is there on the road?"

"A new roadblock has been established by the police below Loitokitok. All vehicles are being searched."

"How do you feel this morning?"

"I do not feel well, my brother."

"I will give you a purgative."

"I do not think that a purgative alone would cure me."

"I'll give you two purgatives."

"Brother, be kind to me. I have worked hard and well."

"You pour it," I said. "It is only for your health."

"Naturally," he said. "To your health and to that of Memsahib."

"Today is a busy day," I said. "I want you to get a ride up to Loitokitok and report to me anything you see and hear and everything that you hear said after we fly over the town."

"I go at once. May I say, brother, that your fiancée is happier and more tranquil."

"I have no fiancée and I do not know to whom you refer. Take this ten shillings for expenses and go. Continue to be the splendid informer that you are."

"Thank you, brother. Only ten?"

"Only ten. A further reward, perhaps, based on the accuracy of your information."

"Good-bye, my brother. You will never have a more devoted informer than me. I would inform on anyone. I fear no man. There is a mission boy from beyond Loitokitok waiting to see you. He claims that his shamba was destroyed by elephants."

"Do you know him?"

"No, brother."

"Leave and send him in."

The mission boy came in and bowed at the door and said, "Good morning, sir."

He was tall, not bad looking, not good looking, nose a little wide, very dark, good teeth, white shirt and white trousers and shoes. I did not remember ever having seen him around Loitokitok and I shook hands to see if his hands were calloused. They were not. He gave me his name when we shook hands and I gave him mine. I saw he had the town Mau Mau style of haircut, parted on the side with the part cut out with a razor. But that could mean nothing.

"These elephants?" I asked.

"They came last night and destroyed my shamba," he said. "I believe it is your duty to control them. I would like you to come tonight and kill one to drive them away."

And leave the camp unguarded and this nonsense on, I thought. The people out in the shambas and I leave the camp and all the stuff here with the amount of Mau Mau we know to be in and around Loitokitok. How stupid can you be, mission boy, I thought.

"Thank you for the report on the elephants," I said. "A plane is arriving here shortly and we will take you with us and make a reconnaissance of the damage done to your shamba and attempt to locate the elephants. You will show us your shamba and the exact damage done."

"But I have never flown, sir."

"You'll fly today. And you will find it both interesting and instructive."

"But I have never flown, sir. And I could be ill."

"Sick," I said. "Not ill. One must respect the English language. Sick is the word. But paper containers will be provided. Aren't you interested in seeing your property from the air?"

"Yes, sir."

"It will be most interesting. It will be almost as though you had an aerial map of your domain. You will have a knowledge of its topographical features and its contours impossible to acquire in any other way."

"Yes, sir," he said. I was feeling a little bit ashamed but there was the manner that the hair was cut and there were the soft hands and the camp had enough stuff in it to be well worth a raid in force and if Arap Meina and Ngui and I were sucked off from it on an elephant and bull story it would be easy to rush.

Then he tried once more not knowing that each time he made it a little worse.

"I do not think that I should fly, sir."

"Look," I said. "Everyone of us here has flown or has wished to fly. It is a privilege for you to see your own country from the air. Have you never envied the birds? Have you never wished to be the eagle or even the hawk?"

"No, sir," he said. "But today I will fly."

Then I thought even if he is our enemy or a crook or merely wants an elephant killed for meat he has made the correct and dignified decision. But I knew just enough to ask him to wait in the mess tent and sit down and then I stepped out and told Arap Meina that this man was under arrest and not to inform him but guard him properly and not allow him to leave the camp nor to look into the tents and that we were taking him up in the ndege.

"He is guarded," Arap Meina said. "Do I fly too?"

"No. You flew enough last time. Ngui flies today."

"Mzuri," Arap Meina said and grinned. Ngui grinned too and said, "Mzuri sana." I told him I would send the mission boy out and I asked Ngui to go down and check on the windsock and spook any animals off the homemade landing strip in the meadow.

CHAPTER 9

Mary came out to the mess tent in her fresh bush kit that Mwindi had washed and ironed for her. She looked as new and young as the morning and noticed that I had drunk beer with or before breakfast.

"I thought you only did that when G.C. was here," she said.

"No. Often I drink it in the morning before you're awake. I'm not writing and it's the only time of day it's cold."

"Did you find out anything about the lion from all those people who were here talking?"

"No. There's no news of the lion. He didn't talk in the night."

"You did," she said. "You were talking to some girl that wasn't me. What was it that there was no remedy for?"

"I'm sorry I talked in my sleep."

"You were talking in Spanish," she said. "It was all about there being no remedy."

"Must be no remedy then. I'm sorry I don't remember the dream."

"I never asked you to be faithful to me in dreams. Are we going to hunt the lion?"

"Honey, what's the matter with you? We agreed we wouldn't hunt the lion even if he came down. We were going to lay off him and let him get confident."

"How do you know he won't go away?"

"He's smart, honey. He always moves on after he kills cattle. But he gets confident after he kills game. I'm trying to think in his head."

"Maybe you ought to think in your own head a little."

"Honey," I said, "would you maybe order breakfast? There's Tommy liver and bacon."

She called Nguili and ordered her breakfast very graciously.

"What were you smiling about in your sleep after you had your tea?"

"Oh that was my wonderful dream. I met the lion and he was so nice to me and so cultured and polite. He'd been at Oxford, he said, and he spoke with practically a BBC voice. I was sure I had met him before someplace and then suddenly he ate me up."

"We live in very difficult times," I said. "I guess when I saw you smiling was before he ate you up."

"It must have been," she said. "I'm sorry I was cross. He ate me up so suddenly. He never gave any sign that he disliked me. He didn't roar or anything like the Magadi lion."

I kissed her and then Nguili brought in the beautiful small slices of browned liver with upcountry bacon spread across them, fried potatoes, and coffee and tinned milk and a dish of stewed apricots.

"Please have one piece of the liver and bacon," Mary said. "Are you going to have a rough day, darling?"

"No. I don't think so."

"Will I be able to fly?"

"It doesn't look like it. But maybe if there's time."

"Is there a lot of work?"

I told her what we had to do and she said, "I'm so sorry I came in cross. It was just the lion eating me up, I think. Eat the liver and bacon and finish the beer, honey, and take it easy until the ndege comes. Nothing has reached the no hay remedio stage. Don't ever even think it in your sleep."

"Don't you ever think about the lion eating you up either."

"I never do in the daytime. I'm not that sort of girl."

"I'm not a no hay remedio boy really."

"Yes. You are a little bit. But you're happier now than when I first knew you, aren't you?"

"I'm truly happy with you."

"And you be happy with everything else too. My, it will be wonderful to see Willie again."

"He's much better than either of us."

"But we can try to be better," Mary said.

We did not know what time the plane would be in nor even if it would surely come. There had been no confirmation of the signal the young police officer had sent but I expected the plane from one o'clock on although if there was any weather building over the Chyulus or on the eastern flank of the mountain Willie might come earlier. I got up and looked at the weather. There was some cloud over the Chyulus which was natural but the mountain looked good.

"I wish I could fly today," Mary said.

"You'll fly plenty, honey. Today's just a job."

"But will I fly over the Chyulus?"

"I promise. We'll fly anywhere you want."

"After I kill the lion I'd like to fly into Nairobi to get the things for Christmas. Then I want to be back in time to get a tree to have it beautiful. We picked out a fine tree before that rhino came. It will be really beautiful but I have to get all the things for it and everybody's presents."

"After we kill the lion Willie can come down with the Cessna and you can see the Chyulus and we'll go way up the mountain if you want and we'll check the property and then you go back to Nairobi with him."

"Do we have enough money for that?"

"Sure."

"I want you to learn and to know about everything so we won't have just wasted the money. Truly I don't care what you do as long as it's good for you. All I want is that you love me the most."

"I love you the most."

"I know it. But please don't do other people harm."

"Everybody does other people harm."

"You shouldn't. I don't care what you do as long as you don't hurt other people or spoil their lives. And don't say 'no hay remedio.' That's too easy."

I didn't know anything to say because I did not know how any of this was handled. There were many tribal things I did not understand and I took everything naturally and acted the way I felt. I had not looked for the trouble but neither had I turned it away, nor was I turning it away now nor was I seeking it. Mary understood this and it was kind and understanding for her to do so.

Then she said, "When it is all fantastic and you all make up your lies and live in this strange world you all have then it is just fantastic and charming sometimes and I laugh at you. I feel superior to such nonsense and to the unrealness. Please try to understand me because I'm your brother too. That dirty Informer isn't your brother."

"He invented that."

"Then suddenly the nonsense gets so real that it is like having somebody chop your arm off. Chop it off truly. Not like chop it off in a dream. I mean chop it off truly the way Ngui uses a panga. I know Ngui is your true brother. Then there's the way everyone laughs when you kill. No one is even respectful to the animal. Yesterday it was just a joke on poor dear Charo because he was a Mohammedan and you are all your own special sort of pagans or whatever you all are."

I didn't say anything.

"Then when you speak so harshly to that girl. When you speak like that it's like watching Ngui butcher. It's not the lovely life we have where everyone has fun."

"Haven't you been having fun?"

"I never was as happy in my life ever ever. And now that you have confidence in my shooting I'm really happy today and confident except I only hope it will last."

"It will last."

"But you see what I mean about how it suddenly becomes so different from the lovely dream way it is? The way it is when it is like a dream or the loveliest part of when we were both children? We being here with the mountain every day more beautiful than anything and you people with your jokes and everyone happy. Everyone is so loving to me and I love them too. And then there is this other thing."

"I know," I said. "It's all a part of the same thing, Kittner. Nothing is as simple as it looks. I'm not really rude to that girl. That's just being sort of formal."

"Please never be rude to her in front of me."

"I won't."

"Nor to me in front of her."

"I won't."

"You're not going to take her up to fly in the aircraft, are you?"

"No, honey. I promise you that truly."

"I wish Pop were here or that Willie would come."

"So do I," I said and went out and looked at the weather again. There was a little more cloud over the Chyulus but the shoulder of the mountain was still clear.

"You're not going to drop that mission boy out of the aircraft are you? You and Ngui?"

"Good God, no. Will you believe me that I hadn't thought of it?"

"I'd thought of it when I heard you talking to him this morning."

"Who's getting to have bad thoughts now?"

"It's not that you think things so bad. All of you do things in that sudden awful way as though there were no consequences."

"Honey, I think a lot about consequences."

"But there's that strange suddenness and the inhumanness and the cruel jokes. There's death in every joke. When will it start being nice and lovely again?"

"Right away. This nonsense only goes on for a few days more. We don't think those people are coming down here and they'll be caught wherever they go."

"I want it to be the way it was when every morning we woke and knew something wonderful would happen. I hate this hunting men."

"This isn't hunting men, honey. You've never seen that. That's what goes on up in the North. Here everybody is our friend."

"Not in Loitokitok."

"Yes, but those people will be picked up. Don't worry about that."

"I only worry about all of you when you are bad. Pop was never bad."

"Do you really think so?"

"I mean bad the way you and G.C. are. You and Willie even are bad when you're together."

I went outside and checked the weather. There was just the steady building up of cloud over the Chyulus and the flank of the mountain was clear. As I watched I thought I heard the plane. Then I was sure and called out for the hunting car. Mary came out and we scrambled for the car and started out from camp and on the motorcar tracks through the new green grass for the landing strip. The game trotted and then galloped out of our way. The aircraft buzzed the camp and then came down, clean silver and blue, lovely wings shining, with the big flaps down and for a moment we were keeping almost abreast of it before Willie smiling out through the Plexiglas as the blur of the prop passed us, touched the aircraft down so that she landed strutting gently like a crane, and then wheeled around to come fanning up to us.

Willie opened the door and smiled, "Hello, you chaps." He looked for Mary and said, "Get the lion yet, Miss Mary?"

He spoke in a sort of swinging lilting voice that moved with the rhythm that a great boxer has when he is floating in and out with perfect, soft, unwasting movements. His voice had a sweetness that was true but I knew it could say the most deadly things without a change of tone.

"I couldn't kill him, Willie," Miss Mary called. "He hasn't come down yet."

"Pity," said Willie. "I have to get a few odds and ends out here. Ngui can give me a hand. Pots of mail for you, Miss Mary. Papa has a few bills. Here's the mail."

He tossed the big manila envelope to me and I caught it.

"Good to see you retain some sign of basic reflexes," Willie said. "G.C. sent his love. He's on his way."

I handed the mail to Mary and we commenced to unload the plane and put the packages and boxes into the hunting car.

"Better not do any actual physical labor, Papa," Willie said. "Don't tire yourself. Remember we're saving you for the Main Event."

"I heard it was canceled."

"Still on, I believe," Willie said. "Not that I'd pay to see it."

"Even you and Willie," Mary said.

"Come on, let's go to campi," she said to Willie.

"Coming, Miss Mary," Willie said. He came down now in his white shirt with the sleeves rolled up, his blue serge shorts, and his low brogues and smiled lovingly at Miss Mary as he took her hand. He was handsome with fine merry eyes, an alive tanned face, and dark hair and shy without any awkwardness. He was the most natural and best mannered person I have ever known. He had all the sureness of a great pilot; he was modest and was doing what he loved in the country he loved.

We had never asked each other any questions except about aircraft and flying. Everything else was supposed to be understood. I assumed he had been born in Kenya because he spoke such fine Swahili and was gentle and understanding with Africans, but it never occurred to me to ask him where he was born and he might have come out to Africa as a boy for all that I knew. G.C. had grown up in Africa as a boy but he was a very special type and also in government service.

Willie secured the aircraft after we had pushed her around to where he wanted her and we left one of the men, who had served in the K.A.R., with a rifle to guard her.

"I came down a little early, Papa, because I didn't know just what the shauri was," Willie said in the hunting car. "No bad news, I hope, Miss Mary?" Mary was reading letters.

"Not in any of these," Mary said. "Will you and Papa have lunch before you go up?"

"What's the drill, Papa?"

"Let's have some lunch if you like the weather."

"The weather's very good," Willie said. "Nothing gone awkward, Papa?"

"No. All routine."

"Old G.C. put ideas in my head. He's coming down in a most warlike way."

"He's warlike," I said. "I wish I was more so."

"I don't," Miss Mary said. "I like gentle people like Willie."

"Very kind of you, Miss Mary."

We drove slowly into camp in order not to raise dust and got out under the big tree between the tents and the lines. Miss Mary went over to see Msembi the cook to have him make lunch at once and Willie and I walked over to the mess tent. I opened a bottle of beer that was still cold in the canvas bag that hung against the tree and poured some in each of our glasses.

87

"What's the true gen, Papa?" Willie asked. I told him.

"I saw him," Willie said. "Old Arap Meina seemed to have him under fairly close arrest. He does look a little bit the type, Papa."

"Well, we'll check his shamba. Maybe he has a shamba and maybe they had elephant trouble."

"We'll check the elephants too. That will save time and then we'll drop him off here and then have a general look around on the other thing. You're not taking Meina again, are you?"

"No. Meina's had it from the ndege. He's too old for that type of flying."

"How long was he out, Papa?"

"Most of the night. All night really. He got conscious around daylight."

"Habit we all have. You must have been a little relieved."

"I was. I'm taking Ngui. If there are elephant and we have to work it out, Meina knows all that country and he and Ngui and I will do it and Ngui and I will have made the recon."

"It all seems sound," Willie said. "You fellows do keep quite busy here for a quiet area. Here comes Miss Mary."

Mary came in delighted with the prospect of the meal.

"We're having Tommy chops, mashed potatoes, and a salad. And it will be here right away. And a surprise. Thank you so much for finding the Campari, Willie. I'm going to have one now. Will you?"

"No, thank you, Miss Mary. Papa and I are drinking a beer."

"Willie, I wish I could go. But anyway I'll have all the lists made and write the checks and the letters ready and after I kill the lion I'll fly in with you to Nairobi to get the things for Christmas."

"You must be shooting very well, Miss Mary, from that beautiful meat I saw hanging in the cheesecloth."

"There's a haunch for you and I told them to change it around carefully to be in the shade all day and then wrap it well for you just before you go back."

"Too good of you, Miss Mary. Are you sure you have plenty?"

"Really, Willie. Papa killed it too dead to halal. Tell us what's new in town."

"There's nothing you won't find in the papers. I think I brought them all. All your friends that I saw were healthy. Your outfitter's still alive he says."

"He stays alive by worrying about when he's going to get all those boxes back," I said. "That and the super hunting car."

"He sent some Pan-Yan pickles," Willie said. "And a box of sweets for Miss Mary."

"Papa gives the sweets to his fiancée," Mary said. "Never tell the outfitter that."

"How is everything at the shamba, Papa?" Willie asked.

"My father-in-law has some sort of combination chest and stomach ailment," I said. "I've been treating it with Sloan's Liniment and Opele. Sloan's came to him as rather a shock the first time I rubbed it in."

"Ngui told him it was part of Papa's religion," Mary said. "They all have the same religion now and it's reached a point where it is basically awful. They all eat kipper snacks and drink beer at eleven o'clock and explain it is part of their religion. I wish you'd stay here, Willie, and tell me what really goes on. They have horrible slogans and dreadful secrets."

"It's Gitchi Manitou the Mighty versus All Others," I explained to Willie. "We retain the best of various other sects and tribal law and customs. But we weld them into a whole that all can believe in. Naturally Miss Mary coming from the Northern Frontier Province, Minnesota, and never having been to the Rocky Mountains until we were married, is handicapped."

"Papa has everybody but the Mohammedans believing in the Great Spirit," Mary said. "The Great Spirit is one of the worst characters I've ever known. I know Papa makes up the religion and makes it more complicated every day. He and Ngui and the others. But the Great Spirit frightens even me sometimes."

"I try to hold him down, Willie," I said. "But he gets away from me."

"How does he feel about ndeges?" Willie asked.

"I can't reveal that before Mary," I said. "When we are airborne I'll give you the word."

"Anything I can do to help *you*, Miss Mary, count on me," Willie said.

"I just wish you could stay around or that G.C. or Mr. P was here," Mary said. "I've never been present at the birth of a new religion before and it makes me nervous."

"You must be something along the lines of the White Goddess, Miss Mary. There's always a beautiful White Goddess, isn't there?"

"I don't think I am. One of the basic points of the faith as I gather it is that neither Papa nor I are white."

"That is timely."

"We tolerate the whites and wish to live in harmony with them as I understand it. But on our own terms. That is, on Papa's and Ngui's and Mthuka's terms. It's Papa's religion and it is a frightfully old religion and now he and the others are adapting it to Wakamba custom and usage."

"I was never a missionary before, Willie," I said. "It is very inspiring and I've been very fortunate that we have Kibo here that is almost the exact counterpart of one of the foothills of the Wind River Range where the religion was first revealed to me and where I had my early visions."

"They teach us so little at school," Willie said. "Could you give me any gen on the Wind Rivers, Papa?"

"We call them the Fathers of the Himalayas," I explained modestly. "The main lower range is approximately the height of that mountain Tenzing the Sherpa carried that talented New Zealand beekeeper to the top of last year."

"Could that be Everest?" Willie asked. "There was some mention of the incident in the *East African Standard*."

"Everest it was. I was trying to remember the name all day yesterday when we were having evening indoctrination at the shamba."

"Jolly good show the old beekeeper put up being carried so high so far from home," Willie said. "How did it all come about, Papa?"

"No one knows," I said. "They're all reluctant to talk."

"Always had the greatest respect for mountaineers," Willie said. "No one ever gets a word out of them. They're as tight-mouthed a lot as old G.C. or you yourself, Papa."

"Nerveless too," I said.

"Like us all," Willie said. "Should we try for that food, Miss Mary? Papa and I have to go out and have a little look around the estate."

"It should have been here, Willie. Nguili," she called. "Leti chakula."

"Ndio, Memsahib."

CHAPTER 10

When we were airborne and flying along the side of the mountain watching the forest, the openings, the rolling country, and the broken ground of the watersheds seeing the zebra always fat looking from the air running foreshortened below us, the plane turned to pick up the road so that the alleged mission boy who sat beside Willie might orient himself as we spread the road and the village before him. There was the road that came up from the swamp behind us and now leading into the village where he could see the crossroads, the stores, the fuel pump, the trees along the main street, and the other trees leading to the white building, high-wire fenced, of the police boma where we could see the flagpole with the flag in the wind.

"Where is your shamba?" I said in his ear and as he pointed Willie turned and we were over the boma and beside the flag and up and along the flank of the mountain where there were many clearings and cone-shaped houses and fields of mealies growing green out of the red-brown earth.

"Can you see your shamba?"

"Yes." He pointed.

Then his shamba roared up at us and spread green and tall and well watered ahead and behind the wing.

"Hapana tembo," Ngui said very low in my ear.

"Tracks?"

"Hapana."

"Sure that's your shamba?" Willie said to the man.

"Yes," he said.

"Looks in pretty good shape to me, Papa," Willie called back. "We'll have another dekko."

"Drag her good and slow."

The fields roared up again but slower and closer as though they might hover next. There was no damage and no tracks.

"Don't have to stall her."

"I'm flying her, Papa. Want to see the other side of it?"

"Yes."

This time the fields came up gently and softly as though they were maybe a green formally arranged desk being raised gently for our inspection by a skilled and gentle servant. There were no damage and no elephant tracks. We rose fast and turned so I could see the shamba in relation to all of the others.

"Are you very sure that is your shamba?" I asked the man.

"Yes," he said and it was impossible not to admire him.

None of us said anything. Ngui's face had no expression on it at all. He looked out of the Plexiglas window and drew the first finger of his right hand carefully across his throat.

"Let's make a general recce for elephant and then go home. He's only sandbagging now," I said to Willie.

"Where, Papa?"

"Small area search. Conscience money."

"Is this journey necessary?" Willie said. "Don't want to show the flag over the village?"

"Not today."

We started to search the part of the mountainside where we knew elephant might be at that time of day. If they were in the truly deep forest we could not see them but there were two stream courses and some inaccessible open wooded country where we often found them. Ngui and I looked as carefully as though we were glassing a mountain for rams. We found no elephants. We saw no campsites either nor anything out of order.

"We might as well wash this and go home," I said.

Ngui put his hand on the side of the plane as though grasping the handle of the door and made a motion as though turning it. I shook my head and he laughed.

When we landed at the meadow and taxied up to where the hunting car was waiting by the windsock on the leaning pole the man got out first. No one spoke to him.

"You watch him, Ngui," I said.

Then I went over to Arap Meina and took him aside.

"Yes," he said.

"He's probably thirsty," I said. "Give him some tea."

Willie and I rode over to the tents of the camp in the hunting car. We were sitting on the front seat. Arap Meina was in the back with our guest. Ngui had stayed behind with my .30-06 to guard the plane.

"Seems a little on the sticky side," Willie said. "When did you make up your mind, Papa?"

"The law of gravity business? Before we went out."

"Very thoughtful of you. Bad for the company. Put me out of business."

"Not necessarily."

"It was thoughtful though."

"Aren't I always thoughtful?"

"Better ask Miss Mary that. I don't mean you can't think. My conscience is clear on the recce and the look about."

"The recce is solid."

"More than. Do you think Miss Mary would care to fly this afternoon? That would put us all up and we could have an interesting, instructional, and educational flight in pursuit of your duties and all of us be airborne until I leave."

"Mary would like to fly."

"We could have a look at the Chyulus and check the buff and your other beasts. G.C. might be pleased to know where the elephant really are."

"We'll take Ngui. He's getting to like it."

"Is Ngui very high in the religion?"

"His father once saw me changed into a snake. It was an unknown type of snake never seen before. That has a certain amount of influence in our religious circles."

"It should, Papa. And what were Ngui's father and you drinking when the miracle occurred?"

"Nothing but Tusker's beer and a certain amount of Gordon's."

"You don't remember what type of snake it was?"

"How could I? It was Ngui's father who had the vision."

"Well, all we can do at the moment is hope Ngui watches the kite," Willie said. "I don't want it changing into a troop of baboons."

Miss Mary wanted to fly very much. She had seen the guest in the back of the hunting car and she was quite relieved.

"Was his shamba damaged, Papa?" she asked. "Will you have to go up there?"

"No. There was no damage and we don't have to go up."

"How will he get back up there?"

"He's hitchhiking, I think."

We had some tea and I took a Campari and Gordon's with a splash of soda.

"This exotic life is charming," Willie said. "I wish I could join in it. What does that stuff taste like, Miss Mary?"

"It's very good, Willie."

"I'll save it for my old age. Tell me, Miss Mary, have you ever seen Papa turn into a snake?"

"No, Willie. I promise."

"We miss everything," Willie said. "Where would you like to fly, Miss Mary?"

"The Chyulus."

So we flew to the Chyulus going by Lion Hill and crossing Miss Mary's private desert and then down over the great swampy plain with the marsh birds and the ducks flying and all the treacherous places that made that plain impassable clearly revealed so that Ngui and I could see all of our mistakes and plan a new and different route. Then we were over the herds of eland on the far plain, dove colored, white striped, and spiral horned, the bulls heavy with their awkward grace breaking away from the cows that are the antelope cast in the form of cattle.

"Pof," Ngui said in Kamba. Eland were his great illusion. They were what we always would have hunted. Then as the plain fed into the breaks in the blue hills there were the oryx. There were more oryx than you could ever see, the slanted long black straight horns, the odd face markings as of a shield black on buff, and the thin, long tufted ears, the bodies of great wild asses trotting and then kneeing into a gallop, each pair of horns separate and each outjutting from the herd that closed and spread at the shadow of the plane. Then we flew contours in the folds of the hills and Mary counted fifteen different rhino, there were families and cows and nearly grown calves and one old bull looking up and snorting at the plane, and coming home we found the two buffalo herds that were working back toward our own country following the new grass and found the elephants under the trees by the small river that fed the swamp plain of the Chyulus. Willie flew delicately and careful not to frighten the game and the buffalo were solid in their migratory formation and unpanicked and the elephants continued feeding in the trees and did not run. We broke away from them and came back by way of Lion Hill and then the small desert and the glades to the meadow that was our airstrip.

"I hope it wasn't too dull, Miss Mary," Willie said. "I was trying not to disturb any of G.C.'s and Papa's stock. Only to see where it was. I didn't want to frighten any creatures away from here or disturb your lion."

"It was lovely, Willie."

Then Willie was gone, first coming down the truck path at us bouncing into a roar as the widespread crane-like legs came joggling closer to clear the grass where we stood and rise into an angle that creased your heart to take his course as he diminished in the afternoon light.

"Thank you for taking me," Mary said as we watched Willie until the plane could no longer be seen. Ngui and Mthuka could still see it but we could not.

"Thank you for going."

"We didn't bother the animals did we?"

"No, truly."

"The buff are awfully impressive. And they are such a big and complicated family. I couldn't believe some of the bulls."

"I wonder what they believe themselves. They are not stupid, you know. And they've had to figure out hunters with guns and now ndeges. But nobody ever killed them like the rinderpest. And who brought the rinderpest?"

"I don't even know about the rinderpest. Let's just go now and be good lovers and friends and love Africa however it is. I love it more than anything."

"So do I."

CHAPTER 11

In the night we lay together in the big cot with the firelight outside and the light from the lantern I had hung on the tree making it light enough to shoot. Mary was not worried but I was. There were so many trip wires and booby snares around the tent that it was like being in a spider web. We lay close together and she said, "Wasn't it lovely in the plane?"

"Yes. Willie flies so gently. He's so thoughtful about the game too."

"But he frightened me when he took off."

"He was just proud of what she can do, and remember he didn't have any load."

"We forgot to give him the meat."

"No. Mthuka brought it."

"I hope it will be good this time. He must have a lovely wife because he's so happy and kind. When people have a bad wife it shows in them quicker than anything."

"What about a bad husband?"

"It shows too. But sometimes much slower because women are braver and more loyal."

"What about so-and-so?"

"That doesn't count. Rummies don't count. They are just poor boring people."

"They certainly are boring."

"Do you know, darling, that on this whole trip we haven't had anyone who repeats stories or anecdotes or observations? Hasn't it been wonderful?"

"There was one man."

"Yes, but we got rid of him. Blessed Big Kitten, will we have a sort of normal day tomorrow and not all these mysterious and bad things?"

"What's a normal day?" I asked watching the firelight and the unflickering light from the lantern.

"Oh, the lion."

"The good kind normal lion. I wonder where he is tonight."

"Let's go to sleep and hope he's happy the way we are."

"You know he never struck me as the really happy type."

"We don't know about anything," Mary said sleepily. "I knew that this afternoon when we saw the buffalo. But maybe we will learn. The Chyulus are the only thing I've ever seen that's even more wonderful than when you see it far away. But the plane made my gerenuk country so small. I always thought it was a huge great country."

"You go to sleep, my kitten."

"I am and I am happy and in the Chyulus. Thank you and Willie so much for taking me. Good night, my blessed."

Then she was really asleep and breathing softly and I bent my pillow over to make it hard and double so I could have a better view out of the open door of the tent. The night noises all were normal and I knew there were no people about. After a while Mary would need more room to sleep truly comfortably and would get up without waking and go over to her own cot where the bed was turned down and ready under the mosquito netting and when I knew that she was sleeping well I would go out with a sweater and mosquito boots and a heavy dressing gown and build up the fire and sit by the fire and stay awake.

There were all the technical problems. But the fire and the night and the stars made them seem small. I was worried though about some things and to not think about them I went to the dining tent and poured a quarter of a glass of whiskey and put water in it and brought it back to the fire. Then having a drink by the fire I was lonesome for Pop because we had sat by so many fires together and I wished we were together and he could tell me about things. I knew the way things were going at the moment that I had done very right or very wrong and I hoped G.C. would come in early in the day. There was enough stuff in camp to make it well worth a full-scale raid and G.C. and I were both sure that there were many Mau Mau in Loitokitok and the area. He had signaled them more than two months before only to be informed that it was nonsense. I believed Ngui that the Wakamba Mau Mau were not coming our way. But I thought they were the least of our problems. It was clear that the Mau Mau had missionaries among the Masai and were organizing the Kikuyu that worked in the timber-cutting operations on Kilimanjaro. But whether there was any fighting organization we would not know. I had no police authority and was only the Acting Game Ranger and I was quite sure, perhaps wrongly, that I would have very little backing if I got into trouble. But the young police officer had called us in three times now and we were an armed force whether we liked it or not. It was like being deputized to form a posse in the West in the old days. I hoped G.C. would bring some sound news and some orders. He did.

He turned up after breakfast his beret over one eye, his boy's face gray and red with dust, and his people in the back of the Land Rover as trim and dangerous looking and cheerful as ever.

"Good morning, General," he said. "Where is your cavalry?"

"Sir," I said, "they are screening the main body. This is the main body."

"I suppose the main body is Miss Mary."

I shook hands with his people and we went into the dining tent and I told him what I had done and he was pleased. Then I told him why I did not think we had to worry about the Wakamba Mau Mau coming here and he agreed.

"They should come out by you the other way. That's the old underground."

"I'm getting back there. I'm sure that's how they'll go. Will get some sort of signal to you. You haven't strained yourself thinking this all out have you?"

"You look a little battle fatigued yourself."

"I'm damned tired actually. But there's some good news. Our pals in Loitokitok are all going in the bag finally."

I told him about the unmolested shamba and owner.

"Don't be sucked off by anything. I'll give you the word and then be back as soon as I can."

He told me some things that I should know and I asked him if the local nonsense were all right as set up.

"Perfect. It was what I was going to ask you to do."

"Any orders, Gin Crazed?"

"Just continue the exercise, General. We'll drink a cold one and I must see Miss Mary and be off."

"Aren't you going up the hill?"

"To scare the fish in the pool and talk balls with child policemen?"

"Did you drive all night?"

"I don't remember. Will Mary be over soon?"

"I'll get her."

"Where's the lion?"

"He's coming down."

"Don't wait for me on him. But with luck I'll be back. How is she shooting?"

"God knows," I said piously.

"We'd better have a short code," G.C. said. "I'll signal shipment received if they come out the way they should."

98

"I'll send the same if they show up here."

"If they come this way I imagine I'll hear of it through channels." Then as the mosquito bar opened, "Miss Mary. You're looking very lovely."

"Thank you, G.C.," she said. She gave him a kiss and he looked at her lovingly. "How are you and how is my idol Mr. Chungo?"

"I'm well and your idol is very well."

"How long can you stay? Will you be here for my lion?"

"We're off right away. But we'll be back."

"Please get back for the lion."

"I want to," G.C. said. "But we have this nonsense on. Is your husband behaving himself?"

"If he didn't have Arab Minor kill a man yesterday."

"He didn't. And you don't need to preach at us before breakfast."

"You will stay for breakfast? I'll go out and see about it now."

She went out and G.C. said, "Her morale's excellent. How is she shooting?"

"I told you."

"High or low?"

"Fourteen-inch-high error at twenty-five yards."

"I'll be damned. She was shooting perfectly when I turned her over to you."

"I know. And she was shooting perfectly when I turned her over to you at Kajiado."

"'S right," G.C. said mimicking a comic character who had been in Kenya recently. "But I'm not sure it's so comic. She was shooting like an angel when you turned her over to me too."

"'S right," I said. "I'll stall on the bloody lion until you get back."

"It won't be easy."

"Maybe she'll go into Nairobi with Willie to buy the Christmas things."

"You could always double with her on the lion."

"She's too smart for that and the lion means too much to her. You don't know how much."

"I think I do," G.C. said. "Let's have a real drink. I'll sleep an hour or so in the Land Rover. There are two good drivers."

"That's sound. I miss you very much, Mr. Gin Crazed."

"Not just about some bloody lion, I hope."

"No nor about Mickey Mice or lack of."

I made the two Camparis and Gordons and G.C. said, "I miss you and Mary and our good life and I get quite impossible with myself and impossible with other people. It's not going to be too much fun when we are all separated. I'll wash now if I may. We really have to roll."

"Mwindi brought water and towels when he saw you. Want to bet?"

"No," he said and went over to the tent. "Do any of these wires go off?" he called.

"Only at night," I said. "And probably not then."

"Do you take a pair of wire cutters every time you step out to see a man about a dog?"

"Criticize your own establishment," I said.

Mary came to the tent at the same time as the breakfast. "My," she said. "I love Chungo. It's absolutely platonic and I'll assure G.C. of that and write a note to Government House if it's necessary so I won't have to be shipped out of the colony on the first boat. I love nearly all of G.C.'s people. And they're all so neat and so military and so beautiful and not like your bandit outlaws."

"I'd fight mine against his if he'd give me Tony."

"He wouldn't give you Tony of course. Tony is one of his best men and so much better than anything you have."

"Tony is a fine man and we are quite good friends."

"Don't you go and start corrupting him now I know you have secrets too. But Tony is too noble to be with your ruffians. It makes me feel so wonderful to see G.C.'s splendid people. And everyone stands at attention when they speak to me. And they're like guardsmen. They all call me Memsahib Miss Mary."

"The Informer calls you Memsahib Lady Miss Mary."

"Oh damn the Informer and his old shawl and porkpie hat. God bless G.C.'s splendid people and God bless G.C. too. You wouldn't find him drinking Campari and gin this time of morning. He just shone with goodness this morning and his splendid spirit showed."

G.C., having heard everything, came into the tent just then, clean faced, hair slicked, eyes delicately touched with gin, holding his empty glass of Campari and Gordon's as though it were a sword hilt.

"Good morning again, Miss Mary," he said. "Memsahib Miss Mary, I mean." He bowed over her hand. "Thank you for inspecting the troops. You're their Honorary Colonel, you know. I'm sure they were all most honored. I say, can you ride sidesaddle?"

"Are you drinking too?"

"Yes, Miss Mary," G.C. said gravely. "And may I add no charges of miscegenation will be preferred for your avowed love for Game Ranger Chungo. The D.C. will never hear of it."

"You're both drinking and making fun of me."

"No," I said. "We both love you."

"But you're drinking though," Miss Mary said. "What can I make you to drink?"

"A little Tusker with the lovely breakfast," G.C. said. "Do you agree, General?"

"It says in the last *Punch*, 'And please may I have whisky instead and make it White Label if you please?' But I don't like White Label especially and I will join you in a little Tusker. By the way I saw one quite good tusker from the air yesterday. He was under a hundred but he might go eighty."

"You're scaling them very accurately this morning, General."

"He was a big bull, G.C., and he had beautiful tusks," Mary said.

"Bigger than the one we saw together?"

"They looked much bigger."

"He'd go over eighty then. Which way were they going, Papa?"

"They were resting about fifteen miles east-northeast of here on the river that runs into the marsh."

"They might work up to the Wakamba shamba then of course. They could. Did you see many?"

"No. One small bunch and the one good bull with his askari with him. We didn't spook them."

"Thoughtful of you. Did you see the buff?"

"Both herds. Working this way."

"Good."

"I'll go out," Miss Mary said. "If you want to talk secrets. Or drink beer without being uncomfortable."

"Honey," I said, "I know that in the war the people in charge of the war used to tell you everything about it before it happened. But there are many things G.C. doesn't tell me about. And I am sure there are people who don't tell G.C. things too long ahead of time. Also when people told you all about everything in the war you weren't camped in the heart of possibly enemy country. Would you want to be wandering around by yourself knowing projects?"

"Nobody ever lets me wander around by myself and I'm always looked after as though I were helpless and might get lost or hurt. Anyway I'm sick of your speeches and you all playing at mysteries and dangers. You're just an early-morning beer drinker and you get G.C. into bad habits and the discipline of your people is disgraceful. I saw four of your men who had obviously been on a drinking bout all night. They were laughing and joking and still half-drunk. Sometimes you're preposterous."

"It was a splendid breakfast," G.C. said standing up. "Thank you so much, Mary. It was lovely seeing you again. I'll be back as soon as I can."

"Thank you very much for the breakfast," I said. I should have just kept my mouth shut and gone out of the tent.

"Why do *you* thank me for the breakfast? Just to be annoying? Isn't it enough to hurt my feelings and treat me like a fool? And you lied to me yesterday and you know it."

"Probably I did," I said. "I don't remember when. But I'm sorry."

"You lie so much you wouldn't remember when."

"It was a lovely breakfast," G.C. said. "Thank you again, Mary."

There was a heavy cough outside the door of the tent. I went outside and there was the Informer, taller and more dignified than ever and impressive in his shawl-wrapped, porkpie-hatted drunkenness.

"Brother, your Number One Informer is present," he said. "May I enter and make my compliments to the Lady Miss Mary and place myself at her feet?"

"I don't think it is the day for it," I said. "Bwana Game is talking with Miss Mary. He'll be out directly."

"Has Bwana Game said anything about the increase in my wages?"

"No and I doubt if it would be wise to mention it to him."

At this moment Bwana Game came out of the mess tent and the Informer bowed. G.C.'s usually merry and kind eyes closed like a cat's and peeled the layer of protective drunkenness from the Informer as you might slice the outer layers from an onion or strip the skin from a plantain.

"You silly sod," he said. "Why are you not at so-and-so?"

"I have been here under the orders of the Bwana."

"Any truth in that?" G.C. asked me.

"Yes," I said.

"Very well, you silly sod. Remain under the orders of Bwana until he releases you. Then get to where I have ordered you or I'll run you. Do you understand?"

"I am at your orders, Bwana Game. I am at the orders of Bwana until he releases me. I am at his orders under your orders. When he releases me from his direct command which is under your orders I then return to your sole and unique command and proceed with my mission as you have ordered."

"Bugger off and don't talk like a babu," G.C. said. Then he turned to me. "Did you want to ask him anything?"

"What's the word from town, Informer?" I asked.

"Everyone was surprised that you did not fly down the main street nor show Britain's might in the air."

"Spell it 'mite,'" G.C. said.

"To respectfully inform I did not spell it. I enunciated it," the Informer went on. "All of the village knows that the Bwana Mzee was in search of

102

marauding elephants and had no time for aerial display. A mission-educated boy returned to the village late in the afternoon having flown with
the ndege of Bwana and he is being tailed by one of the children of the bar
and duka run by the bearded Sikh. The child is intelligent and all contacts
are being noted. There are between 150 and 220 certifiable Mau Mau in the
village or within short outlying districts. Arap Meina appeared in the village shortly after the arrival of the airborne mission boy and devoted himself to his usual drunkenness and neglect of duty. He is voluble in talking
about the Bwana Mzee in whose presence I stand. His story, which has
wide credence, is that the Bwana occupies a position in America similar to
that of the Aga Khan in the Muslim world. He is here in Africa to fulfill a
series of vows he and Memsahib Lady Miss Mary have made. One of these
vows deals with the need for the Memsahib Lady Miss Mary to kill a certain cattle-killing lion indicated by the Masai before the Birthday of the
Baby Jesus. It is known and believed that a great part of the success of all
things known depend on this. I have informed certain circles that after
this vow has been performed the Bwana and I will make the visit to Mecca
in one of his aircraft. It is rumored that a young Hindu girl is dying for the
love of Bwana Game. It is rumored—"

"Shut up," said G.C. "Where did you learn the word 'tailed'?"

"I also attend the cinema when my small wages permit. There is much
to learn in the cinema for an informer."

"You are almost forgiven," G.C. said. "Tell me. Is the Bwana Mzee regarded as sane in the village?"

"With all respect, Bwanas, he is regarded as mad in the greatest tradition of Holy Men. It is rumored too that if the Honorable Lady Miss Mary
does not kill the marauding lion before the Birthday of the Baby Jesus the
Memsahib will commit suttee. Permission, it is said, has been obtained for
this from the British Raj and special trees have been marked and cut for
her funeral pyre. These trees are those from which the Masai make the
medicine which both of you Bwanas know. It is said that in the event of
this suttee, to which all tribes have been invited, there will be a giant ngoma lasting a week after which Bwana Mzee will take a Wakamba wife.
The girl has been chosen."

"Is there no other news from town?"

"Almost none," the Informer said modestly. "Some talk about the ritual
killing of a leopard."

"You are dismissed," G.C. said to the Informer. The Informer bowed
and retired to the shade of a tree.

"Well, Ernie," G.C. said, "Miss Mary had better bloody well kill this lion."

"Yes," I said. "I've thought so for some time."

"No wonder she is a little irascible."

"No wonder."

"It's not the Empire nor White Prestige since you seem to have rather withdrawn from us palefaces for the moment. It's become rather personal. Of course if we do have to have the suttee," he began to muse happily, "we have those five hundred rounds for unknown calibers that your outfitter sent out rather than hang if they were found on him. I think they might be impressive in a suttee in the very center of the pyre. I don't know the drill unfortunately."

"I'll get it from Mr. Singh."

"It puts a little heat on Miss Mary," G.C. said.

"I understand suttee always does."

"There's no question of suttee. She'll kill the lion. But make good peace with her and handle it sweetly and well and try to make him confident."

"That was the plan."

"How's Arap Meina?"

"Wonderful."

"Ernie, go on up to town. Don't change anything. Don't let anyone's attention be diverted. No harm in being seen with the promised bride. After all what was the great tradition he said you were in?"

"Skip it maybe?"

"We skip it. A few wedding fineries wouldn't be out of place. You can always make a settlement from where you are in the hierarchy. Ngui would marry her."

"We are rivals. Honest rivals."

"No wonder Miss Mary was irascible."

"No wonder."

"Always try to remember it is serious. Eddy Shaw's sergeant was pangaed in two last week. Don't be too confident because this area is out of the war. Think how you'd feel if someone pangaed Ngui."

"I know. It wasn't my lack of precautions that browned off Miss Mary."

"I have no criticism of your show," G.C. said. "I wouldn't care to walk into it. It's pleasant that you've made it comic. But now it has gone a little far and we have to make good on it."

"Only two beasts," I said. "Including the ritual leopard. He's the hardest. But we will get him. Then what you let me feed them for the no-suttee Birthday of the Baby Jesus."

"They'll be well fed," G.C. said. "Don't worry about that. It goes under Christmas good will. We can use a little good will now."

We were walking out to the lines and the men who had been at the drinking shambas were just leaving with the lorry for firewood.

"I'm sorry about the ritual leopard," G.C. said. "Probably you should have gone back to Magadi to make sure of him. People have gone a long time without getting their leopard. It was bad luck you had to make that commitment."

"You know how it was. It wasn't straight without it. I *have* to get him. Mary will get the lion all right."

"I may get back right away," G.C. said. "I'll take a short way back. Did you get any sleep last night?"

"No."

"Get some today."

I spoke to G.C.'s people and Tony and I made a few jokes and they were off driving wide around the camp to keep from raising dust. Keiti and I talked about the camp and the way things were going and he was very cheerful so I knew everything was all right. He had walked down to the river and across to the road while the dew was still fresh and had seen no tracks of people. He had sent Ngui on a wide circle up past the meadow where the airstrip was and he had seen nothing. No one had come to any of the shambas.

"They will think I am a careless fool that the men go twice in a row to drink at night," he said. "But I told them to say that I had fever. Bwana, you must sleep today."

"I will. But I must go now and see what Memsahib wishes to do."

At the camp I found Mary sitting in her chair under the biggest tree writing in her diary. She looked up at me and then smiled and I was very glad.

"I'm sorry I was cross," she said. "G.C. told me a little about your problems. I'm just sorry they come at Christmas time."

"I am too. You've put up with so much and I want you to have fun."

"I'm having fun. It's such a wonderful morning and I'm enjoying it and watching the birds and identifying them. Have you seen that wonderful roller? I'd be happy just watching the birds."

"But isn't there something special that you'd like to do?"

"No. But do you think maybe before the day gets too warm we might just go for a little hunt up to the gerenuk country? I think I understand it better now we've seen it from the air."

But the gerenuk country was as difficult as ever on the ground. The plane had made it simple. But the plane made everything simple and on the ground Miss Mary had grown no taller and the bush was as tall as ever. She hunted hard and Ngui and I stayed as far away as we could so that I was nervous. But I had seen no rhino in there yesterday and we saw no fresh spoor and we had seen the rhino and her calf and the two bulls that were in there by a mud wallow in a different patch of country. I felt bad about Mary having the feeling she was never allowed to hunt alone and I stretched the safety limit as far as I dared. Then I remembered my obligation to Pop and moved up too close to be popular. She did not seem to mind and we moved close enough so that there was no chance taking. Then we saw rhino track that was fresh and I sent Ngui back to the car and, with the big gun, moved up close to Mary. It was not a really dangerous country the way Magadi was, but it was spooky enough to make me sweat. Charo and I heard the purr that is like a fluttering tongue or the sound of a quail rising. I looked back and could see Ngui standing on the top of the hunting car and pointing off to our left. Then Charo touched Miss Mary's arm and we all moved off across the wind to our right and in a small clear place we waited until the car came up.

"Dume," Ngui said. "A big bull. But the horn is short and wide."

"Can I see him?" Mary asked.

Charo and Ngui helped her up on the roof and she looked at the rhino, huge and gray in the brush, almost white from the dried mud of the wallow. His head was up and his ears swung forward as his nose searched the wind.

"Do you want to take his picture?"

"No. He's too far away to mean anything."

"We can't bring him closer. The hunting car couldn't get away from him in this. I'll find you another one where we can let him chase us in the open."

"Every time there's something to spoil the gerenuk hunting. We're close to the best place now."

I had been scared, as always, being responsible for Mary where there was a rhino in thick cover. I knew rhino were stupid and they charged the scent and were easy to outmaneuver. They were half-blind, but some saw better than others and when they came through the bush like a crazy locomotive they were always impressive. They were easy to kill. But I had shot one through the heart with the .577 and had him go a hundred yards at top speed before he went into the swirl of his death. If I was alone I was not frightened of them because the .577 would always turn them even if the solid did not hit bone and break them down. But in thick country you never knew where the other one was and it was the other one with these animals that could kill you. So I was looking at the incredibly armored, stupid, bad-tempered, and unlovely animal who yet looked oddly beautiful in his coat of white dried mud and his belligerence that stood like a baffled piece of armor. They have to live all their life with the turret buttoned down, I thought.

"You're sure he wouldn't make a picture?" I asked.

"No," Miss Mary said. "You have to get close to get pictures."

So we let it go at that and we moved off to another more open-bushed piece of country where the hunting of the gerenuk resumed. This time I did not give a damn if I were criticized or told I was playing the nursemaid or the overgunned governess and stayed exactly where I should stay and moved as Pop had taught me. I had realized long before why white hunters were paid as well as they were and I understood why they shifted camp to hunt their clients where they could protect them accurately. Pop would never have hunted Miss Mary here, I knew, and would have taken no nonsense. But I remembered how women almost always fell in love with their white hunters and I hoped something spectacular would come up where I could be my client's hero and thus become beloved as a hunter by my lawful wedded wife instead of her unpaid and annoying bodyguard.

Such situations do not come up too often in real life and when they do they are over so quickly, since you do not permit them to develop, that the client thinks they were extremely facile. On this last stage of the usual unsuccessful, and doomed to unsuccess forever, unless gerenuks became crazy or women walked on stilts as people do in the Landes, gerenuk hunt I had that detached clarity of mind which comes from lack of sleep and from having had drink before breakfast. When we had worked the country over and started back to camp I had become automatic in my reflexes and had disassociated myself from the exercise. It seemed natural if I should be reprimanded for this and it was certainly not the way a white hunter, that iron-nerved panderer to what a woman expects, should behave. But instead Miss Mary was very gracious and said that it had been an exciting hunt, that I had been so good and understanding about not keeping too close, how wonderful the rhino had looked in his white armor, and that we did not really need a gerenuk anyway. It was the hunting that counted, not the killing, and that she was glad the gerenuk were safe and happy. I never had known how happy a gerenuk was, browsing on semidry brush and beset by enemies both day and night and the last one I had killed, which bore a marvelous pair of horns, for a gerenuk, and that is saying very little, was so old, so tired, so rotted with foul diseases and pus that his hide was unusable and his meat had to be burned. We did not want the vultures spreading whatever maladies he suffered from, or simply maintained. But in my suspended sleepiness I was delighted that we had participated in a good hunt and I hoped the lion would get down to the plain and become just a little bit confident and that we might get it over with.

CHAPTER 12

It was quiet around camp and everyone had settled into the normal life. Miss Mary wrote her diary and seemed quite happy. She had gone out and hunted and something unexpected, though undramatic, had happened. There was a huge pile of firewood that the drinkers had brought and they were all sleeping off their work of the night before. The young policeman had come and gone and we had exchanged our news and views. Ngui had asked me if we were going out in the car before five o'clock as he would like to take a walk up the road and bathe in the river. He said he would get the word from the shambas and make a general check. I asked him to take it easy on the general check aspect and to check whether baboons had been raiding any of the shambas. He could make the general check with his eyes and not his mouth.

Arap Meina came in from Loitokitok. He had gotten quite drunk but remembered everything he had seen and heard and it was very interesting. He did not think there was any likelihood of a raid on the camp but there was always the possibility. He had a low opinion of the Loitokitok Mau Mau and said the Masai Mau Mau missionary was a coward and a bluff and that the Masai did not take him or Mau Mau seriously. He said the local Masai were corrupted by drink as we had seen. He was well loved and respected in the district and I took everything he said very seriously. He said it would be a good thing if he and I went together to Loitokitok and both became a little drunk. He said many people had asked why I had not come into town lately. He said that the Informer had lost any real usefulness since the widow had cuckolded him. He explained that a man who has the status of the protector of a widow if he is publicly and notoriously made a cuckold by the widow he protects loses all caste. He thought it would be a sound idea if I protected the widow and disciplined her. The widow wished this, he said, and stated that it was only because the Informer was impotent that she had made him a cuckold. He said the widow was really a fine woman and would like to be under my protection and wished that the Informer might be sent to some distant place if it were impossible to have him hanged.

I explained that I had no authority to hang the Informer or anyone else. He took this as a pleasantry and I asked him about the lion. He said the lion had killed once more on his way down to the swamp and the plain and we would have him any day now.

After that we had a drink together and I told him to get some sleep and come to camp before dark and we would take watch and watch during the night. I took some of his snuff and packed it under my upper lip and went to sleep in the big chair under the tree.

When I woke the clouds had come down from the Chyulus and were black across the flank of the mountain. The sun was still out but you could feel the wind coming and the rain behind it. I shouted to Mwindi and to Keiti and by the time the rain hit, coming across the plain and through the trees in a solid white, then torn, curtain, everyone was pounding stakes, loosening and tightening guy ropes, and then ditching. It was a heavy rain and the wind was wild. For a moment it looked as though the main sleeping tent might go but it held when we pegged the windward end heavily. Then the roar of the wind was gone and the rain held steadily. It rained all that night and nearly all of the next day.

During the rain of the first evening a native policeman came in with a message from G.C., "Shipment Passed Through." The askari was wet and had walked from where a truck was stranded up the road. The river was too deep to cross. The native policeman did not think that they could get up the road that night but that they could make one of the shambas and wait for the road to dry.

I wondered how G.C. had the word so quickly and had been able to send it back. He must have run into a scout who was bringing it to him and sent it back by one of the Hindu lorries. There was no more problem so I went out in my raincoat through the driving rain walking in the heavy mud and around the running streams and lakes of water to the lines and told Keiti. He was surprised that there had been a signal so soon but happy that the alert was over. It would have been a difficult problem as conditions were to continue the exercise in the rain. I left word with Keiti to tell Arap Meina he could sleep in the mess tent if he showed up and Keiti said Arap Meina was too intelligent to show up to keep watch by a fire in this rain.

We were all spoiled by too much perfect weather and the older men were more uncomfortable and intolerant of the rain than the young outfit. Also they did not drink, being Mohammedans, and so you could not give them a shot to warm them when they were soaked through. There had been much discussion as to whether this rain could also have fallen in their own tribal lands in the Machakos area and the general opinion was that it had not. But as it kept up and rained steadily all night everyone was cheered that it was probably falling in the North as well.

As it turned out Arap Meina turned up, really wet, having walked all the way from the shamba in the worst of the storm. I gave him a drink and asked him if he did not want to stay and put on dry clothes and sleep in the mess tent. But he said that he would rather go back to the shamba where he had dry clothes and that it was better for him to be there because this rain would last another day and maybe two days. I asked him if he had seen it coming and he said that he had not and neither had anyone else and that if they said they had they were liars. For a week it had looked as though it would rain and then it had come with no warning. I gave him an old cardigan of mine to wear next to his skin and a short waterproof skiing jacket and put two bottles of beer in the back pocket and he took a small drink and set off. He was a fine man and I wished that I had known him all my life and that we had spent our lives together. I thought for a moment about how odd our lives would have been in certain places and that made me happy.

Mary was not depressed or upset by the rain. It was so violent that it was a spectacle and she knew what it would do to the plain and all the open glades that she loved. She thought she knew, but nobody could know what it really did in the end. We had seen all the dusty and parched country turn green after a short but heavy rain and seen how the animals moved into the country that had been barren and abandoned. But she had never seen the great changes that come to the land with a really heavy rain that the earth has waited too long for. I knew her lion would be here and many other lions too. But neither of us knew how it would be. In the meantime the rain kept on and on.

It was a good thing that it rained, in a way, because nobody could move about at all so there were no mysterious happenings to upset her; the young policeman could not get through with his Land Rover to bring good or bad news; we were cut off from the shamba and Mary had to take an enforced rest. She hated to rest, as always, and hated inactivity. But there was nothing she could do about the rain. It rained so that the bushy trees in front of the mess tent looked as though they were growing out of a lake. The elephant skull outside of the tent door seemed like a boulder showing above water.

It was pleasant in the mess tent with the heavy beating of the rain and I read and drank a little and did not worry at all about anything. Everything had been taken out of my control and I welcomed, as always, the lack of responsibility and the splendid inactivity with no obligation to kill, pursue, protect, intrigue, defend, or participate and I welcomed the chance to read. We were getting a little far down into the book bag but there were still some hidden values mixed in with the required reading and there were twenty volumes of Simenon in French that I had not read. If you are to be rained in while camped in Africa there is nothing better than Simenon and with him I did not care how long it rained. You draw perhaps three good Simenons out of each five but an addict can read the bad ones when it rains and I would start them, mark them bad or good, there is no intermediate grade with Simenon except when he is tired, and then having classified a half-dozen and cut the pages I would read, happily transferring all my problems to Maigret, bearing with him in his encounters with idiocy and the Quai de l'Horloge and happy in his sagacity, true understanding of the French, a thing only a man of his nationality could achieve, since Frenchmen are barred by some obscure law from understanding themselves sous peine de travaux forcés à la perpétuitée.

Miss Mary seemed resigned to the rain which was steadier now and no less heavy and she had given up writing letters and was reading something that interested her. It was *The Prince* by Machiavelli. I wondered what it would be like if it should rain three days or four. With Simenon in the quantities that I possessed of him I was good for a month if I stopped reading and thought between books, pages, or chapters. Driven by continuing rain I could think between paragraphs, not thinking of Simenon but of other things and I thought I could last a month quite easily and profitably even if there should be nothing to drink and I should be driven to using Arap Meina's snuff or trying out the different brews from the medicinal trees and plants we had come to know. Then watching Miss Mary, her attitude exemplary, her face beautiful in repose as she read, I wondered what would happen to a person who since little past her adolescence had been nurtured on the disasters of daily journalism, the problems of Chicago social life, the destruction of European civilization, the bombing of large cities, the confidences of those who bombed other large cities of the King's enemies, and the large- and small-scaled disasters, joys, problems, and incalculable casualties of a happy marriage which are only relieved by unguent or a primitive remedy against the pox by new and finer violences, changes of scene, extensions of knowledge, exploration of the different arts, the places, and knowing the people, the beasts, and the sensations; I wondered what a six-week rain would be to her. But then I remembered how good and fine and brave she was and how much she had put up with through many years and I thought she would be better at

it than I would. Thinking this I saw her put down her book, go and un-
hook her raincoat, put it on, put on her floppy hat, and start out in the
straight-up-and-down rain to see how her troops were.

I'd seen them in the morning and they were uncomfortable but fairly
cheerful. The men all had tents and there were picks and shovels for ditching and they had seen and felt rain before. It seemed to me that if I were
trying to keep dry under a pup tent and live through a rain I would want
as few people in waterproof clothing, high boots, and hats inspecting my
living conditions as possible especially since they could do nothing to better them except see that some local grog was served. But then I realized
this was no way to think and that the way to get along on a trip was not to
be critical of your partner and, after all, visiting the troops was the only
positive action there was to offer her.

When she came back and flapped the rain from her hat, hung her Burberry on the tent pole, and changed her boots for dry slippers, I asked
how the troops were.

"They're fine," she said. "It is wonderful how they keep the cooking
fire sheltered."

"Did they come to attention in the rain?"

"Don't be bad," she said. "I just wanted to see how they cooked in this
rain."

"Did you see?"

"Please don't be bad and let's be happy and have a good time since we
have the rain."

"I was having a good time. Let's think about how wonderful it will be
after the rain."

"I don't have to," she said. "I'm happy with being forced to do nothing.
We have such a wonderful exciting life every day that it is good to be
forced to stop and appreciate it. When it is over we are going to wish we'd
had time to appreciate it more."

"We'll have your diary. Do you remember how we used to read it in
bed and remember that wonderful trip through the snow country out
around Mount Montpellier and the east end of Wyoming after the blizzard and the tracks in the snow and how we would see the eagles and
racing with the streamliner that was the Yellow Peril and all the way along
the border in Texas and when you used to drive? You kept a lovely diary
then. Do you remember when the eagle caught the possum and he was so
heavy he had to drop him?"

"This time I'm always tired and sleepy. Then we'd stop early and be in
a motel with a light to write by. It's harder now when you've been up
since daylight and you can't write in bed and have to write it outside and

so many unknown bugs and insects come to the light. If I knew the names of the insects that interfere with me it would be simpler."

"We have to think about poor people like Thurber and how Joyce was when finally they get so they can't even see what they write."

"I can hardly read mine sometimes and thank God no one else can read it with the things we put down."

"We put in rough jokes because this has been a rough-joking outfit."

"You and G.C. joke so very rough and Pop jokes quite rough too. I joke rough too I know. But not as bad as all of you."

"Some jokes are all right in Africa but they don't travel because people don't realize what the country and the animals are like where it is all the world of the animals and they have predators. People who have never known predators don't know what you are talking about. Nor people that never had to kill their meat. Nor if they don't know the tribes and what is natural and normal. I put it very badly, I know, Kittner, but I'll try and write it so it can be understood. But you have to say so many things that most people will not understand or conceive of doing."

"I know," Mary said. "And the liars write the books and how can you compete with a liar? How can you compete with a man who writes how he shot and killed a lion and then they carried him to camp in a lorry and suddenly the lion came alive? How can you compete with the truth against a man who says the Great Ruaha was maggoty with crocodiles? But you don't have to."

"No," I said. "And I won't. But you can't blame the liars because all a writer of fiction is really is a congenital liar who invents from his own knowledge or that of other men. I am a writer of fiction and so I am a liar too and invent from what I know and what I've heard. I'm a liar."

"But you would not lie to G.C., or Pop, or me on what a lion did, or a leopard did, or what a buff did."

"No. But that is private. A man who writes a novel or a short story is a liar ipso facto. His only excuse is that he makes the truth as he invents it truer than it would be. That is what makes good writers or bad. If he writes in the first person, stating it is fiction, critics now will still try to prove these things never happened to him. It is as silly as trying to prove Defoe was not Robinson Crusoe so therefore it is a bad book. I'm sorry if I sound like speeches. But we can make speeches together on a rainy day."

"I love to talk about writing and what you believe and know and care about. But it's only on a rainy day that we can talk."

"I know it, Kittner. That's because we're here in a strange time. It's maybe as rough a time as there has ever been. Not for hardship but with the new strangeness. But we're happy in it and it's better than anywhere else."

"I wish I'd known it in the old days with you and Pop."

"I was never here in the real old days. They just seem old now. Actually now is much more interesting. We couldn't have been friends and brothers the way we are now in the old days. Pop never would have let me. When M'Cola and I got to be brothers it wasn't respectable. It was just condoned. Now Pop tells you all sorts of things he never would have told me in the old days."

"I know. I'm very honored that he tells me."

"Honey, are you bored? I'm perfectly happy reading and not being wet in the rain. You have to write letters too."

"No. I love for us to talk together. It's the thing I miss when there is so much excitement and work and we're never alone except in bed. We have a wonderful time in bed and you say lovely things to me. I remember them and the fun. But this is a different kind of talking."

The rain was still a steady, heavy beating on the canvas. It had replaced all other things and it fell without varying its beat or its rhythm.

"Lawrence tried to tell about it," I said. "But I could not follow him very well because there was so much cerebral mysticism. I never believed he had slept with an Indian girl. Nor even touched one. He was a sensitive journalist sightseeing in Indian country and he had hatreds and theories and prejudices. Also he could write beautifully. But it was necessary for him to become angry to write after a time. He had done some things perfectly and he was at the point of discovering something most people do not know when he began to have so many theories."

"I follow it pretty well," Miss Mary said. "But what does it have to do with the shamba? I like your fiancée very much because she is quite a lot like me and I think she'd be a valuable extra wife if you need one. But you don't have to justify her by some writer. Which Lawrence were you talking about, D. H. or T. E.?"

"OK," I said. "I think you make very good sense and I'll read Simenon."

"Why don't you go to the shamba and try living there in the rain?"

"I like it here," I said.

"She's a nice girl," Miss Mary said. "And she may think it's not very genteel of you to not turn up when it rains."

"Want to make peace?"

"Yes," she said.

"Good. I won't talk balls about Lawrence and dark mysteries and we'll stay here in the rain and the hell with the shamba. I don't think Lawrence would like the shamba too much anyway."

"Did he like to hunt?"

"No. But that's nothing against him, thank God."

"Your girl wouldn't like him then."

"I don't think she would. But thank God that's nothing against him either."

"Did you ever know him?"

"No. I saw him and his wife once in the rain outside of Sylvia Beach's bookshop in the rue de l'Odeon. They were looking in the window and talking but they didn't go in. His wife was a big woman in tweeds and he was small in a big overcoat with a beard and very bright eyes. He didn't look well and I did not like to see him getting wet. It was warm and pleasant inside Sylvia's."

"I wonder why they didn't go in."

"I don't know. That was before people spoke to people they did not know and long before people asked people for autographs."

"How did you recognize him?"

"There was a picture of him in the shop behind the stove. I admired a book of stories he wrote called *The Prussian Officer* very much and a novel called *Sons and Lovers*. He used to write beautifully about Italy too."

"Anybody who can write ought to be able to write about Italy."

"They should. But it's difficult even for Italians. More difficult for them than for anyone. If an Italian writes at all well about Italy he is a phenomenon. Stendhal wrote the best about Milan."

"But he wrote well about France too."

"Sure. But you don't get him every day. But he wrote terrible tripe sometimes."

"The other day you said all writers were crazies and today you say they're all liars."

"Did I say they were all crazies?"

"Yes, you and G.C. both said it."

"Was Pop here?"

"Yes. He said all game wardens were crazy and so were all white hunters and the white hunters had been driven crazy by the game wardens and the writers and by motor vehicles."

"Pop is always right."

"He told me never to mind about you and G.C. because you were both crazy."

"We are," I said. "But you mustn't tell outsiders."

"But you don't really mean that all writers are really crazy."

"Only the good ones."

"But you got angry when that man wrote a book about how you were crazy."

"Yes. Because he did not know about it nor how it worked. Just as he knew nothing about writing."

"It's awfully complicated," Miss Mary said.

"I won't try to explain it. I'll try to write something to show you how it works."

"Pop's very interested in it. He said you were a crazy and always had been but that he trusted you absolutely and I should trust you too. Sometimes it all gets discouraging. But I'm not discouraged and I love our life. Can I make you a drink? You read now. We don't have to talk."

"Do you want to read?"

"Yes. I'd love to. And us both have a drink and listen to the rain."

"We'll have a lovely time when it's over."

"We're having a lovely time now and I only worry about the animals getting so wet."

So I sat for a while and reread *La maison du canal* and thought about the animals getting wet. The hippos would be having a good time today but it was no day for the other animals and especially for the cats. The game had so many things that bothered them that the rain would only be bad for those that never had known it and those would only be the beasts born since the last rain. I wondered if the big cats killed in the rain when it was as heavy as this. They must have to to live. The game would be much easier to approach but the lion and leopard and cheetah must hate to get so wet when they hunted. Maybe the cheetah not so much because they seemed part dog and their coats were made for wet weather. The snake holes would be full of water and the snakes would be out and this rain would bring the flying ants too.

I thought how lucky we were this time in Africa to be living long enough in one place so that we knew the individual animals and knew the snake holes and the snakes that lived in them. When I had first been in Africa we were always in a hurry to move from one place to another to hunt beasts for trophies. If you saw a cobra it was an accident as it would be to find a rattler on the road in Wyoming. Now we knew many places where cobras lived. We still discovered them by accident but they were in the area where we lived and we could return to them afterwards and where, by accident, we killed a snake he was the snake who lived in a particular place and hunted his area as we lived in ours and moved out from it. It was G.C. who had given us this great privilege of getting to know and live in a wonderful part of the country and have some work to do that justified our presence there and I always felt deeply grateful to him.

The time of shooting beasts for trophies was long past with me. I still loved to shoot and to kill cleanly. But I was shooting for the meat we needed to eat and to back up Miss Mary and against beasts that had been out-lawed for cause and for what is known as control of marauding animals, predators, and vermin. I had shot one impala for a trophy and an oryx for meat at Magadi which turned out to have fine enough horns to make it a trophy and a single buffalo in an emergency which served for meat at Magadi when we were very short and which had a pair of horns worth keeping to recall the manner of the small emergency Mary and I had shared. I remembered it now with happiness and I knew I would always remem-ber it with happiness. It was one of those small things that you can go to sleep with, that you can wake with happy in the night and that you could recall if necessary if you were ever tortured.

"Do you remember the morning with the buff, Kittner?" I asked.

She looked across the mess table and said, "Don't ask me things like that. I'm thinking about the lion."

So now we had her lion coming up as soon as the rain would be over and there was the leopard I had promised and guaranteed to kill, honor-ably, by a certain date.

Those were the only fixed engagements in the book. There would be many duties and interruptions I knew. But those were the two fixtures. So we sat reading in the rain knowing that those were two things that must happen.

They must happen and they would happen but first it must stop rain-ing. In the meantime Mary was getting a good rest, if I could keep her from getting restless, and I was enjoying the irresponsibility the rain brought.

That night after cold supper we went to bed early, since Mary had writ-ten her diary in the late afternoon, and lay in bed listening to the heavi-ness of the rain on that taut canvas.

"I know it's wonderful and that we need it. But it would be nice if it stopped."

"If it's only raining up at the Reserve," I said. "Everyone is worried about the crops."

"It must be. This can't be a local rain. My, it's nice that we don't have to move camp in it."

"You be careful and use your flashlight if you get up in the night. Al-most anything could have crawled in here."

"I'll be careful. And I'll call you."

"Keep your net tucked in well."

"I will. You sleep well, darling, and have good dreams."

"You too, my blessed kitten."

But in spite of the steady noise of the rain I did not sleep well and I woke twice sweating with nightmares. The last one was a very bad one and I reached out under the mosquito net and felt for the water bottle and the square flask of gin. I brought it into the bed with me and then tucked the netting back under the blanket and the air mattress of the cot. In the dark I rolled my pillow up so I could lie back with my head against it and found the small balsam needle pillow and put it under my neck. Then I felt for my pistol alongside my leg and for the electric torch and then unscrewed the top of the flask of gin.

In the dark with the heavy noise of the rain I took a swallow of the gin. It tasted clean and friendly and made me brave against the nightmare. The nightmare had been about as bad as they come and I have had some bad ones in my time. I knew I could not drink while we were hunting Miss Mary's lion; but we would not be hunting him tomorrow in the wet. Tonight was a bad night for some reason. I had been spoiled by too many good nights and I had come to think that I did not have nightmares anymore. Well I knew now. Perhaps it was because the tent was so battened down against the rain that there was no proper ventilation. Perhaps it was because I had had no exercise all day.

I took another swallow of the gin and it tasted even better and more like the old Giant Killer. It had not been such an exceptional nightmare, I thought. I've had much worse than that. But what I knew was that I had been through with nightmares, the real ones that could drench you in sweat, for a long time and I had only had good or bad dreams and most of the nights they were good dreams.

Then I heard Mary say, "Papa, are you drinking?"

"Yes. Why?"

"Could I have some too?"

I reached the flask over from under the net and she put her hand out and took it.

"Do you have the water?"

"Yes," I said and reached it over too. "You have yours too by your bed."

"But you told me to be careful about things and I did not want to wake you with the light."

"Poor Kitten. Haven't you slept?"

"Yes. But I had the most awful dreams. Too bad to tell before breakfast."

"I had some bad ones too."

"Here's the Jinny flask back," she said. "In case you need it. Hold my hand tight, please. You aren't dead and G.C. isn't dead and Pop isn't dead."

"No. We're all fine."

"Thank you so much. And you sleep too. You don't love anybody else do you? White, I mean?"

"No. Not white nor black nor red all over."

"Sleep well, my blessed," she said. "Thank you for the lovely midnight drink."

"Thank you for killing the nightmares."

"That's one of the things I'm for," she said.

I lay and thought about that for a long time remembering many places and really bad times and I thought how wonderful it would be now after the rain and what were nightmares anyway and then I went to sleep and woke sweating again with the horrors but I listened carefully and heard Mary breathing softly and regularly and then I went back to sleep to try it once more.

CHAPTER 13

In the morning it was cold with heavy cloud over all the mountain. There was a heavy wind again and the rain came in patches but the heavy solid rain was over. I went out to the lines to talk with Keiti and found him very cheerful. He was wearing a raincoat and an old felt hat. He said the weather would probably be good by the next day and I told him we would wait until Memsahib woke before driving in the tent pegs and loosening the wet ropes. He was pleased that the ditching had turned out so well and that neither the sleeping tent nor the mess tent had been wet. He had already sent for a fire to be built and everything was looking better. I told him I had a dream that it had rained heavily up in the Reserve. This was a lie but I thought it was good to weigh in with a good heavy lie in case we had good news from Pop. If you are going to prophesy it is good to prophesy with the odds in your favor and I thought this dream was much sounder to weigh in with than one of my nightmares. I knew the nightmares would impress Ngui and Mthuka but they might take them too literally.

Keiti heard my dream through with attention and with simulated respect. Then he told me that he had dreamed that it had rained heavily all the way to the Tana River, which was on the edge of the desert and that six safaris were cut off and would not be able to move for weeks. This, as it was calculated to do, made a very small thing of my dream. I knew that my dream had been registered and would be checked on but I thought I ought to back it up. So I told him, quite truly, that I dreamed that we had hanged the Informer. Recounting this I gave him the exact procedure: where, how, why, how he had taken it, and how we had taken him out, afterwards, in the hunting car to be eaten by the hyenas.

Keiti hated the Informer and had for many years and he loved this dream but was careful that I should know that he himself had not dreamed of the Informer at all. This was important, as I knew, but I gave him some more details of the execution. He was delighted with them. But he said, wistfully, but in full judgment, "But you must not do."

"I cannot do. But maybe my dream will do."

"You must not be shaitani."

"I am not shaitani. Have you ever seen me harm a man or a woman?"

"I did not say you were shaitani. I said you must not be and that it cannot be to hang the Informer."

"If you wish to save him I can forget the dream."

"Good dream," Keiti said. "But make too much trouble."

The day after a heavy rain is a splendid day for the propagation of religion while the time of the rain itself seems to turn men's minds from the beauty of their faith. All rain had stopped now and I was sitting by the fire drinking tea and looking out over the sodden country. Miss Mary was still sleeping soundly because there was no sun to wake her. Mwindi came to the table by the fire with a fresh pot of hot tea and poured me a cup.

"Plenty rain," he said. "Now finished."

"Mwindi," I said. "You know what the Mahdi said. 'We see plainly in the laws of nature that rain comes down from the heavens in the time of need. The greenness and verdure of the earth depend upon heavenly rain. If it ceases for a time the water in the upper strata of the earth gradually dries up. Thus we see that there is an attraction between the heavenly and the earthly waters. Revelation stands in the same relation to human reason as heavenly water does to the earthly water.'"

"Too much rain for campi. Plenty good for shamba," Mwindi announced.

"'As with the cessation of heavenly water earthly water begins gradually to dry up; so also is the case of the human reason which without the heavenly revelation loses its purity and strength.'"

"How I know that is Mahdi?" Mwindi said.

"Ask Charo."

Mwindi grunted. He knew Charo was very devout but not a great theologist.

"If hang Informer better let police hang," Mwindi said. "Keiti ask me to say it."

"That was only a dream."

"Dream can be very strong."

"I never send with dream."

"Can kill with dream like bunduki."

"I'll tell Informer dream. Then it has no power."

"Shaitani," Mwindi said. Shaitani kubwa sana."

"Hapana shaitani."

Mwindi broke it off and asked almost brusquely if I wanted more tea. He was looking over at the lines with his old Chinese profile and I saw what it was he wanted me to see. It was the Informer.

"Hapana shaitani," he said pensively.

"Please take my tea to the mess tent and send him over," I said.

"Send girl too?" Mwindi said dead-faced.

"Hapana girl," I said.

The Informer came in wet and not happy. His style and his gallantry were not gone but they had been dampened. He coughed his cough at once so there would be no doubt of it and it was a legitimate cough.

"Good morning, brother. How have you and my lady endured the weather?"

"It rained a little here."

"Brother, I am a sick man."

"Do you have fever?"

"Yes."

He was not lying and his pulse was 120.

"Sit down and have a drink and take an aspirin and I'll give you medicine. Go home and go to bed. Can the hunting car get through the road?"

"Yes. It is sandy to the shamba and the car can go around the pools."

"How is the shamba?"

"It did not need the rain because it is irrigated. It is a sad shamba with the cold from the mountains. Even the chickens are sad. A girl came with me whose father needs medicine for his chest. You know her."

"I will send medicine."

"She is unhappy that you do not come."

"I have my duties. Is she well?"

"She is well but sad."

"Tell her I will come to the shamba when it is my duty."

"Brother, what is this of the dream that I am hanged?"

"It is a dream that I had but I should not tell it to you before I have eaten breakfast."

"But others have heard it before."

"I had taken early tea. Besides I do not wish to afflict you with it. It is better that you do not hear it. It was not an official dream."

"I could not bear to be hanged," the Informer said.

"I will never hang you."

"But others could misunderstand my activities."

"No one will hang you unless you deal with the other people."

"But I must constantly deal with the other people."

"You understood the sense in which I spoke. Now go to the campfire and get warm and I will make up the medicines."

"You are my brother—"

"No," I said. "I am your friend."

He went off to the fire and I opened the medicine chest and got out Atabrine and aspirin and liniment and some sulfa and some cough lozenges and hoped I had made a small blow against shaitani. But I could remember all the details of the execution of the Informer in about the third of the nightmares and I was ashamed of having even such a nocturnal imagination.

I told him what medicines to take and what to give to the father of the girl. Then we walked out to the lines together and I gave the girl two tins of kipper snacks and a glass jar of hard candies and asked Mthuka to drive them to the shamba and then come straight back. She had brought me four ears of corn and never looked up when I spoke to her. She put her head against my chest as a child does and when she got into the car on the offside where no one could see her she dropped her arm and with her whole hand gripped the muscles of my thigh. I did the same thing when she was in the car and she did not look up. Then I thought the hell with it all and kissed her on the top of the head and she laughed as impudently as ever and Mthuka smiled and they drove off. The track was sandy with a little standing water but the bottom was firm and the hunting car went off through the trees and nobody looked back.

I told Ngui and Charo that we would go north on a routine look-around as far as it was possible to go as soon as Miss Mary had wakened and had breakfast. They could get the guns now and clean them after the rain. I told them to be sure and wipe the bores dry of all oil. It was cold and the wind was blowing. The sun was overcast. But the rain was over except for possible showers. Everybody was very businesslike and there was no nonsense.

Mary was very happy at breakfast. She had slept well after she had wakened in the night and her dreams had been happy. Her bad dream had been that Pop, G.C., and I had all been killed. She did not remember the details. Someone had brought the news. She thought it was in an ambush of some kind. I wanted to ask her if she had dreamed about the hanging of the Informer but I thought that would be interference and the important thing was that she had waked happily and looked forward to the day. I thought that I was rough enough and worthless enough to become involved in the things that I did not understand in Africa but I did not want to involve her. She involved herself enough by going out to the lines and learning the music and the drum rhythms and the songs, treating everyone so well and so kindly that they fell in love with her. In the old days I know Pop would never have permitted this. But the old days were gone. No one knew that better than Pop did.

When breakfast was over and the hunting car was back from the shamba we made a trip out as far as the ground was possible to drive over. The earth was drying fast but it was still treacherous and the wheels spun and dug in where tomorrow the car could go with security. This was so even on the hard ground and where the track had been firmed and hardened. To the north where the slippery clay was it was impassable.

You could see the new grass coming bright green across the flats and the game was scattered and paid little attention to us. There had been no great movement of game in yet but we saw the tracks of elephants that had crossed the track early in the morning after the rain stopped going toward the swamp. They were the lot we had seen from the plane and the bull had a very big track even allowing for the spreading by the wetness of the mud.

"If it wasn't so muddy I think we could turn up by the head of the salt lick on the mud flats and probably find them. But we'd get stuck, honey. It's going to have to dry a full day to get up there."

"It doesn't really matter. The light is so bad," Mary said. "It's a worthless light."

"There are fifteen altogether. The big bull and his friend are quite a little way behind the herd. You can see how they weren't even sprinkled on. We just missed seeing them cross."

"It's probably better not to disturb them anyway."

"They may go right on through," I said. "They may go to that elephant country on the way to Amboseli."

"Do you think we should go back?"

It was gray and cold and blowing and all over the flats and in and beside the tracks were the plover running and feeding busily and then calling sharply and wildly as they flew. There were three different kinds only one of which was really good to eat. But the men would not eat them and thought I wasted a cartridge to shoot them. I knew there might be curlew up on the flat but we could try for them another day.

"We can go on a little further," I said. "There is a pretty good piece of fairly high ground where we can turn."

"Let's go on then."

A short way along the trail we found the track of a lioness which had come down the trail toward us and then turned off and a little further was another lioness track. They had also been on the track a half an hour to an hour before.

"You watch for them over on the right side, Kittner," I said.

Further along we saw where a cow rhino and her calf had crossed the trail. But their tracks had been rained on. It began to rain and I thought we had better get turned around where we could and go back to camp before we were stuck in some of the soft places.

Close to camp, which showed happily against the trees and the gray mist, the smoke of the fires rising and the white and green tents looking comfortable and homelike there were sandgrouse drinking at the small pools of water on the open prairie. I got out with Ngui to get some for us to eat while Mary went on to camp. They were hunched low beside the little pools and scattered about in the short grass where the sand burs grew. They clattered up and they were not hard to hit if you took them quickly on the rise. These were the medium-sized sandgrouse and they were like plump little desert pigeons masquerading as partridges. I loved their strange flight which was like a pigeon or a kestrel and the wonderful way they used their long back-swept wings once they were in full flight. Walking them up this way was nothing like shooting them when they came in great strings and packs to the water in the morning in the dry season when G.C. and I would take only the highest crossing birds and high incomers and paid a shilling penalty anytime we took more than one bird to a shot fired. Walking them up you missed the guttural chuckling noise the packs made as they talked across the sky. I did not like to shoot so close to camp either so I took only four brace which would make at least two meals for the two of us or a good meal if anyone dropped in.

The men did not like to eat them. I did not like them as well as lesser bustard, teal or snipe or the spur-winged plover. But they were very good eating and would be good for supper. The small rain had stopped again but the mist and the clouds came down to the foot of the mountain.

Mary was sitting in the dining tent with a Campari and soda.

"Did you get many?"

"Eight. They were a little like shooting pigeons at the club."

"They break away much faster than pigeons."

"I think it just seems that way because of the clatter and because they are smaller. Nothing breaks faster than a really strong racing pigeon."

"My I'm glad we're here instead of shooting at the club."

"I am too. I wonder if I can go back there."

"You will."

"I don't know," I said. "I think maybe not."

"There are an awful lot of things I'm not sure I can go back to."

"I wish we didn't have to go back at all. I wish we didn't have any property nor any possessions nor any responsibilities. I wish we only owned a safari outfit and a good hunting car and two good trucks."

125

"Everybody you know would come and visit you and go on free safaris," Miss Mary said. "I'd be the most popular hostess under canvas in the world. I know just how it would be. People would turn up in their private planes and the pilot would get out and open the door for the man and then the man would say, 'Bet you can't tell me who I am. I'll bet you don't remember me. Who am I?' Sometime somebody is going to say that and I'm going to ask Charo for my bunduki and shoot the man right straight between the eyes."

"And Charo can halal him."

"They don't eat men."

"The Wakamba used to. In what you and Pop always refer to as the good old days."

"You're some sort of a part Wakamba. Would you eat a man?"

"No," I said. "Positively no."

"I'm glad of that," Miss Mary said. "Those are words to live by. Do you know I've never killed a man in my life? Do you remember when I wanted to share everything with you and I felt so terrible because I had never killed a kraut and how worried everyone became?"

"I remember very well."

"Should I make the speech about when I kill the woman who steals your affections?"

"If you'll make me a Campari and soda too."

"I will and I'll make you the speech."

She poured the red Campari bitters and put in some Gordon's and then squirted the siphon.

"The gin is a reward for listening to the speech. I know you've heard the speech many times. But I like to make it. It's good for me to make it and it's good for you to hear it."

"OK. Start it."

"Aha," Miss Mary said. "So you think you can make my husband a better wife than I can. Aha. So you think you are ideally and perfectly suited to one another and that you will be better for him than I am. Aha. So you think that you and he would lead a perfect existence together and at last he would have the love of a woman who understands communism, psychoanalysis, and the true meaning of the word love? What do you know about love, you bedraggled hag? What do you know about my husband and the things we have shared and have in common?"

"Hear. Hear."

"Let me go on. Listen, you bedraggled specimen, thin where you should be robust, bursting with fat where you should show some signs of race and breeding. Listen, you woman. I have killed an innocent buck deer at a distance of 340 estimated yards and have eaten him with no remorse. I have shot the kongoni and the wildebeest which you resemble. I have shot and killed a great and beautiful oryx and that is more beautiful than any woman and has horns more decorative than any man. I have killed more things than you have made passes at and I tell you you will cease and desist in your mealy-mouthed mouthings to my husband and leave this country or I will kill you dead."

"It's a wonderful speech. You wouldn't ever make it in Swahili would you?"

"There's no need to make it in Swahili," Miss Mary said. She always felt a little like Napoleon at Austerlitz after the speech. "The speech is for white women only. It certainly does not apply to your fiancée. Since when does a good loving husband not have a right to a fiancée if she only wishes to be a supplementary wife? That is an honorable position. The speech is directed against any filthy white woman who thinks that she can make you happier than I can. The upstarts."

"It's a lovely speech and you make it more clear and forcible each time."

"It's a true speech," Miss Mary said. "I mean every word of it. But I've tried to keep all bitterness and any sort of vulgarity out of it. I hope you didn't think 'mealy-mouthed' had anything to do with mealies."

"I didn't think so."

"That's good. Those were really nice mealies she brought you too. Do you think one time we could have them roasted in the ashes of the fire? I love them that way."

"Of course we can."

"Is there anything special about her bringing you four?"

"No. Two for you and two for me."

"I wish someone was in love with me and brought me presents."

"Everybody brings you presents every day and you know it. Half the camp cuts toothbrushes for you."

"That's true. I have lots of toothbrushes. I still have plenty from Magadi even. I'm glad you have such a nice fiancée though. I wish everything was as simple always as things are here at the foot of the mountain."

"They're not really simple at all. We're just lucky."

"I know. And we must be good and kind to each other to deserve all our luck. Oh I hope my lion will come and I'll be tall enough to see him clearly when the time comes. Do you know how much he means to me?"

"I think so. Everybody does."

"Some people think I'm crazy, I know. But in the old days people went to search for the Holy Grail and for the Golden Fleece and they weren't supposed to be silly. A true great lion is better and more serious than any cups or sheepskins. I don't care how Holy or Golden they were. Everybody has something that they want truly and my lion means everything to me. I know how patient you've been about him and how patient everyone has been. But now I'm sure after this rain I'll meet him. I can't wait until the first night that I hear him roar."

"He has a wonderful roar and you'll see him soon."

"Outside people will never understand. But he will make up for everything."

"I know. You don't hate him, do you?"

"No. I love him. He's wonderful and he is intelligent and I don't have to tell you why I have to kill him."

"No. Certainly not."

"Pop knows. And he explained to me. He told me about that terrible woman too that everyone shot her lion forty-two times. I better not talk about it because no one can ever understand."

"We understand and these people that don't we can only be sorry for."

We really did understand too because together one time we had seen the tracks of the first great lion. They were twice the size a lion's tracks should be and they were in light dust that had just been rained on only enough to dampen it so that they were a true print. I had been working up on some kongoni to kill meat for camp and when Ngui and I saw the tracks we pointed with grass stems and I could see the sweat come on his forehead. We waited for Mary without moving and when she saw the tracks she drew a deep breath. She had seen many lion tracks by then and several lions killed but these tracks were unbelievable. Ngui kept shaking his head and I could feel the sweat under my armpits and in my crotch. We followed the tracks, like careful hounds, and saw where he had drunk at a muddy spring and then gone up the draw to the escarpment. I had never seen such tracks, ever, and by the mud of the spring they were even clearer.

I had not known whether to go back and find the kongoni and run the risk of shooting and perhaps having him leave that country with the sound of the rifle shot. But we needed meat and this was a country where there was not much meat and all the game was wild because there were so many predators. You never killed a zebra that did not have black, riven lion claw scars on his hide and the zebra were as shy and unapproachable as desert oryx. It was a buffalo, rhino, lion, and leopard country and nobody liked to hunt it except G.C. and Pop and it made Pop nervous. G.C. had so many nerves that he ended by having no nerves and he never admitted the presence of danger until he had shot his way out of it. But Pop had said that he never had hunted this country without having trouble and he had hunted it, making the trek across the deadly flats at night to avoid the

heat which could be 120 degrees Fahrenheit in the shade, many years before G.C. had been born or motor cars had been brought to East Africa.

I was thinking of this when we saw the huge, unreal tracks of the lion
and afterwards, when we started to outmaneuver the kongoni, I thought
only of that. But the lion track was in my mind as though it had been brand-
ed there and I knew that Mary, from having seen other lions, had seen him
as he must have looked coming along that trail. We had killed the highly
edible, horse-faced, awkward, tawny kongoni which was as innocent, or
more innocent, than anything could be and Mary had finished it with a
shot where the neck joins the head. She had done this to perfect her shooting and because it was necessary and someone must do it.

Sitting there in the tent I thought how abhorrent this would be to all
vegetarians but everyone who has ever eaten meat must know that someone has killed it and since Mary, having engaged in killing, wanted to kill
without inflicting suffering, it was necessary for her to learn and to practice. Those who never eat fish, not even a tin of sardines, and who will stop
their cars if there are locusts on the road, and have never eaten even meat
broth can condemn those who kill to eat and so that others, who love meat,
and to whom the meat belonged before the white men stole their country,
may eat. But who knows what the carrot feels, or the small young radish,
or the used electric light bulb, or the worn phonograph disc, or the apple
tree in winter? Who knows the feelings of the overaged aircraft, the chewed
gum, the cigarette butt, or the discarded book riddled by woodworms? In
my copy of the Regulations of the Game Department no one of these cases
was treated nor was there any regulation about the treatment of yaws and
of venereal disease which was one of my daily duties. There were no regulations regarding the fallen limbs of trees nor dust nor biting flies, other
than tsetse; see Fly Areas. The hunters who took out licenses to shoot and
were allowed by valid permits to hunt for a limited time in certain of the
Masai countries which had formerly been reserves and were now controlled
areas kept a schedule of what beasts they were permitted to kill and then
paid a very nominal fee which was later paid to the Masai. But the Wakamba, who had always hunted game in the Masai country for meat, were not
permitted to hunt nor take any beasts. They were hunted down as poachers by the Game Scouts, who were also, mostly, Wakamba, and G.C. and
Mary thought the Game Scouts were better loved than they were.

The Game Scouts were nearly all of them a very high type of soldier
who had come from the hunting Wakamba. But things were getting very
difficult in the Wakamba country. They had farmed their land foolishly
and almost criminally, but in their own and their old fashion, and it had
eroded along with all the rest of Africa. Their warriors had always fought

in all of Britain's wars and the Masai had never fought in any. The Masai had been coddled, preserved, treated with a fear that they should never have inspired and been adored by all the homosexuals who ever had worked for the Empire in Kenya or Tanganyika because the men were so beautiful. The men were very beautiful, extremely rich, were professional warriors who, now for a long time, would never fight. They had always been drug addicts and now they were becoming alcoholics.

The Wakamba had no meat anymore because they were not allowed to hunt. Formerly they could kill game on the Masai lands for meat for their families since the Masai never killed game but only cared about their cattle. Trouble between the Masai and the Wakamba was always over cattle stealing, never over the killing of game.

The Wakamba hated the Masai as rich showoffs protected by the government. They despised them as men whose women were completely faithless and nearly always syphilitic and as men who could not track because their eyes were destroyed by filth diseases carried by flies; because their spears bent after they had been used a single time; and finally, and most of all, because they were only brave when under the influence of drugs.

The Wakamba, who liked to fight, really fight, not Masai fight which is, usually, a mass hysteria which cannot come off except under the influence of drugs, lived at lower than subsistence level. They had always had their hunters and now there was no place for them to hunt. They loved to drink and drinking was strictly controlled by tribal law. They were not drunkards and drunkenness was severely punished. Meat was a staple of their diet and it was gone now and they were forbidden to hunt it. Their illegal hunters were as popular as smugglers in England in the old days or as those people were who brought good liquor into the United States in Prohibition.

It had not been this bad when I had been there many years before. But it had not been good. The Wakamba were completely loyal to the British. Even the young men and the bad boys were loyal. But the young men were upset and things were not simple at all. The Mau Mau were suspect because it was a Kikuyu organization and the oaths were repulsive to the Wakamba. But there had been some infiltration. There was nothing about this in the Wild Animal Protection Ordinance.

I had been told by G.C. to use my common sense, if any, and that only shits got in trouble. Since I knew that I could qualify for that class at times I tried to use my common sense as carefully as possible and avoid shithood so far as I could. For a long time I had identified myself with the Wakamba and now had passed over the last important barrier so that the identification was complete. There is no other way of making this identification. Any alliance between tribes is only made valid in one way.

Now, with the rain, I knew that everyone would be less worried about their families and if we got some meat everyone would be happy. Meat made men strong; even the old men believed that. Of the old men in camp I thought Charo was the only one who might possibly be impotent and I was not sure about him. I could have asked Ngui and he would have told me. But it was not a proper thing to ask and Charo and I were very old friends. Wakamba men, if they have meat to eat, retain their ability to make love well after they are seventy. But there are some sorts of meat that are better for a man than others. I do not know why I had started to think about this. It had started with the killing of the kongoni the day we had first seen the track of the huge escarpment lion and then it had wandered around like an old man's tale.

"What about going out and getting a piece of meat, Miss Mary?"

"We do need some, don't we?"

"Yes."

"What have you been thinking about?"

"Kamba problems and meat."

"Bad Kamba problems?"

"No. In general."

"That's good. What did you decide?"

"That we needed meat. Let's you and I and Ngui and Charo go without the car and you kill an impala."

"Why an impala? There are no good heads here."

"That's what the old men want. And the Mohammedans didn't get any meat the last time we killed before the big rain."

"But I want to get a wonderful impala head. Or anyway a good one. You promised me one from Salengai."

"There are too many impala here. And I have to kill a leopard and that will save a hundred head of game in a year."

"And help how many baboons to live and eat the crops of the shambas?"

"I'm going to kill enough baboons to make up for what the leopard would kill. They're too smart for him anyway and he's started killing goats."

"You never kill many baboons when I'm around."

"It's too messy."

"I've seen you and G.C. try hard enough."

"That's not the way to hunt them. I've figured out how to hunt them."

"I hate baboons," Mary said. "Well, should we go for the meat?"

"It's a good time to start. If you'd like to walk."

"I'd love to walk. When we come home we'll have a bath and change and there will be the fire."

We had found the herd of impala that were usually close to the road where it crossed the river and Mary had killed an old buck that had one horn. He was very fat and in good shape and my conscience was clear about taking him for meat as he would never have provided the Game Department with a trophy to dispose of and, since he had been driven out of the herd, he was no use anymore for breeding. Mary had made a beautiful shot on him hitting him in the shoulder exactly where she had aimed. Charo was very proud of her and he had been able to butcher absolutely legally by perhaps a hundredth of a second. Mary's shooting, by now, was regarded as completely in the hands of God and since we had different Gods Charo took complete credit for the shot. Pop, G.C., and I had all seen Miss Mary come into perfect form shooting and make astounding and lovely shots. Now it was Charo's turn.

"Memsahib piga mzuri sana," Charo said.

"Mzuri. Mzuri," Ngui told her.

"Thank you," Mary said. "That's three now," she said to me. "I'm happy and confident now. It's strange about shooting, isn't it?"

I was thinking how strange it was and forgot to answer.

"Poor old buck," Mary said. "With only one horn. But did you see how fat he was when Ngui opened him up?"

"I've never seen an impala so fat."

"They ought to be happy with him at camp."

"They will be. We'll be happy with him too."

"It's wicked to kill things. But it's wonderful to have good meat in camp. When did meat get so important to everybody?"

"It always has been. It's one of the oldest and most important things. Africa's starved for it. But if they killed the game the way the Dutch did in South Africa there wouldn't be any."

"But do we keep the game for the natives? Who are we taking care of the game for, really?"

"For itself and to make money for the Game Department and keep the white hunting racket going and to make extra money for the Masai."

We were walking toward camp on the sandy road. It was wet and there were some pools of water in the low spots and Ngui and I were checking it for tracks. Charo had stayed behind with the buck so that the three cheetahs that lived in that corner of the bush-spotted plain or any early evening hyenas would not hit it. We would send the hunting car back to bring it in.

"I love our protecting the game for the game itself," Mary said. "But the rest of it is sort of shoddy."

"It's very mixed up," I said. "But did you ever see a more mixed-up country?"

"No. But you and your mob are all mixed up too."

"I know it."

"But do you have it straight in your head yourself, really?"

"Not yet. We're on a day-to-day basis now."

"Well, I like it anyway," Mary said. "And after all we didn't come out here to bring order into Africa."

"No. We came out to take some pictures and write some captions for them and then to have fun and learn what we could."

"But we certainly got mixed up in it."

"I know. But are you having fun?"

"I've never been happier."

Ngui had stopped and was pointing at the right-hand side of the road. "Simba," he said.

There was the big track, too big to believe. The left hind foot clearly showed the old scar. He had crossed the road quietly more or less at the time Mary had shot the buck. He had gone on into the broken bush country.

"Him," Ngui said. There was no doubt of it at all. With luck we could have met him on the road. But he would have been careful and let us pass. He was a very intelligent and unhurried lion. The sun was almost down and with the clouds there would be no light to shoot in another five minutes.

"Now things aren't so complicated," Mary said very happily.

"Go to camp for the motorcar," I told Ngui. "We'll go back to wait with Charo with the meat."

CHAPTER 14

That night when we had gone to our own beds but were not yet asleep we heard the lion roar. He was north of the camp and the roar came low and mounting in heaviness and then ended in a sigh.

"I'm coming in with you," Mary said.

We lay close together in the dark under the mosquito bar, my arm around her, and listened to him roar again.

"There's no mistaking when it's him," Mary said. "I'm glad we're in bed together when we hear him."

He was moving to the north and west, grunting deeply and then roaring.

"Is he calling up the lionesses or is he angry? What is he really doing?"

"I don't know, honey. I think he's angry because it's wet."

"But he roared too when it was dry and we tracked him in the dust."

"I was just joking, honey. I only hear him roar. I can see him when he sets himself and tomorrow you'll see where he tears the ground up."

"He's too great to joke about."

"I have to joke about him if I'm going to back you up. You wouldn't want me to start worrying about him, would you?"

"Listen to him," Mary said.

We lay together and listened to him. You cannot describe a wild lion's roar. You can only say that you listened and the lion roared. It is not at all like the noise the lion makes at the start of Metro-Goldwyn-Mayer pictures. When you hear it you first feel it in your scrotum and it runs all the way up through your body.

"He makes me feel hollow inside," Mary said. "He really is the king of the night."

We listened and he roared again still moving to the northwest. This time the roar ended with a cough.

"Just hope he kills," I said to Mary. "Don't think about him too much and sleep well."

"I have to think about him and I want to think about him. He's my lion and I love him and respect him and I have to kill him. He means more to me than anything except you and our people. You know what he means."

"Too bloody well," I said. "But you ought to sleep, honey. Maybe he is roaring to keep you awake."

"Well then let him keep me awake," Mary said. "If I'm going to kill him he has a right to keep me awake. I love everything he does and everything about him."

"But you ought to sleep a little bit, honey. He wouldn't like you not to sleep."

"He doesn't care about me at all. I care about him and that's why I kill him. You ought to understand."

"I understand. But you ought to sleep good now, my kitten. Because tomorrow in the morning it starts."

"I'll sleep. But I want to hear him speak once more."

She was very sleepy and I thought that this girl who had lived all her life never wishing to kill anything until she had fallen in with bad characters in the war had been hunting lions too long on a perfectly straight basis which, without a professional to back her up, was not a sound trade or occupation and could be very bad for one and obviously was being that at this moment. Then the lion roared again and coughed three times. The coughs came from the earth where he was direct into the tent.

"I'll go to sleep now," Miss Mary said. "I hope he didn't cough because he had to. Can he catch cold?"

"I don't know, honey. Will you sleep well and good now?"

"I'm asleep already. But you must wake me long before first, first light, no matter how asleep I am. Do you promise?"

"I promise." Then she was asleep and I lay far against the wall of the tent and felt her sleeping softly and when my left arm began to ache I took it from under her head and felt her to be comfortable and then I occupied a small part of the big cot and then listened to the lion. He was silent until about three o'clock when he killed. After that the hyenas all started to speak and the lion fed and from time to time spoke gruffly. There was no talk from the lionesses. One I knew was about to have cubs and would have nothing to do with him and the other was her girlfriend. I thought it was still too wet to find him when it was light. But there was always a chance.

Long before it was light in the morning Mwindi woke us with the tea. He said, "Hodi," and left the tea outside the door of the tent on the table. I took a cup in to Mary and dressed outside. It was overcast and you could not see the stars.

Charo and Ngui came in the dark to get the guns and the cartridges and I took my tea out to the table where one of the boys who served the mess tent was building up the fire. Mary was washing and getting dressed, still between sleeping and waking. I walked out on the open ground beyond the elephant skull and the three big bushes and found the ground was still quite damp underfoot. It had dried during the night and it would be much drier than the day before. But I still doubted if we could take the car much past where I figured the lion had killed and I was sure it would be too wet beyond there and between there and the swamp.

The swamp was really misnamed. There was an actual papyrus swamp with much flowing water in it that was a mile and a half across and perhaps four miles long. But the locality that we referred to as the swamp also consisted of the area of big trees that surrounded it. Many of these were on comparatively high ground and some were very beautiful. They made a band of forest around the true swamp but there were parts of this timber that had been so pulled down by feeding elephants that it was almost impassable. There were several rhino that lived in this forest, there were nearly always some elephant now, and sometimes there was a great herd of elephant. Two herds of buffalo used it. Leopards lived in the deep part of this forest and hunted out of it and it was the refuge of this particular lion when he came down to feed on the game of the plains.

This forest of great, tall, and fallen trees was the western boundary of the open and wooded plain and the beautiful glades that were bounded on the north by the salt flats and the broken lava rock country that led to the other great marsh that lay between our country and the Chyulu Hills. On the east was the miniature desert that was the gerenuk country and further to the east was a country of bushy broken hills that later rose in height toward the flanks of Mount Kilimanjaro. It was not as simple as that but that was how it seemed from camp or from the center of the plain and the glades country.

The lion's habit was to kill on the plain or in the broken glades during the night and then, having eaten, retire to the belt of forest that lay to the westward. Our plan was to locate him on his kill and stalk him there or to have the luck to intercept him on his way to the forest. If he got enough confidence so that he would not go all the way to the forest we could track him up from the kill to wherever he might lie up after he had gone for water.

While Mary was dressing and then making her way on the track across the meadow to the belt of trees where the green canvas latrine tent was hidden I was thinking about the lion. We must take him on if there was any chance of success. Mary had shot well and was confident. But if there was only a chance of frightening him or of spooking him into high grass or difficult country where she could not see him because of her height we should leave him alone to become confident. I hoped we would find that he had gone off after he had fed, drunk at some of the surface water that still lay in the mudholes of the plain, and then gone to sleep in one of the brush islands of the plain or the patches of trees in the glades.

The car was ready with Mthuka at the wheel and I had checked all the guns when Mary came back. It was light now but not light enough to shoot. The clouds were still well down the slopes of the mountain and there was no sign of the sun except that the light was strengthening. I looked through the sights of my rifle at the elephant skull but it was still too dark to shoot. Charo and Ngui were both very serious and formal.

"How do you feel, Kitten?" I said to Mary.

"Wonderful. How did you think I'd feel?"

"Did you use the Eygene?"

"Of course," she said. "Did you?"

"Yes. We're just waiting for it to get a little lighter."

"It's light enough for me."

"It isn't for me."

"You ought to do something about your eyes."

"I told them we'd be back for breakfast."

"That will give me a headache."

"We brought some stuff. It's in a box back there."

"Does Charo have plenty of ammo for me?"

"Ask him."

Mary spoke to Charo who said he had "Mingi risasi."

"Want to roll your right sleeve up?" I asked. "You asked me to remind you."

"I didn't ask you to remind me in an evil bad temper."

"Why don't you get angry at the lion instead of me?"

"I'm not angry at the lion in any way. Do you think there is enough light for you to see now?"

"Kwenda na simba," I said to Mthuka. Then to Ngui, "Stand up in back to watch."

We started off, the tires taking hold very well on the drying track, me leaning out with both boots outside the cutout door, the morning air cold off the mountain, the rifle feeling good. I put it to my shoulder and aimed a few times. Even with the big yellow light-concentrating glasses I wore there was not enough light yet to shoot safely. But it was twenty minutes to where we were going and the light was strengthening every minute.

"Light's going to be fine," I said.

"I thought it would," Mary said. I looked around. She was sitting with great dignity and she was chewing gum.

We drove on up the track past the improvised airstrip. There was game everywhere and the new grass seemed to have grown an inch since the morning of the day before. There were white flowers coming up too, solid in the spread of the grass and making the whole fields white. There was still some water in the low parts of the tracks and I motioned to Mthuka to turn off the track to the left to avoid some standing water. The flowered grass was slippery. The light was getting better all the time.

Mthuka saw the birds perched heavily in the two trees off to the right beyond the next two glades and pointed. If they were still up it should mean the lion was on the kill. Ngui tapped on the top of the car with the palm of his hand and we stopped. I remember thinking that it was strange that Mthuka should have seen the birds before Ngui when Ngui was much higher. Ngui dropped to the ground and came alongside of the car crouching so his body would not break its outline. He grabbed my foot and pointed to the left toward the belt of forest.

The great black-maned lion, his body looking almost black and his huge head and shoulders swinging, was trotting into the tall grass.

"You see him?" I asked Mary softly.

"I see him."

He was into the grass now and only his head and shoulders showed, then only his head, the grass swaying and closing behind him. He had evidently heard the car or else he had started for the forest early and seen us coming up the road.

"There's no sense you going in there," I said to Mary.

"I know all that," she said. "If we'd have been out earlier we would have found him."

"It wasn't light enough to shoot. If you had wounded him I'd have had to follow him in there."

"We'd have had to follow him."

"The hell with the we stuff."

"How do you propose to get him then?" She was angry, but only angry with the prospect of action and a termination gone and not stupid in her anger so that she could expect to demand to be allowed to go into grass taller than her head after a wounded lion.

"I expect him to get confident when he sees us drive on now without even going over to his kill." Then I interrupted to say, "Get in Ngui. Go ahead poli poli, Mthuka." Then feeling Ngui beside me and the car proceeding slowly along the track with two friends and brothers watching the vultures perched in the trees I said, "What do you think Pop would have done? Chased him into the grass and the down timber and taken you in where you're not tall enough to see? What are we supposed to do? Get you killed or kill the lion?"

"Don't embarrass Charo with your shouting."

"I wasn't shouting."

"You ought to hear yourself sometime."

"Listen," I whispered.

"Don't say 'listen' and don't whisper. And don't say 'On your own two feet' and 'When the chips are down.'"

"You certainly make lion hunting lovely sometimes. How many people have betrayed you in it so far?"

"Pop and you and I don't remember who else. G.C. probably will too. If you know so much, you lion-hunting general who knows everything, why haven't the birds come down if the lion's left the kill?"

"Because either one or both of the lionesses are still on it or lying up close to it."

"Aren't we going to see?"

"From further up the road and so as not to spook anything. I want them all to be confident."

"Now I'm getting a little tired of the phrase 'I want them to be confident.' If you can't vary your thinking you could try to vary your language."

"How long have you been hunting this lion, honey?"

"It seems like forever and I could have killed him three months ago if you and G.C. would have let me. I had an easy chance and you wouldn't let me take him."

"Because we didn't know he was this lion. He might have been a lion that had come from Amboseli with the drought. G.C. has a conscience."

"Both of you have the conscience of bushwhacky delinquents," Miss Mary said. "When will we see the lionesses?"

"To your right bearing forty-five degrees about three hundred more yards up this track."

"And what force is the wind?"

"About force two," I said. "Honey, you are a little lion whacky."

"Who has more right to be? Of course I am. But I take lions seriously."

"I do too, really. And I think I care as much about them as you do even if I don't talk about it."

"You talk about it plenty. Don't worry. But you and G.C. are just a pair of conscience-ridden murderers. Condemning things to death and carrying out the sentence. And G.C. has a much better conscience than you too and his people are properly disciplined."

139

I touched Mthuka on the thigh so that he would stop the car. "Look, honey. There is what's left of the zebra kill and there are the two lionesses. Can we be friends?"

"I've always been friends," she said. "You just misinterpret things. May I have the bini, please?"

I handed her the good binoculars and she watched the two lionesses. The one was so big with cubs that she looked to be a maneless lion. The other was possibly her grown daughter, perhaps only a devoted friend. They each lay under the shelter of an island of brush, the one calm, dignified, and prematronly, her tawny jaws dark with blood, the other young and lithe and equally dark about the jowls. There was not much of the zebra left but they were protecting their property. I could not have told from the sounds I had heard in the night whether they had killed for the lion or whether he had killed and they had joined him.

The birds perched heavily in both of the small trees and in the biggest tree in one of the green islands of bush there must have been a hundred more. The vultures were heavy, hump-shouldered, and ready to drop but the lionesses were too close to the striped quarter and neck of the zebra that lay on the ground. I saw a jackal, looking neat and handsome as a fox, at the edge of one of the patches of bush and then another one. There were no hyenas in sight.

"We shouldn't spook them," I said. "I favor not going near it at all."

Mary was friends now. Seeing any lions always excited and pleased her and she said, "Do you think they killed or he killed?"

"I think he killed and ate what he wanted and they came much later."

"Would the birds come in the night?"

"No."

"There are an awful lot of them. Look at the ones stretching their wings to dry like the buzzards do at home."

"They're awfully ugly to be Royal Game and when they have rinderpest or other cattle diseases they must spread it terribly with their droppings. There are certainly too many of them for this area. The insects and the hyenas and the jackals could clean up after any kills made here and the hyenas can kill what is sick or too old and eat on the spot and not spread it all over the countryside."

Seeing the lionesses in their shelter and the truly horrible vultures clumped in such numbers in the trees had made me talk too much, that and that we were friends again and that I would not have to pit my truly loved Miss Mary with the lion until another day. Then, too, I hated vultures and I believed their true utility as scavengers was greatly overrated.

Someone had decided that they were the great garbage disposers of Africa and they had been made Royal Game and could not be held down in numbers and their role as spreaders of disease was heresy against those magic words "Royal Game." The Wakamba thought it was very funny and we always called them King's birds.

They did not look funny now though perched obscenely above the remains of the zebra and when the big lioness rose and yawned and went out to feed again two big vultures dropped as soon as she was on the meat. The young lioness flicked her tail once and charged them and they rose running and heavy-winged as she slapped at them as a kitten slaps. She then lay down by the big lioness and started to feed and the birds stayed in the trees but the closest ones were almost overbalanced with hunger.

It would not take the lionesses long to finish off what was left of the zebra and I told Mary it was probably better to leave them feeding and drive on up the road as though we had not seen them. Ahead of us there was a small bunch of zebra and beyond were wildebeest and many more zebra.

"I love to watch them," Mary said. "But if you think it's better we can go on up and see how the salt flats are and maybe see the buff."

So we went up as far as the edge of the salt flats and saw no tracks of buffalo and no buffalo. The flats were still too wet and slippery for a car and so was the ground to the eastward. We found the tracks of the two lionesses at the edge of the salt flats headed in the direction of the kill. They were fresh tracks and it was impossible to tell when they had hit the kill. But I thought it must have been the lion who killed and Ngui and Charo agreed.

"Perhaps if we just drive back the way we've come he'll get used to seeing the car," Mary said. "I don't have a headache but it would be fun to have breakfast."

It was what I had been hoping she would suggest.

"If we don't shoot at all—" I stopped because I would have said that it would give him confidence.

"Maybe he will think it is a car that just goes up and down," Mary finished for me. "We'll have a lovely breakfast and I will do all the letters I should write and we'll be patient and good kittens."

"You're a good kitten."

"You are. I'm sorry I was cross. We're good friends now, aren't we?"

"We always were. Did you see how huge and black he was?"

"Yes. And how smart."

"Do you see why I love him and respect him?"

"I always did, you dog."

"It is more fun without anybody even if we get cross at each other. Isn't it?"

"Much more for me."

"We'll drive back to camp like tourists and see the new wonderful green fields and breakfast feels so good in advance."

But when we got to camp for breakfast there was the young policeman in his mud-spattered Land Rover waiting for us. The car was under a tree and his two askaris were back at the lines. He got out of the car as we came up and his young face was lined with his great cares and responsibilities.

"Good morning, Bwana," he said. "Good morning, Memsahib. Been making an early patrol I see."

"Will you have some breakfast, Harry?" I asked.

"If I'm not in the way. Turn up anything interesting, gov'nor?"

"Just checking on the stock. What's the word from the boma?"

"They nailed them, gov'nor. They got them over on the other side. North of Namanga. You can call in your people."

"Much of a show?"

"No details yet."

"Pity we couldn't have fought here."

Miss Mary looked at me warningly. She was not happy at having the young policeman for breakfast but she knew he was a lonesome boy and while she was intolerant with fools she was feeling kindly until we had seen the policeman exhausted in his mud-covered vehicle.

"It would have meant a lot to me. Gov'nor, we had almost the perfect plan. Perhaps it was the perfect plan. The only aspect I worried about was the little Memsahib here. If you'll pardon my saying it, ma'am, this is no work for a woman."

"I wasn't in it at all," Mary said. "Would you have some more kidneys and bacon?"

"You were in it," he said. "You were a part of The Screen. I'm mentioning you in my report. It's perhaps not the same as a Mention in Dispatches. But it's all part of one's record. Someday those who fought in Kenya will be very proud."

"After wars I've found that the people are usually just crashing bores," Miss Mary said.

"Only to those who did not fight," young Harry said. "Fighting men and, with your permission, fighting women have a code."

"Try some beer, young Harry," I said. "Have any gen on when we'll fight again?"

"You'll have the word, gov'nor, before anyone else has it."

"You're too kind to us," I said. "But I suppose there is glory enough for all."

"Too true," the young policeman said. "In a way, gov'nor, we're the last of the Empire builders. In a way we're like Rhodes and Dr. Livingstone."

"In a way," I said.

"Will you two gentlemen excuse me?" Miss Mary asked. "I don't want to handicap you if you are going to talk shop."

The young policeman rose and bowed to her and when she was gone he uttered her epitaph, "A great lady and a sensible woman."

"Thank you," I said. "And a great shot when both her feet are on the ground and the chips are down."

"I know it. Or I would have asked you to send her to the boma rather than keeping her with The Screen."

We drank a glass of Tusker to Miss Mary, The Boma, and The Screen.

"Gov'nor, when I drove in, no dust mind you, I saw the chief of that Wakamba village of yours waiting in the lines. Looks the very finest type of chap."

"Should we have him in?"

"It would be useful for me to know him."

"I'll send for him."

The Informer entered and stood at attention. He was a little drunk but he was nobody's fool and he did not commit himself. He had known police before, and if his luck held, he would know them many times again.

"The bwana of the police," I said. "The chief of our Wakamba village."

The young policeman remembering he was not interrogating but governing rose to acknowledge the introduction.

"Sit down, chief," I said. "How is the village?"

"All present and accounted for," the Informer said, remaining standing. He knew that his height was his greatest asset next to his paisley shawl.

"You have relieved the patrols?"

"As you ordered, sir."

"The state of emergency has passed. The Women's Auxiliary returns to Condition Blue. Condition Red is canceled."

"The bwana of the police has brought great news for my village."

"Were you ready to fight, chief? To fight for the Empire?"

"I and my people were ready."

"I will include the chief's name in my report," the young policeman said.

"Under the circumstances don't you think we might offer the chief some libation?" I asked.

"It's your shauri."

"Chief, have you taken strong drink?"

"Never. But I would take it for my King Emperor."

"It's the Queen now," I said sternly.

"For my beloved and gracious Queen Empress."

"Perhaps beer is better for you as a Wakamba," I suggested.

"As a chief I wish to pledge my loyalty and my authority in the strongest possible way," the Informer said. I had never seen him finer nor more noble. The young policeman watched him with admiration.

"Pour for yourself as you would by tribal law and custom."

The Informer, now promoted to Chief, looked at the different bottles on the wooden cases and appeared to recognize none of them. Then he filled a half tumbler and like a disinterested African picked up at hazard the bitters and without looking at the glass snowed a rusty color into the pure colorless fluid he had selected.

"To our Queen!" he said and drained the glass. He then saluted and left the dining tent. I was very proud of him and fonder of him than ever.

"Take your time with the beer, Harry," I said. "I have a minor item I have to check on."

Outside I walked to the lines with the Informer. It was a terrific dosage for him to have taken but he had never been a chief before and it made up for his status at being the protector of a widow and a renegade in an alien tribe.

"How do you feel, brother?" I said.

"All right for the moment. Did you see, brother, that I took the Canadian gin?"

"You are a fine and noble man," I said. "Is everything all right at the shamba?"

"No."

"I'll send you back with the hunting car. Now I must go back with the child of the police."

"He is not a bad child," the Informer said. "He was very nice to me."

"Do you want to throw up?" I said. His gait was lurching.

"No," he said. "No man would throw up his capital."

CHAPTER 15

That afternoon I went to the shamba to see the Informer. He had a very severe cold in his chest and I dosed him with the usual remedies. His morale was not good and a Masai with bad morale is very sad. I gave him twenty B-complex vitamin capsules which I told him were the nearest thing to the great remedy he had read about in the *Reader's Digest*. It was a shame that I had no testosterone as any injection is a great comfort in Africa and if it had been successful it would have won many converts to our new religion.

"Will they really do any good, brother?" he asked me.

"We are of the same circumcision group and I use them myself and I am well."

"But you have led a better life than I have."

"I wouldn't bet on that, brother."

"I never gamble. It is a vice I never could afford."

"You were wonderful as a chief."

"It was not difficult. I should have been a chief if I had not made errors. It was the bwanas and a Somali woman who ruined me."

"How does a Somali woman ruin you, brother?"

"She takes away everything. She even takes away your manhood. She is not happy until she has taken that."

"Do they always do that?"

"Always, brother. And men are enslaved by it. Finally they take everything else and go before the D.C. Brother, never take a Somali woman as a wife."

"I had not planned on it. But thank you, Informer brother."

It was a cold afternoon since the sun was under the cloud of the mountain and a heavy wind was blowing from the heights where all the rain that had fallen on us must now be snow. The shamba was at about 6,000 feet and the mountain was over 19,000 feet high. Its sudden cold winds, when heavy snow had fallen, were punishing to those who lived on the upland plain. Higher, in the foothills, the houses, we did not call them huts, were built in the folds of hills to have a lee against the wind. But this shamba had the full force of the wind and on this afternoon it was very cold and bitter with the smell of not-quite-frozen dung and all birds and beasts were out of the wind.

The man who Miss Mary referred to as my father-in-law had a chest cold too and bad rheumatic pains in his back. I gave him medicine and then rubbed him and applied Sloan's Liniment. None of us Wakamba regarded him as the father of his daughter but he was technically such and by tribal law and custom I was bound to respect him. We treated him in the lee of the house with his daughter watching. She was carrying her sister's child on her hip and was wearing my last good woolly sweater and a fishing cap which had been given me by a friend. My friend had ordered my initials embroidered on the front of the cap and this had some significance with all of us. Until she had decided that she wanted it the initials had always been an embarrassment. Under the woolly sweater she wore the last and too-many-times-washed dress from Loitokitok. It was not correct etiquette for me to speak to her while she was carrying the child of her sister and, technically, she should not have watched the treatment of her father. She handled this by keeping her eyes downcast at all times.

The man who was known by a name which means potential father-in-law was not particularly brave under the ordeal of Sloan's Liniment. Ngui, who knew Sloan's well and had no regard for the men of this shamba, wanted me to rub it in and signaled once that I let a few drops fall where they should not go. Mthuka with his beautiful and undeniable tribal scars on both cheeks was completely happy in his deafness watching what he considered to be a worthless Kamba suffer in a good cause. I was completely ethical with the Sloan's to the disappointment of everyone including the daughter and all lost interest.

"Jambo, tú," I said to the daughter when we left and she said with her eyes down and her chest up, "No hay remedio."

We got into the car, no one waving to anyone, the cold closing in with the formality. There was too much of both and we all felt bad to see such a beautiful shamba so miserable.

"Ngui," I asked, "how can they have such miserable men and such wonderful women in this shamba?"

"Great men have passed through this shamba," Ngui said. "Formerly this was the route to the south until the new route. I tell you this as a blood brother."

"We never made blood brothers."

"It is not necessary. On any day." He was angry with the men of the shamba because they were worthless Kamba.

"Do you think we ought to take this shamba?"

"Yes," he said. "You and I and 'Thuka and the young men."

We were going into the African world of unreality that is defended and fortified by reality past any reality there is. It was not an escape world or a day-dreaming world. It was a ruthless real world made of the unreality of the real. If there were still faru, and we saw them every day while it was obviously impossible for there to be such an animal, then anything was possible. If Ngui and I could talk to faru, who was incredible to start with, in his own tongue well enough for him to answer back and I could curse and insult faru in Spanish so that he would be humiliated and go off, then unreality was sensible and logical beside reality. Sometimes faru would not be insulted and humiliated, and we never tried these games, which were much too rough when Miss Mary was around. But many times he was turned and humiliated by a mixture of his own language and Spanish.

Spanish was regarded as Mary's and my tribal language and it was considered to be the all-purpose language of the country where we came from. They knew we also had an inner or secret tribal language. We were not supposed to have anything in common with the British except the color of our skin and a mutual tolerance. While Mayito was with us he was greatly admired, aside from his excellent qualities as a hunter and a gentleman, because of his very deep voice, the way he smelled, his great courtesy, and because he had arrived in Africa speaking both Spanish and Swahili. They also revered his scars and as he spoke Swahili with a strong Wakamba and Camagüey accent and looked like a bull he was, truly, almost revered.

I had been asked many questions about him and had explained that he was the son of the king of his own country, in the time when it had great kings, and had described the thousands of acres of land that he owned and its quality, the number of cattle I had known that he owned and the quantities of sugar that he produced. Since sugar was the universally sought food by the Wakamba after meat and since Pop had backed me up to Keiti that these things were true and since Mayito was obviously a sound cattleman who knew exactly what he spoke of and, when he spoke of it, spoke in a voice very similar to that of a lion and had never been unjust, rude, contemptuous, or boastful he was really loved. In all the time he was in Africa I only told one lie about Mayito. This was in respect to his wives.

Mwindi who was a true admirer of Mayito asked me, flat out, how many wives Mayito had. Everyone had wondered and it was not the sort of statistic they could get from Pop. Mwindi was in one of his gloomy days and there had evidently been a discussion. I did not know which side he had taken but it was evidently a question that he had been asked to settle.

I thought the question and the aspects of the strangeness over and said, "In his own country no one would wish to count them."

"Ndio," Mwindi said. This was the proper language of mzees.

Mayito had one wife actually. She was very beautiful. Mwindi went out as gloomy as ever.

Now today, coming back from the shamba, Ngui and I were engaged in that characteristic occupation of men, planning the operation which will never take place.

"All right," I said. "We take it."

"Good."

"Who takes Debba?"

"She is yours. She is your fiancée."

"Good. After we take it how do we hold it when they send a company of K.A.R.?"

"You get troops from Mayito."

"Mayito is in Hong Kong now. In China."

"We have aircraft."

"Not that kind. What do we do without Mayito?"

"We go up into the mountain."

"Very cold. Too damn cold right now. Also we lose the shamba."

"War is shit," Ngui said.

"I'll sign that," I said. We were both happy now. "No. We take the shamba day by day. The day is our unit. Now we are having in our belief what the old men believe they have when they die. Now we hunt good; eat good meat; drink well once Memsahib kills the lion; and make the happy hunting grounds while we are alive."

"We have to kill chui too."

"We'll kill that chui. I saw it already in a dream."

"Did you dream about simba?"

"No," I said truthfully.

"Everybody dreams too much about simba," Ngui said. "Everybody."

"Let him dream about himself," I said. "Memsahib kills him this week."

"Truly?"

"I know."

"Much better. Then we make happy hunting ground."

Mthuka was too deaf to hear anything we said. He was like a motor which is functioning perfectly but the gauges have cut out. This usually only happens in dreams but Mthuka had the finest sight of any of us, was the best wild driver, and he had, if such a thing exists, complete extrasensory perception. As we drove up to the camp and stopped the car Ngui and I knew he had not heard a word we had said but he said, and he was very distant from a yes-man, "It is better, much, much better."

"Tu," I said to him. He had pity and kindness in his eyes and I knew he was a better and kinder man than I could ever be. He offered me his snuff box. It was semi-normal snuff with none of the strange additions of Arap Meina but it tasted very good and I put a big three-fingered pinch of it under my upper lip.

None of us had been drinking at all. Mthuka always carried himself rather like a crane in cold weather with his shoulders hunched. The sky was overcast and the cloud was down to the plain and as I handed him back the snuff box he said, "Wakamba tu."

We both knew it and there was nothing to do about it and he covered the car and I walked over to the tent.

"Was the shamba in good shape?" Miss Mary asked.

"It's fine. It's a little cold and rough."

"Is there anything I can do for anyone there?"

You good, lovely, kind kitten, I thought and I said, "No. I think everything is fine. I'm going to get a medicine chest for the widow and teach her to use it. It's awful for the kids' eyes not to be cared for when they're Wakamba."

"If they are anybody," Miss Mary said.

"My God, it's cold."

"Take a good hot bathi and then we'll sit by the fire and have drinks."

"Have you bathed?"

"Yes, while I waited for you. Mwindi is heating your water."

"You know it must have really snowed an awful lot on the mountain."

"It had to with all that rain. When do you think we'll see it?"

"In the morning, I hope."

"I'm going out to talk to Arap Meina. Would you please ask Mwindi to call me when the bath is ready?"

Arap Meina did not think that the lion would kill that night. I told him he had looked very heavy when he had gone off into the forest that morning. He doubted if the lionesses would kill that night either although they might and the lion might join them. I asked him if I should have made a kill and tied it up or covered it with brush to try to hold the lion. He said the lion was much too intelligent and we remembered how we had killed for him several months before and he had left the country. He had then been with a lioness that was in heat. He was fascinated by her and they paid no attention to us at all. The lion was so big and so beautiful that we, not knowing him nor his history, had believed that he must be a picture lion which had wandered out from the National Park and that it would be murder for Mary to kill him. He was in the open under a tree and the lioness was teasing him. So it had looked like a wonderful chance to take photographs but when a piece of meat had been brought close to the tree he and the lioness had gone off into the edge of the belt of forest and had never come back. This was the time that Mary felt we had deprived her of him. But G.C. did not wish to take any chance of our killing a lion that had not been condemned and I agreed with him absolutely.

It was more than three months since Mary had first seen him with his lioness and since it is about three months and three weeks between breeding and the birth of the cubs this could be the same mate he had then. I was sure he was the same lion and so was Arap Meina but there was no way we could know about the lioness since she had altered in appearance so by being with cubs. Now she looked big enough to be a maneless lion.

Anyway food was plentiful now for the lions as more game was coming in from the direction of the Chyulus as the grass grew higher and Arap Meina was sure Mary's lion would be here for at least two weeks if unmolested. Other lions would certainly come in. But there was no possibility of confusing them with him. If we killed him it would satisfy the Masai and if cattle killing continued by any of the other lions, which seemed doubtful with so much game coming in, we would find the lion that did it and Arap Meina and I would kill him.

A large part of time in Africa is spent in talk. Where people are illiterate this is always true. Once you start the hunt hardly a word is spoken. You all understand each other and in hot weather your tongue is stuck dry in your mouth. But in planning a hunt in the evening there is usually much talking and it is quite rare that things come off as they are planned, especially if the planning is too complicated.

That night the lion proved us all to be wrong. He roared in the night to the north of the field where we had made the airstrip. Then he moved off roaring from time to time. Then another and less impressive lion roared several times. Then it was quiet for a long time. After that we heard the hyenas and from the way they called and from the high, quavering, laughing noise they made I was sure some lion had killed. After that there was the noise of lions fighting. This quieted down and the hyenas started to howl and laugh.

"You and Arap Meina said it was going to be a quiet night," Mary said very sleepily.

"Somebody killed something," I said.

"Well, we came to Africa on purpose," Mary said.

"I tell you what I think they are doing—"

"You and Arap Meina tell each other in the morning. I have to go to sleep now to get up early. I want to sleep well so I won't be cross."

I was out by the fire in the morning. The stars were out and it promised to be a good day. Mwindi brought the tea an hour before it would be light. He slumped along in his green robe and took tea in to Mary and I heard him say, "Hodi, Memsahib," then brought me mine and put it on the table. He had heard Arap Meina and me talk together and it made him cheerful even at this hour.

"Jambo, Bwana. Bwana sleep well?"

"Very well."

"No hear simba?"

"Hear plenty simba."

"One simba come by three four days before rain. One old mzee simba. Young simba kill wildebeest. Two manamuki simba come. Old man simba and nanyake simba make big fight. Nanyake simba go away. Old man simba eat. Go away. Manamuki simba eat. Go away. Young dume simba come back eat then go away. Fisi eat up everything. Keiti says so too. You see."

"Thank you very much for telling me."

"You see. I listen all night. Keiti listen. Charo listen. We talk this morning. You listen?"

"Yes. But how do you know he killed a wildebeest?"

"Hear wildebeest talk. Old men not stupid. Make safari before young men born."

"Was the nanyake lion hurt badly?"

"Not much hurt. Make much talk. Then little fight. Then run away."

"What else happened?"

"Keiti want to go out with you in hunting car to see if all true."

"What else happened last night?"

"Chui kill goats at shamba."

He had been saving this.

"How many goats?"

"You find out when Informer comes to tell you."

I had known Mwindi very morose, very cynical, and very disenchanted but I had never seen him as happy or as talkative as this morning except sometimes when he was teaching me Kamba and showing me how wrong I was in basic theology or ignorant of tribal law.

"Bwana, old men very old maybe but not drink. Hunt since toto. Hear everything at night."

"Did you ever see me not respect an old man?"

"No. You always respect old man. But Keiti wants to go to see if what we say is true."

"Do you want to go?"

"Some day on hunt. Today too much work. Leti chai, Bwana?"

"Yes. Tell Mthuka and the gunbearers we will move out at first light with Keiti."

"Want sanlich?"

"No. Tell Nguili bring me pieces of cold meat. I'll eat some now."

I sat there by the fire and drank the tea and thought that this was a very fine and well-mounted counterattack by the old men. I knew what a fine hunter Keiti was and how beautifully he tracked and I thought that if he wanted to take on so much responsibility of prediction and had put it all so flatly this would be a morning to learn from. The only place where he might have tricked was the part about the shamba. He could have heard that from someone. But I could check on that.

We were off just before there was enough light to shoot. The light would come early and if Keiti should be wrong it might be possible to intercept the lion. The new grass was much higher and seemed almost double the height of yesterday and the track was firm. Keiti sat in the back with Mary and Charo. He was shy and smiling and not at all showing off.

We reached and passed the place where the lions had killed the day before and I had checked my sights for shooting light and the light was quite possible. The magazine and the shell in the chamber I always checked when we got into the car.

Then, to the right of the track and about four hundred yards away we could see birds on the ground in an open glade, more vultures dropping, and others in the trees. I touched Mthuka's arm to stop and we got out. It probably would have been sounder to drive over in the car but I thought, since it was so early, the lion might be lying down in one of the islands of bush between us and where the birds were going down. I had not seen his tracks crossing the tracks made by the motorcar wheels and I had been watching very carefully on one side and Charo on the other. But as we walked toward the patch of moving, pulling, flapping vultures on the new green grass, Mary ahead, me behind her and to her left, and Ngui to my left, Ngui found his tracks. We motioned Keiti over and when I saw that they were the tracks of the big lion and that they were headed toward the high dead grass and the forest, I took my binoculars from Charo and glassed all of that country. There were several islands of brush where he might have lain up before the high grass came close to the trail so I told Keiti we would go back to the car and drive up the road and see if he had crossed the road. If he had not I planned for us to come back against the wind and check the various bush islands where he might be. The wind had already started to blow lightly. It was useless to track him downwind and I wanted to know as soon as possible whether he had crossed the trail and gone into the forest.

We got back into the car and drove on up the trail. Ngui, Keiti, Mary, and Mthuka were watching for the lion and I was watching for tracks on one side and Charo was watching on the other. We saw the tracks at the same time. He had gone across the trail and into the high, dead, yellow grass.

The wind was blowing, very lightly, from us toward him. The grass was higher than Mary's chest. I could see the spread trail of his passage as he had shouldered through the grass.

"Should we follow him in there?" I said to Keiti. It was an academic question.

"Hapana," Keiti shook his head and smiled.

"Kittner," I said. "We'll go back in the car and take a look at the kill. We'll have to kill for him this afternoon to get him onto something further away from the swamp and the forest. He's too smart and those lionesses are awfully hungry."

"I had him once. Just under that tree up there? Do you remember?"

"I should."

We drove over to the kill and put up all the Royal Game which took to the trees or flew away flopping obscenely to coast to a halt on the grass when we stopped. There was nothing left of a wildebeest cow but the ribs and the head and horns. There could have been nothing to hold the birds there except yearning for contact that brings ex-royalty together at such places as certain towns in Portugal and occasionally in Switzerland.

"Thin day for the Royal Game," I said. "I think the syndicated hyenas cleaned it up pretty well."

"I'm not going to get out," Mary said. "It's too foul."

It was foul and as feathery as an ill-kept hen yard.

Keiti and Charo were walking around outside the perching and jostling area. I was willing to believe anything and had lost all taste for the demonstration.

"You might tell the great detectives that the two lionesses are lying up down under that tree at the far end of this glade," Mary said.

"They've seen them," I said. "That's their re-entry. They want me to point them out so they can tell me how long ago they saw them."

"Hiko hapa," Keiti called to me. I went over and he showed me the track of the young lion. It was a fair-sized lion track.

"Dume," Keiti said. The lion had gone off bleeding slightly.

"Gone to the old manyatta," I said.

"Ndio," Keiti said. "Mingi fisi."

"Plenty of hyenas," I agreed. "We both heard them."

Keiti was moving in a circle around the bird-fouled area.

"See the two lionesses?" I asked.

"Of course."

"Exactly as advertised," I said. Keiti had picked up the outgoing trail of the big lion. He leaned down and with the quill of a shed vulture plume scraped under the surface and picked up some hairs. They were obviously from the mane of the younger lion where the big lion had cuffed him. Keiti handed them to me.

I held them and asked him for the plume. Then with the plume I scratched an arrow on the ground pointing toward the swamp. I found a hind-foot track that showed the scar and dug the impress of the scar out with the quill and holding it in the palm of my hand laid it on the scratched arrow, then marked a cross over the dirt. I looked at the hairs from the young lion and shook my head, rubbed the whole thing out with my boot, and put the hairs in the slit of a piece of bark on the tree trunk.

"Everything was as you said," I told Keiti. "Asante sana. Kwenda na campi."

We all got into the car and Mthuka turned her around toward the trail.

"What kind of mumbo jumbo were you making?" Mary asked.

"Hapana mumbo jumbo. Hapana woi. Only a small proving. Does no harm."

"Sus amigos estuvo un poco inquieto."

"Mejor."

"Don't carry things too damned far," she said very rapidly in Spanish. "You could you know."

"Things are carried just far enough."

"When am I going to kill the lion?" she asked in English.

"Within three days," I said knowing Keiti understood what was said in English. "Didn't you see the three hairs that stayed stuck in the bark?"

"Well, I hope G.C. gets here to help out."

"He arrives tonight."

"How do you know that?" she asked in Spanish.

"Intuition, my magic powers, and an appreciation of the state of the roads."

"I hope he makes it."

"One of the Indian lorries got through."

"How did you know?"

"Heard it."

When we got back to camp there was a note for me from G.C. Arap Meina had it from the lorry that had come through. G.C. expected to get in that afternoon. Arap Meina said a leopard had gotten into the boma at the shamba and killed a single goat and jumped out with him.

Keiti was smiling happily at this.

"Only one," I said. "Mwindi said goats not a goat."

"I said a goat." He was really very happy. "I did not hear any sound of big killing. The others were frightened but they were not stricken."

"Your tracking was excellent," I said. I was sorry now I had been a showoff. We also were going to all live together for some time and age feuds were no good. Rivalries were healthy and Keiti was a beautiful tracker and a fine hunter and had always been a loyal friend. "I'm sorry I had to make my own medicine about the lion."

"You have medicines you have to make. I did not say woi. It was Bwana said it."

"I said hapana woi."

"That is true."

I put out my hand and we shook hands. Woi was a very bad word to use and I should never have said it in front of Mary anyway. She did not know what it was but when I said it she felt the difference. Shaitani was a joke. But woi could lead to kingole.

"Hapana woi," Keiti said.

"Hapana mbongolo," I answered.

Keiti shook his head and walked away. It was as rough a joke as I dared to make to a man who was my elder. But it was a good rough joke in Kamba and he liked it. The point, though, was that I had been respectful and that I appreciated his skills and that we were friends.

"What were you two talking about?" Mary asked. "What is woi?" Arap Meina turned his head away. He had come close to tell me about the leopard having retired while Keiti and I talked.

I did not use the word again but said, "It is the worst kind of wizard who can and does kill people on order or for choice."

"You're not one, are you?"

"I positively am not."

"But you don't pretend to be, do you?"

"No."

"Tell me about it another time. I wish they'd bring breakfast. Arap Meina wants to talk to you."

Mary sat down to breakfast and I stayed outside the dining tent to talk with Meina. He said after the leopard had killed the goat and jumped the thorn fence with him he had dragged him away to some brush and eaten

155

what he wanted of him and then gone off. There was not enough left for a bait. It was not a big goat.

"We'll kill some baboons for baits," I said. "Now I must go in and eat with Memsahib."

"Memsahib will kill the lion in three days."

"How do you know that?"

He winked, saluted, and went off to the lines.

I sat down to the eggs and bacon, the toast, coffee, and jam. Mary was on her second cup of coffee and seemed quite happy. "Witchcraft and all nonsense aside," she said, "are we really getting anywhere?"

"Yes."

"But he outsmarts us every morning and he can keep it up forever."

"No, he can't. We're going to start to move him a little too far out and he'll make a mistake and you'll kill him."

"Is it all right if I don't go to hunt baboons? I know I need the practice but if I start to miss at that sort of shooting it could put me off."

"No. I think that's a good idea."

"And you aren't really that awful thing. It sounds worse than a were-wolf."

"No. You ask the baboons."

The baboon, when he knows he is being hunted, can be a very difficult animal to destroy. We were supposed to keep the population of baboons down to protect the shambas but we had been doing it in a rather stupid way trying to catch the bands in the open and fire on them as they made for the shelter of the forest. This gave difficult and sporting shots, if there is any such thing as a sporting shot, but it did not do away with many baboons. After you followed them into the forest you nearly always got some in the trees. But you did not get the smart baboons nor the leaders. Baboon hunting, so far as I know, has never been the Sport of Kings and I have yet to see the baboon listed as Royal Game although if enough true baboon lovers organize he may be Royal Game in time and the Africans simply be moved away from their shambas in some vast resettlement scheme. It might be simplest for the baboon lovers to have legislation put through prohibiting the African from planting mealies and then a compromise could be reached putting the baboon on the Game Department lists as a Game Animal with a fairly high license fee. Spurred on by white hunters' tales of the baboon's wiliness, and his ferocity, and there is no lack of true tales, the baboon might be built up into one of the great beasts of the big game hunter. So far there have been few tales of a big game hunter being mauled by baboons, but these would come.

The way British East Africa is going which could be summed up as to Hell, fast, I look forward to heading an All-Girl Safari or an All-Juvenile Delinquent Safari on a Dog Baboons Only basis. Women who have never yet shot their husbands and little tots who have never been permitted to stomp someone to death in Brooklyn under the rigorous policing of recent administrations would have the hunt of a lifetime.

"What are you thinking about and smiling at?" Miss Mary asked.

"Baboons."

"I hate them."

"I won't hunt anywhere near the forest so we won't spook the lion. I know a turnoff on the main road where we can get some."

"Are you going to use your secret scheme on them?"

"No. I can't use the secret scheme until after the lion."

"Can't you tell me about the secret scheme?"

"No, honey. It's a surprise. I think we can only do it once."

"We'll have fun after the lion. My, I wish we could get him tomorrow."

"In three days."

"Do you really believe that?"

"I do. Really."

"It will be nice to have G.C. here and his people and the music all the time out at their camp. I love it alone but it's fun with G.C. You and he won't do crazy things at night this time, will you?"

"No. Because we have to get the lion."

That afternoon after lunch we hunted baboons for leopard baits. In order neither to sadden nor enrage baboon lovers I will give no details. We were not charged by the ferocious beasts and their formidable canine teeth by the time we reached them were stilled in death. When we got back to camp with the four disgusting corpses G.C. had already arrived.

He was muddy and he looked tired but happy.

"Good afternoon, General," he said. He looked into the back of the hunting car and smiled. "Babooning, I see. Two brace. A splendid bag. Going to have them set up by Roland Ward's?"

"I'd thought of a group mounting, G.C., with you and me in the center."

"How are you, Papa, and how is Miss Mary?"

"Isn't she here?"

"No. They said she'd gone for a walk with Charo."

"She's fine. The lion's been a little on her mind. But her morale is good."

"Mine's low," G.C. said. "Should we have a drink?"

"I love a drink after babooning."

"We're going in for big-time babooning on a large scale," G.C. said. He

157

took off his beret and then reached into his tunic pocket and brought out a buff envelope. "Read this and memorize our role."

He called to Nguili to bring drinks and I read the operation orders.

"This makes good sense," I said. I read it on skipping, temporarily, the parts that had nothing to do with us and that I would have to check on the map, looking for where we came in.

"It does make sense," G.C. said. "My morale's not low because of it. It's what's holding my morale up."

"What's the matter with your morale? Moral problems?"

"No. Problems of conduct."

"You must have been a wonderful problem child. You have more damned problems than a character in Henry James."

"Make it Hamlet," G.C. said. "And I wasn't a problem child. I was a very happy and attractive child only slightly too fat."

"You're slightly plump now."

"The only place I'm plump is in my bloody awful face. I haven't a great belly like you. Go ahead and read your bloody orders."

I read on until I came to our role. We did not come in until the action was completed and the trap had been sprung.

"We don't seem to do much until they start to break back over the beaters."

"Some could try to come through," G.C. said. "They almost promise it."

Nguili had come and gone and I read of our role. "That's definite enough. We can fight on that."

"It's very definite."

"Do you want me to digest it all?"

"Please, when you have time."

I felt happy and relaxed with the drink and it was so pleasant to have G.C. back. We could talk about his problems later. Now I wanted to get all the shop over before Mary came back.

"How did you do on the Machakos mickies?"

"I had one interesting day in the hills. Two or three long shots."

I let it go at that.

"Seen any friends?"

"A good friend of yours got the chop." He told me about it. I thought about it.

"Thanks. I didn't know."

"Bill Curtis's sergeant got the chop."

"I didn't really know him."

"It was as though it had happened to Ngui with you. They did it the nasty way."

158

"Will we be seeing Bill?"

"He might be in tonight or tomorrow."

"He's one of the finest men and best policemen I ever knew."

"That anyone ever knew ever," G.C. said. "Don't mention his sergeant. How's your local colleague?"

"Comic," I said. "But it's not very comic if you think about it."

"The lion?"

I told him everything I knew, thought, and hoped about the lion and just how things had gone.

"I don't think you've made any mistakes," G.C. said judicially.

"Thank you, General."

"We must put out a bait far enough out into the plain so there is a chance to intercept him in the morning."

"How long are you going to be here, G.C.?"

"I can stay three days. Thank you for setting up things here on that problem. Bill was pleased too. I'm sure it would have worked."

"Maybe."

"I have considerable faith in your bad boys."

"But naturally your people are better."

"Naturally. Better trained, better disciplined—"

"G.C., I hear that so much from Miss Mary."

"Mary's no one's fool," G.C. said. "I'm going to wash the worst of the mud off now before she gets back. Bathe when we get home after we find a bait."

"Do you want meat for your people?"

"Yes. Are yours properly fed?"

"We'll kill tomorrow and if you don't mind I'll send and get these baboons strung up. I want them to ripen down by the shamba."

"What happened there?"

"One leopard killed one goat."

"The gentlemanly type," G.C. said.

"I'm going to show the flag by hanging up these baboons. Leopard ought to eat the free butchered baboon rather than molest the innocent goat. Do you agree?"

"Heartily. But he won't if you hang them too close to the shamba. You'll bait up all the leopards in the country."

"Get them to concentrate," I said.

"I'm glad I'm back, Papa. If you are starting to concentrate leopards it's time I was back."

"Mary was wishing you were back only this noon."

"Sensible girl," G.C. said.

Mary came in with Charo. We saw them coming across the new bright-green grass of the meadow, the same size, Charo as black as a man could be wearing his old soiled turban and a blue coat, Mary bright blond in the sun, her green shooting clothes dark against the bright green of the grass. They were talking happily and Charo was carrying Mary's rifle and her big bird book. Together they always looked like a numero from the old Cirque Medrana.

G.C. came out from washing up without a shirt on. His whiteness contrasted with the rose brown of his face and neck.

"Look at them," he said. "What a lovely pair."

"Imagine running onto them if you'd never seen them before."

"The grass will be over their heads in a week's time. It's nearly to their knees now."

"Don't criticize the grass. It's only three days old."

"Hi, Miss Mary," G.C. called. "What have you two been up to?"

Mary drew herself up very proudly.

"I killed a wildebeest."

"And who gave you permission to do that?"

"Charo. Charo said to kill him. He had a broken leg. Really badly broken."

Charo shifted the big book to his other hand and flopped his arm to show how the leg had been.

"We thought you would want a bait," Mary said. "You did, didn't you? He's close to the road. We heard you come by afterwards, G.C. But we couldn't see you."

"You did quite right to kill him and we did need a bait. But what were you doing hunting alone?"

"I wasn't. I was identifying birds and I have my list. Charo wouldn't take me where there were any bad beasts. Then I saw the wildebeest and he was standing looking so sad and his leg looked awful with the bone sticking out. Charo said to kill him and I did."

"Memsahib piga. Kufa!"

"I hit him right behind the ear."

"Piga! Kufa!" Charo said and he and Miss Mary looked at each other proudly.

"It's the first time I ever had the responsibility of killing without you or Papa or Pop along."

"May I kiss you, Miss Mary?" G.C. asked.

"You certainly may. But I'm awfully sweaty."

They kissed and then we kissed and Mary said, "I'd like to kiss Charo too but I know I shouldn't. Do you know the impala barked at me just as though they were dogs? Nothing is afraid of Charo and me."

160

She shook hands with Charo and he took her book and her rifle over to our tent. "I'd better go and wash too. Thank you for being so nice about my shooting the beast."

"We'll send the truck for him and then put him out where he should be."

I went over to our tent and G.C. went to his tent to dress. Mary was washing and changing her shirt too and then after the safari soap smelled her fresh shirt that had been washed with a different soap and dried in the sun. We each liked to watch the other bathe but I never watched her when G.C. was around because it could be sort of hard on him. I was sitting on a chair in front of the tent reading and she came over and put her arm around my neck.

"Are you all right, honey?"

"No," she said. "I was so proud and Charo was so proud and it was one shot, *whack*, like the pelota ball hitting the wall of the frontón. He couldn't have heard the shot even and Charo and I were shaking hands. You know what it's like to do something yourself for the first time with all the responsibility. You and G.C. know and that's why he kissed me."

"Anybody'd kiss you any time."

"Maybe if I wanted them to. Or made them. But this wasn't like that."

"Why do you feel bad, honey?"

"You know. Don't pretend you don't know."

"No, I don't," I lied.

"I held straight on the center of his shoulder. It was big and black and shiny and I was about twenty yards from him. He was half toward me and looking toward us. I could see his eyes and they looked so sad. He looked as though he would cry. He looked sadder than anything I've ever seen and his leg looked awful. Honey, he had such a long sad face. I don't have to tell G.C., do I?"

"No."

"I didn't have to tell you. But we're going after the lion together and now my goddamn confidence is gone again."

"You'll shoot beautifully. I'm proud to be with you with the lion."

"The awful thing is that I can shoot properly too. You know it."

"I remember all the beauty shots you made. And all the wonderful times you shot better than anyone at Escondido."

"You just help me get back my confidence. But there's such a short time."

"You'll get it back and we won't tell G.C."

We sent the lorry for the wildebeest. When they came back with him G.C. and I climbed up to have a look at him. They are never a handsome animal when dead. He lay big-paunched and dusty, all his bluff gone and his horns gray and undistinguished.

"Mary took an awfully fancy shot at him," G.C. said. The wildebeest's eyes were glazed and his tongue out. His tongue was dusty too and he had been drilled behind the ear just at the base of the skull.

"Now where do you suppose she actually held?"

"She shot him from only twenty yards. She had a right to hold up there if she wanted to."

"I'd have thought she'd have taken him through the shoulder," G.C. said.

I didn't say anything. There was no use trying to fool him and if I lied to G.C. he would not forgive me.

"What about that leg?" I asked.

"Someone chasing at night with a car. Could be something else."

"How old would you say it was?"

"Two days. It's maggoty."

"Somebody up the hill then. We've heard no cars at night. He'd come downhill with that leg anyway. He certainly wouldn't climb with it."

"He's not you and me," G.C. said. "He's a wildebeest."

"A wounded animal goes downhill."

"Usually goes downhill."

"All right. But there haven't been any cars around nights because, a, we would have heard them and, b, we would have seen their tracks."

"I know you would. I was just wondering how he broke his leg."

"Maybe he put his foot in a bat-eared foxhole or a leaping harehole while the lions were panicking them."

"That possibly makes sense. Anyway Mary put an end to his suffering and we have a bait."

We went out with Mary in the front seat between us and G.C. driving and his Chief Game Scout in back with Ngui to drive up the same old track toward the salt lick to select a place for the bait. We agreed on a solitary tree that was three-quarters of a mile further out into the gladed country than where the lions had killed the night before and then drove up to the salt flat and turned around and came home down the same track. The mountain was out now as we drove home facing it and it looked as though the snow came a third of a way down from the top. The sun was at our backs and the mountain seemed close and huge. It never could look anything but big but sometimes it seemed very far away. But this evening it seemed to rise just behind the camp. We were driving in G.C.'s Land Rover and the top was down, of course, and we watched the game feeding quietly, then looking up and trotting away in the green grass, and the Tommies switching their tails and turning their heads to look at us and

162

then going back to feeding. There were several herds of zebra strangely colored against the evening light and on both sides of us there were herds of black wildebeest feeding. A few tossed their heads and bucked and ran galloping as the low car passed. But others only turned their big heads at us and then dropped them as they fed hungrily on the new grass. Always we were driving straight into the great height of the mountain with the shining whiteness of the snow.

"Take the good quarter of that wildebeest and there's enough for your people," I said to G.C.

"I don't believe we should mutilate the bait for that type of lion."

"OK. There's enough meat in camp to hold them for tonight. We'll eat up everything there is and start new tomorrow. I don't want to shoot tonight."

"Will your people have enough?"

"Sure. Miss Mary can make us spaghetti. Would you mind, Kitten?"

"I'd love to."

"Can I help, Miss Mary?" G.C. asked. "I love your spaghetti."

We were coming up to camp now the grass whishing against the wheels and the tents green against the newer green of the trees.

"I'll have to tell Mbebia now so as not to upset him. I've never made spaghetti here in the dark."

"He'll do everything."

"I brought sauces and cheese," G.C. said. "But we can wait until tomorrow, Miss Mary."

We had stopped under the hitching-post tree and were all getting out. G.C. and I went over to the truck which still held the wildebeest and he explained to his Chief Game Scout and the other scouts who had come up where we wanted the bait tied up. It was only to be dragged up to the tree from the road and then hung up out of reach of hyenas. The lions would pull it down if they came to it. It was to be dragged past where last night's kill had been. They were to go up and get it up as quickly as possible and return to camp. My people had all the baboon baits hung up and I told Mthuka to wash the car out well. He said he had stopped at the stream and washed it.

We all took our baths. Mary took hers first and I helped dry her with a big towel and held her mosquito boots for her. She put a bathrobe on over her pajamas and went out to the fire to have a drink with G.C. before they started their cooking. I stayed with them until Mwindi came out from the tent and said, "Bathi, Bwana," and then I took my drink into the tent and undressed and lay back in the canvas tub and soaped myself and relaxed in the hot water.

"What do the old men say the lion will do tonight?" I asked Mwindi who was folding my clothes and laying out pajamas, dressing gown, and my mosquito boots.

"Keiti says Memsahib's lion maybe eats on bait maybe not. What does Bwana say?"

"The same as Keiti."

"Keiti says you mganga with the lion."

"No. Only a little good medicine to find out when he dies."

"When he die?"

"In three days. I could not find out which day."

"Mzuri. Maybe he dies tomorrow."

"I don't think so. But he may."

"Keiti don't think so either."

"When does he think?"

"In three days."

"Mzuri. Please bring me the towel."

"Towel right by your hand. Bring him if you like."

"I'm sorry," I said. There is no word for "I'm sorry" in Swahili.

"Hapana sorry. I just say where it was. You want me rub back?"

"No. Thank you."

"You feel good?"

"Yes. Why?"

"Hapana why. I ask to know."

"Feel very good." I stood up and got out of the tub and started to dry myself. I wanted to say that I felt good and very relaxed and a little sleepy and did not feel much like talking and would have preferred fresh meat to spaghetti but had not wished to kill anything and that I was worried about all three of my children for different causes and that I was worried about the shamba and I was a little worried about G.C. and quite worried about Mary and that I was a fake as a good witch doctor, but no more a fake than the others were, and that I wished Mr. Singh would keep out of trouble and that I hoped the operation we were committed in as from Christmas Day would go well and that I had some more 220 grain solids and that my brother had written a better book and that Simenon would write fewer and better books and that my friend had not been killed. I did not know all the things Pop would discuss with Keiti when he had his bath but I knew Mwindi wanted to be friendly and so did I. But I was tired tonight for no reason and he knew it and was worried.

"You ask me for Wakamba words," he said.

So I asked him for Wakamba words and tried to memorize them and then I thanked him and went out to the fire to sit by the fire in an old pair of pajamas from Idaho, tucked into a pair of worn mosquito boots made in Hong Kong, and wearing a warm wool robe from Pendleton, Oregon, and drank a whiskey and soda made from a bottle of whiskey Mr. Singh had given me as a Christmas present and boiled water from the stream that ran down from the mountain animated by a syphon cartridge made in Nairobi.

"I'm a stranger here," I thought. But the whiskey said no, and it was the time of day for the whiskey to be right. Whiskey can be as right as it can be wrong and it said I was not a stranger and I knew it was correct at this time of night. Anyway my boots had come home because they were made of ostrich hide and I remembered the place where I had found the leather in the bootmaker's in Hong Kong. No it was not me who found the leather. It was someone else and then I thought about who had found the leather and about those days and then I thought about different women and how they would be in Africa and how lucky I had been to have known fine women that loved Africa. I had known some really terrible ones who had only gone there to have been there and I had known some true bitches and several alcoholics to whom Africa had just been another place for more ample bitchery or fuller drunkenness.

The bitches only hunted men although they shot other animals and the alcoholics blamed their rummyhood on the altitude. But they were just as drunk at sea level.

The alcoholics always had some great tragedy which had caused them to drink beyond reason but all of those I had known before their great tragedies had been rummies then too. The white male rummies in Africa were about as boring as the ex-rummies. With one exception I know no greater bore than the former alcoholic. Beside him the impotent man, the former forger, the retired panderer, the reformed card cheat, the ex-chief of police, the former Labor government minister, a former non-career ambassador to a Central American country, an aging official of Moral Rearmament, an interim French premier, ex-royalty, a former radio political commentator, a retired evangelist, a dedicated Big Game angler complete with statistics, an unfrocked priest, a professional ex-communist, or a retired non-practicing pederast are figures of blinding interest and charm.

I thought of that last former alcoholic I had met in Nairobi. He was very hearty and at once asked me to have a drink. They hang about bars at crowded hours taking up the place that might be occupied by an honest drinker and while they sip their tomato juice or barley water and nutmeg they look at the drinkers with that look of the ex-alcoholic which is compounded of Moral Rearmament crossed with one-third marabou stork and a third of the curiosity of the fashionable undertaker who is a little overdrawn at his bank.

"Old Hem," my great old friend said. "Dear old boy. What are you drinking?"

"Whatever you are."

"But this is barley and nutmeg."

"What I've been needing. Bartender, a barley and nutmeg and a double pink gin."

"I don't think I'd mix them, old boy."

"All right. I'll drink them separately. What do you hear from old Stevens?"

"Bad. Bad. Couldn't be worse. Shaking like a leaf. Went down the Tana and got up on an absolutely wonderful bull. Two hundred pounder he said. You know it makes them all lie of course."

"Naturally."

"Missed the elephant completely at twenty yards. He's gone. Doubt if he'll ever go out again."

"Any word from old Dorch?"

"He's gone. Doesn't even know who he's with nor where. Tragic case. Saw him in Jamaica. He just stared at me. Thought I was your brother."

"Poor old Dorch. Nothing we can do for him?"

"You might do something for him."

"I'll think it over. I always liked old Dorch."

"Gone though. Absolutely extinguished. Doubt if he knows whether it's night or day."

"Well it could be night here and day there if he's in Jamaica."

"Quite. But he's not in Jamaica now. He's back in London."

The barley water and nutmeg came and I drank it. It had a heady quality but not too full bodied.

"It is good. I see your point now." I drank a sip of the pink gin. "This cuts those long whiskers on the barley. Forgot how they stick in the throat."

"Are you feeling fit?" my dear old friend asked.

"Very."

"You look better than I'd heard."

"Splendid. Like a fiddler's bitch."

"I'd heard you'd been celebrating a bit. Better not to overdo it."

"You mean you heard I was drunk?"

"No. Just celebrating a bit. The stuff's a deadly poison you know."

"Who told you?"

"The head waiter."

"That's true. I was in here with young G.C. We were celebrating."

"An anniversary?"

"No. A recent event."

"Can you tell me?"

"No."

"Sorry. I didn't mean to be rude."

"Any word on Old Hormones?"

"He's gone. He won't last three months. He may be gone already."

"We'd have heard. You get the *Telegraph* don't you? The air edition. Old Hormones would have been in it if he'd gone."

"True. You're right. It's my favorite paper actually. Any number of the old timers in it. Boozed their lives away."

"Not completely. I wouldn't say Old Hormones did nothing but fondle the bottle."

"No," he said. "One mustn't be unfair."

"The Tempest wasn't exactly designed for drunkards. It weighed seven tons and it landed almost as fast as a Spitty flew."

"Not quite, old boy. Not quite."

"Nowhere near. I was just trying to remind you."

"Great days," he said. "Great chaps. Surprising how they go though now. It is a poison though you know. It's been proved. Not too late for you to stop it, old Hem."

"Actually it's too bloody early for me to stop it. I like it and I get good value from it. What are you having because I have to run ?"

"The same. Look, no offense, eh?"

"None."

"You'll get in touch with me if I can ever be of any help?"

"Absolutely."

"That must have been something interesting you and that youngster, what's his name, K.G., were celebrating, eh?"

"It was the non-death of an elephant which was terrorizing the marble quarries which supply the tombstones for Nairobi."

"That must have been a show. Could you work me in on that type of show? What did the tusks go?"

"Not weighed yet."

"Go to the Game Department of course on a show like that. I'll see them there."

"I'd hold it up a little. You might have misunderstood me."

"I see," he said. "But be careful old boy. See if you can work me in."

"I count on you, Harry," I said. I paid for the drinks and he slipped something into the pocket of my jacket.

"What's that?"

"Read them. Can't do any harm."

That was three months ago in the crowded, high-pitched, overpistoled, pleasant noonday crush at the bar of the New Stanley and now, waiting by the fire for the spaghetti cookers to come in for their drink, I thought God pity rummies but God please save us from the ex-rummy, and from all tracts, for or against, deliver me.

Then I saw them coming from the cook fire looking, in their bathrobes tied around the waists, like a young monk and a small bright-haired fake monk coming lightly and happily toward our big fire.

They were delighted, like children, about their cooking of the spaghetti. The cook had been happy about it too. He loved Miss Mary and liked to have her around his fires. This was strange in a cook but he was a strange Wakamba. He had been cook for a Governor General and was an expert at British cookery which he regarded amiably as an eccentric way of spoiling good food. But he took great pride in being a master of the process and delighted in producing Government House dishes on safari. He loved safari and he loved jokes and secrets and new dishes. He was a non-devout Mohammedan and had learned Mohammedanism just as he would learn a new dish and he served as a sort of cushion between us heathen and the members of the new and unknown religion and the other elders who were all conservative Mohammedans. I think he was the only man in camp who was not in awe of Keiti's authority and seniority. He had a sort of mincing false dignity that was almost a parody of a Somali and he loved to mystify and hint at unspeakable secrets.

"How did it go?" I asked Mary.

"Wait till you taste it. G.C. bought out half Nairobi."

It was a very fine spaghetti cooked perfectly, just a little hard and with a sauce that was so thick and complicated and mysterious and full of chopped onions and garlic browned with the ground Tommy meat and still tasting cleanly of tomato and oregano that it was really wonderful. We drank Chianti with it and ate two big plates apiece. Afterwards we had tinned peaches and fruitcake.

I was very happy to have G.C. back in camp and so was Mary. He was happy to be back too because we had become a family and we always missed each other when we were apart. He loved his job and believed in it and its importance almost fanatically. He loved the game and wanted to care for it and protect it and that was about all he believed in, I think, except a very stern and complicated system of ethics.

He was a little younger than my oldest son and if I had gone to Addis Ababa to spend a year and write back in the middle thirties as I had planned I would have known him when he was twelve since his best friend then had been the son of the people I was going out to stay with. But I had not gone because Mussolini's armies had gone instead and my friend that I had been going out to stay with had been moved to another diplomatic post and so I had missed the chance to know G.C. when he was twelve. By the time I met him he had a long and very difficult and unrewarding war behind him plus the abandonment of a British Protectorate where he had made the start of a fine career. He had commanded irregular troops which is, if you are honest, the least rewarding way there is to make a war. If an action is fought perfectly so that you have almost no casualties and inflict large losses on the enemy it is regarded at headquarters as an unjustified and reprehensible massacre. If you are forced to fight under unfavorable conditions and at too great odds and win but have a large butcher bill the comment is, "He gets too many men killed."

There is no way for an honest man commanding irregulars to get into anything but trouble. There is some doubt as to whether any truly honest and talented soldier can ever hope for anything except to be destroyed.

By the time I met G.C. he was well started in another career in another British colony. He was never bitter and he did not look back at all. But he was intolerant of fools and of the British white trash that sometimes come out to the colonies posing as civil servants. There are many of these and they must be good enough at their specialties or they would not have been graduated from the dreary educational institutions which produce them. But they are not much fun to be with after working hours. It is best never to attempt to joke and for G.C. this was very cramping. He had always joked, as all brave men do, and he had been well brought up and so knew that bad words are used in the best circles.

Over the spaghetti and the wine he told us of how he had been reproved by some newly arrived, bespectacled young bureau master for, having come in from a patrol involving shooting with human beings, using a bad word which might be overheard by this young man's wife. I had seen the wife and felt that a few sound words of the type G.C. had uttered, if put in practice by her husband, might have done the marriage no end of good.

I explained this to G.C. and Mary gave him a list of words which let drop outside of the hearing of the husband might cause the wife to question him about their meaning and eventually, perhaps, produce some laudable action. We pictured the wife asking the husband what these strange terms meant and his embarrassment as he looked them up in the appropriate regulations. All of them were good words long hallowed in the language and G.C. was cheered at hearing them with Mary's clear diction.

I hated for G.C. to have to be bored by these people who, if you were to describe them, no one would believe. The old pukka sahib ones have been often described and caricatured. But no one has dealt much with these since *Nineteen Eighty-four*. I wished Orwell was alive and I told G.C. about the last time I had seen him in Paris in 1945 after the Bulge fight and how he had come in what looked something like civilian clothes to room 117 of the Ritz where there was still a small arsenal to borrow a pistol because "they" were after him. He wanted a small pistol easily concealed and I found one but warned him that if he shot someone with it they probably would die eventually but that there might be a long interval. But a pistol was a pistol and he needed this one more as a talisman than a weapon I thought.

He was very gaunt and looked in bad shape and I asked him if he would not stay and eat. But he had to go. I told him I could give him a couple of people who would look after him if "they" were after him. That my characters were familiar with the local "theys" and would never bother him nor intrude on him. He said no, that the pistol was all he needed. We asked about a few mutual friends and he left. I sent two characters to pick him up at the door and tail him and check if anybody was after him. The next day their report was, "Papa, nobody is after him. He is a very chic type and he knows Paris very well. We checked with so-and-so's brother and he says no one pursues him. He is in touch with the British Embassy but he is not an operative. This is only hearsay. Do you want the timetable of his movements?"

"No. Did he amuse himself?"

"Yes, Papa."

"I'm happy. We will not worry about him. He has the pistol."

"That worthless pistol," one of the characters said. "But you warned him against it, Papa?"

"Yes. He could have had any pistol he wished."

"Perhaps he would have been happier with a stinger."

"No," the other character said. "A stinger is too compromising. He was happy with that pistol."

We let it go at that.

G.C. did not sleep well and often would lie awake most of the night reading. He had a very good library at his house in Kajiado and I had a big duffel bag full of books that we had arranged in empty boxes in the mess tent as a library. There was an excellent bookstore in the New Stanley Hotel in Nairobi and another good one down the road and whenever I had been in town I bought most of the new books that looked worth reading. Reading was the best palliative for G.C.'s insomnia. But it was no cure and I would often see his light on all night in his tent.

Because he had a career as well as because he had been brought up properly he could have nothing to do with African women. He did not think they were beautiful either nor attractive and the ones I knew and liked the best did not care for him either. But there was an Ismailia Indian girl who was one of the nicest people I have ever known and she was completely and hopelessly in love with G.C. She had convinced him that it was her sister, who was in strictest purdah, who loved him and she sent him gifts and messages from this sister. It was a sad but also clean and happy story and we all liked it. G.C. had nothing to do with the girl at all except to speak pleasantly to her when he was in her family's shop. He had his own European girls that he was fond of and I never talked with him about them. Mary probably did. But we had no personal gossip among the three of us on serious personal things.

In the shamba it was different. There and in the lines there were no books to read, no radio, and we talked. I asked the widow and the girl who had decided she wished to be my wife about why they did not like G.C. and at first they would not tell me. Finally the widow explained that it was not polite to say. It turned out that it was a question of smell. All people with the color of skin I had smelled very bad usually.

We were sitting under a tree by the bank of a river and I was waiting for some baboons that, by their talking, were working down toward us.

"Bwana Game smells good," I said. "I smell him all the time. He has a good smell."

"Hapana," the widow said. "You smell like shamba. You smell like smoked hide. You smell like pombe." I did not like the smell of their pombe and I was not sure I liked smelling like it.

The girl put her head against the back of my bush shirt which I knew was salty with dried sweat. She rubbed her head against the back of my shoulders and then the back of my neck and then came around for me to kiss her head.

"You see?" the widow asked. "You smell the same as Ngui."

"Ngui, do we smell the same?"

"I don't know how I smell. No man knows. But you smell the same as Mthuka."

Ngui was sitting against the opposite side of the tree looking downstream. He had his legs drawn up and was resting his head against the tree. He had my new spear beside him.

"Widow, you talk to Ngui."

"No," she said. "I look after girl."

The girl had laid her head in my lap and was fingering the pistol holster. I knew she wanted me to trace the outline of her nose and her lips with my fingers and then touch the line of her chin very lightly and feel the line where she had her hair cut back to make a square line on the

171

forehead and the sides and feel around her ears and over the top of her head. This was great delicacy of courtship and all I could do if the widow was there. But she could explore too, gently, if she wished.

"You hard-handed beauty."

"Be good wife."

"You tell widow go away."

"No."

"Why?"

She told me and I kissed her on top of the head again. She explored very delicately with her hands and then picked my right hand up and put it where she wished it. I held her very close and put the other hand where it should be.

"No," the widow said.

"Hapana tu," the girl said. She turned over and put her head face down where it had been and said something in Kamba that I could not understand. Ngui looked down the stream and I looked up it and the widow had moved behind the tree and we lay there with our fused, implacable sorrow and I reached up the tree and got the rifle and laid it by my right leg.

"Go to sleep, tú," I said.

"No. I sleep tonight."

"Sleep now."

"No. Can I touch?"

"Yes."

"As a last wife."

"As my hard-handed wife."

She said something in Kamba that I did not understand and Ngui said, "Kwenda na campi."

"I have to stay," the widow said. But as Ngui went off walking with his careless walk and casting a long shadow through the trees she walked a little way with him and spoke in Kamba. Then she took up her post about four trees back and looking downstream.

"Are they gone?" the girl asked.

I said yes and she moved up so we lay tight and close together and she put her mouth against mine and we kissed very carefully. She liked to play and explore and be delighted at the reactions and at the scars and she held my ear lobes between her thumb and forefinger where she wanted them pierced. Hers had never been pierced and she wished me to feel where they would be pierced for me and I felt them carefully and kissed them and then bit them a little very gently.

"Really bite them with the dog teeth."

"No."

She bit mine a little bit to show me the place and it was a very nice feeling.

"Why did you never do it before?"

"I don't know. In our tribe we do not do it."

"It is better to do it. It is better and more honest."

"We will do many good things."

"We have already. But I want to be a useful wife. Not a play wife or a wife to leave."

"Who would leave you?"

"You," she said.

There is, as I said, no word for love and no words for I am sorry in Wakamba. But I told her in Spanish that I loved her very much and that I loved everything about her from her feet to her head and we counted all the things that were loved and she was truly very happy and I was happy too and I did not think I lied about any one of them nor about all of them.

We lay under the tree and I listened to the baboons coming down toward the river and we slept for a while and then the widow had come back to our tree and she whispered in my ear, "Nyani."

The wind was blowing down the stream toward us and a troop of baboons were crossing the stream on the rocks of the ford coming out of the bush toward the fence of the mealie shamba where the maize (our field corn) was twelve and fourteen feet high. The baboons could not smell us and they did not see us lying in the broken shade under the tree. The baboons came out of the bush quietly and started to cross the stream like a raiding party. There were three very big old-man baboons at the head, one bigger than the others, walking carefully, their flattened heads and long muzzles and huge heavy jaws swinging and turning. I could see their big muscles, heavy shoulders, and thick rumps and the arched and drooping tails and the big heavy bodies and behind them was the tribe, the females and the young ones still coming out of the bush.

The girl rolled away very slowly so I was free to shoot and I raised the rifle carefully and slowly and still lying down stretched it out across my leg and pulled the bolt back, holding it by the knurl with my finger on the trigger and then letting it forward to the cocked position so there was no click.

Still lying down I held on the shoulder of the biggest old dog baboon and squeezed very gently. I heard the thump but did not look to see what had happened to him as I rolled over and got to my feet and started to shoot at the other two big baboons. They were both going back over the rocks toward the bush and I hit the third and then the second as he jumped over him. I looked back at the first baboon and he was lying face down in the water. The last one I had shot was screaming and I shot and finished him. The others were out of sight in the brush. I reloaded and Debba asked if she could hold the rifle. She stood at attention with it imitating Arap Meina. "It was so cold," she said. "Now it is so hot."

At the shots people had come down from the shamba. The Informer was with them and Ngui came up with the spear. He had not gone to camp but to the shamba and I knew how he smelt. He smelt of pombe.

"Three dead," he said. "All important generals. General Burma. General Korea. General Malaya. Buona notte."

He had learned buona notte in Abyssinia with the K.A.R. He took the rifle from Debba who was now holding it very demurely and looking out at the baboons on the rocks and in the water. They were not a handsome sight and I told the Informer to tell the men and boys to haul them out from the stream and sit them up against the fence of the mealie plantation with their hands crossed in their laps. Afterwards I would send some rope and we would hang them from the fence to frighten away the others or place them as baits.

The Informer gave the order and Debba, very demure, formal, and detached watched the big baboons with their long arms, obscene bellies, and really bad faces and dangerous jaws being pulled out of the water and up the bank and then being composed in death against the wall. One of the heads was tipped back in contemplation. The other two were sunk forward in the appearance of deep thought.

"Great generals. Important generals," Ngui said. "Kwenda na campi?"

We walked away from this scene toward the shamba where the car was parked. Ngui and I walked together, I was carrying the rifle again, the Informer walked to one side, and Debba and the widow walked behind.

"How are you feeling, Informer, old-timer?" I asked.

"Brother, I have no feelings. My heart is broken."

"What is it?"

"The widow."

"She is a very good woman."

"Yes. But now she wants you to be her protector and she does not treat me with dignity. She wishes to go with you and the small boy that I have cared for as a father to the Land of Mayito. She wishes to care for the Debba who wishes to be the assistant wife to the Lady Miss Mary. Everyone's thought is bent in this direction and she talks of it to me all night."

"That's bad."

"The Debba should never have carried your gun." I saw Ngui look at him.

"She did not carry it. She held it."

174

"She should not hold it."

"You say this?"

"No. Of course not, brother. The village says it."

"Let the village shut up or I will withdraw my protection."

This was the sort of statement which was valueless. But the Informer was moderately valueless too.

"Also you had no time to hear anything from the village because it happened a half an hour ago. Don't start to be an intriguer." Or finish as one, I thought.

We had come to the shamba with the red earth and the great sacred tree and the well-built huts. The widow's son butted me in the stomach and stood there for me to kiss the top of his head. I patted the top of his head instead and gave him a shilling. Then I remembered the Informer only made sixty-eight shillings a month and that a shilling was close to half a day's wages to give to a little boy, so I called the Informer to come away from the car and I felt in the pocket of my bush shirt and found some ten shilling notes that were sweated together.

I unfolded two and gave them to the Informer.

"Don't talk balls about who holds my gun. There isn't a man in this shamba that could hold a shitpot."

"Did I ever say there was, brother?"

"Buy the widow a present and let me know what goes on in town."

"It is late to go tonight."

"Go down to the road and wait for the lorry of the Anglo-Masai."

"If it does not come, brother?"

Ordinarily he would have said, "Yes, brother." And the next day, "It did not come, brother." So I appreciated his attitude and his effort.

"Go at daylight."

"Yes, brother."

I felt bad about the shamba and about the Informer and the widow and everyone's hopes and plans and we drove off and did not look back. On the way home we killed a warthog. A warthog is a brave, gallant, and extremely attractive animal with a fine serious-minded trot. But he is excellent to eat and I shot him as he trotted across a meadow his tail held high. There was no nonsense about halalling him as the Mohammedans could not eat him and I stuck him with the spear to bleed him. The blade slipped in like going into butter and I wiped the spear on his back, dust gray and with the coarse black hairs, and then slipped it back in its sheath. Ngui and Mthuka and I lifted him into the back of the hunting car and we drove on into camp. I felt bad about the warthog too.

That had been several days ago before the rain and before the lion came back and there was no reason to think of it now except that tonight I was sorry for G.C. who because of custom, law, and choice too perhaps had to live alone on safari and had to read all night. One of the books we had brought with us was Alan Paton's *Too Late the Phalarope*. I had found it almost unreadable due to the superbiblical style and the amount of piety in it. The piety seems to be mixed in a cement mixer and then carried in hods to the building of the book and it was not that there was an odor of piety; piety was like the oil on the sea after a tanker had been sunk. But G.C. said it was a good book and so I would read on in it until my brain would feel that it was not worth it to spend time with such stupid, bigoted, awful people as Paton made with their horrible sense of sin because of an act passed in 1927. But when I finally finished it I knew G.C. was right because Paton had been trying to make just such people; but being more than a little pious himself he had bent backwards trying to understand them until finally in his greatness of soul he approved of them or, at least, could not condemn them except by more scripture. I saw what G.C. meant about the book though; but it was a sad thing to think of.

G.C. and Mary were talking happily about a city called London that I knew of largely by hearsay and knew concretely only under the most abnormal conditions and I was happy to let them talk of it. They knew very different parts and most of them I did not know at all. So I could listen to them talk and think about Paris. That was a city that I knew under almost all circumstances. I knew it and loved it so well that I never liked to talk about it except with people from the old days. In the old days we all had our own cafés where we went alone and knew no one except the waiters. These cafés were secret places and in the old days everyone who loved Paris had his own café. They were better than clubs and you received the mail there that you did not wish have come to your flat. Usually you had two or three secret cafés. There would be one where you went to work and read the papers. You never gave the address of this café to anyone and you went there in the morning and had a café creme and brioche on the terrace and then, when they had cleaned the corner where your table was, inside and next to the window, you worked while the rest of the café was being cleaned and scrubbed and polished. It was nice to have other people working and it helped you to work. By the time the clients started to come to the café you would pay for your half-bottle of Vichy and go out and walk down the quay to where you would have an aperitif and then have lunch. There were secret places to have lunch and also restaurants where people went that you knew.

The best secret places were always discovered by Mike Ward. He knew Paris and loved her better than anyone I knew. As soon as a Frenchman discovered a secret place he would give a huge party there to celebrate the secret. Mike and I hunted secret places that had one or two good small wines and had a good cook, usually a rummy, and were making a last effort to make things go before having to sell out or go into bankruptcy. We did not want any secret places that were becoming successful or going up in the world. That was what always happened with Charley Sweeny's secret places. By the time he took you there the secret had been so revealed that you had to stand in line to get a table.

But Charley was very good about secret cafés and he had a wonderful security consciousness about his own and yours. These were of course our secondary or afternoon and early evening cafés. This was a time of day when you might want to talk to someone and sometimes I would go to his secondary café and sometimes he would come to mine. He might say he wished to bring a girl he wanted me to meet or I might tell him I would bring a girl. The girls always worked. Otherwise they were not serious. No one, except fools, kept a girl. You did not want her around in the daytime and you did not want the problems she brought. If she wanted to be your girl and worked then she was serious and then she owned the nights when you wanted her and you fed her evenings and gave her things when she needed them. I never brought many girls to show them off to Charley who always had beautiful and docile girls, all of whom worked and all of whom were under perfect discipline because at that time my concierge was my girl. I had never known a young concierge before and it was an inspiring experience. Her greatest asset was that she could never go out, not only in society, but at all. When I first knew her, as a locataire, she was in love with a trooper in the Garde Republicaine. He was the horsetail-plumed, metal breastplate, mustached type and his barracks was not very far away in that quarter. He had regular hours for his duty and he was a fine figure of a man and we always addressed each other formally as "Monsieur."

I was not in love with my concierge but I was very lonely at night at that time and the first time she came up the stairs and in through the door, which had the key in it, and then up the ladder that led to the sort of loft where the bed was beside the window that gave such a lovely view over the cemetery Montparnasse and took off her felt-soled shoes and lay on the bed and asked me if I loved her I answered, loyally, "Naturally."

"I knew it," she said. "I've known it too long."

She undressed very quickly and I looked out at the moonlight on the cemetery.

Unlike the shamba she did not smell the same but she was clean and fragile out of sturdy but insufficient nourishment and we paid honor to the view which neither saw. I had it in my mind however and when she said that the last tenant had entered and we lay and she told me that she could never love a member of the Garde Republicaine truly. I said that I thought Monsieur was a nice man, I said un brave homme et tres gentil, and that he must look very well on a horse. But she said that she was not a horse and also there were inconveniences.

So I was thinking this about Paris while they were talking of London and I thought that we were all brought up differently and it was good luck we got on so well and I wished G.C. was not lonely nights and that I was too damned lucky to be married to somebody as lovely as Mary and I would straighten things out at the shamba and try to be a really good husband.

"You're being awfully silent, General," G.C. said. "Are we boring you?"

"Young people never bore me. I love their careless chatter. It keeps me from feeling old and unwanted."

"Balls to you," G.C. said. "What were you thinking about with that semi-profound look? Not brooding are you or worrying about what the morrow will bring?"

"When I start worrying about what the morrow will bring you'll see a light burning in my tent late at night."

"Balls to you again, General," G.C. said.

"Don't use rough words, G.C.," Mary said. "My husband is a delicate and sensitive man and they repugn him."

"I'm glad something repugns him," G.C. said. "I love to see the good side of his character."

"He hides it carefully. What were you thinking about, darling?"

"A trooper in the Garde Republicaine."

"You see?" G.C. said. "I always said he had a delicate side. It comes out completely unexpectedly. It's his Proustian side. Tell me was he very attractive? I try to be broad-minded."

"Papa and Proust used to live in the same hotel," Miss Mary said. "But Papa always claims it was at different times."

"God knows what really went on," G.C. said. He was very happy and not at all taut tonight and Mary with her wonderful memory for forgetting was happy too and without any problems. She could forget in the loveliest and most complete way of anyone I ever knew. She could carry a fight overnight but at the end of a week she could forget it completely and truly. She had a built-in selective memory and it was not built entirely in her favor. She forgave herself in her memory and she forgave you too. She was a very strange girl and I loved her very much. She had, at the moment, only two defects. She was very short for honest lion hunting and she had too good a heart to be a killer and that, I had finally decided, made her either flinch or squeeze off a little when shooting at an animal. I found this attractive and was never exasperated by it. But she was exasperated by it because, in her head, she understood why we killed and the necessity for it and she had come to take pleasure in it, after thinking that she never would kill an animal as beautiful as an impala and would only kill ugly and dangerous beasts. In six months of daily hunting she had learned to love it, shameful though it is basically, and unshameful as it is if done cleanly but there was something too good in her that worked subconsciously and made her pull off the target. I loved her for it in the same way that I could not love a woman who could work in the stockyards or put dogs or cats out of their suffering or destroy horses who had broken their legs at a racecourse.

"What was the trooper's name?" G.C. asked. "Albertine?"

"No. Monsieur."

"He's baffling us, Miss Mary," G.C. said.

They went on talking about London. So I started to think about London too and it was not unpleasant although much too noisy and not normal. I realized I knew nothing about London and so I started to think about Paris and in greater detail than before. Actually I was worried about Mary's lion and so was G.C. and we were just handling it in different ways. It was always easy enough when it really happened. But Mary's lion had been going on for a long time and I wanted to get him the hell over with.

Finally, when the different dudus, which was the generic name for all bugs, beetles, and insects, were thick enough on the dining tent floor so that they made a light crunching when you walked, we went to bed.

"Don't worry about the morrow," I said to G.C. as he went off to his tent.

"Come here a moment," he said. We were standing halfway to his tent and Mary had gone in to ours. "Where did she aim at that unfortunate wildebeest?"

"Didn't she tell you?"

"No."

"Go to sleep," I said. "We don't come in until the second act anyway."

"You couldn't do the old husband and wife thing?"

"No. Charo's been begging me to do that for a month."

"She's awfully admirable," G.C. said. "You're even faintly admirable."

"Just a lot of admirals."

"Good night, Admiral."

"Put a telescope to my blind eye and kiss my ass, Hardy."

"You're confusing the line of battle."

Just then the lion roared. G.C. and I shook hands.

"He probably heard you misquoting Nelson," G.C. said.

"He got tired of hearing you and Mary talk about London."

"He is in good voice," G.C. said. "Go to bed, Admiral, and get some sleep."

In the night I heard the lion roar several more times. Then I went to sleep and Mwindi was pulling on the blanket at the foot of the cot.

"Chai, Bwana."

It was very dark outside but someone was building up the fire. I woke Mary with her tea but she did not feel well. She felt ill and had bad cramps.

"Do you want to cancel it, honey?"

"No. I just feel awful. After the tea maybe I'll be better."

"We can wash it. It might be better to give him another day's rest."

"No. I want to go. But just let me try and feel better if I can."

I went out and washed in the cold water in the basin and washed my eyes with boric, dressed, and went out to the fire. I could see G.C. shaving in front of his tent. He finished, dressed, and came over.

"Mary feels rocky," I told him.

"Poor child."

"She wants to go anyway."

"Naturally."

"How'd you sleep?"

"Well. You?"

"Very well. What do you think he was doing last night?"

"I think he was just going walkabout. And sounding off."

"He talks a lot. Want to split a bottle of beer?"

"It won't hurt us."

I went and got the beer and two glasses and waited for Mary. She came out of the tent and walked down the path to the latrine tent. She came back and then walked down again.

"How do you feel, honey?" I asked when she came over to the table by the fire with her tea. Charo and Ngui were getting the guns and the binoculars and shell bags out from under the tents and taking them to the hunting car.

"I don't feel good at all. Do we have anything for it?"

"Yes. But it makes you feel dopey. We've got Terramycin too. It's supposed to be good for both kinds but it can make you feel funny too."

"Why did I have to get something when my lion's here?"

"Don't you worry, Miss Mary," G.C. said. "We'll get you fit and the lion will get confident."

"But I want to go out after him."

She was in obvious pain and I could see it coming back on her again.

"Honey, we'll lay off him this morning and rest him. It's the best thing to do anyway. You take it easy and take care of yourself. G.C. can stay a couple of more days anyway."

G.C. shook his hand, palm down, in negation. But Mary did not see him.

"He's your lion and you take your time and be in shape to shoot him and all the time we let him alone he will be getting more confident. If we don't go out at all this morning it's much better."

"I can go out and I will go out. It's only this thing hits you. I'm sorry," she said and she was gone.

"Let's hope it isn't amoebic," I said to G.C. "That's the worst she could draw. It could be ptomaine from just one sliver of that meat ground for the spaghetti. That meat was hung a couple of days."

"She shouldn't go out this morning anyway," G.C. said. "Giving him a rest is good. But I can't stay more than tomorrow and the next day. You know that."

"We might possibly kill him if you weren't here."

"Don't be rude. We're partners. The thing to do now is look after Miss Mary."

I went over to the car and then said we were not going out. Then I went and found Keiti by the fire. He seemed to know all about it but he was very delicate and polite.

"Memsahib is sick."

"I know."

"Maybe spaghetti. Maybe dysentery."

"Yes," Keiti said. "I think spaghetti."

"Meat too old."

"Yes. Maybe little piece. Made in the dark."

"We leave lion alone take care of Memsahib. The lion gets confident."

"Mzuri," Keiti said. "Poli poli. You shoot kwali or kanga Mbebia make Memsahib broth."

CHAPTER 16

After we were sure that the lion would have left the bait if he had been on it, G.C. and I went out to have a look at the country in his Land Rover. Beasts were accustomed to seeing this vehicle and we thought the lion if he saw it might not connect it with the hunting car whose silhouette he knew. Many years ago I had discovered, or believed I had, that lions have no depth of vision and see only in silhouette. I had experimented with this, and later gambled on it, in photographing wild lions at close range in the old days before the Serengeti was a Game Reserve, and I was convinced that it was true. In those days I did not have the respect for lions that I should and Pop was along to back me up if I was wrong. Now I knew much more about lions and respected them much more but I still thought this was a valid theory. G.C. wanted to go in the Land Rover anyway. So it did not make much difference.

Miss Mary had said that what she wanted was to rest and be by herself. I had given her some Chlorodyne in water and she had kept it down. She was also going to try some tea again. I wanted to stay with her but she hated being ill and if she were sick she wanted to be by herself.

"You and G.C. go. Please go. Mwindi will look after me. But don't spook the lion. The only good thing about me being this way is that we give him a rest."

I promised her we wouldn't even get out at the bait and we started over to the Land Rover and got in with G.C.'s head Game Scout and Ngui in the back. The head Game Scout was a tall, handsome, very soldierly Wakamba with a mustache. He was very good at his work and fanatically devoted to G.C. He was also devoted to Miss Mary and I always had a strong feeling that he thought I was not good enough for her. He would like to have seen her married to the Governor General at least. Ngui usually tried to look as unsmart as possible when he and the head Game Scout were together.

The grass seemed to have doubled in height in the night and it was a lovely clear cool morning with almost no wind. There seemed to be about three sorts of grass and one was a rather weedy sort that was growing faster than the others. There was more game than ever and we moved along the tire tracks as though through a park. There was game everywhere.

When we were about opposite where the bait had been taken well over to our right we hit the tracks of the big lion crossing the tire tracks to go into the woods across the dead grass field to our left. The tracks were fresh and there was no dew on them. Some of the weedy grass was bruised and the sap was fresh on the cracked stems. There were dry places on the tall grass where he had gone in shoulder high.

"How long ago?"

"An hour," Ngui said. "Not much more." He looked at the chief Game Scout who nodded.

"They are very fresh," he said in English.

"He stayed out maybe an hour longer, G.C.," I said.

"We're getting him, Papa," G.C. said. "I don't think we'll go near the bait. It's all gone now. We'll feed him tonight same place."

"Good thing Mary doesn't know he crossed here in plenty good light."

"It's the best thing she could have," G.C. said. "We're getting ahead of him now."

"Two more days."

"You said you could deal with him."

"We bloody well can too."

"Don't be cross. You don't mind me being along though?"

"Let's not talk rot."

"Let's talk sense then. Suppose Miss Mary hits him and he doesn't come. If he comes I grant you kill him but you have your wife to think about and she has to stand where she is because if she runs he'll go for her. This is all fine. You play the heroic type and bring him down at your feet. Or he brings you down ass over apple cart. Is that the correct American expression?"

"Quite correct. Only now they say, 'And then the shit went into the electric fan.'"

"I'll make a note of that."

"Be worthless. They'll be saying something else the next time you have Americans on your hands. People are hired to make up those expressions. They're called gag writers."

"OK," G.C. said. "You are my gag writer. Now you've just entered the electric fan."

"Thanks."

"Now," G.C. said, "I'm the contemplative type. I'm more the strategic type."

"The hell you are. You're the emotional instant-decision type who's only alive because he shoots twice as fast as Wyatt Earp and Doc Holliday combined."

The Land Rover was stopped now under some green and yellow trees with tall wide branches and in the shade we were both looking across the gray of the mud flats, dry now, toward the greens of the papyrus swamp and the green-brown hills beyond.

"All right," G.C. said. "There isn't anything out there except just the usuals. So I can shoot faster than you. I'm glad to hear that admitted. But here you are the brusque, semi-heroic, outmoded miracle type who brings them down like the bowmen at Crecy. Now suppose Miss Mary hits this lion somewhere and instead of coming he has a little sense and breaks for better cover where you will have to go in and dig him out and every one of the miraculous shots that you throw after him throws dust behind his ass and he makes the island of thick cover."

"You know what I have to do then."

"Do you like it?"

"Not even with you."

"But we do it."

"I go in with the pump full of buckshot and you stay on his most likely exit route and Chungo on his next and Arap Meina on his next and Miss Mary is on the top of a truck whether she likes it or not. I go in with Ngui to see if he can see him before he comes."

"Do you like it?"

"I'll buy it."

"What if all this starts at eighteen hundred hours and you have one half an hour of light to complete the operation?"

"Do you have to get morbid?"

"No," G.C. said. "I'm the contemplative type and I was only contemplating."

"Let's get him so confident that he'll come out any time."

"I couldn't agree more fully. Do you think we've earned a drink?"

"Beer."

"Did you really bring some?"

I asked Ngui for a bottle. It was wrapped in a wet sack and was still cold from the night and we sat in the Land Rover in the shade of the tree and drank it out of the bottle and looked off across the dried mud flat and watched the small Tommies and the black movement of the wildebeest and the zebra that looked gray white in this light as they moved out across the flat to the grass on the far side and at the end toward the Chyulu Hills. The hills were a dark blue this morning and looked very far away. Turning to look back at the great mountain it looked very close. It seemed to be just behind camp and the snow was heavy and bright in the sun.

"We could hunt Miss Mary on stilts," I said. "Then she could see him in the tall grass."

"There's nothing in the Game Laws against it."

"Or Charo could carry a stepladder such as they have in libraries for the higher stacks."

"That's brilliant," G.C. said. "We'd pad the rungs and she could take a rest with the rifle on the rung above where she stood."

"You don't think it would be too immobile?"

"It'd be up to Charo to make it mobile."

"It would be a beautiful sight," I said. "We could mount an electric fan on it."

"We could build it in the form of an electric fan," G.C. said happily. "But that would probably be considered a vehicle and illegal."

"If we rolled it forward and had Miss Mary keep climbing in it like a squirrel would it be illegal?"

"Anything that rolls is a vehicle," G.C. said judicially.

"I roll slightly when I walk."

"Then you're a vehicle. I'll run you and you'll get six months and be shipped out of the Colony."

"We have to be careful, G.C."

"Care and moderation have been our watchwords, haven't they?"

"Any more in that bottle?"

"We can share the dregs."

"A pair of dreg sharers out in the blue."

"The Chulis *are* blue."

They were very blue and very beautiful.

"Chyulus," G.C. corrected. "Tell me what is The Wild Blue Yonder that your air force has a song about?"

"It is a Challenge To Man."

"I know a beautiful airline stewardess that is a Challenge To Man."

"She's probably the one they're talking about in the song."

"Here," G.C. said handing the empty bottle over his shoulder. "Wrap that carefully and save it for Mr. Singh."

"Which way do you want to go?"

"Should we drive up by the old manyatta and try to find some kwali for Miss Mary? We're too far from camp to shoot a bait. No sense to bring a truck way up here."

We started off through the new grass to the edge of the mud flat. The heat haze was starting and there was a shimmer over the game. Later there would be beautiful lakes of water on the mud flats and the game would seem to be drinking at them or wading in them with their heads down. But now the flats were still normal and there was just the beginning of the heat haze.

We wanted to stay away from the country where the lions were living and circle well around it, on our way back to camp and find some of the francolin or spurfowl, the partridges that the East Africans grouped under the name kwali, around the old manyattas or deserted corrals and villages. There were three of these old manyattas but one quite large one where the partridges came to dust. There were often lion around the old manyattas but they were in the opposite direction from where Mary's big lion spent the day in the forest so we did not worry about frightening him. G.C. said that there were two and possibly three more lion that should be killed in the district but we looked forward to hunting them after Mary had killed the bad lion and when we had time to find out which were the troublemakers or the ones that should be eliminated. If there were any emergencies about them while G.C. was away I was to deal with them. We both enjoyed hunting lion very much when it was necessary that they should be killed and we loved to hunt together and loved to hunt alone. Mary's lion was something entirely different from ordinary hunting and hunting by ourselves or together would be a holiday from responsibility.

It was getting late to find francolin but we finally found some near the abandoned village that ran and flew into the bush. G.C. stopped the car and we got out and took the shotguns and went to look for them. Ngui followed with my rifle and G.C.'s Game Scout went with him. The birds flushed on our side almost at once and I shot one that came down head first and hit another that ran when he came down. I shot him running as he crossed the clearing, swinging ahead of him like a hare. They were heavy plump birds, red-necked francolin, bigger than partridges. Ngui carried them with the rifle slung over his shoulder. We hunted the rest of the bush but no more birds flew.

I could not see G.C. who was on the right but I heard him shoot twice and then calling something to the Game Scout and then shoot twice again. Ngui and I sat down in the shade and I took the two birds from him and hefted them in my hand and admired them. The breeze was coming off the mountain now and I was hoping Mary was feeling better. We would have enough birds to make a good broth for lunch and dinner. We would get some camp meat and a bait in the afternoon. G.C. wanted this lion killed and he had been condemned so it was all right to kill a bait for him.

The other lions would kill if we did not kill for them so that was all right. Nothing would be killed that would not be killed anyway. But this way we could select it. You can sit under a tree in a cool breeze and justify anything, I thought. You should wait and let G.C. say all this. I took my shirt off and dried my sweat with it and then Ngui spread it over a bush to let it dry in the sun.

The breeze felt good on my bare chest and I asked Ngui if it was not bad to let a wet shirt dry in the sun if it was wet with your sweat. He said no. I told him it was bad with us in the land of Mayito and that the old men believed that if you let a shirt wet with sweat dry in the sun your own sweat would dry in your body. He said nobody believed that because the old men had not worn shirts so there was no belief about it. I said to let the shirt dry in the sun. We both knew this was wrong so he put the shirt in the shade for the wind to dry it. We sat back and waited for the other hunters. We heard two more shots quite a distance away and I told Ngui to go to the car and bring one of the pint bottles of beer. He had put in a quart bottle of Tusker and three Carlsbergs and we drank one of the Carlsbergs together.

Ngui and I and Mthuka and Pop's gunbearer loved to drink beer together. We never did it in front of white people. Pop knew we drank together but as long as he didn't see it he did not mind. It was a part of being brothers and because Ngui and I were full brothers it would have been insulting to have used a glass.

Finally we saw G.C. and his scout coming out of the broken bush. Ngui handed me the bottle and I lifted it up and drained it.

G.C. was red-faced and sweating and the Game Scout was carrying four good heavy-looking birds.

"You solitary drinker," he said. "What did you shoot?"

"One brace."

"How many is that in American?"

"Two. A he and a she."

"We had a hell of a time finding them. Never did find one."

"That's a pas trouvé. The French game books are full of them."

"Leave any beer?"

"One Carlsberg for you. One for the troops."

"Leti pombe," G.C. said to the Game Scout who brought the two bottles wrapped in the still moist sack. "Draw the birds and wrap them in the sack. Do you want any beer?"

"No, Bwana," the Game Scout said and shook his head.

"I usually give some to Ngui," I said. "Probably wrong."

"Ngui, do you want some beer?" G.C. asked.

"After Bwana, perhaps," Ngui said. He opened both bottles and handed one to G.C. and one to me. We were just short of even on the first one and I made a mark with my thumb on what I decided was the just level and drained it to there, carefully wiped the mouth and neck on my sweat-stained shirt and handed the bottle to Ngui.

"Thank you, Bwana," he said.

G.C. was about as far from stupid as people can be and when Ngui and the Game Scout had gone over to the car to draw the birds he said, "What are you two up to?"

"His father and I used to drink beer together when you were ten years old."

"I'm not ten years old now."

"That's correct. And we're going to have your birthday party pretty soon. Did you shoot well?"

"Yes. But they fell in the damnedest stuff."

"Cool out a little and we'll drive in and see how Miss Mary is and organize the next move."

Back in the camp we found that Miss Mary was much better. But she was weak and she did not feel well and it was natural that she should not be in a good temper. She was nearly always in wonderful temper in Africa and we had not had a fight since Fig Tree camp in the Magadi area where I had turned on the shortwave radio to listen to the World Series and then fallen asleep while listening. This was an irritating enough thing to do since we should have been sleeping soundly in order to get up rested and fresh before daylight to hunt the lion that Mary was then engaged in pursuing instead of me lying asleep by a radio which kept Mary awake. Someone, undoubtedly me, had smashed the radio antenna and we had gone to meet the appointment, which the lion had not kept, with a certain amount of grimness. Several weeks later I found out how the Series came out. That night I had my cot moved out of the tent and slept in the open. This was fun. But Mary pointed out, quite rightly, that it left her in the tent at the mercy of any beast that wandered in. We compromised finally, I believe, by putting my cot outside in a way that blocked the entrance of beasts by the front flap of the tent.

The latrine tent was not far astern of our sleeping tent in an intensely wooded area through which a path had been pangaed or chopped out. It was not until G.C., going to do his morning duties, had been chased off this path and into the pebbly bed of the charming little stream that came down from the escarpment and then rechased out of the stream bed that we had come to take the beasts with proper respect. After that I had always preceded Miss Mary to the latrine tent and mounted guard outside with the big gun and then escorted her back to the tent and the clearing under the huge fig trees.

After Pop had been forced, by ill health, to return for a time to Nairobi and G.C. had to leave because of duty and Miss Mary and I were left alone to hunt there without transport we became very close friends and the radio was not even remembered. I had expected to be killed in the Magadi area as it was, partly, such thick cover that no one could crawl through the tunnels that were game trails in the solid, creeper-woven bush without eventually running, unexpectedly, onto the animals that had made them. It was a bad trouble country. But when Mary and I were alone we had hunted the pleasant and moderately open parts. There were always enough stuffy places getting home, though, and camp itself was so overbeasted that the loss of the World Series and all other spectator sports assumed a proper place in my values.

On this day Mary was angry with me and I knew that I could do nothing right to offset all the wrong things I had probably done all of my life. When it was definitely decided, always through my own fault; a lack of courtesy; talking too fast or too rough when an order was made; the lack of appreciation of the lovely qualities of some old friend who was always kind and gentle and loving and never rude; always forgetting the qualities of this old dear friend; the cigarette butts he left always wet with the liquor he spilled; his bleary, maundering gossip, his foul breath, his bright sweet red eyes, his passing out almost shyly, and the delicate lift of his shoulders and the sweet hang of his spittled chin, his misremembered anecdotes, and his campy sweetness as he held his little hands like a contrite monkey. There was always this old friend to bring up. "Who am I writing to? I'm writing to Teddy. One of my best friends. Do you mind?"

You did not mind or pretended you did not mind and after the letter was written you might be re-received into the status of a member of the human race. But it was best not to be too sure because you might yet be due to be accused of those atrocities you had committed against a former wife. In some ways these atrocities, on which there was a certain difference of opinion but on which Miss Mary had received the authorized version by the wife, might have been considered to have been, in a way, if not expiated at least to have come under some statute of limitations. But this was not so. They were as fresh and alive as though they were in the morning mail if there had been a morning mail. They did not fade nor pale as the atrocities of the first war did and no matter how many times you had been convicted and fined for them they were as fresh as the first launching of the bayoneted Belgian babies.

So it was to be one of those days of "Would you mind giving me that book? That happens to be the book that I am reading."

Or "Do you know that the camp is completely out of meat due to your carelessness or incapacity? Everyone has complained to me about your thoughtlessness. We *are* allowed to have meat to feed the boys, aren't we, G.C.?"

Or "Did you take small envelopes out of this box? No?"

This to be followed by elaborate and obvious industry to show that there was someone around this camp who was serious and did not take her duties lightly or sloppily, frequent trips to the green tent at the edge of the fever trees, which, it is true, had not been built with possible dysentery in mind but had been placed there since it was the nearest shade and shelter apart from the clump of trees which shaded the camp and the lines. I felt terrible that Mary felt ill and I did not blame her for being in a bad temper but for the moment there was nothing to do. The best thing was to get out of her sight but there is no place to go in Africa at high noon except the shade and so I took a chair in the mess tent which, with its heavy fly and the breeze that came through, was cool and comfortable. It would have been nice to take the road up the slope of the mountain and sit in the back room of Mr. Singh's and read and listen to the sawmill. But that would have been desertion.

We had one of those lunches finally where the hostess is quietly heroic and wonderful to the guest and the husband would be better off eating in the lines. I wished that Ngui and I had gone off toward the Chyulus and killed an eland. I was hungry for eland and so was he but I tasted the broth and it was good, completely unseasoned, and sure to be healthy and G.C. and I ate a bird and mashed potatoes and I ate a mealie that had been brought from the shamba. I had seen Debba and the widow out at the lines but had not gone over to speak to them. G.C. and I ate some cheese that he had brought. But the shadow of all my sins, past, present, and future lay spread across the table and catsup and mustard on the cheese did not help them. I had enjoyed my actual sins, those I had committed rather than those I had been accused of, and I could never be contrite about them because I knew that I might well commit them again. I was not convinced, in the daylight, that they were sins and today I did not care very much. I knew we had prepared Miss Mary's lion for her as well as possible and I knew I was going to have to find and butcher meat when the sun was low in the afternoon and kill a bait. G.C. had to write his monthly report. Mary was going to help with the typing.

While they ate and were charming and polite to each other I thought whether I could take Debba out to hunt with me. I had thought about this while we were eating the mealies. But I decided against it because we had to take a legitimate Mohammedan for the camp meat and it was no good to take Debba with one of the elders along. After the meal was over and Miss Mary had gone to lie down in her tent I checked with G.C. on what to kill for meat and the bait he wished killed. Then I walked out to the lines and woke Ngui and told him what time we would start and to bring Charo to halal. Debba and the widow had gone and I went back to camp and sat in the good shade and slept.

When we started out Arap Meina wanted to go too and so did the mess attendant who wanted to learn to be a hunter. Miss Mary was sleeping and G.C. was working on his report and we all pulled out very quietly and away from the lion country. It was a wonderful late afternoon and there was only a light belt of cloud across the mountain. The great snow at the top looked furrowed in the old volcanic channels. But the snow lay heavy like cake frosting and the mountain rose straight up above us. It could come close or go away as though by magic.

"Go by shamba?" Mthuka asked hopefully

"No," I said looking at Charo.

"Ndio," Charo said and smiled. It was very nice of him. He was always kind and polite and this was nothing against his religion.

"Hapana," I said.

"Mzuri," he said and smiled again charitably and kindly and with all old friendship.

"Hapana," I said. "Asante sana."

He shook his head and smiled. I smiled too because we had always been very good friends and I know that after twenty years he had never given up converting me to the church. We had made one Ramadan together.

Ngui wanted to get on with the hunt. He didn't give a damn about any woman when he was hunting and he was like a hound. We decided to hunt in the broken bush toward the Chyulus but further towards the mountain than the Chyulu trail. We found zebra and Ngui and I circled and stalked to within twenty-five yards. I picked out a young stallion, watched him look at me with the painted black stripes circling his muzzle, his jaw, and his head and with his eyes on me, he still unknowing, and the stripes looking as wide as though they were new and wide and perfectly stenciled. I slid my right hand back slowly for Ngui to see until my thumb touched the base of the jaw and then shot him there. The bullet lifted him very slightly and he fell head first, neck bent, his neck hitting with his shoulders. After the car came up we all lifted him in the back and that was the bait.

Ngui wanted to hunt eland and so did I. But we found none and worked back to one of the parks far away from the lion country and I shot another of the animals G.C. had said we might kill for meat. I picked an old ram with a bad head and made a close stalk and then, with Charo with me this time, shot him with a solid in order not to spoil the meat and in a place where Charo would have time to halal. I had held his head while Charo slit his throat and then bent it back and cracked his spine and Charo looked at me and brought his hand down sharply and shook his head.

We had to get the other piece of meat for camp and finally I found an old wildebeest bull. Everybody was against the choice of this animal and I gave in and we finally took a young fat bull. Charo halalled him too because he produced a grunt when Ngui knelt on him and held his neck back.

He was heavy and hard to lift into the back but we got him up and rolled him in. The boy who wanted to be a hunter lifted the most. The Mohammedans would not wish to eat him anyway. But times might get bad. We drove fast back to camp as the bait was still to be put out. Ngui, Mthuka, and I in the front seat made a sort of sniffing noise when we started to laugh. This is the extremity of Wakamba laughter. None of us took the killing of nondangerous game very seriously except as an indication of whether you were shooting properly or not. It meant something though as an augury. Mostly, though, it only meant training and a chance to shoot.

Then Arap Meina, from the rear seat, put his arms around my neck and kissed me. It was evident that he had access to the Jinny flask which was in one of the shotgun shell bags hung on the back of the seat.

"Shaitani," Arap Meina said and sat back and went to sleep in an erect and soldierly position.

Charo handed the remains of the Jinny flask up to Ngui. He handed it to me and I emptied some into my hand and rubbed it on the spot Arap Meina had kissed me. This was a good Wakamba joke and I took a small drink out of the corner of my mouth to show there was no hard feeling and we drove on into camp and pulled up at the lines.

Keiti was pleased about the meat and I found G.C. still working on his report and he sent his people out to rig the bait with Mthuka driving the hunting car. There was still plenty of time to put it out. G.C. was worried about Mary and we both agreed that she probably had the start of dysentery as well as the ptomaine.

I went to see her and she asked if we had gotten any food for the camp. I said that we had. She inquired what and I told her.

"Did you shoot well?"

"Moderately."

"You can go into rhapsodies about it if you want to. I'm here to listen."

"I've been out butchering for the camp. That's all."

"Then why talk so much about it? Wasn't everyone delighted and amazed and overwhelmed by how wonderfully you shot?"

"They didn't mention it. Arap Meina kissed me."

"You'd gotten him drunk I suppose?"

"Actually not. He'd found the Jinny flask."

"I suppose you're drunk too?"

"No. Decidedly not."

"But you will be."

"You may have something there."

"G.C. hasn't brought his report yet for me to type."

"He's another son of a bitch," I said. "The camp's full of them. Are you running any fever?"

"No. I just have bad cramps and feel awful."

"Do you feel as though you'd be going out in the morning?"

"I'd go out no matter how I feel."

I went and found G.C. He was sitting under the fly of his tent working on the report. We had an absolute privacy rule so I left him.

"Bugger it," he said. "Let's have a drink and watch the sunset. What are we doing in camp anyway?"

"I'm cheering up Miss Mary. But she isn't having any of it."

"Poor girl."

"I think she'll get the bastard tomorrow."

"Why call him a bastard?"

"Just for friendliness."

"She's going out in the morning?"

"Complete with handles."

"Splendid," G.C. said. "Lovely Miss Mary."

So on the next day Miss Mary killed her lion.

CHAPTER 17

The day that Miss Mary shot her lion was a very beautiful day. That was about all that was beautiful about it. White flowers had blossomed in the night so that with the first daylight before the sun had risen all the meadows looked as though a full moon was shining on new snow through a mist. Mary was up and dressed long before first light. The right sleeve of her bush jacket was rolled up and she had checked all the rounds in her Mannlicher .256. She said she did not feel well and I believed her. She acknowledged G.C.'s and my greetings briefly and we were careful not to make any jokes. I did not know what she had against G.C. except his tendency to lightheartedness in the face of undeniably serious work. Her being angry at me was a sound reaction, I thought. If she were in a bad mood I thought she might feel mean and shoot as deadly as I knew she knew how to shoot. This agreed with my last and greatest theory that she had too kind a heart to kill animals. Some people shoot easily and loosely; others shoot with a dreadful speed that is still so controlled that they have all the time they need to place the bullet as carefully as a surgeon would make his first incision; others are mechanical shots who are very deadly unless something happens to interfere with the mechanics of the shooting. This morning it looked as though Miss Mary was going out to shoot with grim resolution, contemptuous of all those who did not take things with appropriate seriousness, armored in her bad physical condition which provided an excuse if she missed, and full of rigid, concentrated do-or-die deadliness. It seemed fine to me. It was a new approach.

We waited by the hunting car for it to be light enough to start and we were all solemn and deadly. Ngui nearly always had an evil temper in the very early morning so he was solemn, deadly, and sullen. Charo was solemn, deadly, but faintly cheerful. He was like a man going to a funeral who did not really feel too deeply about the deceased. Mthuka was happy as always in his deafness, watching with his wonderful eyes for the start of the lightening of the darkness.

We were all hunters and it was the start of that wonderful thing, the hunt. There is much mystic nonsense written about hunting but it is something that is probably much older than religion. Some are hunters and some are not. Miss Mary was a hunter and a brave and lovely one but she had come to it late instead of as a child and many of the things that had happened to her in hunting came as unexpectedly as being in heat for the first time to the kitten when she becomes a cat. She grouped all these new knowledges and changes as things we know and other people don't.

It was a good enough grouping and the four of us who had seen her go through these changes and had seen her now, for months, hunting something grimly and seriously against every possible sort of odds were like the cuadrilla of a very young matador. If the matador was serious the cuadrilla would be serious. They knew all the matador's defects and they were all well paid in different ways. All had lost completely any faith in the matador and all had regained it many times. As we sat in the car or moved around it waiting for it to be light enough to set out I was reminded very much of how it is before a bullfight.

Our matador was solemn; so we were solemn, since, as is unusual, we loved our matador. Our matador was not well. This made it even more necessary that he be protected and given even a better chance in everything he chose to do. But as we sat and leaned and felt sleep drain from us we were as happy as hunters. Probably no one is as happy as hunters with the always new, fresh, unknowing day ahead and Mary was a hunter too. But she had set herself this task and being guided and trained and indoctrinated into absolute purity and virtue of killing a lion by Pop, who had made her his last pupil and given her ethics he had never been able to impose on other women so that her killing of her lion must not be the way such things are done but the way such things should ideally be done; Pop finding finally in Mary the spirit of a fighting cock embodied in a woman; a loving and belated killer with the only defect that no one could say where the shot would go. Pop had given her the ethics and then it was necessary that he go away. She had the ethics now but she only had G.C. and me and neither of us was to be really trusted as Pop was. So now she was going out again to her corrida that always was postponed.

Mthuka nodded to me that the light was beginning to be possible and we started off through the fields of white flowers where yesterday all the meadows had been green. As we came even with the trees of the forest with the high, dead, yellow grass on our left Mthuka slid the car to a quiet stop. He turned his head and I saw the arrow-shaped scar on his cheek and the slashes. He said nothing and I followed his eyes. The great black-maned lion, his head huge above the yellow grass, was coming out toward us. Only his head showed above the stiff, tall, yellow grass.

"What you say we circle easy back to camp?" I whispered to G.C.

"I quite agree," he whispered.

As we spoke the lion turned and moved back toward the forest. All you could see of him was the movements of the high grass.

When we got back to camp and had breakfast Mary understood why we had done what we did and agreed that it was right and necessary. But the corrida had been called off again when she was all set and tense for it and we were not popular. I felt so sorry that she felt ill and I wanted her to let down in tension if she could. There was no use going on talking about how the lion had made a mistake finally. Both G.C. and I were sure we had him now. He had not fed during the night and had come out to look for the bait in the morning. He had gone back into the forest again. He would lie up hungry and, if he were not disturbed, he should be out early in the evening; that is he should be. If he were not, G.C. had to leave the next day no matter what happened and he would revert back to Mary and me on our own. But the lion had broken his pattern of behavior and made a very grave mistake and I did not worry anymore about our getting him. I might have been happier to hunt him with Mary without G.C. but I loved to hunt with G.C. too and I was not so stupid as to want any sort of bad show to happen with me alone with Mary. G.C. had pointed out too well how it could be. I always had the great illusion of Mary hitting the lion exactly where she should and the lion rolling over like anything else as I had seen them do so many times and be as dead as only a lion can be. I was going to drive two into him if he rolled over alive and that was that. Miss Mary would have killed her lion and been happy about it always and I would only have given him the puntilla and she would know it and love me very much forever world without end amen. It was now the sixth month that we had looked forward to this.

G.C.'s chief Game Scout and Arap Meina went out to bring back the word. I had wanted to go out with G.C. but we had decided that too many white men stinking up the ground with a smart lion was not worthwhile. Some people say lions have no sense of smell and some people can be wrong. We sat around and talked shop and made jokes and G.C. went to work on his report. I went over to see Miss Mary but she just felt bad and did not want company and I went out to the lines and spoke to Keiti and the cook and we spoke of various things. Keiti had heard the lion roar in the night but in the direction of the forest. He had heard other lions hunting well to the north, towards the salt lick he thought. Keiti said he was sure we would get the big lion now and I told him my medicine had already told me so and that I expected Miss Mary to kill him this afternoon or evening. Keiti smiled and said nothing. Then he said, "Mzuri."

Everybody who had been up early was sleeping except Mwindi who was ironing bush shirts and trousers that he had washed and looking very disillusioned. I knew better than to speak to him and so I checked the meat and then walked back to the mess tent to read a book by a man who had been very heroic in command of a submarine, then very lucky, then very insubordinate finally and wrote with false modesty and bitterness. That year you had the choice between escapers, climbers, underwater men, ex-R.A.F. types, submariners of all nationalities, African adventurers, explainers of Mau Mau, and an exceptionally good book by Colonel, as he was then, Lindbergh which made him seem human and the air over the Atlantic a dangerous, strange, and interesting place. There were also accounts of prisoners of the Japs, of buggery in Burma at platoon level, believable and unbelievable stories of elephants and those who hunted and trained them. It was not too bad a year for books. Fiction was almost uniformly worthless except for books about nasty characters who suffered heart attacks or were apprehended by the police in England and about professors and instructors in American universities who did or did not live up to their ideals and were all brought down in the end by various committees. Chambers was emptying his pot; a man named McCarthy was gathering a following and being attacked; some Lord had come out either for or against a man named Hiss; it was hard to determine. But none of us book readers cared too much for Hiss, McCarthy, or Chambers. It was difficult to imagine them in the area.

Just then a new Land Rover, one of the new, larger, and faster models we had never seen before, drove into camp through the wonderful field of white flowers that had been dust a month ago and mud one week before. This car was driven by a red-faced man of middle height who wore a faded khaki uniform of an officer in the Kenya police. He was dusty from the road and there were white smile wrinkles at the corners of his eyes that cracked the dust.

"Anybody home?" he asked coming into the mess tent and taking off his cap. Through the open, muslin-screened end that faced toward the mountain I had seen the car come up.

"Everybody home," I said. "How are you, Mr. Harry?"

"I'm quite well."

"Sit down and let me make you something. You can stay the night, can't you?"

He sat down and stretched his legs and moved his shoulders as pleasantly as a cat does.

"Couldn't drink anything. No proper people drink at this hour."

"What do you want?"

"Would you share a beer?"

I opened the beer and poured it out and watched him relax and smile with his dead-tired eyes as we raised the glasses.

"Have them put your gear in young Pat's tent. It's that green one that's empty."

"How is his wife?"

"She's quite well. He's had a go of fever. Thank you very much for handling the signals."

"It's a pity he couldn't have stayed here with you. Did you have good fun before he had to leave?"

"Wonderful. Should I call the boy and have your gear moved in?"

"Later. We can stay the night. What's on with you?"

"Mary's hunting a great bastard of a lion that people say has been misbehaving for a very long time."

"People say so many things," Harry said. "How'd he misbehave?"

"Kills cattle."

"Cattle are money," Harry said. "But they won't spend their money. Not my business. Yours and the Duke's. The Duke's and yours rather. How is the Duke?"

"He's very well. He should be over now."

"I think I saw him going down the garden path to the latrine."

"I hope he hasn't got it."

"Why? Is the Memsahib ill?"

"Not too well."

"I'm sorry. You OK?"

"Very."

"That's something," he said and I poured the glasses full again. "The flowers are very beautiful, aren't they? I wish my Memsahib could see them."

Harry Dunn was shy, overworked, kind, and ruthless. He was fond of Africans and understood them and he was paid to enforce the law and carry out orders. He was as gentle as he was tough and he was not revengeful nor a hater nor was he ever stupid or sentimental. He did not hold grudges in a grudge-holding country and I never saw him be petty about anything. He was administering the law in a time of corruption, hatreds, sadism, and considerable hysteria and he worked himself, each day, past the limit that a man can possibly go, never working to seek promotion or advancement because he knew his worth at what he was doing. Miss Mary one time said that he was a portable fortress of a man.

Today he was a tired fortress and I thought of the first time I had ever seen him when he was only a shape at the wheel of a motorcar on a very dark night in a vehicle which had not answered a challenge after curfew and G.C. had ordered me, "Shoot the man at the wheel." And I had covered him and taken up the slack on the trigger but had challenged again being sure something was wrong and it had turned out to be Harry Dunn with three converted Mau Mau with him. He had never been stuffy about that and had complimented G.C. on his efficiency. But he was the only man I had ever known that I had held a rifle on at twelve yards and started to squeeze off on who had been completely without bitterness.

On this day I knew that he had lost a sergeant that he felt about as I felt about Ngui; in the last week the sergeant had been chopped into pieces and mutilated and we did not speak about this not because of any traditions of good form or the stiff upper lip but because it does no good to talk about the death of those we love or care for deeply. If he wished to speak about it in any practical way of imparting knowledge he would do so. Until then it was his and the sergeant's shauri.

"How is the boy up on the hill?"

"Worthless," I said. "Hopeless maybe."

"He's down with fever. That's why you haven't seen him."

"I'm sorry. I'll go up and see him."

"No hurry. It's just a go of fever. Think it's his first though. You could drop in when you go up. I hear you've made a lot of friends up there."

"One friend. I know quite a few people."

"Would you guaranty your friend?"

"No," I said. "Only as a friend. I'd like to see him stay in business though. There ought to be some place for the bad boys to get together."

"Don't worry about him. We're not all bloody fools."

"I'm a bloody fool."

"I wouldn't say so. Not yet. I'll let you know in plenty of time. Are you having fun here?"

"Very much."

"I've heard a little. What's this about having to kill the leopard before the Birthday of the Baby Jesus?"

"That's for that picture story for that magazine we were making the pictures for in September. Before we met. We had a photographer and he took thousands of pictures and I've written a short article and captions for the pictures they use. They have a beautiful picture of a leopard and I shot him but he isn't mine."

"How does that work?"

"We were after a big lion that was very smart. It was over on the other side of the Guaso Nyiro beyond Magadi under the escarpment."

"Well off my beat."

"We were trying to work up on this lion and this friend of mine climbed up a little rocky kopje with his gunbearer to look ahead to see if the lion had showed. The lion was for Mary because he and I had both killed lions. So we didn't know what the hell had happened when we heard him shoot and then something was down in the dust roaring. It was a leopard and the dust was so deep that it rose solid in a cloud, and the leopard kept on roaring and nobody knew which direction he was coming out of the dust. This friend of mine, Mayito, had hit him twice from up above and I had shot into the moving center of the dust and ducked and moved to the right where it was natural he would break out. Then he showed his head up just once out of the dust still talking bad and I hit him in the neck and the dust started to settle. It was sort of like a gunfight in the dust outside of an old time saloon out west. Except the leopard didn't have any gun but he was close enough to have mauled anyone and he was awfully worked up. The photographer took pictures of Mayito and him and of all of us and him and of me and him. He was Mayito's because Mayito hit him first and hit him again. So the best picture of him was the one with me and the magazine wanted to use it and I said they couldn't unless I killed a good leopard alone by myself. And so far I've failed three times."

"I didn't know the ethics were so rigid."

"Unfortunately they are. It's the law too. First blood and continuous pursuit."

"Is it perfectly all right if I don't understand you and the Duke completely?"

"I think something would be wrong if you did, Harry. Try to find out sometime if the Duke understands himself?"

"Don't you understand him?"

"Hell no. His ethics are too complicated for me."

"By God, none of us is safe," Harry said. "Perhaps we should share another beer. But you're a writer. Writers are supposed to understand things. That's what they implied in the book of words."

"Africa is very complicated, Harry."

"You know," he said. "That idea had occurred to me. Perhaps I was just at the point of grasping it. You were good to put it so clearly."

Just then G.C. came in. He had the triumphal look of a man who has completed his monthly report. He was beautifully turned out in fresh-washed, sharply pressed kit and his face looked like a rather mature but delinquent cherub.

"Who is this character called the Duke that this visiting policeman has been mentioning? Does he have a permit for this area?"

"An eavesdropper," I said to Harry.

"Good afternoon, your grace," Harry said. "I have the hangman with his lorry outside. Do you mind if I bring him to lunch?"

"Do you really have the hangman?" G.C. asked pouring himself a glass of Tusker.

"No," Harry said. "He's broken down up the road."

"The General here has been hanging baboons lately. Care to turn off a few baboons to amuse this policeman while we have lunch, General?"

"I can turn off a few for hospitality's sake," I said. "Call the baboon wallah."

G.C. called, "Baboon wallah," several times. Finally Nguili came. He had been putting on his green serving gown and he was grinning. He was happy that we were happy. He did not know what a baboon wallah was but it sounded like a good joke.

"I'll stick to the beer," Harry said.

"It slows the General and me," G.C. said. "We never know when we may have to do the impossible. Do you feel up to the impossible today, General?"

"The partially or the totally?"

"We're not poltroons," G.C. said. "The absolute impossible."

"I'm glad there's something you're not," Harry said. "Now hear me out, Duke. What did the General mean when he stated that Africa was very complicated?"

"You can run him under the Official Secrets Act on that."

"Africa is vast," I said. "It is mysterious."

"You see?" G.C. said. "He's a subversive. Fortunately he has a faithful wife that will bring him around in the end."

"Are you mixed up in his new religion?"

"Not I," said G.C. "I don't want to even hear about it."

"He doubts Gitchi Manitou the mighty," I said. "Can you believe that, Harry?"

"It's a wonder he hasn't been turned into a pillar of salt."

"I'd thought of turning him but I was afraid you might run me under the Witchcraft Ordinance."

"Never worry. Turn him any day you like. Might do him no end of good. Have to put in a return on the salt though. I'll see you get the necessary forms."

"The General's predicted a miracle on Miss Mary's lion for today," G.C. said happily. "Half his followers are out praying to Gitchi Manitou now.

The other half are despondent. He has a rooster out there by the cook tent that's mixed up in the religion and even the rooster is despondent."

"Is the rooster in the religion?"

"Only in the nicest way."

"It might not be a bad idea to teach him to crow thrice," G.C. said.

"You leave our religion alone. Don't fool with it. Any really good religion has it a little rough at the start."

"Just don't mention any names," Harry said. "It's bad luck Mrs. H. isn't feeling fit. Will she be up for lunch?"

"I'll go and see," I said. I thought he and G.C. might want to talk business and it would be better if I left them alone. The religion joking was good and rough and pleasant but it was a little close to the bone after the rooster had come into it. I did not think that G.C. meant it to have any edge but we always joked so very rough that I did not want our jokes to hurt each other especially on a day like today. I have many presentiments of things that do not happen. But I never thought ever that a day was going to be rougher than this day was going to be and I knew Ngui felt lower than I did.

Arap Meina and the chief Game Scout had brought back the word that the two lionesses and the young lion had killed far up on the edge of the salt flat. The bait had not been uncovered except where hyenas had pulled at it and the two scouts had recovered it carefully. There were birds in the trees around it that would surely draw the lion but the birds could not get at the remains of the zebra which were high enough to draw the lion surely. He had not fed nor killed in the night, and since he was not hungry and had not been disturbed we might, almost surely, find him in the open in the evening. This was all good and my bad feeling came from something else.

"How do you feel, honey?" I asked Mary.

"I'm sorry, Big Kitten," she said. "I can make it to lunch all right. But I feel really awful."

"It's a lovely day and the lion should almost surely be out."

"I know it. That's what's so awful. I just feel terrible. I'm wearing that path out. The flowers are so beautiful and the mountain is so wonderful and I just feel too awful."

"Does the Chlorodyne do any good?"

"I don't think so. It just makes me feel sick at my stomach. Are you having fun with Harry Dunn?"

"Yes. But I wish you felt well."

"I don't," she said. "And the lovely day with the big high clouds and my lion coming to meet me and I feel sick to the bone. Maybe it isn't fair."

"It certainly isn't."

"What should I eat?"

"I'll see about some clear soup and mashed potatoes with just meat-juice gravy and some dry toast."

I went back to speak to the cook about the food and then to the dining tent turning wide and coming in from well out in front so I would not come in on any police shop. I saw they were talking seriously and so I swung wide again over to the big tree that was out of earshot of the tent and sat there in one of the camp chairs and looked out over the white fields with the green islands of trees and bush in them. Later G.C. would tell me what he wanted me to know. I liked it better that way. There were enough problems of status without complicating it and I had no ambition and very few illusions. It was like all of those jobs. If you did what you were asked to do well you would have the reward of doing some other job and you had certain privileges and many favors from the people that liked you. If you did anything badly you would be accused of interfering where you weren't wanted and of acting without authority. It was an old and familiar pattern and I did not mind it in the least. There were always some people who liked you very much and others who disliked you as much or more and I had drawn cards in this sort of game for so long that I had learned to feel quite impersonal about the ones who would eventually knife you. So now I sat in the shade under the tree and thought about how much I liked Harry Dunn and G.C. and I had no curiosity about what they were talking about. Eventually I would hear about it and that would probably be too soon. I knew neither one of them was going to knife me and I trusted them more than I did myself. I had a pretty good idea who would try it, I thought. But it did not look to build up very quickly and perhaps I was thinking morbidly. I decided I was and walked over to the dining tent.

The talk was over. Harry stood up and smiled. "I'm going to wash up," he said.

"You can bathe," I said. "There's plenty of water."

"No. I'll take a good wash-up and bathe tonight."

After he had gone G.C. said to me, "You didn't have to stay out of it, Ernie."

"Oh balls," I said.

"I'll give you the gen. Harry asked me to. We were discussing personalities."

"I don't want the gen except as it concerns what you want me to do while you're here and after you're gone."

"Don't be so bloody. What are you peed off about?"

"I'm not, G.C. I feel bastardly about Mary not feeling well and I've got black ass."

"So have we all," said G.C.

"It isn't right on a day like this. And the only one who has any right to have it is Harry."

"I don't think that's been disputed."

"I'm sorry, G.C."

Mary came in then and nodded to us and said, "Where's Harry Dunn?"

"He went to wash, Miss Mary," G.C. explained. "We're both here."

"So I saw," she said. I went over to the sideboard table and poured a gimlet and put some water in it from the cool thin canvas neck of the water bag. I picked up an airmail edition of the London *Daily Telegraph* that was two weeks old and went out to sit in the chair under the tree. Goddamn it, I thought. She was friendly half an hour ago. What have we done since then? Maybe she'll cheer up when Harry comes in. He hasn't done anything yet.

We had lunch, finally, and Mary was very cheerful and gracious with all of us. I believe she even asked me if I wanted any more of the cold meat. When I said no thank you, that I had enough, she said it would be good for me, that any man who drinks a great deal needs to eat. This was not only a very old truth but had been the basis of an article in the *Reader's Digest* that we all had read. That number of the *Digest* was down in the latrine tent now. I said that I had decided to run on a platform of true rummyhood and deceive none of my constituents. Churchill drank twice what I did if you could believe the accounts and had just been awarded the Nobel Prize for Literature. I was simply trying to step up my drinking to a reasonable amount when I might win the Prize myself; who knows?

G.C. said that the Prize was as good as mine and that I ought to win it for bragging alone since Churchill had been awarded it, at least partially, for oratory. Harry said that he had not followed the Prize awards as closely as he should but that he felt I might well be awarded it for my work in the religious field and for my care of the natives. Miss Mary suggested that if I would try to write something, occasionally, I might win it for writing. This moved me very deeply and I said that once she had the lion I would do nothing but write; just to please her. She said that if I wrote even a little it would certainly please her. Harry asked me if I planned to write something about how mysterious Africa was and that if I planned to write in Swahili he could get me a book on up-country Swahili that might be invaluable to me. Miss Mary said that we already had the book and that she thought even with the book it would be better if I tried to write in English. I suggested that I might copy sections of the book to help me get an up-country style. Miss Mary said I could not write one correct sentence in Swahili nor speak one either and I agreed with her very sadly that this was true.

"Pop speaks it so beautifully and so does G.C. and so does Harry and you are a disgrace. I don't know how anyone can speak a language as badly as you do."

I wanted to say that at one time, years before, it had looked as though I were going to speak it quite well. But that I had been a fool not to have stayed on in Africa and instead had gone back to America where I had killed my homesickness for Africa in different ways. Then before I could get back came the Spanish war and I became involved in what was happening to the world and I had stayed with that for better and for worse until I had finally come back. It had not been easy to get back nor to break the chains of responsibility that are built up, seemingly, as lightly as spider webs but that hold like steel cables. I had thought about these things for a long time and about how we writers were the lowest slave laborers of the State, taxed in advance on money we could never guaranty to make. The theory and the position, perhaps untenable, if fully stated, would ruin any lunch and we were salvaging something from this one so I said nothing serious nor defensive but admitted I was very bad at all languages, which I knew to be a lie, but which might pass as modesty with G.C. and Harry and might cheer Miss Mary up. I was thinking how easy it is when you are Mary's age and G.C.'s and Harry's to learn another language and how hard it was at mine with two languages beside your own, embedded and dug deep into your mind, one so deeply that you were liable to think in it when you were tired even if you thought with errors of grammar. Miss Mary was a snob about grammar as G.C. and I were snobs about various other things. Harry was not a snob about anything. He found life quite hard enough without playing complicated games under strange rules to increase the difficulties and keep out those who have had no chance to learn that particular game as some men play at court tennis.

They were all having a good time now joking and making fun of one another and I joked a little but was careful to be very modest and contrite hoping to win back Miss Mary's favor and hoping to keep her in a good humor in case the lion would show. I had been drinking Bulwer's Dry Cyder which I had found to be a marvelous drink. G.C. had brought some in from Kajiado from the Stores. It was very light and refreshing and did not slow you down at all shooting. It came in full quarts and had screw-in tops and I used to drink it in the night when I woke instead of water. Mary's extremely nice cousin had given us two small square sacking-covered pillows filled with balsam needles. I always slept with mine under my neck or, if I slept on my side, with my ear on it. It was the smell of Michigan when I was a boy and I wished I could have had a sweet grass basket to keep it in when we traveled and to have under the mosquito net in the bed at night. The cider tasted like Michigan too and I always remembered the cider mill and the door which was never locked but only fitted with a hasp and wooden pin and the smell of the sacks used in the pressing and later spread to dry and then spread over the deep tubs where the men who came to grind their wagonloads of apples left the mill's share. Below the dam of the cider mill flume there was a deep pool where the eddy from the falling water in turning cut back in under the dam. You could always catch trout if you fished there patiently and whenever I caught one I would kill him and lay him in the big wicker creel that was in the shade and put a layer of fern leaves over him and then go into the cider mill and take the tin cup off the nail on the wall over the tubs and pull up the heavy sacking from one of the tubs and dip out a cup of cider and drink it. This cider that we had now reminded me of Michigan, especially with the pillow.

Neither Ngui nor Mthuka nor our other brother who was Pop's gun-bearer liked cider. They were beer men. But they all thought that the smell of the pillow was wonderful. I let Ngui smell it first inside the tent one time when he had brought back the guns from cleaning them. I showed him the different designs of the trees that were embroidered on them. One tree for men and one tree for women. Also the difference in the way the trees were made that distinguished my tribe from the tribe of Miss Mary. Afterwards Ngui asked me if the two other brothers could smell my pillow. It had a formal Indian design of a pine tree on it in green and black wool. Miss Mary's had a balsam tree branch in embroidered green and brown wool. The green made the needles and the brown was the branch. They noticed that mine had a square in green around the tree and that Miss Mary's had not. Naturally they did not touch Miss Mary's but they held mine very carefully when I handed it to them and smelled it very deeply and acted the way people do in church. Their tribal religion was founded on a tree too.

Sitting now at the table I was pleased Mary seemed to be feeling better and I hoped the lion would show in the late afternoon and that she would kill him dead as snake shit and be happy forever after. Then I hoped that I might get the leopard quickly and then that we might all relax and have fun the way we knew how to have it. After Miss Mary's lion we would start to have fun. I knew of three different leopards in the area and there were probably more and if I hunted intelligently I could certainly find one and if I didn't I would go down to Fig Tree camp beyond Magadi where I knew there was one that believed he owned the country around there. I planned to go down with Ngui and Pop's gunbearer, maybe, and we would not need any camp but just hunt there until we got him. If I could have stayed there one more day I am quite sure I would have killed him. But no sentence that starts with "if" is any good in Africa and most sentences start that way.

We finished lunch and everybody was very cheerful and we all said we would take a nap and I would call Miss Mary when it was time to go to look for the lion.

CHAPTER 18

Mary went to sleep almost as soon as she lay down on her cot. The back of the tent was propped open and a good cool breeze blew down from the mountain and through the tent. We ordinarily slept facing the open door of the tent but I took the pillows and placed them at opposite ends of the cot and doubling them over and with the balsam pillow under my neck lay on the cot with my boots and trousers off and read with the good light behind me. I was reading a very good book by Gerald Hanley who had written another good book called *The Consul at Sunset*. This book was about a lion who made much trouble and killed practically all the characters in the book. G.C. and I used to read this book in the mornings on the latrine to inspire us. There were a few characters the lion did not kill but they were all headed for some other sort of bad fate so we did not really mind. Hanley wrote very well and it was an excellent book and very inspiring when you were in the lion-hunting business. I had seen a lion come, at speed, once and I had been very impressed and am still impressed. On this afternoon I was reading the book very slowly because it was such a good book and I did not want to finish it. I was hoping the lion would kill the hero or the Old Major because they were both very noble and nice characters and I had gotten very fond of the lion and wanted him to kill some upper-bracket character. The lion was doing very well though and he had just killed another very sympathetic and important character when I decided it would be better to save the rest and got up and pulled on my trousers and put my boots on without zipping them up and went over to see if G.C. was awake. I coughed outside his tent the way the Informer always did outside the mess tent.

"Come in, General," G.C. said.

"No," I said. "A man's home is his castle. Are you feeling up to facing the deadly beasts?"

"It's too early yet. Did Mary sleep?"

"She's still sleeping. What are you reading?"

"Lindbergh. It's damned good. What were you reading?"

"*The Year of the Lion*. I'm sweating out the lion."

"You've been reading that for a month."

"Six weeks. How are you coming with the mysticism of the air?"

That year we were both, belatedly, full of the mysticism of the air. I had given up on the mysticism of the air finally in 1945 when flying home in an overaged, unreconditioned flight-weary B-17.

I finished telling G.C. about this and then went over to the tent to see Mary.

"Do you want to go out, honey? We're going out in Harry's new big Land Rover."

"I feel too bad really."

"All right. We'll be careful not to disturb anything and if we see him we'll come back and get you."

"I'm worthless," she said. "And I feel terrible."

"Try to rest and take it as easy as you can."

"How can I rest and take it easy when my lion is going to come out and I'll not be there to meet him?"

"We'll be back for you if he's out."

"And he'll be gone back into the forest."

I walked over to where G.C. and Harry were waiting in the new car under the tree and climbed in the front with them. G.C. was driving and we went out through the meadow of white flowers to the airstrip. G.C. turned onto the tracks that were grown up with the flowers and drove the length of the strip toward the Kilimanjaro end and then made a turn and drove back beside his tracks. The flowers came up to the hubs of the wheels. It was late afternoon and when we had driven up the strip the mountain was huge and white beyond the dark-green trees of camp. Now we were driving into the late sun with the mountain behind us.

"We'll have to put the lorry up and down there a few times," I said to G.C. "Those flowers are getting a little high for Willie."

"Something will eat the flowers up," Harry said. "Something always does. Do you like her, Duke?"

G.C. nodded happily. He was completely absorbed in the new car.

"Can I take her back up the strip and open her up, Harry?"

"Probably best not to open her up quite yet," Harry said. "Strip's a bit short too."

The strip had always seemed to G.C. and me like a very marvelous speedway and it was at night too. I had thought of it for some time, privately, as the Kilimanjaro measured mile and testing course and having to realize that it was nowhere near a mile in length and completely unsuitable for testing anything at all made me feel very parochial.

"You can open her up on the Kajiado-Sultan Hamud road," Harry said. "She'll have enough miles on her by then."

G.C. seemed sort of glazed with contentment with a new car and we moved off the airstrip speedway and onto what I thought of as the Great North Road, the tire tracks that paralleled the forest and led up toward the mud flats, the salt licks, and the buffalo swamp. Ngui and G.C.'s chief Game Scout were in back and they were watching for the lion. So was I and so were G.C. and Harry.

"If he's out," I told Harry, "really out, he'll be over in one of those clumps of trees on the right."

We drove on, very slowly and quietly now with no one speaking. The sun was on our left now over the hills behind the forest. G.C.'s Game Scout reached forward and put his hand on G.C.'s shoulder. He did not point but looked and G.C. stopped the car softly.

"There he is, Harry," he said very low.

"I see him."

I could not believe it when I saw him. Neither could Ngui. The lion lay on top of an anthill looking away from us. It was a broad-topped gray mound and the lion was molded on its top as though he were sculpted there. The mound was in the shade of a wide-topped thorn tree and I had never seen a lion look so big nor so black. His great head was black and his mane swept in a black wedge over his back into the tawny gray of his flanks.

I had never seen a lion looking that way except in a painting or in a heroic sculpture. What was he doing there? He who had been so wary and so intelligent? Why had he gotten up in plain sight like that?

The wind was blowing toward us and he had not heard us nor seen us. G.C. let in the clutch very quietly and turned the car and we went back down the road and when we were out of sight of the lion he drove as fast as we could go for camp.

"What the hell put him up there?" I asked G.C.

"He got confident. He finally got confident. He went up there to look over his country and enjoy himself. It *is* his country."

"He's a hell of a lion," Harry said. "I can see why the Memsahib is worked up about him. Does he really kill cattle or did you just make that up to feed the troops?"

"He kills cattle," I said.

In camp I got Mary up while the gunbearers got Mary's rifle and my big gun from under the beds and checked the solids and the soft-nosed and then ran to the big Land Rover.

"He's there, honey. He's there and you'll get him."

"It's late. Why didn't you take him? It's so damned late."

"Don't think about anything. Just get out in the car."

"I have to put my boots on. You know that."

I was helping her on with them.

"Where's my damned hat?"

"Here's your damned hat. Walk. Don't run to the nearest Land Rover. Don't think about anything but hitting him."

"Don't talk to me so much. Leave me alone."

Mary and G.C. and Harry were in the front seat with Harry driving. Ngui, Charo, and I were in the open back with the Game Scout. I was checking the cartridges in the barrel and the magazine of the .30-06, checking those in my pockets and checking and cleaning the rear-sight aperture of any dust with a toothpick. Mary was holding her rifle straight up and I had a fine view of the new-wiped dark barrel and the Scotch tape that held her rear-sight leaves down, of the back of her head and her disreputable hat. The sun was just above the hills now and we were out of the flowers and going north on the old track that ran parallel to the woods. Somewhere on the right was the lion.

When we came up in sight of the high rounded cone of the anthill he was gone. The car stopped and everyone got out except Harry who stayed at the wheel. The lion's tracks went off to the right toward a clump of trees and brush on our side of the lone tree where the bait was covered by a pile of brush. He was not on the bait and there were no birds on it either. They were all up in the trees. I looked back at the sun and it did not have more than ten minutes before it would be behind the far hills to the west. Ngui had climbed the anthill and looked carefully over the top. He pointed with his hand held close by his face so that you could hardly see it move and then came fast down from the mound.

"Hiko hapa," he said. "He's there. Mzuri motocah."

G.C. and I both looked at the sun again and G.C. waved his arm for Harry to come up. We climbed into the car and G.C. told Harry how he wanted him to go.

"But where is he?" Mary asked G.C.

G.C. put his hand on Harry's arm and Harry stopped the car.

"We leave the car back here," G.C. told Mary. "He must be in that far clump of trees and brush. Papa will take the left flank and block him off from breaking back to the forest. You and I will move straight in on him."

The sun was still above the hills as we moved up toward where the lion must be. Ngui was behind me and on our right Mary was walking a little ahead of G.C. Charo was behind G.C. They were walking straight toward the trees with the thin brush at their base. I could see the lion now and I kept working to the left, walking sideways and forward. The light showed the lion huge black and long tawny gray-gold and he was watching us. He was watching us and I thought what a bad place he had gotten himself into now. Every step I made I was blocking him worse from his safety that he had retreated into so many times. He had no choice now except to break toward me, to come out toward Mary and G.C., which he did not figure to do unless he were wounded, or to try for the next island of heavy cover, trees and thick brush, that was 450 yards away to the north. To reach there he would have to cross open flat plain.

Now I figured that I was far enough to the left and began moving in toward the lion. He stood there thigh deep in brush and I saw his head turn once to look toward me then it swung back to watch Mary and G.C. His head was huge and dark but when he moved it the head did not look too big for his body. His body was heavy, great, and long. I did not know how close G.C. would try to work Mary toward the lion. I did not watch them. I watched the lion and waited to hear the shot. I was as close as I needed to be now to have room to take him if he came and I was sure that if he were wounded he would break toward me as his natural cover was behind me. Mary must take him soon, I thought. She can't get any closer. But maybe G.C. wants her closer. I looked at them from the corner of my eyes, my head down, not looking away from the lion. I could see Mary wanted to shoot and that G.C. was preventing her. They were not trying to work closer so I figured that from where they were there were some limbs of brush between Mary and the lion. I watched the lion and felt the change in his coloring as the first peak of the hills took the sun. It was good light to shoot now but it would go fast. I watched the lion and he moved very slightly to his right and then looked at Mary and G.C. I could see his eyes. Still Mary did not shoot. Then the lion moved very slightly again and I heard Mary's rifle go and the dry whack of the bullet. She had hit him. The lion made a bound into the brush and then came out of the far side headed for the patch of heavy cover to the north. Mary was firing at him and I was sure she hit him. He was moving in long bounds, his great head swinging. I shot and raised a puff of dirt behind him. I swung with him and squeezed off as I passed him and was behind him again. G.C.'s big double was firing and I saw the blossomings of dirt from it. I fired again picking the lion up in the sights and swung ahead of him and a bunch of dirt rose ahead of him. He was running now heavy and desperate but beginning to look small in the sights and almost certain to make the far cover when I had him in the sights again, small now and going away fast, and swung gently ahead and lifting over him and squeezed as

I passed him and no dirt rose and I saw him slide forward, his front feet plowing and his great head down before we heard the thunk of the bullet. Ngui banged me on the back and put his arm around me. The lion was trying to get up now and G.C. hit him and he rolled onto his side.

I went over to Mary and kissed her. She was happy but something was wrong.

"You shot before I did," she said.

"Don't say that, honey. You shot and hit him. How could I shoot before you when we'd waited all that time?"

"Ndio. Memsahib piga," Charo said. He had been right behind Mary.

"Of course you hit him. You hit him the first time in the foot, I think. You hit him again too."

"But you killed him."

"We all had to keep him from getting into that thick stuff after he was hit."

"But you shot first. You know you did."

"I did not. Ask G.C."

We were all walking up to where the lion lay. It was a long walk and the lion grew larger and deader as we walked. With the sun gone it was getting dark fast. The shooting light was gone already. I felt wrung-out inside and very tired. G.C. and I were both wet with sweat.

"Of course you hit him, Mary," G.C. told her. "Papa didn't shoot until he went into the open. You hit him twice."

"Why couldn't I have shot him when I wanted to when he was just standing there and looking at me?"

"There were branches that could have deflected the bullet or broken it up. That was why I made you wait."

"Then he moved."

"He had to move for you to shoot him."

"But did I really hit him first?"

"Of course you did. Nobody would have shot at him before you did."

"You're not just lying to make me happy?"

This was a scene that Charo had seen before.

"Piga," he said violently. "Piga, Memsahib. PIGA."

I slapped Ngui on the hip with the side of my hand and looked toward Charo and he went over.

"Piga," he said harshly. "Piga, Memsahib. Piga bili."

G.C. came over to walk by me and I said, "What are *you* sweating for?"

"How far did you hold over him, you son of a bitch?"

"A foot and a half. Two feet. It was bow-and-arrow shooting."

"We'll pace it when we walk back."

"Nobody would ever believe it."

"We will. That's all that matters."

"Go over and make her realize she hit him."

"She believes the boys. You broke his back."

"I know."

"Did you hear how long it took for the sound of the bullet hitting to come back?"

"I did. Go over and talk to her. Here comes Harry." The Land Rover pulled up behind us.

Now we were there with the lion and he was Mary's and she knew it now and she saw how wonderful and long and dark and beautiful he was. The camel flies were crawling on him and his yellow eyes were not dull yet. I moved my hand through the heavy black of his mane. Harry had stopped the Land Rover and come over and shaken Mary's hand. She was kneeling by him.

"He's a beautiful lion," he said. "I've never seen one so big or so dark." Then we saw the lorry coming out across the plain from camp. They had heard the shooting and Keiti had come out with everyone except two guards that they had left in camp. They were singing the lion song and when they piled out of the lorry Mary had no more doubt about whose lion it was. I have seen many lions killed and many celebrations. But not one like this. I wanted Mary to have all of it. I was sure it was all right with Mary now and I walked on to the island of trees and thick brush the lion had been making for. He had nearly made it and I thought of what it would have been like if G.C. and I had to go in there to dig him out. I wanted a look at it before the light was gone. He would have made it there in sixty more yards and it would have been dark when we got up to it. I thought about what could have happened and went back to the celebration and the picture taking. The headlights of the lorry and the Land Rover were centered on Mary and the lion and G.C. was making the photographs. Ngui brought me the Jinny flask from the shell bag in the Land Rover and I took a small swallow and handed it to Ngui. He took a small drink and shook his head and handed it to me.

"Piga," he said and we both laughed. I took a long drink and felt it warm and felt the strain slip off me like a snake shedding his skin. Until that moment I had not realized that we had the lion finally. I knew it technically when the unbelievable long bow-and-arrow shot had hit and broken him down and Ngui had hit me across the back. But then there had been Mary's worry and being upset and walking up to him we had been as unemotional and as detached as though it were the end of an attack. Now with the drink and the celebrating going on and the photography, the hated and necessary photography, too late at night, no flash, no professionals to do it properly to make Miss Mary's lion immortal now on film, seeing her shining happy face in the glare of the headlights and the lion's great head that was too heavy for her to lift, proud of her and loving the lion, me feeling as empty inside as an empty room, seeing Keiti's gashed slant of a smile as he bent over Mary to touch the lion's unbelievable black mane, every one cooing in Wakamba like birds and each man individually proud of this our lion, ours and belonging to all of us and Mary's because she had hunted him for months and had hit him in that barred phrase standing on her own two feet and when the chips were down, and now happy and shining in the headlights looking like a small, not quite deadly, bright angel and everyone loving her and this our lion, I began to relax and to have fun.

Charo and Ngui had told Keiti how it was and he came over to me and we shook hands and he said, "Mzuri sana, Bwana. Shaitani tu."

"It was lucky," I said, which God knows it had to be.

"Not lucky," Keiti said. "Mzuri. Mzuri. Shaitani kubwa sana."

Then I remembered that I had given this afternoon for the lion's death and that it was all over now and that Mary had won and I talked with Ngui and Mthuka and Pop's gunbearer and the others of our religion and we shook our heads and laughed and Ngui wanted me to take another drink from the Jinny flask. They wanted to wait until we would get to camp for beer but they wanted me to drink now with them. They only touched the bottle with their lips. Mary stood up now after the photography and saw us drinking and she asked for the flask and drank from it and passed it to G.C. and to Harry. They passed it back and I drank and then lay down by the lion and talked to him very softly in Spanish and begged his pardon for our having killed him and while I lay beside him I felt for the wounds. There were four. Mary had hit him in the foot and in one haunch. While I stroked his back I found where I had hit him in the spine and the larger hole G.C.'s bullet had made well forward in his flank behind the shoulder. All the time I was stroking him and talking to him in Spanish but many of the flat, hard camel flies were shifting from him to me so I drew a fish in front of him with my forefinger in the dirt and then rubbed it out with the palm of my hand.

"Mzuri," Mthuka said. He had not understood the ceremony but he approved. He had seen the fish. "Samaki mzuri," he nodded. Keiti nodded solemnly too. So did Charo. Evidently the fish was dignified and good. I said good-bye to the lion in Spanish and then said, "Kwisha," and walked over to where Mary and G.C. stood with their arms around each other.

"Now are you happy?" I asked Mary.

"Oh yes. Everybody says I hit him."

"I saw you hit him twice."

"I could see you hit him from way back where I was," Harry said. "The old man didn't shoot at him until he broke out."

"Were you watching with glasses?"

"With and without. I take it you were just firing to speed him on his way, Duke. Is that part of the game as you chaps play it? Are you sure it was quite sporting for old Hemingstein to break his back that way? I thought the two of you were just sort of trying to speed him up so that he'd go into the brush and you could go in after him. Isn't that the type of situation you're always trying to bring about?"

"Death to the police," I said.

"All in good time," Harry said. "I've always been curious to see one of these things. Wouldn't it be more interesting though if the lion ran toward you? They do that sometimes don't they, Duke? You must forgive my ignorance."

"Let's take his ignorance to camp and wet it," G.C. said. "We must have them lift him very carefully into the lorry and be careful that the hide's not rubbed and careful of his mane."

"Are you still speaking of me or of the lion?" Harry asked.

"The lion," G.C. said. "I'll speak to Keiti and then we'll go in and have a proper drink."

On the way into camp Ngui and Charo and I did not talk. I heard Mary once ask G.C. if I had not really shot before she did and heard him tell her that she had gotten her lion. That she had hit him first and that these things did not always go off ideally and that when an animal was wounded he had to be killed and that we were damned lucky and she should be happy. But I knew that her happiness came and went because it had not been as she had hoped and dreamed and feared and waited for all of six months. I felt terrible about how she felt and I knew it made no difference to anyone else and it made all the difference in the world to her. But if we had to do it over again there was no way we could have done it differently. G.C. had taken her up closer than anyone but a great shot had a right to take her. If the lion had charged when she hit him, G.C. would have had time for only one shot before the lion would have been on them. His big gun was as deadly and efficient if the lion came as it was a handicap if he had to shoot it at two and three hundred yards. We both knew that and had not even joked about it. Taking the lion at the range she did Mary had been in great danger and both G.C. and I knew that at the distance he had brought her to she had, recently, a possible error of eighteen inches on live game. This was not the time to talk about that but Ngui and Charo knew it too and I had slept with it for a long time. The lion, by deciding to make his fight in the thick cover, where he was heavy odds on to get someone had made his choice and had very nearly won. He was not a stupid lion and he was not cowardly. He wanted to make his fight where the odds were in his favor.

We came into camp and sat in chairs by the fire and stretched our legs out and drank tall drinks. Who we needed was Pop and Pop was not there. I had told Keiti to break out some beer for the lines and then I waited for it to come. It came as suddenly as a dry streambed filling with the high, foamcrested roar of water from a cloudburst. It had only taken time enough for them to decide who was to carry Miss Mary and then the wild, stooped dancing rush of Wakamba poured in from behind the tents all singing the lion song. The big mess boy and the truck driver had the chair and they put it down and Keiti dancing and clapping his hands led Miss Mary to it and they hoisted her up and started dancing around the fire with her and then out toward the lines and around the lion where he had been lain on the ground and then through the lines and around the cook fire and the men's fire and around the cars and the wood truck and in and out. The Game Scouts were all stripped to their shorts and so was everyone else except the old men. I watched Mary's bright head and the black strong fine bodies that were carrying her and crouching and stamping in the dance and then moving forward to reach up and touch her. It was a fine wild lion dance and at the end they put Mary down in the chair by her camp chair at the fire and everyone shook hands with her and it was over.

She was happy and we had a fine happy meal and went to bed.

CHAPTER 19

In the night I woke and could not get back to sleep. I woke very suddenly and it was absolutely quiet. Then I heard Mary's regular, smooth breathing and I had a feeling of relief that we would not have to pit her against the lion every morning. Then I began to feel sorrow that the lion's death had not been as she hoped it would be and as she had planned it. With the celebration and the really wild dance and the love of all her friends and their allegiance to her the disappointment that she felt had been anaesthetized. But I was sure that after the more than a hundred mornings that she had gone out after a great lion the disappointment would return. She did not know the danger she had been in. Maybe she did and I did not know. Neither G.C. nor I wanted to tell her because we had both cut it too fine and we had not soaked in sweat that way in the cool of the evening for nothing. I remembered how the lion's eyes had looked when he had looked toward me and turned that down and then looked toward Mary and G.C. and how his eyes had never left them. I lay in the bed and thought how a lion can come one hundred yards from a standing start in just over three seconds. He comes low down to the ground and faster than a greyhound and he does not spring until he is on his prey. Mary's lion would weigh well over four hundred pounds and he was strong enough to have leaped out over a high thorn boma carrying a cow. He had been hunted for many years and he was very intelligent. But we had lulled him into making a mistake. I was happy that before he died he had lain on the high, yellow, rounded mound with his tail down and his great paws comfortable before him and looked off across his country to the blue forest and the high white snows of the big mountain. Both G.C. and I wanted him to be killed by Mary's first shot or, wounded, charge. But he had played it his own way. The first shot could not have felt more than a sharp, slapping sting to him. The second that passed high through a leg muscle while he was bounding toward the heavy cover where he would make his fight would, at most, have felt like a hard slap. I did not like to think what my long thrown

218

running shot that was thrown at all of him hoping to rake him and bring him down must have felt like when it by chance took him in the spine. It was a 220-grain solid bullet and I did not have to think how it would have felt. I had never yet broken my back and I did not know. I was glad G.C.'s wonderful distance shot had killed him instantly. He was dead now and we would miss hunting him too. But it was a great relief that he was dead because today I would have been hunting him alone with Mary without G.C. and so there would have been nobody to block in the place I had blocked last evening. He was so crafty that something could always have gone wrong with him.

Mary was still breathing regularly and I looked out at the night and the glow of the coals of the fire when the breeze stirred the ashes and I was very glad the responsibility of hunting Mary on lion was over. There was nothing I could do about her disappointment when she woke. But maybe it would wear off. If it didn't she could kill another great lion some other time. But not right now, I thought, please not right now.

I tried to go to sleep but I started to think about the lion and what the moves would have been if he had reached the heavy cover remembering other people's experiences under the same circumstances and then I thought the hell with all that. That's stuff for G.C. and me to talk over together and to talk with Pop. I wished Mary would wake and say, "I'm so glad I got my lion." But that was too much to expect and it was three o'clock in the morning.

I remembered how Scott Fitzgerald had written that in the something something of the soul something something it is always three o'clock in the morning. For many months three o'clock in the morning had been two hours, or an hour and a half, before you would get up and get dressed and put your boots on to hunt Miss Mary's lion. I untucked the mosquito net and reached for and found the cider bottle. It was cool with the night and I built up the two pillows by doubling them over and then leaned back against them with the rough square balsam pillow under my neck and thought about the soul. First I must verify the Fitzgerald quotation in my mind. It had occurred in a series of articles in which he had abandoned this world and his former extremely shoddy ideals and had first referred to himself as a cracked plate. Turning my memory back I remembered the quotation. It went like this: "In a real dark night of the soul it is always three o'clock in the morning." And I thought sitting up awake in the African night that I knew nothing about the soul at all. People were always talking of it and writing of it but who knew about it? I did not know anyone who knew anything of it nor whether there was such a thing. It seemed a very strange belief and I knew I would have a very difficult time trying to explain it to Ngui and Mthuka and the others even if I knew anything about it. Before I woke I had been dreaming and in the dream I had a horse's body but a man's head and shoulders and I had wondered why no one had known this before. It was a very logical dream and it dealt with the precise moment at which the change came about in the body so that they were human bodies. It seemed a very sound and good dream and I wondered what the others would think of it when I told it to them. I was awake now and the cider was cool and fresh but I could still feel the muscles I had in the dream when my body had been a horse's body. This was not helping me with the soul and I tried to think what it must be in the terms that I believed. Probably a spring of clear fresh water that never diminished in the drought and never froze in the winter was closest to what we had instead of the soul they all talked about. I remembered how when I was a boy the Chicago White Sox had a third baseman named Harry Lord who could foul off pitches down the third base-line until the opposing pitcher was worn out or it would get dark and the game be called. I was very young then and everything was exaggerated, but I can remember it beginning to get dark, this was before there were lights in ballparks, and Harry still fouling them off and the crowd shouting, "Lord, Lord, save your soul." This was the closest I had ever come to the soul. Once I had thought my own soul had been blown out of me when I was a boy and then that it had come back in again. But in those days I was very egotistical and I had heard so much talk about the soul and read so much about it that I had assumed that I had one. Then I began to think if Miss Mary or G.C. or Ngui or Charo or I had been killed by the lion would our souls have flown off somewhere? I could not believe it and I thought that we would all just have been dead, deader than the lion perhaps, and no one was worrying about his soul. The worst part would have been the trip to Nairobi and the inquiry although that would be easier because Harry Dunn had been present and he was a policeman. But all I really knew was that it would have been very bad for G.C.'s career if Mary or I had been killed. It would have been bad luck for G.C. if he had been killed. It would have certainly been very bad for my writing if I had been killed. Neither Charo nor Ngui would have liked to be killed and if she had been killed it would have come as a great surprise to Miss Mary. It was something to be avoided and it was a relief to not have to put yourself in a position where it could happen day after day.

But what did this have to do with "In a real dark night of the soul it is always three o'clock in the morning, day after day"? Did Miss Mary and G.C. have souls? They had no religious beliefs as far as I knew. But if people had souls they must have them. Charo was a very devout Mohammedan so we must credit him with a soul. That left only Ngui and me and the lion.

Now here it was three o'clock in the morning and I stretched my recent horse's legs and thought I would get up and go outside and sit by the coals of the fire and enjoy the rest of the night and the first light. I pulled on my mosquito boots and put on my bathrobe and buckled the pistol belt over it and went out to the remains of the fire. G.C. was sitting by it in his chair.

"What are we awake about?" he said very softly.

"I had a dream I was a horse. It was very vivid."

"Did you train well? Or had you been retired to stud?"

"There was something about stud. But I woke up before that."

"I had bloody nightmares."

"What kind?"

"I can't remember them."

"Do you think we're getting to be the nervous irascible type?"

"You maybe. Me never."

"You're the home-loving, faithful husband, rather inarticulate type."

"Am I not. Whose husband am I faithful to?"

"Miss Mary's."

"That bastard. What was it you dreamed you were? A horse's ass?"

"It will seem funny not to hunt the old bastard anymore."

"It will. I have to talk to you about something."

"You're sure I should hear it?"

"Yes. I thought if I came out here you'd probably show up."

"I didn't hear you."

"You probably did and didn't notice it."

"Could be but I don't think so."

We sat and watched the light early morning winds from the mountain blow on the coals of the fire until the wood caught that I had put on it and G.C. told me what I needed to know about the next police operation that we were involved in. It seemed very sound and could be very effective. When he finished he asked me if I had any questions and I said I thought I understood it.

"You just go on as you are unless you have word from me or from Harry or that infant police asks you for help. But he mustn't do anything until the trap's pulled."

"Good," I said. "He's sick anyway."

"I shouldn't have any contact with him up there nor let anyone there see you with him before this show."

"I won't."

221

We sat and watched the fire that was burning brightly now and lighting the tents and the trees. It was half past three or a quarter to four by now or maybe four. I told G.C. about Scott Fitzgerald and the quotation and asked him what he thought of it.

"Any hour can be a bad hour when you wake," he said. "I don't see why he picked three especially. It sounds quite good though."

"I think it is just fear and worry and remorse."

"We've both had enough of those, haven't we?"

"Sure; to peddle. But I think what he meant was his conscience and despair."

"You don't ever have despair do you, Ernie?"

"Not yet."

"You'd probably have had it by now if you were going to have it."

"I've seen it close enough to touch it but I always turned it down."

"Speaking of turning things down, should we share a beer?"

"I'll get it."

The big bottle of Tusker was cold too in the canvas water bag and I poured beer into two glasses and set the bottle on the table.

"I'm sorry to have to go, Ernie," G.C. said. "Do you think she'll take it really badly?"

"Yes."

"You ride it out. She may take it perfectly all right."

"She won't. I wish Pop were here. He can con her into anything. He's had women shooting lions for years and they were always happy. I wish he were here so that she could complain to him about us if nothing more."

"You be good and she'll get it all straightened out. Be kind and patient."

"Like you."

"You're older. You're supposed to have all sorts of splendid traits I haven't."

"How many times did you shoot?"

"We'll count the shells. You?"

"Six."

"You hitting him wasn't any miracle. I was sure you'd hit him. But hitting him where you did was a bloody first-class miracle and the luck of a son of a bitch."

"At your service."

"Did you see how the boys were about it?"

"It did the religion a lot of good."

"Did it not. You try for another miracle now with Miss Mary."

"It's going to be bad," I said. "But she'll get over it like everything else."

"Do you really think we get over everything?"

"We have so far, haven't we?"

"*We've* not had anything to get over. All we've had is a bloody wonderful time. We've had too good a time."

"I'm not talking about that. I'm talking about what we've come through to be able to be happy now."

"That's worthless to talk about this time of morning. You won't have any trouble getting that leopard. He's a control leopard, you know, and you can take him any way you want to."

"No. I have to take him straight."

"That's right. I'd forgotten. But you've plenty of time."

"I'm not worried about him."

"I wish I could stay another day. The scouts want to make a real ngoma. That might just do the trick with Mary."

It was beginning to get light now and I heard the noise of a lorry a long way off on the road.

"Now who would that be?" G.C. asked.

"Some character that must have followed orders and camped for the night and then got going early."

"He must have a guilty conscience."

"Probably Mr. Singh then."

"Not necessarily."

We listened to the lorry come down the hill and then on the flat. Then we heard it stop and then start again and go off again on the flat road.

"That was odd," G.C. said.

"We've had odder. Here, have the rest of this."

We sat and watched it get light and Mwindi and G.C.'s boy brought tea. Harry came out and brought his tea and then Arap Meina came up and saluted and handed G.C. an envelope. "The lorry brought it, Bwana. I met them on the road."

G.C. tore it open and read it then handed it to Harry.

"I'm here another day," G.C. said to me.

"I must get off," Harry said. "You're letting the Memsahib sleep late, I hope. You'll say good-bye for me and thank her so much, will you?"

"When will we see you, Harry?"

"I'll try to get up here after Christmas. Maybe I can bring the wife. She's never been out on a safari."

"That will be wonderful. Mary will be very happy."

"You're sure you wouldn't mind? We'd just drop in."

"We'd be delighted."

"I'll just get something to eat and we'll be off."

We did no shouting or calling. I went back to the lines to give the orders and we talked very low so that Mary would not be wakened. Out at the lines I talked with Keiti and saw that the lion was in the lorry still in the shade of a big tree and it was cool there and his body was cold. I knew Mary wanted to measure him and there would be time to do that after she got up and still be time to skin him while the day was still cool. A lion after he has died and stiffened has little dignity. His mane is flattened and matted and he looks heavy, ugly, too wide, and strangely foreshortened. His eyes were sunken and the lip was drawn back from the long, heavy canine teeth. Looking at him I was glad that we had not killed the great lion under the escarpment out from Fig Tree camp. I could always remember him as he burst out bounding through us, his unbelievable speed and his roaring as he came.

I came back to the mess tent and had breakfast with Harry and G.C. and then Harry's Land Rover was loaded and he was gone with his boy and his two askaris. He did not look back and wave. His two askaris sat very stiffly with their rifles and his personal servant, who was a converted Mau Mau, imitated them.

"He had a good time," G.C. said. "I think it took his mind off things."

"Did he say anything about his sergeant?"

"No. He didn't mention him."

"Is he going on a bad show now?"

"Very."

"I hope he can make it up here after Christmas with his wife."

"So do I," said G.C.

I went into the tent to see if Mary was awake. But she was still sleeping heavily. She had awakened and drunk some of her tea and then gone back to sleep again.

"We'll let her sleep," I said to G.C. "It doesn't make any difference if we don't skin out until half past nine even. She should get all the sleep she can."

G.C. was reading the Lindbergh book but I had no stomach for *The Day of the Lion* this morning and so I read the bird book. It was a good new book called *African Handbook of Birds* and I knew that by hunting one beast too hard and concentrating on him I had missed much in not observing the birds properly. If there had been no animals we could have been quite happy observing the birds but I knew that I had neglected them terribly. Mary had been much better. She was always seeing birds that I did not notice or watching them in detail while I sat in my camp chair and just looked out across the country. Reading the bird book I felt how stupid I had been and how much time I had wasted.

At home sitting in the shade at the head of the pool it made me happy to see the kingbirds dip down to take insects off the water and to watch the gray white of their breasts show green from the reflection of the pool. I loved to watch the doves nesting in the alamo trees and to watch the mockingbirds as they sang. Seeing the migratory birds come through in the fall and the spring was an excitement and it made an afternoon happy to see the small bittern come to drink at the pool and watch him search the gutters for tree frogs. Now here in Africa there were beautiful birds around the camp all of the time. They were in the trees and in the thorn bushes and walking about on the ground and I only half saw them as moving bits of color while Mary loved and knew them all. I could not think how I had become so stupid and calloused about the birds and I was very ashamed.

For a long time I realized I had only paid attention to the predators, the scavengers, and the birds that were good to eat and the birds that had to do with hunting. Then as I thought of which birds I did notice there came such a great long list of them that I did not feel quite as bad but I resolved to watch the birds around our camp more and to ask Mary about all the ones I did not know and most of all to really see them and not look past them.

This looking and not seeing things was a great sin, I thought, and one that was easy to fall into. It was always the beginning of something bad and I thought that we did not deserve to live in the world if we did not see it. I tried to think how I had gotten into not seeing the small birds around camp and I thought some of it was reading too much to take my mind off the concentration of the serious hunting and some was certainly drinking in camp to relax when we came in from hunting. I admired Mayito who drank almost nothing because he wanted to remember everything in Africa. But G.C. and I were drinkers and I knew it was not just a habit nor a way of escaping. It was a purposeful dulling of a receptivity that was so highly sensitized, as film can be, that if your receptiveness were always kept at the same level it would become unbearable. You make out quite a noble case for yourself, I thought, and you know too that you and G.C. drink because you love it too and Mary loves it the same way and we have such good fun drinking. You better go in and see if she is awake now, I thought.

So I went in and she was still asleep. She always looked beautiful asleep. Her face, when she slept, was neither happy nor unhappy. It simply existed. But today the line of it was too finely drawn. I wished that I could make her happy but the only thing I knew to do for this was to let her keep on sleeping.

I went out again with the bird book and identified the shrike, the starling, and the bee-eater and then I heard movement in the tent and went in and found Mary sitting on the edge of her cot putting her moccasins on.

"How do you feel, honey?"

"Awful. And you shot at my lion first and I'd rather not see you."

She put on her dressing gown and started on the trail that ran across the meadow toward the round, slanted-top tent that just showed in the edge of the fever trees.

I went over to the mess tent where G.C. was reading.

"How did Miss Mary wake?"

"She feels bad. Also I shot the lion first and she'd rather not see me."

"You're rather a conspicuous object."

"I'll keep out of sight. After breakfast she better measure him and then they get to skinning. Any bullets are yours."

"She'll feel better."

"She really feels bad, G.C. I know just how she feels. Let's not talk about it. I feel sick about how she feels."

"I can't say to her that if you *had* shot first the lion would have rolled over like a bloody rabbit because of course it mightn't of. But that's the form."

"No, for God's sake don't say that."

"I'll say the truth which is that she fired and hit him and then she hit him again. Does she have any bullets in him?"

"No. They both had exit holes. I checked last night."

"It will turn out all right. You'll see."

"I'll go out babooning or get some meat."

"Take a drink and cheer up. We've been up since three."

"Should we split a beer?"

"I don't think it would harm us."

G.C. poured a gin and shook some bitters in it and poured another one for me. We tipped them down and then each drank a glass of the cool Tusker beer.

"I think the day will come out all right," G.C. said. "Mary's a really wonderful girl."

"I'll just keep out of the way for a while."

I was on the far side of the tent headed for the lines when I heard G.C. say, "Good morning, Miss Mary."

"Good morning, G.C."

"How are you feeling?"

"I'll feel much better. Did Papa go out?"

"Yes. He had something to do."

I felt bad about overhearing so I started back for the tent.

"Did you want me for anything, Kitten?" I asked Mary.

"No. I only wanted to say I was sorry about starting in again on the lion."

"I understand about it. Only I didn't shoot him first."

"Let's not talk about it," she said. "Please, let's not talk about it."

"I'm going out and check some stuff with Arap Meina," I said. "I'll be back after a while. Do you feel better, honey?"

"I'm sure I will."

Out at the lines Keiti told me that the Game Scouts were planning a really big ngoma, everyone in the camp would be dancing, and the whole shamba was coming. Keiti said that we were short of beer and of Coca-Cola and I said I would go up to Loitokitok in the hunting car with Mthuka and Arap Meina and anybody who wanted to buy anything in the village. Keiti wanted some more posho too and I would try to get a sack or a couple of sacks as well as some sugar. The Wakamba liked the cornmeal that was brought in by way of Kajiado and sold by the Indian duka whose owner was a follower of the Agha Khan. They did not like the other type that was sold in the other Indian general stores. I had learned to tell the kind they liked by color, texture, and taste, but I could always make a mistake and Mthuka would check. The Coca-Cola was for the Mohammedans who could not drink beer and for the girls and the women who would come to the ngoma. I would drop Arap Meina off at the first Masai manyatta, and he would tell the Masai to come and see the lion so they would know, surely, that he had been killed. They were not invited to the ngoma which was to be strictly Wakamba.

I told G.C. what I was going to do. Mary had gone off to the tent in the fever trees again after breakfast and G.C. said they were going over to measure and take pictures of the skinning out as soon as she was back. He asked me to pick up the Informer and bring him in if I ran into him and to pick up a piece of meat on my way back. So I took Pop's gunbearer to stay with my rifle and Keiti said he would go along to check on the posho and halal anything I killed so the meat would be legal.

This made us a serious outfit with Keiti along so Mthuka and I did not stop at the shamba or even go through it. I met the Informer on the road and told him to go on into camp, that G.C. wanted to see him. We went on to the turn-off for the first Masai manyatta and I dropped Arap Meina. I knew he would like to have driven in, left his message, and then gone up to town with us but he knew too that we were trying to build up our seriousness with Keiti so I just dropped him off and in his faded khaki uniform and flat-topped Camel Corps cap, his rifle slung he started into the worn trail through the broken brush and we went on along the red road that rose steadily until it started to loop and climb up the side of the lower mountain. We could see the tin roofs and the dark trees of Loitokitok across the rising shoulder of mountain to our left. That was the last shelf before the dark forests rose in the upthrust of the mountain. We were too close now to see any of the high part of the mountain and the snows were far above our vision. It was all dark-blue wooded mountain and as I looked behind us I could see the green forests at the base of the mountain, the plains dotted and broken with trees, the wild broken country toward the Chyulus and the swamp before the far blue hills and the badlands of the red and yellow desert. The road climbed at an easy gradient and then made several steep turns. We stopped and picked up Masai from the man-yattas that we knew until the car was full and then climbed the two steep twisting turns that led to the last climb onto the shelf where the town was strung along the single street. We stopped in front of the gasoline pumps and the duka where we traded and the Masai got down and Keiti got down. I passed my rifle back to Pop's gunbearer Mwengi who locked it in the rack that was built against the back of the front seat. I told Keiti I would go down to Mr. Singh's to order the beer and soft drinks and told Mthuka to get the car filled with petrol and then drive it down to Mr. Singh's and put it in the shade. I did not go into the big general store with Keiti but walked down under the shade of the trees to Mr. Singh's.

It was cool inside and smelled of cooking from the kitchen in the living quarters and of sawdust from the sawmill. Mr. Singh had only three cases of beer but thought he could get two more at a place across the street. Three Masai elders came in from the disreputable drinking place next door. We were friends and greeted each other with dignity and I could smell they had already been drinking Golden Jeep sherry which accounted for the affection that was mixed with their dignity. Mr. Singh had only six bottles of beer cold so I bought two for the three of them and one for my-self and told them Miss Mary had killed the big lion. We drank to each other and to Miss Mary and the lion and then I excused myself because I had business with Mr. Singh in the back room.

There was no real business. Mr. Singh wanted me to eat something with him and drink a whiskey and water with him. He had something to tell me that I couldn't understand and went out and got a mission-educated boy to translate for him. This young man wore trousers and a white shirt, tucked in, and big, heavy, black square-toed boots which were the badge of his education and civilization.

"Sir," he said. "Mr. Singh here requests me to tell you that these Masai chiefs take a constant advantage of you in respect to beer. They congregate at the beer hall next door which calls itself a tearoom and when they see you arrive they come over solely to take an advantage of you."

"I know those three elders and they are not chiefs."

"I used the designation chiefs as one speaks to a European," the mission-educated boy said. "But the observation of Mr. Singh here is exact; they abuse your friendship in respect to beer."

Mr. Singh nodded his head solemnly and handed me the bottle of White Heather. He had understood two words of the mission English: friendship and beer.

"One thing must always be clear. I am not a European. We are Americans."

"But there is no such distinction. You are classified as Europeans."

"It is a classification that will be remedied. I am not a European. Mr. Singh and I are brothers."

I poured water in my glass as did Mr. Singh. We toasted each other and then embraced. We then stood and looked at the oleograph of the original Singh strangling the two lions one in each hand. We were both deeply moved.

"You are a follower of the Baby Jesus I presume?" I asked the mission-educated Chagga.

"I am a Christian," he said with dignity.

Mr. Singh and I looked at each other sadly and shook our heads. Then Mr. Singh spoke to the interpreter.

"Mr. Singh here says he is saving the three cold bottles for you and your people. When the Masai mzees return he will serve them wine."

"Excellent," I said. "Will you see if my people have arrived in my shooting brake?"

He went out and Mr. Singh tapped his head with his forefinger and offered me the White Heather in the square squat bottle. He said he was sorry we had no time to eat together. I told him to keep off the goddamn roads at night. He asked me how I liked the interpreter. I said he was marvelous and had strong black shoes to prove his Christianity.

"Two of your people are outside with the shooting lorry," the interpreter said as he came in.

"Shooting brake," I said and went out to motion Mthuka in. He came in in his check-striped shirt, tall and stooped and long lipped with the beautiful Kamba arrow scars on his cheeks. He saluted Mrs. Singh behind the counter where the bolts of cloth, beads, medicines, and novelty goods were and looked at her appreciatively. His grandfather had been a cannibal and his father was Keiti and he was fifty-five at least. Mr. Singh gave him one of the cold quarts of beer and handed me mine which had been corked up. He drank a third of his and said, "I'll take it out to Mwengi."

"No. We have a cold one for him too."

"I'll take this out now and we will keep watch."

"There are two left," Mr. Singh said. Mthuka nodded.

"Give the interpreter an Orange Crush," I said.

Holding his soft drink the interpreter said, "Before your friends the Masai return may I ask a few questions, sir?"

"Certainly. How is the Orange Crush?"

"Delicious, sir."

"Next year we will have bubble gum."

"There is bubble gum already. But it is very expensive."

"What are the questions?"

"Sir, how many aircraft do you have?"

"Eight."

"You must be one of the richest men in the world."

"I am," I said modestly.

"Why then, sir, do you come here to do the work of a game ranger?"

"Why do some go to Mecca? Why does any man go anywhere? Why would you go to Rome?"

"I am not of the Catholic faith. I would not go to Rome."

"I thought you were not of that faith from the shoes."

"We have many things in common with the Catholic faith but we do not worship images."

"Too bad. There are many great images."

"I would like to be a Game Scout and have employment with you, sir, or with the Bwana Game."

Just then the Masai elders returned bringing with them two new comrades. I had never met them but my oldest friend among the elders told me that they had many problems with lions who not only carried cattle out of the bomas but donkeys, morani, totos, women, and goats. They would like for Miss Mary and me to come and liberate them from this terror. All these Masai were quite drunk by now and one was a little inclined to be rude.

We had known many fine Masai and great ones and unspoiled Masai but drinking was foreign to Masai as it was natural to Kamba and they disintegrated under it and some of the elders could remember when they were a great ruling tribe of warriors and raiders instead of a syphilis-ridden, anthropological, cattle-worshiping curiosity. This new comrade elder was drunk at eleven o'clock in the morning and rude drunk. That was apparent from his first question, and I decided to use the interpreter to make a formal distance between us and also, since the five elders were carrying spears of morani length which showed bad tribal discipline, it was almost certain that the interpreter would be speared first since it was he who would utter the provoking words if there should be such words uttered. If there was an argument with five drunken, spear-carrying Masai in the small front room of a general store one was certain oneself of being speared. But the presence of the interpreter meant that you had a chance to get three of your drunken friends with the pistol instead of one or possibly two. I moved the holster around so it lay on the front of the leg, was pleased that it was buckled down and tripped the buckle on the strap with my little finger.

"Interpret, big shoes," I said. "Interpret accurately."

"He here says, sir, that he has heard that one of your wives, he said women, has killed a lion and that he wonders if in your tribe the killing of lions is left to the womens."

"Tell the great chief who I have never met that in my tribe we sometimes leave the killing of lions to women as in his tribe he leaves to the young warriors the drinking of Golden Jeep sherry. There are young warriors who spend their time drinking and have never killed a lion or a man."

The interpreter was sweating hard at this moment and things were not getting good. The Masai who was a good-looking old man of possibly my own age or possibly older spoke and the interpreter said, "He here says, sir, that if you had wished to be polite and to talk as one chief to another you would have learned his language so that you and he could talk together as man to man."

It was over now and cheap enough so I said, "Say to this chief who I have not known until now that I am ashamed not to have learned his language properly. It has been my duty to hunt lions. The wife I have brought here has the duty to hunt lions. She has killed yesterday and there are two more bottles of cold beer here which I was reserving for my people, but I will drink one of them with this chief and with him only and Mr. Singh will provide wine for all other chiefs."

The interpreter said this and the Masai came forward and shook hands. I buttoned the strap on the holster and patted the gun back against my thigh where it belonged.

"An Orange Crush for the interpreter," I said to Mr. Singh. The interpreter took it but the Masai who had wanted trouble spoke to him earnestly and confidentially. The interpreter took one swallow of his soft drink to clear his throat and said to me, "This chief here asks in absolute confidence how much you paid for this wife who kills lions. He says that such a wife for breeding could be as valuable as a great bull."

"Tell the chief, who I see is a man of great intelligence, that I paid two small airplanes and one larger airplane and one hundred head of cattle for this wife."

The Masai elder and I drank together and then he spoke to me again rapidly and seriously.

"He says that is a great price to pay for any wife and no woman could be worth that. He said you spoke of cattle. Were they cows or were there bulls too?"

I explained that the ndege were not new aircraft but had been used in war. The cattle I said were all cows.

The old Masai said this was more understandable but no woman could be worth that much money.

I agreed that it was a high price but that the wife had been worth it. Now, I said, it was necessary for me to return to the camp. I ordered another round of the wine and left the big beer bottle with the elder. We had drunk from glasses and I set my glass top-down on the counter. He urged me to take another glass and I poured one half-full and drained it. We shook hands and I smelled the leather and smoke and dried dung and sweat smell that is not unpleasant and I went out into the sharp light of the road with the hunting car half-shaded by the leaves. Mr. Singh had five cases of beer in the back of the car and his boy brought out the last cold bottle wrapped in a newspaper. He had figured the beer and the bottle of wine for the Masai on a pad of paper and I paid him and gave the interpreter a five shilling note.

"I would prefer employment, sir."

"I cannot give you employment except as an interpreter. This has been given and paid for."

"I would like to come with you as an interpreter."

"Would you interpret between me and the animals?"

"I could learn, sir. I speak Swahili, Masai, Chagga, and of course English as you see."

"Do you speak Kamba?"

"No, sir."

"We speak Kamba."

"I could learn it easily, sir. I could tutor you to speak proper Swahili and you could teach me hunting and the language of animals. Do not be prejudiced against me because I am a Christian. It was my parents who sent me to the mission school."

"Did you not like the mission school? Remember God is listening. He hears your every word."

"No, sir. I hated the mission school. I am a Christian through instruction and ignorance."

"We will take you out hunting some time. But you will have to come barefoot and in shorts."

"I hate my shoes, sir. I must wear them because of Bwana McCrea. If it were reported to him that I was without my shoes or that I had been with you in Mr. Singh's I would be punished. Even if I had only drunk Coca-Cola. Coca-Cola is the first step, Bwana McCrea says."

"We will take you to hunt sometime. But you are not from a hunting tribe. What good will it do? You will be frightened and you will be unhappy."

"Sir, if you will keep me in your mind I will prove myself to you. With this five shillings I will make a down payment on a spear at Benji's store. I will walk at night without the shoes to toughen my feet as those of a hunter's are. If you ask me for a proof I will make a proof."

"You are a good boy but I do not wish to interfere with your religion and I have nothing to offer you."

"I will make you a proof," he said.

"Kwisha," I said. Then to Mthuka, "Kwenda na duka."

In the duka it was very crowded with Masai shopping and watching others who were buying. The women stared at you boldly from head to foot and the young warriors with their heavy ochered pigtails and bangs were insolent and cheerful. Masai smell good and the women have cold hands and once their hand is in yours they never remove it but delight in the warmth of your palm and explore it happily without movement. Benji's was a cheerful busy place like an Indian trading post at home on a Saturday afternoon or a monthly pay-off day. Keiti had found good posho and all the Coca-Cola and soft drinks that were needed for the ngoma and he was ordering a few unnecessary items from high shelves so that he could watch the lovely and intelligent Indian girl, who was in love with G.C. from a great distance and who we all admired and would have been in love with if it were not useless, reaching them down and bringing them to him. This was the first time that I had seen how Keiti loved to watch this girl and I was happy that it gave us a faint advantage over him. She spoke to me in her lovely voice and asked about Miss Mary and said how happy she was about the lion and while I took great pleasure in seeing her and hearing her voice and in our shaking hands I could not help seeing how far gone Keiti was. It was only then I noticed how smart and fresh and well pressed his clothes were and that he was wearing his best safari uniform and his good turban.

The people from the duka aided by Mthuka started taking the sacks of meal and the cases of soft drinks out and I paid the bill and bought a half-dozen whistles for the ngoma. Then, since the duka was short-handed, I went out to guard the rifle while Mwengi helped with the cases. I would have been glad to help with the loading but it was not considered seemly. When we were alone hunting we always worked together but in town and in public it would have been misunderstood so I sat in the front seat with the rifle between my legs and heard the petitions of the Masai who wanted to ride down the mountain with us. The Chevrolet truck chassis on which the hunting car body had been built had good brakes but with the load we had we could not carry more than about six extra people. I had seen days of a dozen or more. But it was too dangerous on the curves which sometimes made the Masai women sick. We never carried warriors down the mountain road although we often picked them up coming up. At first there had been some bitterness about this but now it was an accepted practice and men we had carried up would explain it to the others.

Finally we had everything stowed and four women with their bags, bundles, gourds, and mixed loads were in the back, three more sat on the second seat with Keiti at the right of them, and myself, Mwengi, and Mthuka in front. We started off with the Masai waving and I opened the cold bottle of beer still wrapped in the newspapers and offered it to Mwengi. He motioned for me to drink and sank lower in the seat to be out of sight of Keiti. I drank and handed it to him and he drank deep using the side of his mouth to not tip the big quart bottle into sight. He handed it back to me and I offered it to Mthuka.

"Later," he said.

"When a woman is sick," Mwengi said.

Mthuka was driving very carefully getting the feel of his load on the steep dropping turns. Usually there would have been a Masai woman between Mthuka and me; one we knew was proof against road sickness and two more being tested out between Ngui and Mwengi in the second seat. Now we all felt three women were being wasted on Keiti. One of them was a famous beauty who was as tall as I was, built wonderfully, and with the coldest and most insistent hands I had ever known. She usually sat between Mthuka and me on the front seat and she held my hand and courted Mthuka lightly and purposefully with her other hand while she looked at us both and laughed when there were reactions to her courtship. She was very classically beautiful with a lovely skin and she was quite shameless. I knew that both Ngui and Mthuka gave her their favors. She was curious about me and loved to provoke visible reactions and when we dropped her off to go to her manyatta someone almost always dropped off with her too and made his way to camp later by foot.

But today we were riding down the road looking out on all our own country. Mthuka could not even have any beer because of Keiti his father sitting directly behind him, and I was thinking about morality and drinking beer with Mwengi, we having torn a mark in the paper covering the bottle to mark the place below which the beer all belonged to Mthuka. According to basic morality it was perfectly all right for two of my best friends to go with this Masai woman, but if I did so while I was on probation as a Wakamba and while Debba and I felt seriously about each other it would have proved me to be irresponsible and profligate and not a serious man. On the other hand if I had not responded, visibly, when in unsought contact or when incited it would have been very bad all around. These simple studies in our tribal moeurs always made the trips to Loitokitok pleasant and instructive but sometimes, until you understood them, they could have been frustrating and puzzling except that you knew that if you wished to be a good Wakamba it was necessary never to be frustrated and to never admit that you were puzzled.

Finally they called out from the back of the car that a woman was sick and I signaled to Mthuka to stop the car. We knew Keiti would take advantage of this halt to go into the brush and urinate so when he did with great dignity and casualness I passed the quart of beer to Mthuka and he drank his share rapidly leaving the rest for Mwengi and me.

"Drink it before it gets hot."

The car loaded up again and with three unloadings we were relieved of our passengers and across the stream and going through the park country toward camp. We saw a herd of impala crossing through the woods, and I got out of the car with Keiti to head them off. They looked red against the heavy green, and a young buck looked back as I whistled almost silently. I held my breath, squeezed softly, and broke his neck, and Keiti ran toward him to halal as the others leaped and jumped floatingly into the cover.

I did not go up with Keiti to see him halal so it was a question of his own conscience and I knew his conscience was not as rigid as Charo's. But I did not want to lose the buck for the Mohammedans any more than I had wanted to shoot up the meat so I walked forward slowly over the springy grass and when I came up he had cut the impala's throat and was smiling.

"Piga mzuri," he said.

"Why not?" I said. "Shaitani."

"Hapana shaitani. Piga mzuri sana."

I told Keiti not to get his clean uniform dirty and Mwengi, Mthuka, and I picked the impala up and swung him into the back of the car where he bled in a quiet and genteel manner onto the cases of Coca-Cola. Mthuka laughed, since I had put his head there, and when we shut the tailgate Mwengi said, "Now we've halalled the Coca-Cola."

We drove into camp and stopped by the lines, and I went to find G.C. and tell him I'd killed an impala for camp meat and for the Mohammedans and to ask him what he needed for camp if he had not picked it up. I saw Mary was lying down in the tent and she looked to be sleeping. I did not disturb her. G.C. was in the mess tent.

"Have a good trip?" he asked. "Mary's morale's much better but she isn't feeling well. She's napping."

"How are you?"

"This nonsense just keeps me on the trail from here to the latrine."

"How's Lindbergh?"

"He's still up there."

"Good thing we know how it came out. What do you want me to get for meat? I shot an impala for us."

"There's your people and my people and my people on the road tomorrow and a few odds and ends for the shamba for the ngoma."

"I'd better get out now. What do you want? A zebra and a wildebeest?"

"I'd think so."

There were three cold quarts of beer in one of the big canvas cooling bags and I said that I would take them and I went into the private stores box and got some tins of kipper snacks and some shrimps. I told Nguili to take these out to the hunting car and then found Ngui and told him to get my binoculars and a shell bag and the big gun. I told him to get Mwengi and Mthuka. We were going out to drink beer and kill some meat.

"Better kill meat and then drink beer," Mwindi said who was standing by us.

"Thank you very much," I said. "Bring me my big hat that is soaked in the water, please."

I went to the stores and found three bottles of Carlsberg beer. They were small and thin and we eased them into the cold, beaded water bag that swung on the side of the car.

"Let's go," I said.

"Where?" Mthuka asked as he turned the car in a half circle out of the lines.

I pointed north toward the open park country and the green and white fields. He took off straight to the north. There were high clouds coming off the mountain now that made passing shadows over the plain, and I thought that we would go up to the northern end of the park-like country and leave the car and sit in the shade and drink beer and wait for some game to graze into range. But it was too close to noon and the game was not moving, so we left the car in the shade and Ngui and I worked up until we were close to some wildebeest and I shot a young bull. The others galloped off then stood to look back. A dozen zebra came by in the opening galloping through the white flowered field and I shot a stallion. He fell, black-striped in the white flowers about fifty yards from where the wildebeest lay black in the field of white. I had not wanted to kill anything and had wanted to put it off. But it was necessary to get the meat. Ngui and I walked up to them and I took out the pistol to shoot the zebra in the back of the neck. He had a beautiful hide and the unsuccessful look of a dead horse. But Ngui touched his eyes with the point of his knife and said, "Hapana." We walked on to the wildebeest and I shot him at the base of the brain with the pistol. He quivered and stretched his legs stiff, then relaxed. The car came toward us leaving dark wheel tracks through the carpet of flowers and the four of us got the wildebeest into the back. He was heavy and as awkward a load as ever to lift and the zebra was heavy too and we had to work to load him. We should have emptied them out but there were people who would come to the ngoma who would value all the tripe and bits and we did not feel like butchering in the hot noon sun. Putting them in the car reminded me of bringing fish in over the stern of the boat except for the heavy lifting at the back. While we were washing our hands with water from the drinking water sack and I was picking ticks off and Ngui picking ticks off my back and shoulders I thought what a damned fool I had been not to bring someone else along to help load but I had been planning a pleasant sort of picnic to make up for the discipline of the trip up the mountain and had forgotten the abattoir realities.

Now we were all back in the car and I opened two of the cold bottles of beer and passed one to Ngui and Mwengi and Mthuka and I took the other. I said we would drive back and cut the track that led from the shamba to camp and pick up anyone coming in to give them a lift. The cold beer tasted very good after the lifting and hauling and we drank it in long double swallows. It was not the way I had planned to drink it. But that could be for another day.

On the track we picked up three women with babies on their way into camp and I heard Ngui and Mwengi talking to them and them laughing. But I could not understand what they said. There were people all under the trees and out behind the lines, the women with their lovely brown heads and faces in their bright cloth top covers and beautiful wide bead collars and bracelets. The big drum had been brought down from the shamba and the Game Scouts had three other drums. It was early yet but the ngoma was starting to take shape. We rode past the people and the preparations and stopped in the shade and the women got out and children came running to see the animals unloaded. I handed the rifle to Ngui to clean and walked over to the mess tent. The wind was blowing quite hard from the mountain now and the mess tent was cool and pleasant.

"You took all our cold beer," Miss Mary said. "What was that about?" She looked much better and more rested.

"I brought one bottle back. It's coming in the bag. How are you, honey?"

"G.C. and I are much better. We didn't find your bullet. Only G.C.'s. My, a lion looks so noble and beautiful when he is white and naked. He's dignified again as when he is alive. Did you have fun at Loitokitok?"

"Yes. We did all the errands."

"I'd like to have gone out with you when you went for the meat. But I was asleep."

"What did you get, Papa?" G.C. asked.

"What you asked for."

"I heard two shots."

"Don't make fun. I'm new here and I'm just trying to get along."

"Make him welcome, Miss Mary," G.C. said. "Show him around and see that he's comfortable. You've seen a ngoma before, haven't you, my good man?"

"Yes, sir," I said. "And we have them in my own country too. We are all very fond of them."

"Is that what they call baseball in America? I always thought that was a form of rounders."

"At home, sir, our ngomas are a sort of harvest festival with folk dancing. It's rather like your cricket I believe."

"Quite," said G.C. "But this ngoma is something new. It's going to be danced entirely by natives."

"What fun, sir," I said. "May I accompany Miss Mary, as you call this charming young lady, to the ngoma?"

"I've been spoken for," Miss Mary said. "I'm going to the ngoma with Mr. Chungo of the Game Scouts Department."

"The hell you are, Miss Mary," G.C. said.

"Is Mr. Chungo that very well-built young man with the mustache and shorts who was fixing ostrich plumes onto his head, sir?"

"That would probably be Mr. Chungo."

"He looked a very good sort, sir. Is he one of your colleagues in the Game Scouts Department? I must say, sir, you have a magnificent body of men."

"I am in love with Mr. Chungo and he is my hero," Miss Mary said. "He told me that you were a liar and had never hit the lion at all. He said all the boys know you are a liar and Ngui and some of the others only pretend to be friends of yours because you give them presents all the time and have no discipline. He said look how Ngui had broken your best knife that you paid so much money for in Paris that day when you came home drunk."

"Yes, yes," I said. "I do remember seeing old Chungo in Paris. Yes. Yes. I remember. Yes. Yes."

"No. No." G.C. said absentmindedly. "No. No. *Not* Mr. Chungo. He's not a member."

"Yes. Yes," I said. "I'm afraid he is, sir."

"Mr. Chungo told me another interesting thing too. He told me that you had been using Wakamba arrow poisoning on your solids and that Ngui makes it for you and that all this risasi moja business of one shot kills is the effect of the arrow poisoning. He offered to show me how fast the arrow poisoning would run up a stream of blood dripping from his own leg."

"Dear, dear. Do you think she had best go to the ngoma with your colleague Mr. Chungo, sir? It may all be absolutely tickety-boo but she still is a memsahib, sir. She still comes under the White Man's Burden Act."

"She'll go to the ngoma with me," G.C. said. "Make us a drink, Miss Mary; or no, I will."

"I can make drinks still," Miss Mary said. "Don't you both look so sinister. I made it all up about Mr. Chungo. Someone has to make jokes here sometimes beside Papa and his pagans and you and Papa and your night wildness and wickedness. What time did you all get up this morning?"

"Not too early. Is it still the same day?"

"The days run into each other and into each other and into each other," Miss Mary said. "That's in my poem about Africa."

Miss Mary was writing a great poem about Africa but the trouble was that she made it up in her head sometimes and forgot to write it down and then it would be gone like dreams. She wrote some of it down but she would not show it to anybody. We all had great faith in her poem about Africa and I still have but I would like it better if she would actually write it. We were all reading the *Georgics* then in the C. Day Lewis translation. We had two copies then but they were always being lost or mislaid and I have never known a book to be more mislayable. The only fault I could ever find with the Mantuan was that he made all normally intelligent people feel as though they too could write great poetry. Dante only made crazy people feel they could write great poetry. That was not true of course but then almost nothing was true and especially not in Africa. In Africa a thing is true at first light and a lie by noon and you have no more respect for it than for the lovely, perfect weed-fringed lake you see across the sun-baked salt plain. You have walked across that plain in the morning and you know that no such lake is there. But now it is there absolutely true, beautiful and believable.

"Is that really in the poem?" I asked Miss Mary.

"Yes, of course."

"Then write it down before it gets to sound like a traffic accident."

"You don't have to spoil people's poems as well as shoot their lions."

G.C. looked up at me like a weary schoolboy and I said, "I found my *Georgics* if you want it. It is the one that hasn't got the introduction by Louis Bromfield in it. That's how you can tell it."

"You can tell mine because it has my name in it."

"And an introduction by Louis Bromfield."

"Who's the man Bromfield?" G.C. asked. "Is it a fighting word?"

"He's a man who writes who has a very well-known farm in America; in Ohio. Because he is well known about the farm the Oxford University had him write an introduction. Turning the pages he can see Virgil's farm and Virgil's animals and Virgil's people and even his own stern and rugged features or figures I forget which. It must be rugged figures if he is a farmer. Anyway Louis can see him and he says it forms a great and eternal poem or poems for every kind of reader."

"It must be the edition I have without Bromfield," G.C. said. "I think you left it in Kajiado."

"Mine has my name in it," Miss Mary said.

"Good," I said. "And your *Up-Country Swahili* has your name in it too and right now it's in my hip pocket and sweated through and stuck together. I'll get you mine and you can write your name in it."

"I don't want yours. I want my own and why did you have to sweat it solidly together and ruin it?"

"I don't know. It was probably part of my plot to ruin Africa. But here it is. I'd advise you to take the clean one."

"This one has words that I'd written in myself that aren't in the original and it has notations."

"I'm sorry. I must have put it in my pocket some morning in the dark by mistake."

"You never make a mistake," Miss Mary said. "We all know that. And you'd be much better off if you studied your Swahili instead of trying to speak all the time in Unknown Tongue and reading nothing but French books. We all know you read French. Was it necessary to come all the way to Africa to read French?"

"Maybe. I don't know. This was the first time I ever had a complete set of Simenon and the girl at the bookshop in the long passageway at the Ritz was so nice to send and then get them all."

"And then you left them down in Tanganyika at Patrick's. All except a few. Do you think they'll read them?"

"I don't know. Pat's sort of mysterious someways like me. He might read them and he might not. But he has a neighbor who has a wife who is a Frenchwoman and they'd be good to have for her. No. Pat would read them."

"Did you ever study French and learn to speak it grammatically?"

"No."

"You're hopeless."

G.C. frowned at me.

"No," I said. "I'm not hopeless because I still have hope. The day I haven't you'll know it bloody quick."

"What do you have hope about? Mental slovenliness? Taking other people's books? Lying about a lion?"

"That's sort of alliterative. Just say 'lying.' Now I lie me down to sleep. Conjugate the verb lie and who with and how lovely it can be. Conjugate me every morning and every night and fire, no sleet, no candlelight and the mountain cold and close when you're asleep and the dark belts of trees are not yews but the snow's still snow. Conjugate me once the snow and why the mountain comes closer and goes farther away. Conjugate me conjugal love. What kind of mealies do you bring?"

It was not a nice way to talk, especially to anyone with Virgil on her mind, but lunch came then and lunch was always an armistice in any misunderstandings and the partakers of it and its excellence were as safe as malefactors once were said to be in churches with the law after them although I had never had much faith in that sanctuary. So we cleaned it up and rubbed it all off the slate and Miss Mary went to take a nap after lunch and I went to the ngoma.

It was very much like other ngomas except extraordinarily pleasant and nice and the Game Scouts had made a huge effort. They were dancing in shorts and they all had four ostrich plumes on their heads, at least at the beginning. Two of the plumes were white and two dyed pink and they kept them on with all sorts of devices from leather straps and thongs to binding them or wiring them into the hair. They wore bell anklets to dance with and they danced well and with beautiful contained discipline. There were three drums and some drumming on tins and empty petrol drums. There were four classic dances and three or four that were improvised. The young women and the young girls and the children did not get to dance until the later dances. They all danced but they did not enter into the figures and dance in the double line until late in the afternoon. You could see from the way the children and the young girls danced that they were used to much rougher ngomas at the Wakamba shamba.

Miss Mary and G.C. came out and took color pictures and Miss Mary was congratulated by everyone and shook hands with everybody. The Game Scouts did feats of agility. One was to start to turn a cartwheel over a coin that was half buried in the earth edge up and then stop the cartwheel when the feet were straight up in the air and to lower the head to the ground, sinking down on the arms, get the coin in the teeth and then come up and spin over to the feet in a single roll. It was very difficult and who was the strongest of the Game Scouts and the most agile, the kindest and the gentlest, did it beautifully.

Most of the time I sat in the shade and filled in on one of the basic beat empty petrol drums working the end with the base of the hand and watched the dancing. The Informer came over and squatted down by me wearing his imitation paisley shawl and his porkpie hat.

"Why are you sad, brother?" he asked.

"I am not sad."

"Everyone knows you are sad. You must be cheerful. Look at your fiancée. She is the queen of the ngoma."

"Don't put your hand on my drum. You deaden it."

"You are drumming very well, brother."

"The hell I am. I can't drum at all. I'm just not doing any harm. What are you sad about?"

"The Bwana Game has spoken to me very roughly and he sends me away. After all our magnificent work he says I do nothing here and he sends me to a place where I may easily be killed."

"You may be killed anywhere."

"Yes. But here I am useful to you and I die happy."

The dance was getting wilder now. I liked to see Debba dance and I didn't. It was as simple as that and, I thought, it must have happened to all followers of this type of ballet. I knew she was showing off to me because she danced down at this end by the petrol-drum bongo.

"She is a very beautiful young girl," the Informer said. "And the queen of the ngoma."

I went on playing until the end of the dance and then got up and found Nguili who had his green robe on and asked him to see the girls had Coca-Cola.

"Come on to the tent," I said to the Informer. "You are sick, aren't you?"

"Brother, I have a fever truly. You can take the temperature and see."

"I'll get you some Atabrine."

Mary was still taking pictures and the girls were standing stiff and straight with their breasts standing out against the scarves that looked like tablecloths. Mthuka was grouping some of the girls together and I knew he was trying to get a good picture of Debba. I watched them and saw how shy and downcast Debba's eyes were standing before Miss Mary and how straight she stood. She had none of the impudence she had with me and she stood at attention like a soldier.

The Informer had a tongue as white as though it were sprouting chalk and when I depressed his tongue with a spoon handle I could see he had a bad yellow patch and a yellow and whitish patch in the back of his throat. I put the thermometer under his tongue and he had a temperature of 101.3.

"You're sick, Informer old-timer," I said. "I'll give you some penicillin and some penicillin lozenges and send you home in the hunting car."

"I said I was sick, brother. But nobody cares. Can I have one drink, brother?"

"It's never hurt me with penicillin. It might do your throat good."

"I am sure it would, brother. Do you think Bwana Game will let me stay here and serve under you now that you can certify that I am sick?"

"You won't be any ball of fire while you're sick. Maybe I ought to send you in to the hospital in Kajiado."

"No please, brother. You can cure me here and I will be available for all emergencies and I can be your eyes and your ears and your right hand in battle."

God help us all, I thought, but he is having these ideas with no liquor in him and no bhang and none of the stuff and with a septic sore throat and possibly quinsy. It is pretty good morale even if it is just from the mouth.

I was making a half-tumbler of half-and-half Rose's lime juice and whiskey that would ease the throat and afterwards I would give him the penicillin and the lozenges and drive him home myself.

The mixture made his throat feel better and with the liquor his morale blossomed.

"Brother, I am a Masai. I have no fear of death. I despise death. I was ruined by the bwanas and by a Somali woman. She took everything; my property, my children, and my honor."

"You told me."

"Yes. But now since you bought me the spear I am starting again in life. You have sent for the medicine that brings youth?"

"It is coming. But it can only bring back youth if youth is there."

"It is there. I promise, brother. I feel it flooding into me now."

"That's the stuff."

"Perhaps. But I can feel youth too."

"I'll give you the medicine now and then I'll drive you home."

"No. Please, brother. I came with the widow and she must go home with me. It is too early for her to go yet. I lost her for three days at the last ngoma. I will wait and go with her when the truck leaves."

"You ought to be in bed."

"It is better that I wait for the widow. Brother, you do not know the danger that a ngoma is for a woman."

I had a sort of an idea of this danger and I did not want the Informer to talk with his throat so bad but he asked, "Could I have just one last drink before the medicine?"

"All right. I think it's OK medically."

This time I put sugar with the Rose's lime juice and made a good big drink. If he was going to wait for the widow it might be a long time and soon the sun would go down and it would be cold.

"We will do great deeds together, brother," the Informer said.

"I don't know. Don't you think we ought to do a few great deeds separately to sharpen up?"

"Name a great deed and I will do it."

"I'll think up a great deed as soon as your throat is well. I have many small deeds I must do myself now."

"Can I help in a small deed, brother?"

"Not in these. These I must do alone."

"Brother, if we do great deeds together will you take me to Mecca with you?"

"I may not be going to Mecca this year."

"But next year?"

"If it be the wish of Allah."

"Brother, do you remember Bwana Mike Cottar?"

"Too well."

"He is dead. So is the father. Tell me is it true that Bwana Blix is dead?"

"He is dead. In the snow and ice of Sweden."

"Brother, many say it is not true that Bwana Blix is dead. They say that he has disappeared until the death of his creditors and that then he will come again to earth like the Baby Jesus. In the theory of the Baby Jesus. Not that he will appear as the actual Baby Jesus. Can there be truth in this?"

"I think there can be no truth in this. The Bwana Blix is truly dead. Friends of mine have seen him dead in the snow with his head broken."

"Too many great men are dead. Few of us remain. Tell me, brother, of your faith that I have heard spoken of. Who is this great Lord who heads your faith?"

"We call him Gitchy Manitou the Mighty. That is not his true name."

"I see. Has he too been to Mecca?"

"He goes to Mecca as you or I might go to the bazaar or enter a duka."

"Do you represent him directly as I have heard?"

"Insofar as I am worthy."

"But you hold his authority?"

"It is not for you to ask that."

"Pardon me, brother, in my ignorance. But does he speak through you?"

244

"He speaks through me if he chooses."

"Can men who are not—"

"Do not ask."

"Can—"

"I will administer the penicillin and you can go," I said. "It is not fitting to speak of religion in a mess tent."

The Informer did not have the confidence in the oral penicillin that I hoped for from a potential doer of great deeds but it may have been disappointment at not being able to show his bravery under the big needle. He liked the pleasant taste though and took two tablespoonfuls with enjoyment. I joined him in a couple of tablespoons just in case he might be poisoned and also because one never knew what might happen at a ngoma.

"It tastes so good that do you think it can be powerful, brother?"

"The Great Manitou uses it himself," I said.

"Allah's will be done," the Informer said. "When do I take the rest of the flask?"

"In the morning when you wake up. If you are awake in the night suck on these tablets."

"Already I am better, brother."

"Go now and look after the widow."

"I go."

All this time we had been hearing the beating of the drums and the thin shaking of the ankle bells and the blowing of the traffic whistles. I still did not feel festive nor like dancing so, when the Informer was gone, I mixed a Gordon's gin and Campari and put some soda in it from the siphon. If this mixed well with the double dose of oral penicillin something would have been established even though not perhaps in the realm of pure science. They seemed to blend harmoniously and, if anything, to sharpen the beat of the drums. I listened carefully to see if the police whistles were any shriller but they seemed unaltered. Taking this to be an excellent sign I found a cool quart of beer in the dripping canvas water bag and made my way back to the ngoma. Someone was playing the head of my metal drum and so I found a good tree to sit against where I was joined by my friend Tony.

Tony was a fine man and one of my best friends. He was a Masai and had been a sergeant in the tank corps and had been a very brave and able soldier. If not the only Masai in the British Army he was at least the only Masai sergeant. He worked for G.C. in the Game Department and I always envied G.C. having him because he was a good mechanic, loyal, devoted, and always cheerful, and he spoke good English, perfect Masai, naturally, Swahili, some Chagga, and some Kamba. He had a very un-Masai build having short rather bandied legs and a heavy, powerful chest, arms, and neck. I had taught him to box and we sparred together quite often and were very good friends and companions.

"It is a very fine ngoma, sar," Tony said.

"Yes," I said. "Won't you dance, Tony?"

"No, sar. It is a Wakamba ngoma."

They were dancing a very complicated dance now and the young girls were dancing too in a very intense copulative figure.

"There are some very pretty girls. Who do you like the best, Tony?"

"Who do you like, sar?"

"I cannot decide. There are four really beautiful girls."

"There is one who is the best. You see who I mean, sar?"

"She's lovely, Tony. Where is she from?"

"From the Wakamba shamba, sar."

She was the best all right and better than the best. We both watched her.

"Have you seen Miss Mary and the Captain?"

"Yes, sar. They were here a short time ago. I am truly happy that Miss Mary has killed her lion. Do you remember from the early days and the lion spearing with the bubble gum Masai, sar? Do you remember from Fig Tree camp? That was a long time, sar, for her to hunt lion. This morning I told her a Masai proverb. Did she tell you?"

"No, Tony. I don't think she did."

"I told her this saying, 'It is always very quiet when a great bull dies.'"

"That is very true. It is quiet now even with the noise of the ngoma."

"Did you notice it too, sar?"

"Yes. I have been quiet inside all day. Do you want any beer?"

"No thank you, sar. Will there be boxing tonight?"

"Do you feel like it?"

"If you do, sar. But there are many new boys to try. We can do it better tomorrow without ngoma."

"Tonight if you like."

"Perhaps it would be better tomorrow. One boy is not a very nice boy. Not bad. But not nice. You know the kind."

"Town boy?"

"A little bit, sar."

"Can he box?"

"Not really, sar. But fast."

"Hit?"

"Yes, sar."

"What is that dance now?"

"The new boxing dance. You see? They make infighting now and left hooks the way you teach."

"Better than I teach."

"Tomorrow is best, sar."

"But you'll be gone tomorrow."

"I forgot, sar. Please excuse me. I am forgetful since the great bull died. We'll make it when we come back. I go now to check the lorry."

I went off to look for Keiti and found him on the outskirts of the dancing. He looked very cheerful and possessive.

"Please send them home in the truck when it gets dark," I said. "Mthuka can take several loads in the hunting car too. Memsahib is tired and we should have dinner early and go to bed."

"Ndio," he agreed.

I found Ngui and he said, "Jambo, Bwana" sarcastically in the dusk.

"Jambo tu," I answered. "Why didn't you dance?"

"Too much law," he said. "It is not my day to dance."

"Nor mine."

"Tomorrow?"

"We hunt leopard at first light."

"Ndio," he said. "You. Me. Rifle. Shotgun."

That night we had a cheerful dinner. Mbebia, the cook, had made breaded cutlets of the lion tenderloin and they were excellent. In September, when we had eaten the first lion cutlets, it had been a matter for discussion and was regarded as an eccentricity or something barbaric. Now everyone ate them and they were regarded as a great delicacy. The meat was white as veal and tender and delicious. It had no gamy flavor at all.

"I don't think anyone could tell it from a cotoletta milanese at a really good Italian restaurant except that the meat is better," Mary said.

I had been sure it would be good meat the first time I had ever seen a lion skinned. M'Cola who was my gunbearer in those days told me that the tenderloin was the best meat there was to eat. But we had been very disciplined then by Pop who was trying to make at least a semi-pukka sahib of me and I had never had the nerve to cut a tenderloin and ask the cook to prepare it. This year, though, when we killed the first lion and I asked Ngui to take the two tenderloins it had been different. Pop said it was barbarous and that no one ever ate lion. But this was almost surely the last safari we would ever make together and we had come to the point where we both regretted things we had not done rather than those we had and so he made only perfunctory opposition and when Mary showed Mbebia how to prepare the cutlets and when we smelled their fine savor and when he saw how the meat cut exactly like veal and how much we enjoyed it he tried some too and liked it.

"You ate bear in America hunting in the Rockies. It's like pork but too rich. You eat pork and a hog will feed fouler than a bear or a lion."

"Don't badger me," Pop had said. "I'm eating the damned stuff."

"Isn't it good?"

"Yes. Damn it. It's good. But don't badger me."

"Have some more, Mr. P. Please have some more," Mary said.

"All right. I'll have some more," making his voice into a high complaining falsetto. "But don't keep staring at me while I eat it."

It was pleasant talking about Pop whom Mary and I both loved and who I was fonder of than any man that I had ever known. Mary told some of the things Pop had told her on the long drive they had made together through Tanganyika when we had gone down to hunt the Great Ruaha river country and the Bohara flats. Hearing these stories and imagining the things he had not told it was like having Pop there and I thought that even in his absence he could make things all right when they were difficult.

Then too it was wonderful to be eating the lion and have him in such close and final company and tasting so good. I was glad Mary's and G.C.'s stomachs were behaving well and I hoped it was more than temporary. My own digestive process fortified by the oral penicillin was functioning perfectly and I wondered how the Informer was. We had sent everybody home early because G.C. had to make an early start in the morning and, with any luck, there would be many more ngomas. Also it gave me a reputation as a moralist which might be useful in the future.

That night Mary said she was very tired and she went to sleep in her own bed. I lay awake for a while and then went out to sit by the fire. In the chair watching the fire and thinking of Pop and how sad it was he had to die and how happy I was that he had been able to be with us so much and that we had been lucky to have three or four things together that were like the old days along with just the happiness of being together and talking and joking I went to sleep. When I woke I remembered that I must start off on foot to hunt leopard as soon as it was light and that I ought to go into the tent and lie down and get some sleep. I went to the open door of the tent and sat on my cot with the mosquito netting still tucked under the air mattress while I took off my boots. It was cold and fresh in the tent and Miss Mary was breathing steadily and gently. Tomorrow I must try to be very good and take good care of her and make her happy. I put my bathrobe at the foot of the bed, pulled up the mosquito netting and crawled inside the sheets and the blankets. I said my prayers for luck and in case they might be of any use to Miss Mary and to ask that she be happy. Then I went to sleep and I was asleep when Mwindi came with the tea.

CHAPTER 20

The sun was not up but that was because of the flank of the mountain it had to rise over and the light was gray but good and Ngui and I were walking through the grass that was wet from the dew. He walked ahead because he knew where the bait had been hung and I watched the trees and his back and the trail his black legs made through the wetness of the grass. We walked silently and the cold wet of the new knee-high grass against my legs was cold and pleasant. Ngui carried the old Winchester pump gun and I carried the Springfield and the only noise that I heard from myself was the light slopping of the tea in my stomach.

We came onto the tracks of the lorry now and I watched Ngui's legs walking in one of the grooves where the grass was bent and crushed. I was watching all of the trees as we came toward them and passed them and then I smelled the sick sweet and sour odor from the bait and saw the hiding place. Ngui looked back and saw that I had seen it and waited for me to come up. We did not speak and I turned my head until I had the location of the bait. He grinned when I twitched my nostrils and took in a full breath. He pointed toward the hide and we went to it very softly but fast, the way a snake would move. Across a small opening in the trees I could see the baboon draped obscenely in the crotch of the tree. Then we both searched the tree and all the other trees. There was no leopard but a leopard had pulled the baboon up from where he had been tied and placed him in the crotch.

"Chakula kidogo," Ngui whispered which meant in shorthand bad Swahili that the leopard had fed on him a little. The leopard was gone now. He should return in the evening since he had found the bait. Neither of us cared much for the place and Ngui was ashamed that the hide was so obvious that I had been able to see it.

"Go on and look at it," I said and Ngui went off out of sight while I studied how the shot would be in the evening. He came back without me hearing him or having seen him and that put him several points up on me. "Chui kidogo," he said. He was a small leopard and he had fed last evening before the dew had fallen. We both knew there was no use trying to find him in the thick stuff as we would only frighten him and perhaps he would not return.

"He probably went to the ngoma," I said.

"There was a chui in camp last night," Ngui said. "Did you hear him?"

"No."

"Charo heard him."

"Old men hear everything."

"Let's go to the other bait."

We walked through the green park country and past a thick patch of bush where a cobra had his hole. The cobra had been out in the night and his track showed like a slim finger drawing through the dew on the grass where he had returned. The light was much stronger now and I knew the sun was climbing behind the slope of the hills that rose to the edge of the mountain. Ngui was wearing a rusty pink shirt and we were moving in a long half-circle toward the second leopard bait. Ngui was bareheaded and I watched the back of his neck and the wide thrust of his neck into his shoulders and the muscles showing under the loose-hanging shirt. He was short as most great Wakamba hunters are and he had his father's beautifully turned legs. His father, when he was an old man, had the handsomest legs I had ever seen on a man. I knew Ngui was the son of his father's youngest wife and I tried to remember how she looked twenty years ago. It was just twenty years ago, give or take a month, and it was easy to remember her and I thought how like Pop it was not to tell me that Ngui was M'Cola's boy and to leave it for me to find out.

All that Pop had said was, "The gunbearers are good boys, I think you'll find. They've all hunted elephant and been in sticky places and done well enough. Your gunbearer is the only one that's ever given me any trouble. But I think you and he will get on. Mary's gunbearer is a good boy. They're all ex-K.A.R."

This was before Mary had loaned her gunbearer to Tommy Shevlin when we had gone down to lower Tanganyika and Pop had found Charo for her. Tommy had needed a gunbearer very badly on a suddenly conceived hunt for a big elephant in difficult dry country below Voi and it had been wonderful luck that Pop had located old Charo who was a much better hunting companion for Mary than the almost too cheerful, gay, and possibly careless Mwengi. He was a good gunbearer for an old head and he was a brave and very keen hunter but Charo was a very old and terribly wise hunter armored in his knowledge and harshly disciplined by his religion.

Now walking in the early morning watching Ngui striding lightly through the grass thinking how we were brothers, in crime, Pop said, but we thought for better or for worse and for always I wished my skin were as dark as his and that M'Cola was my father. I would have preferred for Pop to be my father and my mother either a Somali or a Wakamba. But that seemed a lot to ask of Pop at this hour of the morning. It always seemed stupid to be white in Africa and I remembered how twenty years before I had been taken to hear the Muslim missionary who had explained to us, his audience, the advantages of a dark skin and the disadvantages of the white man's pigmentation. I was burned dark enough to pass as a half-caste.

"Observe the white man," the missionary had said. "He walks in the sun and the sun kills him. If he exposes his body to the sun it is burned until it blisters and rots. The poor fellow must stay in the shade and destroy himself with alcohol and stinghas and chutta pegs because he cannot face the horror of the sun rising on the next day. Observe the white man and his mwanamke, his memsahibs. The woman is covered with brown spots if she goes into the sun, brown spots like the forerunners of leprosy. If she continues the sun strips the skin as from a person who has passed through fire. The white man places his faith in Pan-Yan pickles instead of in Allah and the pickles kill him. He runs from the bowels like an aborted cow. The poor white man worships the horse. If he moves the horse into fly country it dies as does his dog.

"The poor white man," the missionary had said, "has no true skin on the soles of his feet and if he loses his shoes he is dead for he cannot walk barefooted. He is ruled by women. Even the chiefs of the tribes have been women. See the face of the mwanamke on the Maria Theresa thaler. By such mwanamke is the white man ruled. For the space of a man's life the British were ruled by the old woman you can still see on some shilingi. Yet the white man had no shame to be ruled by a woman. Only the Germans were ruled by men and you know what sort of man the Germani are. They are to the English as the morani is to the mtoto. But the German for all his good qualities cannot stand the sun because of his white skin that turns as red or redder than the British.

"The white man is red when he lives among us if he goes out into the sun but in his home countries his face is the color of a salt lick. If he is kept from beer and from whiskey pegs he cannot control his nerves and cries out against his God the Baby Jesus. Let me tell you of the Baby Jesus," the missionary went on. "In this baby worship do we see the childishness of the white man. This is a sickness that gnaws like a worm in his brain and he can only kill it with beer and with whiskey pegs and stingahs until he curses the child that he worships. This Baby Jesus, brothers, had a mother but no father. This the white men themselves admit and I have heard it explained at a so-called mission school I attended to study this childish belief that I might better confront it. This baby was born to a carpenter, an honorable man but who had only been able to acquire one Masai donkey and this one wife who made the Baby Jesus without sleeping with her husband. This the white men really believe and I swear it to you. The announcement of the coming birth was made to this virgin wife by a man wearing the wings of an ndege. An actual ndege, not an airplane. The wings of a bird with feathers. This the white man believes while he calls the true religion superstition and error."

On this lovely morning I did not try to remember further about the Sermon against the White Man. It had been long ago and I had forgotten many of the more lively parts but one thing I had not forgotten was the white man's heaven and how this had been shown to be another of his horrifying beliefs which caused him to hit small white balls with sticks along the ground or other larger balls back and forth across nets such are used on the big lakes for catching fish until the sun overcame him and he retired into the club to destroy himself with alcohol and curse the Baby Jesus unless his mwanamkes were present. Since the mwanamkes believed in the Baby Jesus and were the propagators of the faith except for the missionaries and since the white man feared them he never cursed the Baby Jesus in their presence and if he did he asked their pardon. A white man who habitually cursed the Baby Jesus in the presence of the mwanamkes could be forbidden the club which was comparable to being expelled from the tribe. Such white men, I remembered, who were sent out from the club did become rather like the Wandorobo who had been expelled from their tribes. Some of them even became good hunters by African standards and the missionary told of pitiful cases that I knew personally of such white men who had become bearded and ceased washing altogether and drank gin in their squalid huts in a life that was so degrading that they ceased to speak their own tongue except aloud to themselves and sometimes they became so depressed that they did not even curse the Baby Jesus though this was rare. I myself recalled cases where such men had fallen so low that in their blasphemies they even coupled the name of Our Lord with that of the Honorable Secretary of the Club speaking highly of neither. And I recalled another thing that these men who were cast out from the club were nearly always the type of white man which does not turn red in the sun but rather becomes a badly tanned leather color or the color of uncured hides with a not dissimilar smell and usually dirt in the wrinkles of the neck. But we were coming up on the second leopard bait now. I had seen the wheel tracks in the grass and then noted where the lorry had stopped and the baboon been dragged on a rope to the tree. This trace was all freshly dewed now but I could smell him and when Ngui and I both saw the blind he was disgusted. We went over and into it and looked out through the leaves and saw the grotesque baboon hanging and then turned away and started back for camp.

We could not have had a more unsuccessful nor a less promising morning but we were both so disgusted that it was comical and we did not feel bad. I had a theory that a baboon bait went sour and unattractive immediately after it had reached its first full bloom of decay and begun to enter deliquescence. I did not know either the Swahili or the Kamba for this and so I just thought it over as we walked through the wet grass back toward camp. In an emergency I could have explained it. But this was no emergency. This was the classic return of the disappointed leopard hunters and neither of us felt talkative. Ngui had passed another brush patch where a cobra had his hole. The cobra was either still out or had gone visiting leaving no address. Neither of us were great snake hunters. That was a white man's obsession and a necessary one since snakes, when trodden on, bit the cattle and the horses and there was a standing reward of shillings for them on Pop's farm, both cobras and puff adders. Snake hunting, for pay, was as low as a man could fall. We knew cobras as quick, lithe moving creatures who sought their holes which were so small that it seemed impossible for them to enter them and we had jokes about this. There were tales of ferocious mambas that rose high on their tails and pursued the helpless colonists or intrepid Game Rangers while they were mounted on horses but these tales left us indifferent since they came from the south where hippos with personal names were alleged to wander across hundreds of miles of dry country seeking water and snakes performed biblical feats. I knew these things must be true since they had been written by honorable men but they were not like our snakes and in Africa it is only your own snakes that matter.

Our snakes were shy or stupid or mysterious and powerful. I made a great show of snake-hunting fervor which deceived nobody except, possibly, Miss Mary, and we were all against the spitting cobra since he had spat at G.C. This morning when we found that the cobra was absent and had not returned to his hole I said to Ngui that he was probably the grandfather of Tony anyway and that we should respect him.

Ngui was pleased at this since the snakes are the ancestors of all the Masai. I said the snake might well have been the ancestor of his girl at the Masai manyatta. She was a tall, lovely girl and had a certain amount of snake about her. Ngui being cheered up and slightly horrified at the possible ancestry of his illegal love I asked him if he thought the coldness of the Masai women's hands and the stranger occasional coldness of other parts of their bodies could be due to snake blood. First he said that it was impossible, that Masai had always been like that. Then we were walking side by side now and heading for the high trees of camp that showed etched in yellow and green against the brown wrinkled base and the high snow of the mountain. Camp was not visible but only the high trees marking it. He said that it might be true. Italian women, he said, had cold and hot hands. The hand could be cold and then become warm as a hot spring and in other ways they were as scalding as a hot spring if one could remember it. They had no more bubo, the penalty for relation, than the Masai. Perhaps the Masai did have snake blood. I said that the next time we killed a snake we would all feel the blood and see. I had never felt the outrush of snake blood since they were antipathetic to me and I knew they were to Ngui too. But we agreed to feel the blood and have others, if they could control their repugnance, feel it too. This was all in the interests of our anthropological studies which we pursued each day and we kept on walking and thinking of these problems and of our own small problems which we tried to integrate with the greater interests of anthropology until the tents of camp showed under the yellow and green trees which the first light of the sun was now turning to bright dark green and shining gold and we could see the gray smoke of the fires at the lines and the camp breaking of the Game Scouts and, seated by the fire before our own tents now deep under the trees and the sunlight of the new day, the figure of G.C. seated in a camp chair by a wooden table reading with a bottle of beer at his hand.

Ngui took the rifle and shouldered it with the old shotgun and I walked over to the fire.

"Good morning, General," G.C. said. "Shoot many leopards?"

"Only my share."

"You *were* up early."

"We leopard hunters have it rugged," I said. "We hunt them on our own two feet and the chips are always down."

"Somebody ought to pick the damned chips up sometime. You'll tread on them with your own two feet. Have some beer."

He poured a glass very carefully from the bottle bringing the head up to the point of running over and then delicately holding it bubble by bubble until the glass was full.

"Satan will find work for idle hands to do," I said and lifted the glass which had been filled so that a swell of the amber beer seemed to hang like the lip of an avalanche and conveyed it gently and unspilling to my lips taking in the first sip with the upper lip.

"Not bad for an unsuccessful leopard hunter," G.C. said. "Such steady hands and red-rimmed, bloodshot eyes have made our England's greatness."

"'Neath twisted shards and iron sands we drink it down as God commands," I said. "Are you across the Atlantic yet?"

"I passed over Ireland," G.C. said. "Frightfully green. I can all but see the lights of Le Bourget. I'm going to learn to fly, General."

"Many have said it before. The question is how are you going to fly?"

"I'm going to straighten up and fly right," G.C. said.

"On your own two feet and when the chips are down?"

"No. In the aircraft."

"Probably sounder in the aircraft. And will you carry these principles into Life, son?"

"Drink your beer, Billy Graham," G.C. said. "What will you do when I am gone, General? No nervous breakdowns I hope? No trauma? You're up to it I hope? It's not too late to refuse the flank."

"Which flank?"

"Any flank. It's one of the few military terms that I retained. I always wanted to refuse them a flank. In actual life you're always putting out a defensive flank and anchoring it somewhere. Until I refuse a flank I've been thwarted."

"Mon flanc gauche est protégée par une colline," I said remembering too well. "J'ai les mitrailleuses bien placée. Je me trouve tres bien ici et je reste."

"You're taking refuge in a foreign tongue," G.C. said. "Pour one and we'll go out and get that measuring over while my well-peppered ruffians do whatever it is they do this morning before they are for the town's end to beg during life."

"Did you ever read *Sergeant Shakespeare*?"

"No."

"I'll get it for you. Duff Cooper gave it to me. He wrote it."

"It isn't reminiscences?"

"No."

We had been reading the *Reminiscences* serialized in one of the thin paper airmail editions that came out to Nairobi on the Comets that landed at Entebbe. I had not liked them very much in the newspaper installments. But I had liked *Sergeant Shakespeare* very much and I had liked Duff Cooper without his wife. But there was so much of her in the *Reminiscences* that both G.C. and I had been put off.

"When are you going to write your reminiscences, G.C.?" I asked. "Don't you know old men forget?"

"I hadn't really thought much of writing them."

"You'll have to. There's not many of the really old timers left. You could start on the early phases now. Get in the early volumes. *Far Away and Long Ago in Abyssinia* would be a good one to start with. Skip the University and Bohemian times in London and the Continent and cut to *A Youngster with the Fuzzy Wuzzies* then move into your early days as a game ranger while you can still recall them."

"Could I use that inimitable style you carved out of a walnut stick in *An Unwed Mother on the Italian Front*?" G.C. asked. "I always liked that the best of your books except for *Under Two Flags*. That was yours, wasn't it?"

"No. Mine was *The Death of a Guardsman*."

"Good book too," G.C. said. "I never told you but I modeled my life on that book. Mummy gave it to me when I went away to school."

"You don't really want to go out on this measurement nonsense, do you?" I hoped.

"I do."

"Should we take neutral witnesses?"

"There are none. We'll walk it ourselves."

"Let's get out then. I'll see if Miss Mary's still sleeping."

She was sleeping and she had drunk her tea and looked as though she might well sleep for another two hours. Her lips were closed and her face was smooth as ivory against the pillow. She was breathing easily but as she moved her head I could tell that she was dreaming.

I picked up the rifle where Ngui had hung it on a tree and climbed into the Land Rover beside G.C. There was much new game that had moved in with the grass and G.C. drove fast but careful not to set the game moving. We saw two Granti bucks with almost unbelievable horns and pulled up to admire them. The big Alsatian, who had been a flop-eared puppy when we had first come to Africa this time raised the crest along his back and shivered as we stopped to let them feed off into the trees.

"That's as big a Granti head as I ever saw."

"I've seen bigger," G.C. said. "And you will too. It's a pity you took that one of yours in the dry weather."

"I remember when you could take your choice of four."

"I know but there's only one now. And you can't enforce it if you don't respect it."

"I wasn't thinking of that. I was thinking of the old days before they were measly and how everybody used to watch you when you took one or missed him because it meant the difference between meat and no meat and the heat waves coming off the rifle and the heavy wind blowing and how they'd waver in the sights. And what it meant if you heard the thunk of the piga."

"Foot safari?"

"Yeah. Sideshow, small one. Pop said I'd never know what it was about without a foot safari. Like having to go through sail."

"I learned it on camel safari in the desert."

"Pop said we'd always do the desert. But we never did."

"I love the desert," G.C. said.

We went on now and finally picked up the old tracks and found where Miss Mary had shot the lion. Many things were changed as they always are on any old battlefield but we found her empty cartridges and G.C.'s and off to the left we found mine. I put one in my pocket.

"Now I'll drive to where he was killed and then you pace it on a straight line."

I watched him go off in the car his brown hair shining in the early sun, the big dog looking back at me and then turning to look straight ahead. When the Land Rover made a circle and stopped this side of the heavy clump of trees and bush I put my toe a pace to the left of the most westerly of the ejected shells and started to pace toward the vehicle counting as I paced. I carried the rifle over my shoulder holding it by the barrel with my right hand and when I started the Land Rover looked very small and foreshortened. The big dog was out and G.C. was walking around. They looked very small too and sometimes I could only see the dog's head and neck. When I got to the Land Rover I stopped where the grass was bent where the lion had first lain.

"How many?" G.C. asked and I told him. He shook his head and asked, "Did you bring the Jinny flask?"

"Yes."

We each took a drink.

"We never, never tell anybody," G.C. said. "Drunk or sober with shits or decent people."

"Never."

"Now we'll set the speedometer and you drive it back in a straight line and I'll pace it."

There were a couple of paces difference in our tallies and a slight discrepancy between the speedometer reading and the paces so we cut four paces off the whole thing. Then we drove back to camp watching the mountain and feeling sad because we would not hunt together again until Christmas.

CHAPTER 21

After G.C. and his people were gone I was alone with Miss Mary's sorrow. I was not really alone because there was also Miss Mary and the camp and our own people and the big mountain of Kilimanjaro that everyone called Kibo and all the animals and the birds and the new fields of flowers and the worms that hatched out of the ground to eat the flowers. There were the brown eagles that came to feed on the worms so that eagles were as common as chickens and eagles wearing long brown trousers of feathers and other white-headed eagles walked together with the guinea fowl busily eating the worms. The worms made an armistice among all the birds and they all walked together. Then great flocks of European storks came to eat the worms and there would be acres of storks moving on a single stretch of plain grown high with the white flowers. Miss Mary's sorrow resisted the eagles because eagles did not mean as much to her as they did to me.

She had never lain under a juniper bush up above timberline at the top of a pass in our own mountains with a .22 rifle waiting for eagles to come to a dead horse that had been a bear bait until the bear was killed. Now he was an eagle bait and then afterwards he would be a bear bait again. The eagles were sailing very high when you first saw them. You had crawled under the bush when it was still dark and you had seen the eagles come out of the sun when it had cleared the opposite peak of the pass. This peak was just a rise of grassy hill with a rock outcropping at the top and scattered juniper bushes on the slope. The country was all high there and very easy traveling once you had come this high and the eagles had come from far away toward the snow mountains you could have seen if you had been standing instead of lying under the bush. There were three eagles and they wheeled and soared and rode the currents and you watched them until the sun spotted your eyes. Then you closed them and through the red the sun was still there. You opened them and looked to the side limit of the blind of the sun and you could see the spread pinions and the wide fanned tails and feel the eyes in the big heads watching. It had been cold in the early morning and you looked out at the horse and his too old and too exposed now teeth that you had always had to lift his lip to see. He had a kind and rubbery lip and when you had led him to this place to die and dropped the halter he had stood as he had always been taught to stand and when you had stroked him on the blaze on his black head where the gray hairs showed he had reached down to nip you on the neck with his lips. He had looked down to see the saddled horse you had left in the last edge of the timber as though he were wondering what he was doing here and what was the new game. You had remembered how wonderfully he had always seen in the dark and how you had hung onto his tail with a bear hide packed across the saddle to come down trails when you could not see at all and when the trail led along the rimrock in the dark down through the timber. He was always right and he understood all new games.

So you had brought him up here five days before because someone had to do it and you could do it if not gently without suffering and what difference did it make what happened afterwards. The trouble was, at the end, he thought it was a new game and he was learning it. He gave me a nice rubber-lipped kiss and then he checked the position of the other horse. He knew you could not ride him the way the hoof had split but this was new and he wanted to learn it.

"Good-bye, Old Kite," I said and held his right ear and stroked its base with my fingers. "I know you'd do the same for me."

He did not understand, of course, and he wanted to give me another kiss to show that everything was all right when he saw the gun come up. I thought I could keep him from seeing it but he saw it and his eyes knew what it was and he stood very still trembling and I shot him at the intersection between the crosslines that run from opposite eye to opposite ear and his feet went straight down under him and all of him dropped together and he was a bear bait.

Now lying under the juniper I was not finished with my sorrow. I would always feel the same way about Old Kite all of my life, or so I told myself then, but I looked at his lips which were not there because the eagles had eaten them and at his eyes which were also gone and at where the bear had opened him so that he was sunken now and the patch the bear had eaten before I had interrupted him and I waited for the eagles to come down.

One came, finally, dropping like the sound of an incoming shell and braking, with doubled-forward pinions and feathered legs and talons thrust forward to hit Old Kite as though he were killing him. He then walked pompously around and started working in the cavity. The others came in

259

more gently and heavy winged but with the same long feathered things and the same thick necks, big heads, and dipped beaks and golden eyes.

I lay there watching them eat at the body of my friend and partner that I had killed and thought that they were lovelier in the air. Since they were condemned I let them eat a while and quarrel and go pacing and mincing with their selections from the interior. I wished that I had a shotgun but I hadn't. So I took the .22 Winchester finally and shot one carefully in the head and another twice in the body. He started to fly but could not make it and came down wings spread. The other I had luck with and the eagle had none and I broke a wing and I had to chase him up the high slope. Nearly every other bird or beast goes downhill when it is wounded. But an eagle goes uphill and when I ran this one down and caught his legs above the killing and holding claws and, with my moccasined foot on his neck, folded his wings together and held him with his eyes full of hatred and defiance I had never seen any animal or bird look at me as the eagle looked. He was a golden eagle and full grown and big enough to take the mountain sheep lambs and he was a big thing to hold and as I watched the eagles walking with the guinea fowl and remembered that these birds walk with no one I felt bad about Miss Mary's sorrow but I could not tell her what the eagles meant to me nor why I had killed these three, the last one by smacking his head against a tree down in the timber, nor what their skins had bought at the reservation.

We were out riding in the hunting car when we saw the eagles and the guineas together and it was in the open glades of the forest that had been so damaged when the great herd of more than two hundred elephants had come through early that year and pulled and butted the trees down. We had gone there to check on the buffalo herd and perhaps to run onto a leopard that I knew lived there in the big unharmed trees close to the papyrus swamp. But we had seen nothing except the overrunning of the caterpillars and the strange armistice among the birds. Mary had located a few more possible Christmas trees and I had been thinking too much about eagles and about the old days. The old days were supposed to have been simpler but they were not; they were only rougher. The reservation was rougher than the shamba. Maybe not. I did not really know but I did know that the white people always took the other people's lands away from them and put them on a reservation where they could go to hell and be destroyed as though they were in a concentration camp. Here they called the reservations the reserves and there was much do-gooding about how the natives now called the Africans were administered. But the hunters were not allowed to hunt and the warriors were not allowed to make war. G.C. hated poachers because he had to have something to believe in so he had taken to believing in his job. He would, of course, insist that if he did not believe in his job he would never have taken it and he would be right in that too. Even Pop in one of the greatest rackets of all, the safari swindle, had very strict ethics, the strictest. The customer must be taken for every possible cent but he must be given results. All great white hunters were touching about how they loved the game and hated to kill anything but usually what they were thinking about was preserving the game for the next client that would come along. They did not want to frighten it by unnecessary shooting and they wanted a country to be left so that they might take another client and his wife or another pair of clients into it and it might seem like unspoiled, never shot-over, primitive Africa that they could rush their clients through giving them the best results.

Pop had explained all this to me one time many years before and said when we were up the coast fishing at the end of the safari, "You know no one's conscience would ever let them do this to anyone twice. If they like them I mean. The next time you come out and get some transport, better bring it, and I'll find you the boys and you can hunt anywhere you've been and you'll work out new places and it will cost you no more than to hunt at home."

But it had turned out that rich people liked how much it cost and they came back again and again and it always cost more and was something that others could not do so that it was increasingly attractive. Old rich people died and there were always new ones and the animals decreased as the stock market rose. It was a big revenue-producing industry for the colony too and because of this the Game Department, which had control over those who practiced the industry, had, with its development, produced new ethics that handled, or nearly handled, everything.

It was no good thinking about ethics now and less good to think about the reservation where you sat on a deer hide in front of a tepee with your three eagle tails spread out with the undersides up so that the lovely white ends and the soft plumes showed and said nothing while they were looked at and held your tongue in the bargaining. The Cheyenne who wanted them the most cared nothing anymore except for tail plumes. He was beyond all other things or all other things had been removed. To him eagles on the land of the reservation were as they circled high in the sky and unapproachable when they settled on a pile of gray rock to watch the country. Sometimes they could be found and killed in blizzards when they sat against a rock back against the driving snow. But this man was no good in blizzards anymore. Only the young men were and they were gone.

You sat and did not talk and did not talk and sometimes reached out and touched the tails and stroked the plumes very lightly. You thought about your horse and about the second bear that had come through the pass to the horse after the killing of the eagles while the horse was still a bear bait and how when you had shot him a little too low in the bad light, taking him from the edge of the timber where the wind was right and he had rolled over once and then stood and bawled and slapped both his great arms as though to kill something that was biting him and then come down on all fours and come bouncing like a lorry off a highway and you had shot him twice as he came down the hill and the last time so close you smelled the fur burn. You thought of him and of the first bear. The hide had slipped on him and you took the long curved grizzly claws out of your shirt pocket and laid them out behind the eagle tails. Then you did not talk at all and the trading started. There had been no grizzly claws for many, many years and you made a good trade.

There were not any good trades this morning but the best thing was the storks. Mary had only seen them twice in Spain. The first time was in a small town in Castille on our way across the high country to Segovia. This town had a very fine square and we had stopped there in the heat of the day and gone out of the blinding light into the cool darkness of the inn to get our wineskins filled. It was very cool and pleasant in the inn and they had very cold beer. In this town they had a free bullfight one day each year in the lovely square in which everyone who wished could fight the three different bulls that were turned loose from their boxes. People were nearly always wounded or killed and it was the big social event of the year. I had been a very keen follower of these fights which were known as capeas for many years before I had first gone to Africa and I remembered the reputation of this town and the great size of the bulls that were always used. In this town everyone you met or would meet except the priest, perhaps, or the members of the Guardia Civil had attempted bullfighting with bulls that were lethal at least once. The priest too might have tried it or at least been in the ring before his seminary days and so might the civiles. The square or plaza was converted into a bullring by blocking all exit streets with carts. Amateur fighters when pursued by the bull could refuge in the doorways of the inn, other stores, or private dwellings if these were opened to them. If the bull entered this was the cause of panic, hilarity, and sometimes death. One bull was said to have pursued an amateur into the inn, smashing one of the double doors with his horn and ripping an entire plank out of it. Once inside the inn there were no photographs and each man's account varied. But the bull was said to have tossed one man back into the billiard room where he was later operated on on the green cloth of the billiard table where a sheet had been spread and to have sent another man over the bar where the man smashed the bar mirror when he hit. The bull was said to have had both of his front hooves on the bar and to be looking at himself in the broken mirror when he was treacherously stabbed in the back of the neck by the local butcher. There is no evidence on any of this although a great friend of mine once painted a picture of the bull with his two forefeet on the bar and one of them clutching with some difficulty a glass of the local red wine while the bull stared into the shattered mirror and the sinister figure of the butcher crept up with his puntilla. My friend had been in a period of great spiritual depression when he painted this canvas and entitled it *¿Que futuro tenemos?* I always regretted that it had been destroyed with so many other artistic treasures in the Spanish Civil War and that I didn't have it now to give as a present to Debba, changing the title, perhaps, to *No hay remedio.*

But on this particularly hot day in Castile Miss Mary had discovered the storks nested on top of the tower of the church which had looked down on so many tauric incidents. The wife of the innkeeper had taken her up to a high room of the house where she might photograph them and I was talking at the bar with the owner of the local transport and trucking company. Both he and the proprietor of the inn, a not dissolute but early drinker who had joined us at the historic bar, had friends in common that we were very careful about mentioning since they were dead under varying circumstances. It was better to speak of the bulls and the storks. The storks, naturally, were the luck of the village. There were two young ones and both the male and the female were in good health and were good parents. They hoped my wife would get a good photograph of them and it meant very much to them that she should. I told them how we had read an article that told how the storks were disappearing from Europe and that some scientists laid it to the bombing of northern countries during the war. Then we talked about the different Castilian towns which had always had storks' nests on the churches and from all I could learn from the trucking man these were as plentiful as ever. No one had ever molested storks in Spain. They are one of the few birds that are truly respected.

Then we started to talk about the capeas and the innkeeper told how as a special event last year they had let an enormous bull attack a lorry. The transport owner showed me a photograph from his wallet. Almost any other place except this inn would have had a framed enlargement on the wall. But this was an inn where everyone remembered everything and there was no need of photographs to prove past events. The transport owner's photograph, which was badly worn and creased from showings in other towns where there were doubters, showed the bull tossing and overturning the lorry. This was a very considerable feat because the bull had charged the lorry four times and been held off by the owner who acted as picador for three of these times. But on the fourth charge the bull had overturned the lorry and broken his neck. We all had a tall cold beer at the remembrance of this great event and then the innkeeper told me about a compatriot of mine, an inglés of some sort; they believed him to be a Canadian who had been in the town for some time with a broken-down motorcycle and no money.

He undoubtedly would eventually receive money and he had sent for the part that he needed for his motorcycle to Madrid but it had not come. Everyone liked him in the town and they wished that he were there so I might meet a compatriot who might even be a fellow townsman. He had gone off somewhere painting but they said someone could go off and find him and bring him in. The interesting thing the innkeeper said was that this compatriot of mine spoke absolutely no Spanish at all except one word, joder. He was known as Mister Joder and if I wished to leave any message for him I could leave it with the innkeeper. I wondered what message I should leave for this compatriot with such a decisive name and finally decided to leave a fifty-peseta note folded in a certain way that old travelers in Spain may be familiar with. Everyone was delighted at that and they all promised that Mister Joder would surely spend the ten duros that night without leaving the bar but that he and his wife would be sure to get him to eat something.

I asked them how Mr. Joder painted and the transport man said, "Hombre, he is neither Velásquez nor Goya nor Martinez de León. That I promise you. But times are changing and who are we to criticize? In your youth and my youth it would have caused a scandal if I had piced a five-year-old bull from a camion. Now it is all but forgotten."

Miss Mary came down from the high room where she had been photographing and said that she had taken good and clear pictures of the storks but that they would be worthless because she had no telescopic lens. We paid up and drank cold beer on the house and all said good-bye and drove out of the square and the blinding light of the steep climb above the town to the high country toward Segovia. I stopped above the town and looked back and saw the male stork come in with his lovely flight to the nest on the top of the church tower. He had been down by the river where the women beat the clothes and later on we had seen a covey of partridges cross the road and later in the same lonely high bracken country we had seen a wolf.

That was this same year when we had been in Spain on the way to Africa and now we were in a yellow-green forest that had been destroyed by elephants about the same time that we were riding across the high country to Segovia. In a world where this could happen I had small time for sorrow. I had been sure that I would never see Spain again and I had returned only to show Mary the Prado. Since I remembered all the pictures that I loved truly and so owned them as though I possessed them there was no need for me to see them again before I died. But it was very important that I should see them with Mary if that were possible and could be done without compromise or indignity. Also I wanted her to see Navarre and the two Castiles and I wanted her to see a wolf in high country and storks nesting in a village. I had wanted to show her the paw of a bear nailed onto the door of the church in Barco de Ávila but it was too much to expect that it would still be there. But we had found the storks quite easily and would find more and we had seen the wolf and had looked down on Segovia from a near and pleasant height coming onto it naturally on a road that tourists did not take but that travelers would come by naturally. There are no such roads anymore around Toledo but you can still see Segovia as you would see it if you walked over the high country and we studied the city as though it were being seen for the first time by people who had never known it was there but had always lived to see it.

There is a virginity that you, in theory, only bring once to a beautiful city or a great painting. This is only a theory and I think it is untrue. All the things that I have loved I bring this to each time but it is lovely to bring someone else to it and it helps the loneliness. Mary had loved Spain and Africa and had learned the secret things naturally and hardly without knowing she had learned them. I never explained the secret things to her, only the technical things or the comic things and my own greatest pleasure came from her own discovering. It is stupid to expect or hope that a woman that you love should love all the things that you do. But Mary had loved the sea and living on a small boat and she loved fishing. She loved pictures and she had loved the West of the United States when we had first gone there together. She never simulated anything and this was a great gift to be given as I had been associated with a great simulator of everything and life with a true simulator gives a man a very unattractive view of many things and he can begin to cherish loneliness rather than to wish to share anything.

Now this morning with the day becoming hot and the cool wind from the mountain not having risen we were working out a new trail out of the forest that the elephants had destroyed. After we came out into the open prairie land after having to cut our way through a couple of bad places we saw the first great flock of storks feeding. They were true European storks black and white and red legged and they were working on the caterpillars as though they were German storks and under orders. Miss Mary liked them and they meant much to her since we had both been worried about the article that said that storks were becoming extinct and now we found that they had merely had good sense enough to come to Africa as we had done ourselves; but they did not take away her sorrow and we went on toward camp. I did not know what to do about Miss Mary's sorrow. It was proofed against eagles and proofed against storks against neither of which I had any defense at all and I began to know how great a sorrow it really was.

Ngui noticed that something was wrong and he took out the Jinny flask from the Spanish leather cartridge bag and handed it to me. I passed it back to Miss Mary who was watching the storks rather grimly. I looked at them and decided there were probably too many damned storks and that was why they had no power against her sorrow.

"Aren't you drinking a little early in the day?" she asked. I noticed hopefully that she was holding the Jinny flask.

"I hope not," I said. "For my stomach's sake."

She still retained the bottle and I thought I heard her open it. Ngui nodded imperceptibly.

"Give your damned sorrow a drink and I'll take one too."

"I took a small drink," she said and handed back the bottle. "What have you been thinking of all morning when you've been so uncommonly silent?"

"About birds and places and how nice you are."

"That was nice of you."

"I didn't do it as a spiritual exercise."

"I'll be all right. People don't just jump in and out of bottomless pits."

"They're going to make it an event in the next Olympic Games."

"You'll probably win it."

"I have my backers."

"Your backers are all dead like my lion. You probably shot all your backers one day when you were feeling especially wonderful."

"Look, there's another field of storks."

"Yes," she said. "Look, there's another field of storks."

CHAPTER 22

Africa is a dangerous place for a great sorrow to live very long when there are only two people in a camp and when it gets dark shortly after six o'clock in the evening. There had been the usual problems of medicine and minor surgery, the reports of the presence and absence of predatory beasts, and one serious report by Arap Meina. In the afternoon I had gone to the shamba with Miss Mary and had given the Informer some more penicillin. His morale was low but his condition was better and I touched the bad white buttes and caverns in his throat with silver nitrate. He bore this very well and it pleased the widow to see his fortitude. I did not like the look of his throat but I thought that by the next day the penicillin would be taking hold and that it was probably best to cauterize what I could reach. After the treatment I poured him out a good shot of gin into a glass Ngui had brought and left him the glass to furnish the house. Ngui loved to see me operate and I think he had hopes that we might have to really open up the Informer. Instead we left the Informer cheered and more confident and with two old copies of *Life* to divert him and went out to where Miss Mary was making friends with the children of the shamba. Debba had one of her sister's babies on her hip but she was off under one of the big shade trees of the shamba and did not come near the car. Bringing Miss Mary to the shamba was a little too much like showing the flag. Miss Mary knew this and we left the shamba for a ride back through the edge of the heavy bush and the gerenuk country. It was a cool and pleasant evening.

We saw no gerenuk but after we came out into the park country with the glades of trees Mary and Charo stalked a pair of Tommy rams and Mary made a beautiful shot on the bigger of the two and she and Charo and all of us were happy. Charo had made the ram into legal Moslem meat and there was no meat problem in camp now. There was still plenty of pagan meat and I had cold lion cutlets. We came back into camp at sunset and took our baths and then sat by the fire with drinks before dinner and talked and were happy.

We did not talk about lions nor think about them anymore and the emptiness where Mary's sorrow had lived was filling again with the routine and the strange fine life and the coming of the night. We talked about Spain and about the inn at Montiel in the pass where it was so cool and lovely and pleasant in the afternoon in the shade and then so hot at night that you could not breathe when the breeze stopped and the reflected heat came off the rocks of the mountains. We talked about the harshness of awakening in the morning at the clean but deadly cold and fog-bound hotel at Lecumberri at four in the morning for the drive into Pamplona and then how it was to come out of the mist of the mountains and down onto the plateau and the yellow of the grain fields of Navarre after Irurzun and the road unwinding under the Lancia so that it was almost like flying on the deck if you could keep the aircraft always between the long line of fast passing trees and not have to bring her up for anything. We talked about the advantages of speed and of slowness and how you never knew a country until you had walked it or ridden the roads in an open car or flown over it at treetop level or lower. We talked about the Chyulu Hills and I could not wait to have Willie back with the Cessna so that we could go there together again. We talked about the place down below the market where we went every morning after the bull running in Pamplona for breakfast of bacalao and lobster with smooth high-seasoned sauce you dipped with bread and the light clean-tasting wine with the local drunks singing and dancing and then the steep walk up the hill to the old ramparts and down through the old gate of the fortifications to the shade along the river where the horse fair was spread along the road under the trees. At first it had been difficult to accept the changes in Pamplona and I had been stupid about it. Later I had found the old places that had not been changed and we spent our time there and met our expensive friends at the new places that they liked and learned to enjoy what part of them was enjoyable. 21 in New York is a good restaurant and we always enjoyed eating there and there was no reason not to go to the new Basque versions of 21 that were necessary to our friends. If they knew no better that was what they knew and it made them comfortable and happy to be in each other's company and for things to be prohibitively costly.

We sat in the tent by ourselves at the table and the thousands of insects came against the netted door wishing to die against the petrol lamp and we talked about how wonderful it was that we had not seen a bore for more than five months which could easily be a record in this world where bores can now move from place to place so rapidly. We had seen them of

268

course each time we had been forced into a town. But we had not entertained any nor fed with any. We talked about how important it is not to eat with your enemies. You drink with them in legitimate defense but if you eat with them you are a fool and should be punished as an unsuccessful suicide is punished. It was pleasant to remember how we had gone five months without breaking bread with a wealthy bore and I knew that we owed the Mau Mau a considerable debt for this. Sitting there in the tent with Miss Mary happy again as we were almost always happy when we were alone enough together I began to want the aircraft very much. There was no legitimate excuse for sending for it unless the report Arap Meina had brought me was confirmed and I had spent much more money than I had any right to spend flying. I knew too that I had corrupted Mary into thinking there was no danger in flying on the deck nor around mountains and that I had been more than slightly a bastard by thinking up the slogan "Every Wakamba A Pilot." In our group we knew that this program would take some time and considerable expense but it was at least a goal to strive for and in our friction with the Moslems in the development of our new and definitive religion I had explained that anyone killed in an ndege or aircraft if he had within himself the intention or wish to become a pilot, navigator, or observer went directly to the Happy Hunting Grounds which we were now experimenting here on earth in developing and which was as vastly superior to the Moslem's promised happiness as a good drinking saloon was to a tea room. Keiti had flown more than anyone but we thought that we had him on the question of intention. Had he flown in pursuit of a vocation or had he merely traveled in an aircraft as a convenience? It made a great difference.

Willie had not been enthusiastic about procuring parachutes by which we could be dropped into the Chyulu Hills at locations where no white man or European nor any white woman including Miss Mary had ever been. Ngui was prepared to make this drop with me but the project was dimly viewed by Willie. We had not mentioned the project to G.C. since it was overly illegal but it was really not an unsound project at all and if it had come off and we could have followed it with a few more droppages I still think the religion might have swept the country. On the initial drop I had planned to bring in the highly necessary Tablets of the new religion such as it is always necessary to produce. Since nobody but me in our group could read or write I thought I would probably have to write these in Spanish and keep them as short as possible. We would have to bring back several miraculous things and it would be a long walk back but I was quite sure that Ngui and I could do it all right since there was plenty of water if you could follow the various watercourses and not have to worry about taking a vehicle through the lava boulders and the swamps that guarded the hills.

I was thinking about this and listening to Miss Mary talk about someone in London that neither of us could remember the name of when she suddenly interrupted and said, "I have a wonderful idea."

"What would it be, my good kitten?"

"I just thought we could have Willie come with the Cessna and you and he could check on all your beasts and your problems and then I'd go back with him to Nairobi and see a good doctor about this dysentery or whatever it is and I could buy Christmas presents for everyone and all the things we should have for Christmas."

"We call it the Birthday of the Baby Jesus."

"I still call it Christmas," she said. "And there are an awful lot of things we need. It wouldn't be too extravagant, do you think?"

"I think it would be wonderful. We'll send a signal through Ngong. When would you want the plane?"

"How would day after tomorrow be?"

"Day after tomorrow is the most wonderful day there is after tomorrow."

"I love tomorrow too and the next day and the next day. Aren't we lucky to be in Africa?"

"We're too lucky."

"I feel it too sometimes. But we're lucky kittens."

I knocked on the wood of the table three times with my right forefinger.

"But we are. You don't have to knock."

I knocked again but on the side of the table where she would not notice. She noticed though and said, "Knock if it's better for you. But we *are* lucky kittens."

This time I touched the wood of the pistol butt which was low down on my right leg, three times lightly and then took a chance and said, "Sure we're lucky."

"You're a very strange man," she said. "But it's your religion."

"Does the touching wood really bother you?"

"No," she said thoughtfully. "Why did you give your lucky stone away though? That was a really beautiful lucky stone and it wasn't too heavy for your pocket."

"If you give a lucky stone away you still have it," I explained. "It is only if you lose it or if it is stolen that is bad."

"I hope that's true."

"It's true all right."

"How can you really tell?"

"If you believe it it's true."

270

"It's an awfully primitive religion."

"They are all very primitive until they start to handle money."

"Where does the money always come from?"

"From the faithful."

"Let's talk about something else. I don't like to talk about religion at night."

"Neither do I."

"Anyway your religion is mostly superstitions."

"Beliefs," I said. "Or call it anything you like. Should we go out by the fire for a while before we go to bed?"

"Let's and we'll turn the light out so the poor bugs will stop committing suicide."

CHAPTER 23

When the fire burned down I pulled a long heavy dead tree from the pile of dead wood the lorry had brought in the afternoon onto the coals and we sat in our chairs and watched the night breeze blow the coals up and watched the wood catch fire. This night breeze was a small wind that came off the snows of the mountain. It was so light that you only felt its coolness but you could see it in the fire. You can see the wind in many ways but the loveliest is at night in the brightening and the lowering and rising of the flame in your fire. The lorry driver who was a very gay and charming drunkard and the two big porters who were not hunters and had no way to distinguish themselves except by feats of strength and fortitude loved to bring in loads of dead wood that competed in their oversized trunks and wild extending branches with the unbelievable size and very occasional ferocity of the animals we had to deal with. Loading up a lorry with moderate or reasonable sized pieces of dead wood for a well planned and economical fire meant nothing to them. They liked to come in as though they had killed a huge and unbelievable elephant and throw down logs and whole trees and one of their pleasures and excitements was to see scorpions come out as the rotted portions of the wood would break as they pitched it out. I always shot scorpions with the .22 Colt pistol. This was a part of the wood gathering game and at night when they would hear the small, sharp bark of the pistol coming from the campfire Mary and I would hear the porters laughing from their tents in the lines.

Tonight no scorpions came out of the dead tree trunk and the lines were quiet.

"We're never alone with our fire," Mary said. "I'm glad now there is only us and our fire. Will that log burn until morning?"

"I think so," I said. "If the wind doesn't rise."

"It's strange now without the lion to look forward to in the morning and you haven't any problems or worries now, have you?"

"No. Everything is quiet now," I lied.

"Do you miss all the problems you and G.C. had?"

"No."

"Maybe now we can get some really beautiful pictures of the buffalo and other fine color pictures. Where do you think the buffalo have gone?"

"I think they are over toward the Chyulus. We'll find out when Willie brings the Cessna."

"Isn't it strange how the mountain throwing all those stones hundreds and hundreds of years ago can make a place impossible to get to so that it is absolutely shut off from everyone and no one can reach it since men started to go on wheels?"

"They're helpless now without their wheels. Natives won't go as porters anymore and the fly kills pack animals. The only parts of Africa that are left are those that are protected by deserts and by the fly. The tsetse fly is the animals' best friend. He only kills the alien animals and the intruders."

"Isn't it strange how we truly love the animals and still have to kill almost every day for meat?"

"It's no worse than caring about your chickens and still having eggs for breakfast and eating spring chicken when you want it."

"It is different."

"Of course it is. But the principle is the same. So much game has come now with the new grass that we may not have any trouble lions for a long time. There is no reason for them to bother the Masai when we have so much game now."

"The Masai have too many cattle anyway."

"Sure."

"Sometimes I feel as though we were fools protecting their stock for them."

"If you don't feel like a fool in Africa a big part of the time you are a bloody fool," I said rather pompously I thought. But it was getting late enough at night for generalizations to appear the way some stars showed reluctant in their distance and disinterest and others always seemed brazen in their clarity.

"Do you think we should go to bed?" I asked.

"Let's go," she said. "And be good kittens and forget anything that's been wrong. And when we're in bed we can listen to the night."

So we went to bed and were happy and loved each other with no sorrow and listened to the night noises. A hyena came close to the tent after we had left the fire and I had crawled in under the mosquito net and between the sheets and the blankets and lay with my back against the canvas wall of the tent with Mary comfortable in the main part of the cot. He cried out a few times in the strange rising pitch and another answered him and they moved through the camp and out beyond the lines. We could see the glow of the fire brightening when the wind came and Mary said, "Us kittens in Africa with our faithful good fire and the beasts having their night life. You really love me, don't you?"

"What do you think?"

"I think you do."

"Don't you know?"

"Yes, I know."

After a while we heard two lions coughing as they hunted and the hyenas were quiet. Then a long way away to the north toward the edge of the stony forest beyond the gerenuk country we heard a lion roar. It was the heavy vibrating roar of a big lion and I held Mary close while the lion coughed and grunted afterwards.

"That's a new lion," she whispered.

"Yes," I said. "And we don't know anything against him. I'll be very damned careful about any Masai that talk against him."

"We'll take good care of him, won't we? Then he'll be our lion the way our fire is our fire."

"We'll let him be his own lion. That's what he really cares about."

"We haven't even seen him yet."

"We'll see him. Maybe you should go to sleep, Kitten. I have to get up early to hunt leopard."

"I'm asleep. I'm just talking in my sleep. Is it all right?"

"Don't you want to go in your bed?"

"No. I'll go when you're asleep."

She was asleep now and after a while I was asleep and when I woke and heard the lion again she was gone and I could hear her breathing softly in her bed.

CHAPTER 24

In the morning Ngui and I hunted leopard. It was a new day, as fresh and new as always, but neither of us had any confidence in the baits nor in the hides and I began to remember how leopards would come once to a dead baboon and feed and then not return. I could not blame them and thought this was admirable. Walking home through the wet grass I thought of all the nonsense I had read and heard about hunting leopards. Now that they were Royal Game and not just a beast that you shot for their hide as in the old days the white hunters had built them up into a really terrific animal. They were a fine cat. Perhaps the best and the fastest and strongest for their size and they could be very dangerous when they were wounded. Pop had drilled and redrilled that into me because he thought I did not take them seriously enough because I knew cats and liked them. A lioness was a cat, a true cat, and I always thought that I could think inside of her head. Cats are supposed to be very mysterious but they are not if you have any cat blood. I had a lot of cat blood, too much for my own good, but quite useful around cats. I had bear blood too and could think in a bear's head and talk with a bear and get him to do anything reasonable and I have been drunk with bears many times and never known a bear yet that I could not get along with. I smelled very good to bears and they smelled very good to me and I had never known a bear that I could not be friends with.

Walking in the morning with the day newly made and the pleasant cold wetnesses of your low boots and the wet of your khaki trousers against the calves of your legs it was fun to think about the different cats and about bears. A male lion never really seemed like a cat. He had some other kind of blood and the main cat qualities he had were his laziness and his short, terrible speed. The cheetah too never really seemed like a cat. He had dog blood and his long turn of speed was more like a greyhound's than like any cat. The leopard was a true cat though and a really wonderful one. The white hunters told their clients that you never saw them, or almost never, in the open or except when they came to a bait. This of course made it a great and rare event for a client to see a leopard in the open redounding both to the credit of the white hunter and the extraordinary luck of the client.

The way the white hunters ran safaris now they hung a series of leopard baits in trees, small buck, warthogs, and other animals, and left them to rot. In the evening they would drive by the baits and drop their clients off into the blinds that had been built to conceal them and when it came dark and the leopards climbed the trees to feed the clients would shoot them in the last fading light with the help of their telescopic sights. This was leopard hunting now and the clients were led to believe that there was no other way. The great moment was when the leopard miraculously appeared in the crotch of the tree where the bait was tied. This was a mystical moment which the clients never forgot. That and the leopard's baleful eyes and the fact that he was a spotted animal supplied the mystique. The white hunter did everything but pull the trigger and the leopard toppled dead or else was wounded and went into the bush and was eaten by hyenas. In Tanganyika some white hunters pulled the whole trick off at night with searchlights.

Now no clients would shoot anything without a telescopic sight. It was considered as necessary as a pink coat in the hunting field and with the newest clients nothing was really killed unless it had been struck by the .300 Weatherby Magnum. This piece of ordnance was stated to eliminate the necessity of shooting at the vital parts of any animal. It was said to deliver such a shocking, bone-shattering, tissue-destroying blow that it was only necessary to hit the animal itself and it was, if there was anything left of it, in the pot or its shattered hide en route to the taxidermist. The spectacle of a group of sportsmen clutching their Weatherby Magnums in their clammy hands being dropped off from their Land Rovers to ambush leopards in an endless chain from Narok to some sort of eternity where Weatherby would have it so perfectly organized that no shot from a Weatherby Magnum would blow off some young Tommy ram's hind leg to send him off seemingly gaily on three legs or eviscerating him to run out of range of the sportsman and his car was not good company walking back to camp. So I thought of something else.

I thought of all the leopards I had come on by accident since I had first gone to Africa and how I had never killed one on a bait in my life nor watched one appear noiselessly and quicker than the eye could follow in the fatal crotch of the tree that was the soul-trying mystic moment for the client. It was good to remember the first leopard I had ever seen in Tanganyika while walking along the bank of a stream that could have been a trout stream cutting through a meadow at home. The leopard had killed a small buck and was feeding on it crouched like a cat. I did not see him until he had heard or seen me and for a hundredth part of a second I had seen the two forms, the spotted one and the tawny one melded together and the head and the eyes of the leopard looking at me from twenty feet. I did not have time to see that his eyes were baleful nor for any literary thoughts because the leopard who had been foreshortened and concentrated into himself as he lay on the buck gave a spring that carried him far clear of the buck and into the grass and then moved out in great bounds over the short grass moving so fast with his tail out, not straight but curved, and his head up as he bounded that I could not swing the rifle ahead of him and shot three times behind him as he bounded toward and into the bush, the rifle bullet throwing an eruption of moist red dirt behind him each time I shot. It was impossible for me then to swing the rifle fast enough to get ahead on the crossing shot and I thought the leopard was the fastest animal I had ever seen move and his breaking into that first long bound and top speed one of the most moving things I had ever seen. He was a very big leopard too and I was lucky to see my first leopard that way.

Then I had never seen a cheetah and did not know how much faster a cheetah can run in the open than a leopard. In those days, being new to the country, we still shot cheetah. Now, having gotten to know them, I would never kill one but then we were if not stupider at least more ignorant, and I shot cheetah with the same ignorance and stupidity that a man will shoot a waterbuck. I had, then, just brains enough not to shoot a waterbuck. But that is no excuse for having shot cheetah.

By the time I had taken to shooting cheetah to get hides for a coat for my wife that turned out beautifully I had killed leopard unexpectedly and shot much running game so that I was loose with the rifle and swinging it well. On this particular cheetah who was going at full speed across an open glade I caught him in the sights and swung far ahead of him. He rolled over with the shot and lay quite still with his paws up. There had been no whunk from the bullet striking but only a light crack as a stick might make in breaking and I thought I must have hit him in the skull; perhaps only a glancing shot. When I walked up to him he was breathing and conscious and he looked at me with the look of a disappointed dog; only the eyes were cat's and they were not baleful; they were sad and thinned against the sun. There was no wound apparent and I asked M'Cola for the small 6.5 Mannlicher and shot him behind feeling like an executioner. The cheetah had made no move and had only watched us.

We turned him over and I said, "Where is he hit, M'Cola?"

M'Cola pointed to the tail. I had swung at least three lengths ahead of him and missed the body entirely and hit the bone of the rigid tail halfway to its end and that blow to the bone and the extension of the spinal cord had tumbled him over and he had lain there waiting for us to bring death to him.

This was not much good thinking about either except that I liked to think about M'Cola whose name was pronounced M'Cora, since Wakamba cannot pronounce the letter L. He was Ngui's father and when he was a boy the Wakamba had still been cannibals. This had helped to bridge what could have been a serious gap of understanding. I had no feeling about cannibalism so long as I was not expected to eat the meat myself. It was impossible for me to eat human flesh or the flesh of snakes. But I was sure this was some taboo just as Keiti could not eat the flesh of wildebeest and no one would eat the flesh of lions until Mary and I ate it and the appetizing smell of it cooking spread through the camp. Ngui ate it first because he and I would do anything which was not repulsive and we both affected to despise all taboos, one being the son of M'Cola and the other his apprentice and, finally, good friend. I did not know whether taboos produced the revulsion. That was quite possible. But I had an unbreakable revulsion toward the idea of human flesh or snake flesh. I could eat different lizards, though I disliked doing it. But the other things my stomach would never have retained.

It was strange to think back and remember all my prejudices about eating in boyhood. I drank milk in large quantities, usually from two to four quarts a day, and I could remember the wonderful feeling of drinking a whole quart when I first woke in the morning when we lived in town in the winter and I would bring the dozen quarts cold and almost frozen in from the back steps of the house. We always took twelve quarts of milk and sometimes fourteen and sixteen and as I woke the earliest of anyone in the family it was my duty to bring them in out of the cold before they should freeze and the cream rise high up out of the neck of the bottles with the cardboard caps perched ridiculously on top. The milk could rise like this without breaking the bottle although sometimes a bottle would be cracked but once risen it could not lower as a column when it thawed and it would melt and spill so the milk bottles had to be ranged in the sink until the cook should come and deal with them.

I loved to drink milk and to eat any kind of meat and nearly all fish although the best were perch, rock bass, trout, and sunfish. Whitefish from the Great Lakes was splendid to eat too and smoked it was a great delicacy. I ate the meat of all birds that we shot except birds of prey and all the berries that grew in Michigan in the summer; wild blackberries, raspberries, huckleberries that we picked in the summer and preserved for food in the winter. These and all the fruits I loved to eat but I could eat no vegetables except sweet corn, the mealies of Africa, which we ate roasted in the ashes of a fire. Then I did not like it boiled but I learned to like it later. All other vegetables I had to be forced to eat, usually by holding my nose so that I would not smell the odor of the vegetable. The odor made me violently ill and I could not abide any cooked vegetables and I had, finally, to learn to eat each one separately and with great effort. But I liked corn meal, which is the posho of Africa, and nearly always rolled my fish in it before frying them and we used posho to bake a cake called johnny-cake in a deep cast-iron cooking pot on legs which was placed in the coals and ashes of the fire and was known as a Dutch oven. It was much the way Msembi cooked out at the lines and as we came out into the white-flowered plain and saw the trees of camp against the loom of the moun-tain I could see the thin smoke rising and I was hungry for breakfast. There would be no cold quart of milk though I thought how cool the milk would be if it had hung all night in the canvas water bottle. But there would be good Tommy chops and stewed apricots and an egg and a slice of raw onion and a bottle of cold Tusker beer and a whole good day ahead of us that might bring anything. I would forget about the leopard and not wor-ry about him but would maneuver Mary into leopard country all the time and Ngui and I and Mthuka would be watching all the time and we would run onto a leopard as we had always run onto them with none of the leop-ard assassination setups that were provided for the clients. There were five leopards in this piece of country that I knew of and we would find one casually as we always had.

It would show my power to the Moslems in a much stronger way if we killed the leopard without using a bait, first announcing that we would do so. So when we came into camp I stopped by the cook tent to ask Keiti if everything was in order and if there were any problems or complaints. He said everything went well and that he was going to cut a path out from our tent to the latrine tent so that the Memsahib would not get wet from the high grass. I asked him to have the latrine tent changed from its present position to where I could see into the tops of the three tallest trees while sitting on the wooden seat. He grinned his long slit grin because he knew what that was for and I said to put the tent in earliest morning shade so I would be comfortable. He said yes and that the tree tops would be in the sun but the sun would be behind me. I told him I had a very strong dream in the night that we would kill the leopard without using baits. He was serious at this and asked me how strong the dream was. I said it was strong enough to awaken me three times. He said that this was a very strong dream but that baits were surer and that we should bait with buck and not with baboons. I said we might put up one buck bait to back up my dream

279

but that my dream coming three times was one that must be respected. I said I had a small dream that a leopard had come into the camp and that I had shot him in the tent but this was a black leopard and so I had discarded the dream. This dream had him worried so having asked for my breakfast and arranged for the lorry to go up to Loitokitok with the message that would bring the plane I walked over to the tent.

Mary was still sleeping and there was no particular reason for waking her so I went over to the mess tent and took a cold bottle of beer out of the canvas bucket and sat down to read Bemelmans. This was middle-period Bemelmans with much information and very few tricks and it was excellent breakfast reading after a walk in the early morning. I remembered seeing Bemelmans in the passageway between the Vendôme and the rue Cambon sides of the Ritz in Paris when we had last been in Paris on our way to Africa. I had stopped to speak with the girl who ran the bookstand. She was getting me, gradually and with patience, the complete collection of all published Simenons which I wished to take out to my son for rainy season reading and she told me who it was that was coming toward us along the passageway walled with glass showcases with their precious, elegant, or modish contents walking rather like a hippo moving along his trail from one part of a swamp to another. He looked like a Bavarian hippo who had been taught at an early age to proceed as a biped and I was charmed at this chance of meeting him unexpectedly as he proceeded along the tunnel that linked the two spheres where I had heard him spoken of not always with love by his ex-colleagues who served in the hotel.

I knew that the girl of the bookshop expected me to greet him as one homme des lettres should address another so I bowed and extending my hand told him very truly how much pleasure his books had given me and how pleased I was to see him looking so well. He examined my hand for a moment, bowed almost politely, and continued his progress occasionally stopping to look at some of the more spectacular mountings of jewels.

After saying good-bye to the girl I went on to the bar to compare my homework on the racing form with that of George who had come in early for this rendezvous in which we were comparing information, inspiration, and the element of withholding in past performances before I should go out to represent our two-man syndicate at Auteuil. George was very happy with my account of having finally met Bemelmans. It was in exact accord with the form he had on that writer who had given me so much enjoyment. We spoke of him a little and then went back to our studies.

Now it was pleasant to sit and drink moderately cold Tusker beer and read the Bemelmans of the good days while I ate the breakfast I had been looking forward to. There was another book that I knew I had to read but each time I tried it I became embarrassed and had to put it down. It was a book written by my brother and in an Indian bookshop in Dodoma in Tanganyika I had found the airmail edition of a weekly news magazine from America with a review of this book so cheaply and snidely written and with a photograph of my brother making him look like a hog in sheep's clothing at best and, at the worst, a small whale two days dead along an unfashionable pebbly beach of a tideless sea. The review made me so angry that I could not wait to write my brother of its injustice and share with him some anecdotes about certain reviewers that I knew would make him feel better. I was still bitter against this injustice to my brother who had always been the most idealistic and exemplary male member of our family. It was only he who a well-paying job having been obtained for him felt the absolute need to insult his employer as the sad poltroon the employer indeed was. Only my brother in our family would take a rotted hulk to sea without repairing her bottom and when she sank know that he had done his best. No one I knew but my brother had the courage in our family or in any other family that I had known to navigate using a rather rusted dollar alarm clock for a chronometer and I had never known another man so steeped in the literature of the great solitary navigators that he would lay to a sea anchor when he might as well be running before a fair breeze and then be becalmed for twenty-five days. These are only small feats that my brother accomplished and I, as soon as I could arrange to borrow Miss Mary's typewriter, was going to answer all critics of his seamanship, his unmitigating valor, and his sensitive and underived craftsmanship in writing. I intended, as an example of humility, to try to imitate my brother's prose style so that being refreshed by this contact with something quite new in writing I might experience a manual, tactile, and literary renaissance.

Then when I had finally conned Miss Mary into letting me use her typewriter under the pretext I would produce some durable or endurable prose, my brother's book arrived. It was a splendid book filled and refilled with everything. It brought the late war home to me in such poignant fashion that I had trouble sleeping at night unless I lay down or reclined in a chair. There was a character who resembled my brother and he was of such a goodness, kindness, and purity and thought so exactly as a man should that I felt as when I first read Dostoevsky and knew that in purity and nobility I could never compete with Alyosha until I could learn not to step on people's feet in the clinches and could study how not to let my thumb be drawn as by a lodestone to the right eye of an opponent. As I read further and saw the iniquities of others, both the Germans and those of our own band, and the unmitigated nobility of my brother, I felt overwhelmed by my own crassness and instead of the renewal that I had expected all desire to write left me and I would exchange the chances of attaining literary immortality for a few words with my fiancée at the shamba and the possibility of doing away with half a troop of baboons. Where my brother was born to slay dragoons with a borrowed sword and his integrity so looming through the fog of battle that I would have mistaken it for the Rock of Gibraltar and fallen back on it at once I could see that I was no better than a baboon slayer destined, perhaps, to bring about peace and understanding between the black and other races by an application of the policy of cohabitation in our time. Reluctantly I left my brother's book, excellent though it was, and went back again into the sordidness of our daily lives. I was somewhat consoled to remember that Dostoevsky himself was a gambler and a very poor gambler at that. This cheered me up and I went back to reading the ever instructive Bemelmans until Miss Mary came into the tent.

She was very beautiful and she greeted me cheerfully and asked why I had not waked her earlier. She had been awake quite a long time after her tea and then had gone back to sleep again. Her insides felt better but she was not well yet and we agreed that it was still a good plan for the Cessna to come out and for her to go in to Nairobi. She was happy and excited about the trip but it made her miss the camp and our country and our strange life and she said that she was homesick for it before she had left it.

We asked each other about the dreams we had in the night and she had dreamed a wonderful dream about someone she had known in Bemidji, Minnesota. She could not remember the dream but it had been full of excitement and adventure and she failed to remember it in great detail. I told her I had dreamed of leopards but in very short dreams that might or might not mean something. She said Mwindi had told her I had a very strong and powerful dream about a leopard and I told her that dream was the stuff we fed the troops.

At this we had an argument about whether it was justified to lie and I was caught and cornered maintaining a position that certain lies were truer than the truth and they were a necessity to any form of religion. I said that in Africa you should never lie about any practical thing but that if you did not have the necessary dreams you must invent them. Anyone to have any success in Africa must be able to invent dreams and then make them come true. This was elemental, I said.

"I'm not your dear Watson," Miss Mary said. "And I don't tell any lies to anyone and that is why I am loved and respected."

"I'll remember that," I said. "But are you revered?"

"Yes. I'm probably revered too."

"I'm delighted to know that. How did you find out?"

"Chungo told me," Mary said. "He told me that I was beloved and respected and revered. I wish Chungo was here. He is my hero and he personifies the opposite of everything that your people are."

"He's a company man," I said. "He sold out to the white man. He would have been a scout with George Armstrong Custer."

"You mean to say you think G.C. is like General Custer?"

"No."

"Then what are you trying to say?"

"Too early in the morning," I said. "What would you like to do today, my good tiger kitten?"

"What do you have to do?"

"We ought to have a routine look around and we can do anything you like. You wouldn't like to go up to Loitokitok?"

This was before Mary too had fallen in love with Loitokitok and she said no, that on her last day she would rather go on the general patrol and try to get some really good photographs of the storks and the eagles and check on the new lion and on the lionesses. She would also like to hunt the gerenuk country once more if it was possible.

While she had been eating her breakfast I had been finishing the bottle of Tusker and reading in the Bemelmans which was a big collection of all his hotel stories. I wished a detailist such as Bemelmans could have been with us in Africa to write at my orders as you would use a cameraman. Of course you could not hire people of that category since they were individuals and giant personalities and wished to ruin their talents in their own way and with perfect right to but I thought what splendid discipline it would be for an ex-Kraut hotel employee and how much better things in the end could be produced than the mawkish stuff about the little daughter and Lady Mendl. The picture of Bemelmans squatting out in the lines with Mbebia and the wonderful gossip and scandal that was there for him was dimmed though by the realization of what it would really be like and I thought I was lucky enough to have the splendid hotel memoirs of the German Proust of the back stairways. It was strange to think of the Ritz at breakfast in camp at the edge of the swamp and of the writers who had been associated with that hotel but it was very pleasant too and when Miss Mary had finished her breakfast and made the parade once again through new green grass to the faded green latrine tent and back we set off for the routine patrol.

The hunting car smelled of the old man smell of Charo in the early morning, of the freshly oiled shotguns and the rifles and the smell of oiling and cleaning rags that had cleaned and polished them, of Ngui's and Mthuka's personal odor of clean washed shirts and snuff and of Mary's clean clothes. It also smelled of the leather of the camera cases and the Spanish leather shell cases and of my freshly dubbed boots. As we drove through the fields of flowers they had no smell except when we crushed them and their stems. That was a smell like cutting green hay and the smell the wheels of the mower made in crushing the first stalks of alfalfa. But the flowering stalks of the high plateau grass were not sweet smelling.

We came onto the fields where the storks were spread out feeding, running and darting their heads down, walking slowly and driving their beaks with great speed and noticed that there were many marabou storks with them. They did not mix but fed in flocks of the European storks and groups and clusters of the marabous. We stopped the car and Mary made some excellent pictures and we were excited by the great flocks of storks. Their breasts and necks were a shiny white and their bills were red. The black of their lower backs and drooping tails formed a sharp black mass with their long black wing plumes. Their plumage was very formal and they looked so clean and Middle European beside the ungainly and obscene looking marabous and adjutants. The European storks had such clean white smooth feathered heads and when they flew if Mary walked too close to them they had such a beautiful line of black and white under the wings as their wing beats drove the long necks and bills forward easily and gracefully with full value from each unbroken stroke their legs close tucked up in a straight line or sometimes trailing.

In spite of the storks which fed steadily from just after daylight until just before dark the army worms were doing great damage to the flowers and the grass stripping the stems and working in the fields sometimes so thickly that it seemed as though the fields were moving. The storks kept on appearing in greater quantities all of the time and I wondered where they would go when they left us. They seemed to have such insatiable appetites and to eat such huge quantities of the worms that I wondered that they could ever exist in Europe on the limited quantities of food they would find on the Spanish plateau and in countries like the Black Forest compared to the feed that appeared after the rains in Africa. We knew from the newspapers that locusts had appeared in Arabia and that there were swarms as far down as Abyssinia and I thought that these birds might follow the locusts and the seasonal insect hatchings and perhaps only return to Europe for the breeding season. A great part of them certainly must not even return for the breeding and I hoped that we might find where they nested in Africa.

After Mary had the pictures she wanted we drove on by the old track up to the edge of the gray mud flats and the salt licks. The game was more plentiful than ever and as we drove very slowly they paid little attention to us. The wildebeest were in herds and in bunches and the Grant gazelles and the Tommys were feeding on the new grass as busily as the storks pursued the worms. Only the plover flew up crying wildly. We found tracks where two lionesses had crossed the track and further on the track of a big lion. Ngui and I followed it a while and found where he scuffed and braced himself when he had roared. This was the lion we had heard in the night.

Miss Mary had quite strong cramps so we all left her and the car by a big broken tree and then walked on up toward the mud flats to see if the buffalo showed by the papyrus swamp or if we would cross their trail. We wandered around, each making his small discoveries of what had happened in the night at the places where there was water and a fringe of reeds in the center of the western mud flat. The gray sweep was beginning to shimmer now enough to distort the outlines of the animals that were feeding on the patches of grass that grew in streaks or clumps on the dried mud but not enough to make the mirage of the lake with its reedy shores. The light made a single wildebeest look like a buffalo in the edge of the papyrus but the 8x glasses cut through the distortion and showed the wildebeest clearly.

I looked back toward the car and saw that Mary was in her seat and we turned back. When we came up to the car Mary did not look well and she said she had bad cramps again. I told her we would walk back along the track and for her to touch the klaxon when she wanted Mthuka to come for the car and drive down and pick us up.

When we were all together in the car again Mary said, "I'm so ashamed of being such a nuisance."

"You're no nuisance. Charo remembers when I nearly died of amoebic. Tomorrow you'll be in Nairobi and they'll fix you up."

"But I don't want to lose today. We were going to have such a lovely day and now I'm spoiling it for you."

"Don't be silly, honey. We had a lovely time with the storks and you got some really good pictures. We'll go back to camp where it's cool and take it easy and you rest good."

"I wanted to go and hunt the gerenuk country once before we left."

"You'll hunt the gerenuk country plenty of times. We'll go in now while it's still cool."

Back in camp there was a good strong breeze from the mountain and it was cool and fresh in the mess tent with its double canvas roof. Mary made the walk to the new latrine location and I had Mwindi open up the back of our tent and prop it open so that the wind blew through. Our tent was in the shade and when the back was propped open it was cool and pleasant with the breeze blowing through.

"Memsahib sick?" Mwindi asked as he fixed the pillows so that Mary could lie with her head toward the wide-open end of the tent and tested the air mattress on the cot with the palm of his hand before drawing the sheets smooth over the mattress and folding them tightly under.

"Yes. A little."

"Maybe from eat the lion."

"No. She was sick before kill the lion."

"Lion run very far very fast. Was very angry and sad when he die. Maybe make poison."

"Bullshit," I said.

"Hapana bullshit," Mwindi said gravely. "Bwana Captain Game Ranger eat lion too. He sick too."

"Bwana Captain Game Ranger sick with same sickness long back Salengai."

"Eat lion Salengai too."

"Mingi bullshit," I said. "He sick before I kill lion. Hapana eat lion in Salengai. Eat lion here after safari from Salengai. When lion skinned Salengai all chop boxes packed. Nobody eat that morning. You think back bad."

Mwindi shrugged his shoulders under the long green gown. "Eat lion Bwana Captain Game Ranger sick. Memsahib sick. Bwana Hudson mingi sick."

"Bwana Hudson sick for forty years. You know too bloody well. Who eat lion feel fine? Me."

"Shaitani," Mwindi said. "I see you sick to die before. Many years ago when you young man you sick to die after you kill lion. Everybody know you die. Ndege know. Bwana know. Memsahib know. Everybody remember when you die."

"Did I eat the lion?"

"No."

"Was I sick before I kill that lion?"

"Ndio," Mwindi said reluctantly. "Very sick."

"You and me talk too much."

"We are mzees. All right talk if you wish talk."

"Kwisha talk," I said. I was tired of the pidgin English and I did not think much of the idea that was building up. "Memsahib goes to Nairobi in the ndege tomorrow. Doctor in Nairobi cures her sickness. Come back from Nairobi well and strong. Kwisha," I said again meaning it is finished.

"Mzuri sana," Mwindi said. "I pack everything."

I went out of the tent and Ngui was waiting under the big tree. He had my shotgun.

"I know where there are two kwali. Shoot them for Miss Mary."

Mary was not back yet and we found the two francolin dusting in a patch of dried dirt at the edge of the big fever trees. They were small and compact and quite beautiful. I waved at them and they started to run crouching for the brush so I shot one on the ground and the other as it rose.

"Any more?" I asked Ngui.

"Only the pair."

I handed the gun to him and we started back for camp, me holding the two plump birds, warm and clear eyed with their soft feathers blowing in the breeze. I would have Mary look them up in the bird book. I was quite sure I had never seen them before and that they might be a local Kilimanjaro variety. One would make a good broth and the other would be good for her if she wanted solid food. I would give her some Terramycin and some Chlorodyne to tie things up. I was allergic to Terramycin but she seemed to get no bad reactions from it.

I was sitting in a comfortable chair in the cool mess tent when I saw Mary come up to our tent. She washed and then came over and into the door of the tent and sat down.

"Oh my," she said. "Should we not mention it?"

"I could drive you back and forth in the hunting car."

"No. It's as big as a hearse."

"Take this stuff now if you can hold it down."

"Would it be terrible to have a gimlet for my morale?"

"You're not supposed to drink but I always did and I'm still here."

"I'm not quite sure whether I'm here or not. It would be nice to find out."

"We'll find out."

I made the gimlet and then said that there was no hurry to take the medicine and for her to go in and lie down on the bed and rest and read if she felt like it or I would read to her if she would like.

"What did you shoot?"

"A couple of very small francolin. They're like small partridges. I'll bring them in after a while and you can look at them. They'll make you supper."

"What about lunch?"

"We'll have some good Tommy broth and mashed potato. You're going to knock this thing right away and it's not so bad that you shouldn't eat. They say Terramycin kills it better than Yatren in the old days. But I'd feel better if we had Yatren. I was sure we had it in the medical chest."

"I'm thirsty all the time."

"I remember. I'll show Mbebia how to make rice water and we'll keep it cool in a bottle in the water bag and you drink all of that you want. It's good for the thirst and it keeps your strength up."

"I don't know why I had to get ill with something. We lead such a wonderful healthy life."

"Kitten, you could just as well have got fever."

"But I take my Atabrine every night and I always make you take yours when you forget it and we always wear our mosquito boots in the evening by the fire."

"Sure. But in the swamp after the buffalo we were bitten hundreds of times."

"No, dozens."

"Hundreds for me."

"You're bigger. Put your arms around my shoulders and hold me tight."

"We're lucky kittens," I said. "Everybody gets fever if they go in country where there is a lot of it and we were in two bad fever countries."

"But I took my medicine and I made you remember yours."

"So we didn't get fever. But we were in bad sleeping sickness country too and you know how many tsetse flies there were."

"Weren't they bad though by the Guaso Nyiro? I remember coming home in the evenings and they would bite like a red-hot eyebrow tweezer."

"I've never even seen a red-hot eyebrow tweezer."

"Neither have I but that's what they bit like in that deep woods where the rhino lived. The one that chased G.C. and Kibo into the river. That was a lovely camp though and we had so much fun when we first started hunting by ourselves. It was twenty times more fun than having somebody with us and I was so good and obedient, remember?"

"And we got so close to everything in the big green woods and it was like we were the first people that were ever there."

"Do you remember where the moss was and the trees so high there was almost no sunlight ever and we walked softer than Indians and you took me so close to the impala that he never saw us and when we found the herd of buffalo just across the little river from the camp? That was a wonderful camp. Do you remember how the leopard came through the camp every night just like having Boise or Mr. Willie moving around the Finca at night at home?"

"Yes, my good kitten and you're not going to be sick really now because the Terramycin will have taken hold of that by tonight or in the morning."

"I think it's taking hold now."

"Cucu couldn't have said it was better than Yatren and Carbarsone if it wasn't really good. Miracle drugs make you feel spooky while you are waiting for them to take hold. But I remember when Yatren was a miracle drug and it really was then too."

"I'm going to just lie quiet and feel the breeze from the snow on our mountain. You go and make yourself a drink and read and be comfortable."

"I'll go out to show Mbebia how to make the rice water."

Mary felt much better at noon and in the afternoon she slept again and in the evening felt quite well and was hungry. I was delighted with how the Terramycin had acted and that she had no bad reactions from it and told Mwindi, touching the wood of my gun butt, that I had cured Mary with a powerful and secret dawa but that I was sending her into Nairobi tomorrow in the ndege in order that a European doctor might confirm my cure.

"Mzuri," Mwindi said.

Everyone was happy that Miss Mary was better because they had all seen what dysentery could do in the old days and it was miraculous and lovely when she went out to the cooking fires and joked with Mbebia who always behaved like a combination of a wise old man, a confidant of kings, and a rather disreputable school girl. They both made fun of my rice water which had turned out to be fairly tasteless and repulsive but I knew that Mbebia remembered the days of barley water and more barley water and the evacuations mounting into the hundreds a day and the careful washing of the prolapsed intestine and the reinsertion with the aid of soap and warm water and the sudden spasms of almost true pain. Mbebia, Keiti, Mwindi, and Charo remembered all of this along with the arrival of the vultures and the marabou storks drawn by the odor and they could remember very well the burial details. But now we had miracle drugs for almost everything and it was getting so only the drugs could kill you.

So we ate lightly but well and happily that night and it was a happy camp again and the disease and misfortune, through the eating of lion meat party, which had made a strong bid for power in the morning, dissolved as though the subject never had been raised. There were always these theories that came to explain any misfortune and the first and most important thing was someone or something that was guilty. Miss Mary was supposed to have extraordinary and unexplainable bad luck herself, which she was in the process of expiating, but she was also supposed to bring great good luck to other people. She was also well loved.

Arap Meina actually worshiped her and Chungo, G.C.'s chief Game Scout, was in love with her. Arap Meina worshiped very few things as his religion had become hopelessly confused but he had moved into a worshiping of Miss Mary that, occasionally, reached peaks of ecstasy that were little short of violence. He loved G.C. but this was a sort of schoolboy fascination combined with devotion. He came to care greatly for me carrying this affection to the point where I had to explain to him that it was women that I cared for rather than men though I was capable of deep and lasting friendship. But all his love and devotion which he had scattered over one whole slope of Kilimanjaro with complete sincerity and almost always with returned devotion giving it alike to men, women, children, boys and girls, and to all types of alcohol and the available heroic herbs, and they were many, he now concentrated this great talent for affection on Miss Mary.

Arap Meina was not supremely beautiful although he had great elegance and soldierliness in uniform with his earlaps always coiled neatly over the tops of his ears so that they formed a knot of the sort Greek goddesses wore their hair in, a sort of modified psyche knot. But he had to offer the sincerity of an old elephant poacher gone straight and into a straightness so unimpeachable that he could offer it to Miss Mary almost as though it were a virginity. The Wakamba are not homosexual. I do not know about the Lumbwa because Arap Meina was the only Lumbwa I have ever known intimately but I would say that Arap Meina was strongly attracted by both sexes and that the fact that Miss Mary with the shortest of African haircuts provided the pure Hamitic face of a boy with a body that was as womanly as a good Masai young wife was one of the factors that channeled Arap Meina's devotion until it became worship. He called her not Mama, which is the ordinary way an African speaks of any married white woman when he does not feel up to saying Memsahib, but always Mummy. Miss Mary had never been called Mummy by anyone and told Arap Meina not to address her in that way. But it was the highest title he had salvaged from his contact with the English language and so he called her Mummy Miss Mary, Miss Mary Mummy, or Mummy Mummy, depending on whether he had been using the heroic herbs and barks or had simply made contact with his old friend alcohol.

We were sitting by the fire after dinner talking of Arap Meina's devotion to Miss Mary and I was worrying about why I had not seen him that day and whether what he had told me the day before might have turned out badly when Mary said, "It isn't bad for everybody to be in love with everybody else the way it is in Africa, is it?"

"No."

"Are you sure something awful won't come out of it suddenly?"

"Awful things come out of it all the time with the Europeans. They drink too much and get all mixed up with each other and then blame it on the altitude."

"There is something about the altitude or it being altitude on the equator. It's the first place I've ever known where a drink of pure gin tastes like water. That's really true and so there must be something about the altitude or something."

"Sure there is something. But we who work hard and hunt on foot and sweat our liquor out and climb the damned escarpment and climb around this mountain don't have to worry about liquor. It goes out through the pores. Honey, you walk more going back and forth to the latrine than most of the women who come out here on safari walk in the whole of Africa."

"Let's not mention the latrine. It has a wonderful path to it now and it's always stocked with the best reading matter. Have you ever finished that lion book yet?"

"No. I'm saving it for when you're gone."

"Don't save too many things for when I'm gone."

"That's all I saved."

"I hope it teaches you to be cautious and good."

"I am anyway."

"No, you're not. You and G.C. are fiends sometimes and you know it. When I think of you a good writer and a valuable man and my husband doing what you and G.C. do on those terrible night things."

"We have to study the animals at night."

"You don't either. You just do devilish things to show off to each other."

"I don't think so really, Kitten. We do things for fun. When you stop doing things for fun you might as well be dead."

"But you don't have to do things that will kill you and pretend that the Land Rover is a horse and that you're riding in the Grand National. Neither of you can ride well enough to ride at Aintree on that course."

"That's quite true and that's why we're reduced to the Land Rover. G.C. and I have the simple sports of the honest countryman."

"You're two of the most dishonest and dangerous countrymen I've ever known. I don't even try to discipline you any more because I know it's hopeless."

"Don't talk bad about us just because you're leaving us."

"I wasn't doing that. I was just horrified for a minute thinking about you two and what your ideas of fun are. Anyway thank God G.C. isn't here so you'd be alone together."

"You just have a good time in Nairobi and get checked by the doctor and buy whatever you want and don't worry about this manyatta. It will be well run and orderly and nobody will take any unnecessary risks. I'll run a nice clean joint while you're gone and you'll be proud."

"Why don't you write something so I'll be really proud?"

"Maybe I'll write something too. Who knows?"

"I don't mind about your fiancée as long as you love me more. You do love me more, don't you?"

"I love you more and I'll love you more still when you come back from town."

"I wish you could come too."

"I don't. I hate Nairobi."

"It's all new to me and I like to learn about it and there are nice people too."

"You go to it and have fun and come back."

"Now I wish I didn't have to go. But it will be fun flying with Willie and then I'll have the fun of flying back and coming back to my big kitten and the fun of the presents. You'll remember to get the leopard, won't you? You know you promised Bill you'd have the leopard before Christmas."

"I won't forget but if you'd just as soon I'd rather do it and not worry about it."

"I just wanted to be sure you hadn't forgotten."

"I hadn't forgotten. Also I'll brush my teeth and remember to turn off the stars at night and put the hyena out."

"Don't make fun. I'm going away."

"I know it and it isn't funny at all."

"But I'll be back and I'll have big surprises."

"The biggest and best surprise is always when I see my kitten."

"It's even better when it's in our own airplane. And I'll have a wonderful and special surprise but it's a secret."

"I think you ought to go to bed, Kitten, because even though we are winning now with the stuff you ought to rest well."

"Carry me in to the bed the way I thought you would have to carry me when I thought I might start dying this morning."

So I carried her in and she weighed just what a woman that you loved should weigh when you lifted her in your arms and she was neither too long nor too short and did not have the long dangling crane legs of the tall American beauties. She carried easily and well and she slid into the bed as smoothly as a well launched ship comes down the ways.

"Isn't bed a lovely place?"

"Yes. Bed is our Fatherland."

"Who said that?"

"Me," I said rather proudly. "It's more impressive in German."

"Isn't it nice we don't have to talk German?"

"Yes," I said. "Especially since we can't."

"You were very impressive in German in Tanganyika and at Cortina."

"I fake it. That's why it sounds impressive."

"I love you very much in English."

"I love you too and you sleep well and you'll have a good trip tomorrow. We'll both sleep like good kittens and be so happy that you're going to be all right."

In the night I lay awake for quite a long time happy that Mary was sleeping well and that she was going to be all right. Awake in the night it seemed funny that she should have spoken of the Cessna as our own plane and I thought that if we had bought it on the installment plan instead of chartering it that it would have been our own plane in a few more months. But then it would be one more thing to worry about. I did not like possessions any more except the guns and the precious 220 grain solid ammo for the .30-06 that was so hard to come by and that I always kept in the inside loops of my left breast pocket flap for life insurance. With that you did not need the big gun if you were by yourself and had no one you had to be responsible for. I thought how all we really needed to be happy was ourselves, something to read, two rifles that would shoot where you held them, a .22 pistol and plenty of long rifle ammo for it, and then as I thought the severely restricted essentials dragged out into an inventory of the whole safari. We were living exactly as we liked to live and it was not elaborate but it was very comfortable and tomorrow the plane would be in and Willie and I would case the country. It was a normal night and I listened to the noises and after I heard the new big lion and located him as somewhere this side of the old manyatta on this side of the gerenuk country I went to sleep.

CHAPTER 25

Ngui and I still hunted leopard across and through the park country and along the river moving softly and watching all the possible leopard branches in the likely trees. We hunted with the light against our backs. There was no wind at all yet and when the sun was over the lowest slope of the mountain it was on our backs.

Charo had heard a leopard hunting along the river going toward the swamp early in the morning before it was light when I was still sleeping. We told Charo where we were going to hunt and for him to send Mthuka out to us when he, Charo, should hear me shoot. I planned to kill a piece of meat for Willie to have a quarter or a saddle to take back to Nairobi in the plane for his family. I should have taken Charo instead of Ngui so that Charo could halal for the Moslems but Ngui and I were brothers and I was going to shoot something good for the Moslems anyway and the pagans Mary, Willie, and I could deal with this meat. I had wakened hungry for meat and hungry all the way through and had only drunk a single cup of tea because I did not want to feel it sloshing.

We hunted very soft and easy and I was trying to think like a big leopard who had plenty of game to kill, four shambas in his hunting area with goats, dogs, and chickens, a camp with hung meat to steal from, six or eight troops of baboons and no one, as far as he knew, except for one experience a month before, hunting him. I decided that if a leopard I would not be too careful. I had seen this leopard, the very big one, at a distance of about thirty feet. He was flattened on the limb of a tree at the edge of the swamp in a driving rainstorm. The rain was in my face, I was wearing glasses, and I was just going to wipe the glasses when looking through them as through a rain-pelted windshield I looked into his eyes as he lay crouched facing me with his back against the bole of the tree and the wind and rain. His head looked almost as broad as a lioness and we looked directly into each other's eyes and made our moves at the same time. I raised the rifle to shoot him cocking by pulling back on the knurled bolt as I raised it as fast as in taking a towering bird and in this time he had pivoted so fast that he blurred and was going down the far side of the tree like a snake with never more than a patch of spotted belly showing on either side of the tree. I ran to the right of the tree as he went into the tall papyrus of the swamp in a single bound. Without the rain I would have had a snap shot. Without glasses I would have had a shot in the rain. As it was there was no shot and the biggest leopard I had ever seen had moved the fastest and the most intelligently that I had ever seen a cat move.

We found where he had bedded there and from the claw marks and from hairs on other trees where he had slept. We had baited him once but he had never come to the bait. He had moved up the river and taken to raiding the shamba for goats and now he had stopped killing goats temporarily and was killing game again. I had always wished that I had been carrying the shotgun when we had looked at each other in the rain. But it wasn't a shotgun country except for the snakes. It was a bad rhino and difficult buffalo country and we were not going into it this morning. We were simply hunting the places he might have gone into on a good leopard tree if he had gotten careless again. We picked up his tracks as he traveled along the stream and then lost them on a rocky hillside and turned back to camp.

On our way out in the early morning we had seen a cheetah on a patch of plain and he was still lying in the grass when we came back. I looked at his handsome cat-dog face as he looked out across the plain with its new grass watching the small, grazing, tail-flicking antelope he owned and was glad that I did not shoot cheetahs any more. I remembered the coat that had been made from the cheetah hides by Valentina and how the ruff over the shoulders had been combined in the various hides to make a ruff along the line of the shoulders of the woman who wore it and how beautiful it had been one fall in New York and unlike any other coat. Then I remembered how any coat of that sort was regarded by nearly all women as an evasion of responsibility in that it was neither mink nor sable and was not an investment and without resale value. It was as bad as giving some substitute for jewels. After the good dark wild mink coat of proper length had been given a man might be permitted some fantasies but not before and I looked at the cheetah and the small buck that were his property and I hoped I might see him kill again with his two brothers some evening.

Now that I began to think about that fall in New York and how that cheetah coat ended I did not wish to disturb this cheetah nor the small herd of game he and his two brothers lived on. It was a great pleasure to see them hunt and watch that unbelievable closing rush and their skins belonged on their own backs and not across any woman's shoulders unless Debba was getting cold, I thought, and then I would get her a goat- and chicken-killing leopard except that a woman could not wear a leopard skin in our tribe and it would only make trouble. I would give her enough springhare skins to make a vest of to have against the cold wind of the early morning that could come down colder than the wind came off the snow-topped Guadarramas to Madrid. She could wear it back from ngomas too at night. She had never heard of mink and I could start her in on springhare and serval cat. I'd have to look up in the game regulations to make sure serval cat had not been made Royal Game. Some day they will make the hyena Royal Game, I thought, but maybe not in our time. Her Majesty's Ever Loyal Hyenas led by Bwana Lord Fisi in the March Past. Straighten up there now heads further up and when I say slope I don't mean slope down to your ass.

We had left the cheetah behind and we came onto the clearing in the medium high trees where the two Tommy rams with the beautiful heads with horns that were so big they looked almost like Grant's gazelle grazed. They were friends of ours and we were proud and happy to have them so close to camp and they paid us almost no attention as we crossed the corner of the clearing moving almost knee-deep through the new rich grass. I did not want to frighten these two bucks that we thought of as our friends and I had decided long ago that it was selfish and thoughtless to kill anything that morning that we did not have Charo or another of the good Moslems halal so we worked our way around the game we saw and came into camp across the field with the broken patches of bush.

I could see Mthuka and Charo waiting in the car beyond the tents under the big tree. Mthuka was sitting forward leaning on the wheel, his old slouch hat down over his eyes, and Charo was in the back only his very black face, his ancient blue jacket, and his dirty white turban showing as he sat erect against the seat.

Mary had dressed and was brushing her head. Ngui walked on to the car with the guns saying, "Jambo, Memsahib," as he passed the open tent.

Mary said, "Jambo, Ngui. I didn't hear you shoot."

"Hapana," Ngui said and went on to the car.

We kissed good morning and I asked her if she wanted to go out with us now to get the meat for Willie and for the camp.

"How do you feel, honey?"

"I feel good," she said. "That stuff has fixed me. I'd love to go if I may. But you shoot."

"No. You shoot. I'll shoot plenty while you are away."

"We'll shoot partners and you back me up."

"You won't need any backing up. We can go out now and have breakfast when we come in. Do you have any tea left?"

"No. I drank it all. I was so very thirsty."

"That's natural. Are you sure you want to go, honey?"

"Please. I can get everything ready while you and Willie are flying. I'd love to fly with you but I know I shouldn't."

Since there was no tea ready I drank about a quarter of a bottle of beer and brought the rest of the bottle along for Ngui and Mthuka and me to drink in the car. We went off to the north past the airstrip and then turned east and when we sighted some Tommies mixed with Grant's we stopped the car and let Charo and Mary start their walk away from the car and out of line with the game and then when they were a quarter of a mile away and screened by some trees they started their stalk and we drank the beer. They did not get up right the first time and we opened another bottle that Ngui had brought in a cooler bag not knowing I was bringing the opened bottle.

From a half a mile away we saw Miss Mary raise her rifle to shoot and heard the shot and then the thunk. Charo ran out and we saw Mary walk out of sight beyond the patch of bush. Mthuka started the car and passed the bottle to me. I took a swallow and passed it to Ngui who capped it and put it in the water bag.

We picked up Mary and Charo who was wiping his knife on the Tommy ram and put the dead beast in the back of the car.

"He was such a nice lovely Tommy and I shouldn't have killed him," Mary said. "But he's the one Charo told me to take and I hit him just behind the shoulder where I aimed."

"Piga mzuri," Charo said. "Mzuri sana."

"How far did you take him from, Kitten?"

"I don't know. I thought it was too far but Charo said to piga so I piga-ed him. Anyway he isn't married and has a family. There were three bucks almost the same size and he was the biggest."

"He's fat too."

"I'm so happy I can go to Nairobi now with my insides solid and not a disgrace and knowing I can shoot. Or that I did shoot."

"You don't want any beer do you?"

"I might take a little sip with all the members."

Ngui asked her for her handkerchief and carefully wiped the neck and the mouth of the bottle and Mary took a good drink.

"It's wonderful," she said. "And so refreshing just like the ads with the wholesome looking families at home. Do you suppose we look like a wholesome American family in the beer ads?"

"Sort of," I said. "Except for Charo maybe. He doesn't drink."

"Poor Charo," Mary said and Charo grinned. "Can I have just one more sip?"

She drank and said, "I didn't know what I was missing. Do all of you drink beer in the morning?"

"When we have it and if there isn't any responsibility."

"Now I know how good it is, am I your good brother as well as your wife and provider of meat for everybody?"

"Leave some for your other brothers and you'll be more popular."

"Here, you take it and pass it in the proper order. I don't want to make any mistakes."

I took the quart bottle and drank and passed it to Mthuka who drank and passed it to Ngui who looked at what was left carefully against the sun and finished it.

"I don't want to go away now," Mary said. "I don't want to go away at all ever."

"You'll have a good time and there's the ride both ways with Willie."

"I'd like breakfast now," Miss Mary said. "And then we'll go out and meet Willie at our airstrip. This meat will be properly taken care of, I hope."

"I assure you," I said.

"I'm glad of that. I'd hate to provide meat for my pagan brothers and for my loyal Moslem friends and for the captain of our personal flight and then have it mishandled."

"Do you want it aged, ma'am? It ages very quickly in this climate."

"Age it a little if you think best. No, I think you better keep it as fresh as possible."

"The last piece we gave Willie was so aged and forceful that he said it stepped out of the aircraft by itself and walked into the Aero Club and went up to the bar and ordered a drink."

"Did they serve it?"

"No. Willie said it was too high for them to serve it."

"What was the other terrible thing he said?"

"That some of the boys mistook it for an Old Member who had crashed somewhere in Ruanda-Urundi and had never been found."

"We'll keep this really fresh for Willie."

"Willie will probably say then it was so fresh that it tried to take over the controls and make a dead-stick landing on the dry sand river at Salengai."

"Oh my, it is nice to be with people like Willie and you and G.C. and Pop and people that make jokes and are never solemn."

"I'm glad you like us today. I always love Pop and I love Willie too. He's always so neat and wholesome and fresh looking."

"I'm glad you love some Europeans. It's healthy you know."

"You try and remember your European wife too even if she isn't a real European."

"You are a European. I can swear to it. I've heard you speak French over the telephone."

"Don't make fun of me when I'm going away."

We were back at camp and had breakfast and when Willie buzzed the camp we went out fast to where the windsock hung dead against the skinned tree pole and watched his short delicate landing on the crushed flowers the lorry had flattened for him. We unloaded and loaded the hunting car and I ran through the mail and the cables while Mary and Willie talked in the front seat. I sorted Mary's letters and mine and put the Mr. and Mrs. in Mary's lot and opened the cables. There was nothing really bad and two were encouraging.

In the mess tent Mary had her mail at the table and Willie and I shared a bottle of beer while I opened the worst looking letters. There was nothing that nonanswering would not help.

"How's the war, Willie?"

"We still hold Government House, I believe."

"Torr's?"

"Definitely in our hands."

"The New Stanley?"

"The dark and bloody ground? I heard G.C. put a patrol of airline hostesses as far as the Grill. Chap named Jack Block seems to be holding it. Very gallant effort."

"Who has the Game Department?"

"I shouldn't like to say. From the last gen I had it was rather nip and tuck."

"I know Nip," I said. "But who is this Tuck?"

"A new man I presume. I hear Miss Mary shot a beautiful great lion. Will we be taking him back, Miss Mary?"

"Of course, Willie."

"Papa, the way it looked we might as well go and get our time in over your vast domains whenever you feel up to it. We might have showers over the Chyulus later on. It's building up a little. We can go and look around and I'll fly Miss Mary up to town after the showers if there are any. We'll be back in plenty of time for lunch, Miss Mary."

"Can't I go?"

"Of course if you want to and Papa thinks you should."

"Do you want to go, honey?"

"I'd love to but I don't really think I should. I ought to be getting packed and somebody has to look at the mail."

299

"Read anything of mine you like," I said. "The hell with those white women."

"That's the true spirit, Papa," Willie said. "How's everything at the shamba?"

"My father-in-law is facing up to things. I'm trying to get Rupert Bellville to put him up for White's. Do you think that will please him? I've promised the whole family a trip to Paris and it would be nice for him to have a club if we should pop over to London."

"I'll put him up for the Aero Club," Willie said. "He has his own plane, I suppose?"

"We haven't got delivery of it yet. He's holding out for the Cub with the little wheel in the nose."

"It does look rather African," Willie said. "But we do have bigger flaps on the Cessna. He'd probably like the Cub though."

"It's the name he likes mostly. And that wheel in the nose."

"But, Papa, our flaps are comparable to an old elephant's ears. We'll go over the shamba on our way home and let him have a look at the flaps."

"My fiancée likes it best when we really beat up the shamba and it makes the chickens run and disperses the goats. That's what sends her. She doesn't care about the flaps."

"A pity," Willie said. "But your father-in-law might appreciate them. Does he have you insured, do you know?"

"With Lloyd's. The local man for Lloyd's in Loitokitok spends damned near half his time at the shamba."

"Good chap," said Willie. "That's the spirit we need. Well, Papa, do you think we should get along and become airborne?"

"Are you sure you don't want to go, Kitten?"

"I shouldn't. But don't you fiends go and stunt and scare that nice girl to death. And don't let Willie think I'd read your letters either."

"She doesn't scare. There's a notice says the plane is not licensed for stunting and Willie knows very well you don't read my letters."

"I can respond for all of that, Miss Mary, except whether the girl scares or not. I've never seen her except from the air and she looked quite the steady type."

"From the air don't you think the shamba looks rather like Abbeville?"

"It always reminds me of a marshalling yard near Rheims," Willie said. "What's it look like to you, Miss Mary?"

"You two go and fly," Mary said. "I trusted you to come here and be a good influence, Willie, and now you're both getting into an untrustworthy mood."

"I was just trying to help Papa revive his faded memories in case he was writing a book, Miss Mary."

"I'm taking Ngui and Pop's gunbearer. He wants to fly."

"No Arap Meina?"

"Hapana Arap Meina. He really purchased it from the ndege. He says he'll fly if he has to. But I told him it wasn't necessary. He gave me the gen on what we need to look for."

Ngui and Pop's gunbearer were waiting in the car and we drove out to the aircraft that Arap Meina was guarding. He saluted smartly and watched the four of us get into the plane with unenvious eyes. I told Mthuka to run the hunting car up and down the strip now and then a half dozen times after we were off.

After Willie had taxied down to the end of the strip and turned and held her there while she roared and begged to go we came down the white field of flowers and rose into the air just beside the hunting car and I looked down and saw Mthuka and Arap Meina looking up at us and noticed that the top of the hunting car was scratched. No one had been up there with boots on and I remembered then the place in the thick forest where the heavy branches swept over it. Then the hunting car was small behind us and Willie said, "Where to, Papa?"

"Let's circle wide of the swamp and then take it over to the Chyulus across that boulder country."

"The boulder country it is, Papa. "We looking for mtu or nyama?"

Ngui looked at me and I said, "Both."

We crossed the edge of the lava desert country with the scattered purple brown rocks and then made for Lion Hill with its clump of trees on top. We saw a traveling Masai with his wife and donkey but we did not go down to worry them. Then we swung left again and followed the trail that went off toward the northern plain and the hills. The plain was wonderfully green and the grass was higher than in our own country and the game was everywhere. There were herds of kongoni, zebra, and oryx and we kept away from them in order not to run or frighten them. We circled the game herds and saw no poachers' camps and no shine of meat drying in the sun. There were dark clouds behind the Chyulus and we could see patches where it was raining. Willie took the aircraft over to the Chyulus and we checked the different valleys and the outrun of plain at their base where the rhino were. The rhino were in their usual places and there was no sign of men having been there. There was no smoke of fires nor were there any trace of campsites and we located three rhino that I knew, all with exceptional horns, and they were all there. The count was greater than I had made it before but I knew that we could vary the count anytime by making it at a different time of day and that it was not a census but only an indication. It was clear that no one had been killing the rhino. We saw one cow that we had seen before with an absolutely unbelievable horn even when seen foreshortened from the air.

"Do you want her picture?" Willie asked.

"No. We'll save her for Miss Mary. I only wanted to know she was still here."

We ran into rain and went up and then moved out and around it and then came onto the larger plain and the great eland herds. Across the big swamp with its stream and river courses we could see Lion Hill rising at the edge of the other rolling broken hills and I took a couple of bearings and told Ngui we could always find the eland. He pointed at one gray old bull who held his heavy thick spiraled horns as though they were a load to carry and was so wide and heavy that he could not trot at the pace of the others. Ngui shook his head and licked his lips.

"For Christmas," I said.

"For anytime," Ngui said.

"Your beasts look in good shape," Willie said. "Should we look for elephant?"

"There's some along the river here that I don't want to spook. But let's swing around them and look for the buff."

We swung wide and came back to the river.

"There they are," Willie said.

I saw the rain coming behind us as we turned. The buffalo were crossing an open patch. They were a big herd of cows, calves, and herd bulls. We swung wide of them and went back into the rain and when we came out the rain was just reaching the buffalo and you could see it hitting the broad backs and the muddy flanks and wetting the black gleaming horns. I counted seventy-four but never saw the huge old bull that I was looking for.

We moved around them and were ahead of them and of the rain again. They were following the tracks or moving slightly parallel to the trail of another herd. It looked like a cattle drive where they had crossed a wet patch of ground.

"Do you want to see them?" Willie asked.

"No. I'm sure I know where they are moving. I don't want to spook them."

We went up and moved away from the rain and Willie said, "Where to, Papa?"

"There's some elephant up in that broken country behind the shamba where this same creek comes down from the mountain in the gorge, remember?"

302

"You mean you want to head them off at Eagle Pass, Papa?"

"I want to haze them up the creek a way so they'll cross above the shamba. They're traveling toward that big elephant drop we looked over the last time on the way to Amboseli."

"I think I have the Big Picture," Willie said. "Should we find the shamba and then gen it out from there?"

"What about the rain?"

"It's just rain," Willie said.

We found the elephants and proceeded to move them. There was one lot of eight and another of twenty-two. They were cows, calves, and herd bulls and they did not wish to be moved. But they moved all right and, eventually, in the desired direction. There was one old bull apart from the others who had a young bull with him. This old bull had very heavy tusks and, from the air, everything about him looked enormous. He had been standing under a tree when we first saw him and he did not move off when the others moved. When we came back for him he spread his ears out very wide and raised up his trunk. His askari spread his ears too but not as convincingly. This time I had a very good look at his ivory since he raised it directly toward the aircraft as we came in. It looked almost too heavy for him to lift without effort.

He was not afraid of aircraft, at least not of this aircraft, and he was angry at being disturbed. The younger elephant with him imitated the old bull but I could see that he wanted to move. Ngui was very excited about the tusks that the elephant carried and I was very impressed by them. I wished Arap Meina was along so that I could know if he had ever seen this elephant before. We went up and around again and then came up the stream bed toward the elephant and his friend. He wanted to fight again and this time I said, "Don't try to land on him, Willie."

"Do you think you'll recognize him, Papa?"

"I think so. I know him now like his own dentist."

"Should we see if he stands up to it once more?"

"It's your aircraft."

"I wish it was. What fun we'd have."

We went up and around and this time the rain had caught up with us and when we came onto the elephant again he and his friend were moving on up the narrow stream valley in the rain. I could see the rain pelting his back as we winged over. He did not change his pace and he did not look up at us and the last I saw of him were his tusks, long, heavy, and wet in the rain.

"They're all moving, Papa," Willie said. "Do you have any other chores or housework?"

"No. We're supposed to keep away from the hill."

"The hill wouldn't be much good to us today."

"Let's go home and see Miss Mary."

By the time we were back in camp the rain was there too and we sat in the mess tent and listened to it beat on the canvas. Msembi made me a gimlet and Willie took beer. My letters were all arranged neatly on the table and the newspapers were in a pile.

"Could you see anything in the rain?" Mary asked.

"We could see very well, Miss Mary. They were all local showers and they've only gotten together for a bit now. We'll have good weather in the afternoon."

"Did you do anything useful?"

"Did we, Papa?"

"We were moving elephants," I said.

"You sound like some trucking company. Where were you moving elephants?"

"Up the creek."

"That's correct, Miss Mary. Papa and I and our two loyal Wakamba followers both of them watering at the mouth at the sight of ivory the curse of Africa have been moving elephants in the rain."

"You should have seen the slanting curtain of rain strike the bouldered hillside making a white jagged line and cutting visibility to zero minus zero as we came in for our last desperate pass."

"What's a boulder, Papa?"

"A big round rock."

"Thank you. Miss Mary, this country where Papa keeps these elephants there is a watercourse coming down off Kilimanjaro that is known as the creek. It is guarded on both sides by too many of these big round rocks. It is a place where no white woman has ever been."

"Were there many elephants?" Miss Mary asked.

"We sighted thirty-two. Our mission was to haze them up the creek. Correct, Papa?"

"What happened?"

"We hazed them gently but firmly."

"Did you do something dreadful over the shamba?"

"We did not, Miss Mary," Willie said. "Here we are flying about in the rain caring for the wildlife—"

"The duty I have been gazetted to."

"Right," said Willie. "Gazetted is the word I was seeking."

"When we are subjected, on our return, to a perfectly monstrous interrogation."

"But why did you have to annoy the elephants?"

"We didn't annoy them. We moved them softly and gently so they wouldn't come through the shamba to eat it up and Arap Meina and I have to kill them."

"You noble characters," Miss Mary said.

"We're not appreciated here, Papa. Ordinarily I'd retire to my tent or we'd go into the bar."

"The trouble is you haven't any tent, Willie, and this *is* the bar."

"Don't mind me," Miss Mary said. "I'm just jealous because I didn't fly."

CHAPTER 26

In the afternoon it stopped raining just as Willie said it would and after they had gone in the plane I was very lonesome. I had not wanted to go into the town and I knew how happy I would be alone with the people and the problems and with the country that I loved but I was lonely for Mary and I missed Willie and I missed the aircraft.

It was always lonely after rain; but I was lucky to have the letters which had meant nothing when they came and I arranged them in an orderly manner again and put all the papers in order too. There were the *East African Standard*s, the airmail editions of the *Times* and the *Telegraph* on their paper that was like thin onionskin, a *Times Literary Supplement*, and an air edition of *Time*. The letters opened fairly dull and made me glad I was in Africa.

One letter carefully forwarded by my publisher via airmail at considerable cost was from a woman in Iowa. The first part of it explained in rather confused detail the faults of a book I had written about Venice and the Veneto or, at least, that was the scene of the book. This woman did not like the book in any way and that was her perfect right. If I had been in Iowa I would have refunded her the money she had spent on it as a reward for her eloquence. After demolishing this novel she continued: "Later, 'Old Man of the Sea' was published, and I asked my brother, who is mature, and spent four and a half years in the Army during War LL" (which I took to mean two rather than Long and Lousy) "if this book was any more emotionally mature than River and Trees, and he grimaced and said it wasn't."

It was enjoyable to sit in the empty mess tent alone with my correspondence and imagine the emotionally mature brother grimacing on the porch I hoped, but perhaps in the kitchen over a snack from the Frigidaire, or seated in front of the TV set watching Mary Martin and Leland Hayward as Peter Pan and I thought how kind it was for this lady from Iowa to write me and how pleasant it would be to have her emotionally mature grimacing brother shaking his head here now at this moment.

You cannot have everything, Hemingstein, I said to myself philosophically. What you win on the swings you lose on the roundabouts. You simply have to give up this emotionally mature brother. Give him up, I tell you. You must go it alone, boy. So I gave him up and continued to read Our Lady of Iowa. In Spanish I thought of her as Nuestra Señora de los Apple Knockers and at the surge of such a splendid name I felt a rush of piety and Whitman-like warmth. But keep it directed toward her, I cautioned myself. Don't let it lead you toward the grimacer.

I read on, where a clipping had been inserted: "Maybe I've been slightly stuffy about Hemingway: The most over-rated writer of our time, but still a fine writer. His main faults: (1) scant sense of humor; (2) a juvenile brand of realism; (3) meager idealism, or none; (4) hairy chested bombast; (5) no common sense."

The clipping was from a popular young apple knocker of what would correspond to *The East African Standard of Iowa* and the lady went on to say that she had been meaning for some time to send it to me.

I felt humble and honored and touched by her thoughtfulness and it was exciting to read the tribute of the brilliant young columnist. It had that simple but instant catharsis that Edmund Wilson has called "The Shock of Recognition" and recognizing the quality of this young columnist who indeed would have had a brilliant future on the *East African Standard* had he been born in the Empire and hence been able to secure a work permit I thought again, as one approaches the edge of a precipice, of the well-loved face of the grimacing brother of my correspondent and read on.

Modesty keeps me from quoting all of her letter but it may be permissible to quote the last line. I had bored her greatly in a book that she had never read and I knew that was no mean feat even in the area where she and the grimacer lived. My feelings toward the grimacer had changed now and I was no longer attracted to him as I had been but, rather, saw him seated among the cornstalks his hands uncontrollable in the night as he heard the growth of the stems of the mealies. In the shamba we had mealies that grew as tall as corn grows in the Middle West. But nobody heard it grow in the night because the nights were cool and the corn grew in the afternoon, and at night, even if it had grown at night, you could not have heard it for the talking of the hyenas and the jackals and the lions when they were hunting and the noise the leopard made.

I thought the hell with this stupid Iowa bitch writing letters to people she does not know about things she knows nothing about and I wished her the grace of a happy death as soon as possible. But I remembered her last sentence which was, "Why not write SOMETHING that is worthwhile, before you die?"

And I thought, you ignorant Iowa bitch I have already done this and I will do it again many times and you will still only be able to tell the difference between different grades and sizes of chocolate malted milks and maybe on a day when you are above par your ass.

Scratch one Iowa bitch, I said to Willie who was not there, and read some more letters. Berenson was well, which made me happy, and was in Sicily which worried me unnecessarily since he knew much more about what he was doing than I did. Marlene had problems but had been triumphant in Las Vegas and enclosed the clippings. Both the letter and clippings were very moving. The place in Cuba was OK but there were many expenses. All the beasts were well. There was still money in the New York bank. Ditto the Paris bank but on the feeble side. Everyone in Venice was well except those who had been confined in nursing homes or were dying of various incurable diseases. One of my friends had been badly injured in a motor accident and I remembered the sudden dips into fog no lights could pierce when driving down the coast in the early mornings. From the description of the various fractures I doubted if he, who had loved shooting better than anything, would ever be able to shoot again. A woman I knew, admired, and loved had cancer and was not given three months to live. This information came to me from a friend. Another girl I had known for eighteen years, knowing her first when she was eighteen, and loving her and being friends with her and loving her while she had married two husbands and made four fortunes from her own intelligence and kept them, I hoped, and gained all the tangible and countable and wearable and storable and pawnable things in life and lost all the others wrote a letter full of news, gossip, and heartbreak. It had genuine news and the heartbreak was not feigned and it had the complaints that all women are entitled to. It made me the saddest of all the letters because she could not come out to Africa now where she would have had a good life even if it were only for two weeks. I knew now since she was not coming that I would never see her anymore ever unless her husband sent her on a business mission to me. She would go to all the places that I had always promised to take her but I would not go. She could go with the husband and they could be nervous together. He would always have the long-distance telephone which was as necessary to him as seeing the sun rise was to me or seeing the stars at night was to Mary. She would be able to spend money and buy things and accumulate possessions and eat in very expensive restaurants and Conrad Hilton was opening or finishing or planning hotels for her and her husband in all the cities we had once planned to see together. She had no problems now. She could with the aid of Conrad Hilton take her lost looks to be comfortably bedded never an arm's reach away from the long-distance telephone and when she woke in the night she could truly know what nothing was and what it's worth tonight and practice counting her money to put herself to sleep so she would wake late and not meet another day too soon. Maybe Conrad Hilton would open a hotel in Loitokitok, I thought. Then she would be able to come out here and see the mountain and there would be guides from the hotel to take her to meet Mr. Singh and Brown and Benji and there would be a plaque, perhaps, to mark the site of the Old Police Boma and they could buy souvenir spears from the Anglo-Masai Stores Ltd. There would be hot and cold running White Hunters with every room all wearing leopard-skin bands around their hats and instead of Gideon Bibles by every bedside beside the long-distance telephone there would be copies of *White Hunter, Black Heart* and *Something of Value* autographed by their authors and printed on a special all-purpose paper with portraits of their authors done on the back of the dust jackets so that they glowed in the dark.

Thinking of this hotel and the project of how it might be decorated and run featuring the twenty-four-hour safari, all beasts guaranteed, you sleep in your own room each night with piped in coaxial TV, and the menus and the desk staff all anti-Mau Mau commandos and the better White Hunters, and the little courtesies to guests such as each guest finding by his plate the first night at dinner his commission as an Honorary Game Warden and on his second, and for most the last night, his Honorary Membership in the East African Professional Hunter's Association delighted me but I did not want to work it out too completely until we should have Mary and G.C. and Willie together. G.C. had a splendidly foul mind and great imagination and Willie had a deadly masked wit. Miss Mary having been a journalist had splendid powers of invention. I had never heard her tell a story in the same way twice and always had the feeling she was remolding it for the later editions. We needed Pop too because I wanted his permission to have him mounted full-length and placed in the lobby in the event that he should ever die. There might be some opposition from his family but we would have to talk the entire project over and reach the soundest decision. Pop had never expressed any great love for Loitokitok which he regarded more or less as a sin trap and I believe he wanted to be buried up in the high hills of his own country. But we could, at least, discuss it.

Now, realizing that loneliness is best taken away by jokes, derision, and contempt for the worst possible outcome of anything and that gallows humor is the most valid if not the most durable since it is of necessity momentary and often ill reported, I asked Nguili who had been smiling happily each time I laughed reading the sad letter and thinking about the new Loitokitok Hilton to go and find Arap Meina and send him in to me. The sun was almost down and I knew Mary would be in the New Stanley by now and probably in her bath. I liked to think of her in her bath and I hoped she would have fun in the town tonight. Arap Meina came in and saluted and I told him how we had moved the elephants and asked him if he knew the elephant with the very big ivory.

Arap Meina said Ngui and Pop's gunbearer had told him about the elephants and about this elephant and where we had seen them. He said that he knew this elephant and that he had very big tusks. He said that the best thing would be for me to take out a license and kill him. I said that we might have to kill him if he raided the shamba. Arap Meina said this elephant was much too smart to raid the shamba and that the last time he had come through here he had walked completely around the shamba rather than come through it. He said this elephant had been wounded at least three times that he knew of and had probably been wounded many more. We could find him and stay with him and surely kill him but I should have a license. I said if we killed him raiding a shamba if he had raided and then came back to raid again the ivory would belong to the government but that I could buy it back at auction. Arap Meina said what good would it do me to buy my own elephant.

He told me many crooks had killed elephant on elephant control and been given the ivory for their services. They had also killed the leopards with set gun traps and received their hides. That was why we were now overrun with baboons. He said the Game Department might give me the tusks for killing the elephant or they might not and that I should take out a license and we start to hunt the elephant now.

I explained that I could not do this as I was the acting Bwana Game and I could only kill this elephant if he repeatedly destroyed private property and was a menace to cultivation. Arap Meina said this elephant was too smart for that. I said we would have to let him alone.

It was always pleasant to talk with Meina because he was practical as only a man who had been outside the law can be. He had wisely chosen only one thing to concentrate his reform on animals and in particular elephants. Keiti was bound to tribal things that he could never leave and to his religion as a converted Moslem and his loyalty to Pop, the British Army, and to Pukka-Sahibism and to the preservation of the white hunting and general safari conspiracy. Charo was truly bound to the Moslem religion and I think he had fewer tribal problems than Keiti although I could be wrong. M'Cola had told me many things about Charo when we used to drink beer together in the old days but I could not understand them. I did not want to know about Charo then since it was no part of my business and I did not look up the key words in the dictionary.

Now M'Cola was dead and had lost his nerve before he died and his last son by his fifth wife was my bad and trusted brother Ngui who had five wives of his own and a hunger for meat and, above all, for eland meat that was as strong as an addiction. Well, I thought, we have moved the elephants enough so that I do not think they will hit the shamba. I do not want to kill an eland until Christmas although we had seen so many to-day in the plane that it was upsetting to Ngui and me both. But we knew where they were and I had worked out a way to get to them. Arap Meina had good sense and he knew that I could not go off on an elephant hunt now with the problems we had even though it was this elephant with the heavy-hanging white-brown tusks that had lifted as though powered by some great crane as the aircraft had come in on them. I had never seen ivory being rained on while its owner lifted it and curled his trunk back and spread his ears with the rain driving against the spread of the flaps and I said, "How big is he really, Meina?"

"My father, he is very big."

"How big?"

"Bigger than we think. The right tusk drags on the ground when he is tired."

I remember thinking when he lifted the tusks so slowly that I did not think he could raise them.

"Who wounded him, Meina?"

"Maybe my father. Maybe me."

"Not me."

"No. My mother's husband."

"Did he know this elephant?"

"He knew him when I was a mtoto. Everyone knows this elephant."

"Has Bwana Game seen him?"

"How would he see him without a ndege?"

"Doesn't he come through here?"

"In the night. An elephant with such teeth would not be seen in the daylight."

"Why did he have no fear of the ndege?"

"No one hunts elephants from a ndege. He thinks piga picha."

That was a phrase I hated as it concentrated all the foulness of the bastard language into two words: shoot a picture.

"We'll let his teeth grow."

"Somebody kill him," Meina said. "Wakamba kill him."

"Menos mal," I said in Spanish.

"Wakamba piga mingi bongo. Mingi. Mingi."

"Menos mal," I said since the elephant belonged to the Wakamba long before they were seized for the Crown. It was not proper in my position as Honorary Game Warden and Acting Game Ranger to say this in English or in Swahili so I stated it in Spanish which was the language I was trying to teach our dissident faction.

"No hay remedio," Arap Meina answered giving what amounted to the password.

"No hay no bloody fucking remedio for nothing," I said. This sentence contained the password and two universally known adjectives.

"No hay remedio," Meina said. He saluted and we shook hands and he went out.

In the night I thought about the elephant and his contempt for the Cessna and about the long time he had lived with so many people against him and seeking to kill him for his two wonderful teeth that were now only a great disadvantage to him and a deadly load for him to carry. I loved ivory which is one of the truly satisfying things to touch it being even smoother than the skin of a Chinese girl which is the smoothest and loveliest thing to touch that I know. It had many other strange and satisfying things about it too or it would never have been sought as it has been nor the crimes committed. The sight of the old bull elephant and his unbelievably long and heavy tusks had excited the three of us Wakamba and Willie too as though we had been hunting dogs unleashed on a fresh scent. It was worse than the fresh scent. It was when you sighted the quarry. Lying in the cot, unable to sleep, with the balsam needle pillow under the base of my neck and the sheet and blanket friendly against the cold night I tried to remember what it was that had brought me into such close connection with the tusks so that if I never saw them again I would always possess them and I knew finally in the night that it was the rain on them and the slow terrible effort the elephant made to lift them high into the air and against the aircraft.

In the night I thought where the elephant would be now and what he had said to his friend or askari as the Africans always called the younger companion of an old bull. He certainly would know that he was being scouted and I was quite sure he had defied us when he knew there was nothing else to do but to run. They would have traveled a long way after we were gone. I wondered, in the sharp coldness of the night listening to the talking of the animals, how great a trouble the huge weight of his tusks was to him and whether he was impotent and what sort of comradeship he had with his askari. I knew that the old bulls were driven out of the herds long before they were impotent but I did not know why some were still loved after they had gone by themselves and why others were not.

Tomorrow I knew I must find the buffalo if we could without disturbing them. This was a basic duty. Tomorrow, too, I must hunt leopard as intelligently as possible but using all my luck. My luck was very good and I thought how wonderful it was that Mary had pulled out of her dysentery and her sadness about the lion and gone off happily to Nairobi to confirm her cure and buy gifts and spend money for all the people she loved. I thought about her and where she would probably be now. She did not like the bad dives I frequented and I thought she would probably be at the Travellers Club or some such place and I was glad that it was she who was having that sort of fun and not me. I stopped thinking about her and thought about Debba and that we had promised to take her and the widow to Loitokitok to buy cloth for dresses that they would have for the celebration of the Birthday of the Baby Jesus. This official buying of dresses with my fiancée present and choosing the cloth which I would pay for while forty to sixty Masai warriors and women watched was as formal and definitive an occasion as Loitokitok would offer in this social season or probably any other. Being a writer which is a disgrace but also sometimes a comfort I wondered, being unable to sleep, how Henry James would have handled this situation. I remembered him standing on the balcony of his hotel in Venice smoking a good cigar and wondering what must go on in that town where it is so much harder to keep out of trouble than to get into it and when, in the nights I could not sleep, I always had great comfort thinking of Henry James standing on the balcony of his hotel looking down at the town and people passing, all of them with their needs and their duties and their problems and their small economies and village happinesses and the sound well organized life of the canal, and think of James, who knew no one of the places to go, and stayed on his balcony with his cigar. Happy now in the night where I could sleep or not as I wished I liked to think of both Debba and James and I wondered how it would be if I plucked the consolatory cigar from James's lips and handed it to Debba who might put it behind her ear or perhaps hand it to Ngui who had learned to smoke cigars in Abyssinia where as a rifleman in the K.A.R. opposing, sometimes, white troops and their camp followers and overcoming them he had learned many other things. Then I stopped thinking about Henry James and his exploratory cigar and about the lovely canal which I had been imagining with a fair wind coming to help all my friends and brothers who had to work against the tide and I no longer cared to think of the thick, squat figure with the bald head and the ambulatory dignity and line of departure problems and I thought of Debba and the big skin-covered, smoky, clean-smelling, hand-rubbed wood bed of the big house and the four bottles of sacramental beer I had paid for the use of it, my intentions being honorable, and the beer having its proper tribal custom name; I think it was, among the many ritual beers, known as The Beer for Sleeping in the Bed of the Mother-in-Law and it was equivalent to the possession of a Cadillac in the John O'Hara circles if there be any such circles left. I hoped piously that there were such circles left and I thought of O'Hara, fat as a boa constrictor that had swallowed an entire shipment of a magazine called *Collier's* and surly as a mule that had been bitten by tsetse fly, plodding along dead without recognizing it and I wished him luck and all happiness remembering fairly joyously the white-edged evening tie he had worn at his coming-out party in New York and his hostess's nervousness at presenting him and her gallant hope that he would not disintegrate. No matter how bad things go any human being can be cheered remembering O'Hara at his most brilliant epoch.

Then I started to think about Debba again and some of our social problems on which I would have welcomed James's advice if he had been able to phrase it in such a manner that it would have been perceptible to us both.

One of our problems was the piercing of ears. Debba should have had hers pierced according to custom three months before. She did not want to have her ears pierced unless Miss Mary's were pierced. I thought she was quite right in this. The complicating factor was that both of them wished to have their ears pierced very much. I told Debba this and she believed it but the widow kept telling her that she was waiting too long to have them pierced. This was one of our problems. She had said that neither Ngui nor I had pierced ears, which was true, and we were the only people that she knew who did not have them. This was difficult to explain but I told her that Ngui's taste was his own business and that in my tribe at home the men did not pierce the ears. I was delighted to have it done as a Wakamba, I told her, and we could have it done together if that was permitted, or at least at the same time. She felt very bad because her ears were not pierced because I could not blow through them and she wished mine were pierced so she could blow through them.

It was more interesting to think about these problems than about James on the balcony with his cigar and I knew that I loved Debba very much and realized that it was an injustice that we could not blow through each other's ears. But there was the problem of manners. We had to wait on Miss Mary and no one could ask her out and out to make up her mind and have her ears pierced or not while she was still suffering from dysentery and we were awaiting the celebration of the Birthday of the Baby Jesus which had since our various miracles and feats of magic attained an importance that far passed, tribally, any simple religious significance. I thought about our plans for Christmas which I always loved and could remember in so many countries.

I knew this Christmas was going to be either wonderful or truly awful since we had decided to invite all of the Masai and all of the Wakamba and this was the sort of ngoma which could end ngomas if it were not carried out properly. There would be the magic tree of Miss Mary which the Masai would recognize for what it truly was if Miss Mary did not. I did not know whether we should tell Miss Mary that her tree was really an extra potent type of marijuana-effect tree because there were so many angles to the problem. First Miss Mary was absolutely determined to have this particular type of tree and it had been accepted by the Wakamba as a part of her unknown or Thief River Falls tribal customs along with her necessity to have killed the lion. Arap Meina had confided to me that he and I could be drunk on this tree for months and that if an elephant ate this tree that Miss Mary had selected he, the elephant, would be drunk for a matter of days. He had asked me if I had ever seen a drunken elephant and I had said, never having heard of it before, "But naturally." Arap Meina had then confided to me that these were practically the only type of elephants that the bwanas were ever able to shoot. He had also told me that he had never known a bwana who knew the difference between a drunken and a sober elephant and that nearly all bwanas were so excited when they saw an elephant that they could not see whether the elephant had two tusks or not. He told me, confidentially, that all bwanas smelled so horribly that no game would ever let them approach and that any hunter having anything to do with any bwana could always locate him by simply getting the wind and working upwind until the odor of the bwana became intolerable.

"This is true, Bwana," he told me and when I looked at him he said, "My brother, I used the word unthinkingly and without offense. You and I smell the same as you know."

I did not know but I knew that all I ever smelt of Meina was his strange snuff and that only when he opened the wooden snuff tube with the beaded, leather-capped ends. It was pleasant to think of this and of the dress we would buy for Debba the first day we could go up the mountain and thinking of Debba I thought that I was a damned fool not to be at the shamba or her here but I knew the scandal that would be made if I made a move at this hour. Later, when I had learned that the best hunting was alone at night with a spear in your hand, soft moccasins on your feet, and two other spears across your back to give the illusion of reserves and security, there would have been no scandal. We had moved well away from scandal then because once the taboos of the night had been broken and the night was your own as the day had been and you started to learn about the night, there was never scandal. Then there were only technical problems such as the quality of steel and the problems of the shaft and the setting; then you knew whether your odor was offensive to animals very quickly and you knew that when you rubbed yourself with lion fat you were a lion in the darkness. This was especially true if you had kept a part of the lion and Meina told me so many things about the dark I did not know that I knew more than I could use.

But at this time I still had the miserable traits of a bwana so that Meina had called me that to my face with no other white man present to make it ritual and pardonable and I did not know anything about the night and so I lay awake instead of going out as a man should. I was never driven to the last resource of the bwana, having a light on and reading to keep from knowing how things were. But I knew that Miss Mary must have had a good evening in Nairobi since she was not a fool and it was the only town we had and there was fresh smoked salmon at the New Stanley and an understanding although conniving head waiter. But the fish from the great lakes, the unnamed fish, would be as good as ever and there would be curries but she should not eat them so soon after dysentery. But I was sure she had dined well and I hoped she was in some good nightclub now and I thought about Debba and how we would be going up to buy the material for two lovely hills that she carried so proudly and modestly and how the cloth would emphasize them as she well knew and how we would look at the different prints and how the Masai women with their long hours and the flies and their insane, pretending, beauty parlor husbands would watch us in their unsatisfied boldness and syphilitic cold-handed beauty and how we, Kamba, neither one with our ears even pierced but proud and worse than insolent because of too many things that Masai could not ever know, would feel the stuffs and look at the patterns and buy other things to give us importance in the store. So I thought of this and of other things and the mechanics or the logistics of the next day and then I went to sleep.

CHAPTER 27

When Mwindi brought the tea in the morning I was up and dressed sitting by the ashes of the fire with two sweaters and a wool jacket on. It had turned very cold in the night and I wondered what that meant about the weather for today.

"Want fire?" Mwindi asked.

"Small fire for one man."

"I send Msembi," Mwindi said. "You better eat. Memsahib go you forget to eat."

"I don't want to eat before I hunt."

"Maybe hunt be very long. You eat now."

"Mbebia isn't awake."

"All old men awake. Only young men asleep. Keiti says for you to eat."

"OK. I'll eat."

"What you want to eat?"

"Codfish balls and hash-browned potatoes."

"You eat Tommy liver and bacon. Keiti says Memsahib says to tell you to take fever pills."

"Where are the fever pills?"

"Here," he brought the bottle out. "Keiti says I watch you eat them."

"Good," I said. I ate them.

"What else does Keiti say?"

"Keiti says Memsahib says to remember to piga picha. Not just hunt. Piga mingi picha."

"Oh shit," I said. "Memsahib say how to take bathi and how to limpiar culo?"

"Hapana," Mwindi said. He did not understand Spanish but he knew what limpiar culo meant because it was the two words that would mean that, under the circumstances, in any language.

"You hear the big lion?" Mwindi asked.

"No."

"Keiti, Charo, and I hear him. Very big lion."

"Did you ask him for his papers?"

"Hapana," Mwindi said. "Arap Meina very very drunk."

"Yes?"

"Because you and he do not go to kill the elephant."

"I have my duty."

"You have duty eat now."

"All right why don't they bring it?"

"Chakula comes now. You don't smell it?"

"How can you win?" I asked.

"Very difficult to win against Wakamba," Mwindi said with his thin winner or loser smile.

"Yo también soy Kamba."

"Maybe."

"How do you mean it maybe?"

"Maybe."

Inside the mess tent Msembi had lit the Coleman lantern and I could see him sweeping the dudus of the night before off the table with one hand while he held the breakfast tray in the other. It had the beginning of a good day. The liver and bacon smelled wonderfully and I was sure Mwindi had not smelt them but just had known that they were coming. His back was toward me as Msembi had approached the mess tent. Mwindi had not spoken as an informer about Arap Meina. He knew that when I saw him I would know he had been drunk and he was telling me why. It was a good enough reason to get drunk if you had seen the elephant and three of us had seen him for the first time and Meina had very possibly seen him before any of us were born.

"What you wear?" Mwindi asked.

"Short boots and warm jacket to start and the skin shirt with the solids for when it gets hot."

"I get the other people ready. Today very good day."

"Yeah?"

"Everybody thinks so. Even Charo."

"Good. I feel it is a good day too."

"You don't have any dream?"

"No," I said. "Truly no."

"Mzuri," Mwindi said. "I tell Keiti."

After breakfast we headed straight for the Chyulus by the good trail that went north through the gerenuk country. The sun was not up yet behind the shoulder of the mountain and the country was still cold and fresh from the rain and the cold night. The first part was through park country with good trees for leopard and all five of us watched every tree. Ngui was on top of the car and once he slapped very softly on the wet, rolled up side curtain by my head and I pushed Mthuka with my elbow. He was deaf and could not hear the sound which I barely heard. He stopped the car softly. Charo and Philip's gunbearer in the back had already seen what Ngui had seen and I turned with their eyes and saw the lovely long neck and heavy rising horns of a male gerenuk who looked at us out of the scrub. We all knew this was Miss Mary's long sought and always denied buck and I said, "Kwenda" to Mthuka, and he started the car moving and shook his head.

We went on for the Chyulus until we hit the trail of the first buffalo herd passing over the old motor trail. Here the trace the motorcar followed was on high stony ground that drained well and there was no immediate danger of stalling the car and we all got out and looked at the tracks picking out the big bulls by the split, heart-shaped tracks deep sunk and as big as soup bowls. There was the cattle smell but it was not fresh and the tracks had all been rained on and the dung had been washed over and the dung beetles were working on it already. We had the first of the sun now because we had climbed out of the plain and I took the big gun and went up the trail with Ngui. The first thing we found were the fresh tracks of three elephants that had crossed the trail in the night.

"Where were they? We didn't see them."

"In the rain. Or under the trees," Ngui said.

We went on up the trail until we saw the tracks where the second herd of buffalo had crossed. We could see where they had gone up and over the shoulder of the bouldered hill. I started back to the car and we all waited while Mthuka found a place where he could turn her and then started back on our tracks. Nobody had said anything. Everybody knew where the buffalo were going. No one knew how far they had gone.

We went back on our own tracks and then headed off on a trail to the right that went past an abandoned Masai village called the Old Manyatta. There were eight other old manyattas in the small area as we knew from memorizing it from the air but this was the true Old Manyatta in capital letters since it was there we had found Mayito's lion and the wonderful tracking hunt had started. The trail from the Old Manyatta to the hills where the buffalo should be now as they returned to the swamp was gray with mud and treacherous. But we went on it as far as we could and then we left Mthuka with the car, knowing the mud would be drying in the sun. The sun was now baking the plain and we left it and started up into the steep, small, broken hills covered with lava boulders with the new grass thick and wet from the rain. We did not wish to kill any buffalo but it was necessary to have the two guns as there were rhino in these hills and we had seen three of them the day before from the Cessna. The buffalo should be making their way to the rich new feed at the edge of the papyrus swamp. I wanted to count them and to photograph them if it were possible and to locate the huge old bull with the wonderful horns that we had not seen for more than three months. We did not wish to frighten them or let them know we followed them but only to check on them so that we might photograph them properly and well when Mary came back.

It was very hot in the sun and the abrupt conical hills with the tall wet grass growing between the boulders made me tired and I sweated heavily. I thought several times that it would have been much easier to send Arap Meina to check on the buffalo but I knew too that it was necessary discipline that I must climb and that I had to sweat out the alcohol that G.C. and I gave each other so many valid and invalid excuses for consuming. We worked around up several draws and finally to near the crest of the highest hill and I lay down and wrung my shirt out and sent Ngui with the glasses to crawl up to the crest and look over the country. He went up fast, then froze and then went on like a snake until he froze again, shaded the glasses carefully with his hands and then waved me up with his hand low palm down. I crawled up feeling like a Renoir in the lava and wishing again that I had a black skin like any other Kamba and before I raised my head to look I tied the wet shirt around my shoulders.

We had intercepted the buffalo and the big herd was moving along below us. There were the proud herd bulls, the big old cows, the young bulls, and the young cows and the calves. I could see the curve of the horns and the heavy corrugations, the dried mud and the worn patches of hide, the heavy moving blackness and the huge grayness and the birds, small and sharp billed and busy as starlings on a lawn. The buffalo moved slowly, feeding as they moved, and behind them the grass was gone and the heavy cattle smell came to us and then we had the flies. I had pulled the shirt over my head and I counted one hundred and twenty-four buffalo. The wind was right so that the buffalo did not get our scent. The birds did not see us because we were higher than they were and only the flies found us; but evidently they did not bear tales.

We lay and watched the buffalo pass and Pop's gunbearer and Charo lay in the dead slope of the hill behind us. The huge old bull who was almost white-gray in color and who had the incredible widespread horns was not with this big herd. There was one that was as gray. He was old and massive but his horns were not beautiful. They were worn down and dubbed with huge bosses and blunted points. There were six bulls with exceptional heads. Ngui said eight and he could see better than I could. But the bull we wanted to see was not with them.

I told Ngui we would crawl back and then get up into higher country and try to find the second herd. We worked our way along getting higher all the time. It was very hot and the leather in the sole of one of my boots which were very wet now from the high grass and had probably been dried too close to the fire last night began to squeak. I tried walking on it in different ways but could not keep it from squeaking. The higher we went the worse it squeaked. We were working up a draw with a steep hill on the right when I smelled the buff. It was head high scent and very strong. Ngui nodded and so did Charo. I sat down and took off the boots and hung them over the shoulder of Pop's gunbearer and we worked up the hillside with me in my stocking feet.

They had been good tough feet once but I had not hunted barefoot since I was fifteen and in the hills in Africa it was bad. Later I found I could hunt barefoot at night on the plain except where there were sandburs. But here, in the hills, everything you stepped on seemed to have thorns. Then there were small sharp rocks you could not see in the grass. But with that good trustworthy Spanish boot made in Madrid in the Calle de la Bolsa squeaking as it was you might as well have been hunting preceded by a steam calliope.

We crawled up against the wind with the scent as strong as though you were in a herd of cattle to where there were some small trees at the top of the ridge. As we lay I thought, at first, that the buffalo might be coming up and through us but they turned and moved along the slope below. By the time Charo was up with the camera the great shot was gone and I knew that without a telephoto lens they were just so many buffalo moving along the side of a hill. There were sixty-two in the herd and the fourth from the last was the great bull. We all took turns watching him with the binoculars and we all felt that we owned him but we were saving him for Miss Mary. I piga-ed one picha of him for luck and then two more so my friends would not feel they had carried the cameras for nothing. Then I took the .577 and held low on the point of his fore-shoulder. Shooting prone I knew the .577 could break my shoulder but probably only the collarbone. But it would break the old bull's shoulder. With the safety on I squeezed on him.

Nobody knew whether I was going to shoot him or not except me and to be sure I would not I broke the rifle and took the two shells out. We lay there, under the trees, and watched the buffalo go on toward the swamp and then we moved back from the crest and I sat up and poured a little gin from the Jinny flask on the soles of my feet. Pop's gunbearer helped me get the boots on. The socks had been lost in the stalk.

We backtracked down a way and found one of the socks. I said the hell with the other one and we took a short cut back to the hunting car. We had located both herds of buffalo, knew where they were going, and had not frightened them at all. I felt a fool in the eyes of the Kamba not to have killed the old bull but I knew what a shit I would feel if I had killed him. Then, practically, we could never have gotten the car up there and we would have had to pack out all the meat, and there would be close to a ton of it, and the head, which would take four men to carry it. If the old bull ever was to be killed he could be killed, now, close to the edge of the salt flats. I did not care anything about killing him anymore since we had made two such stalks and we had owned them all. No one was gloomy either and that was good. We had plenty of meat in camp and could get more and we had hunted well and we all knew it.

Mthuka had seen us coming down out of the hills and moved the car along to meet us. The mud was gray baked and flaky now and the car was the first shade we had since we had left the trees. We four drank two bottles of beer between us and Charo drank a Coke while we relaxed in the shade and Mthuka turned the car and drove back on the track toward the Old Manyatta and then into the shade beyond. Ngui told Mthuka about the buff. I could not follow it all but it was favorable.

Once inside the trees with shade, brush, open patches, and much fallen timber we ran into bad luck on the second bottle of beer. A warthog was crossing the open patch to the left trotting briskly, his tusks curving up from his comical head, his tail held straight up like the aerial on a jeep. One of my duties as an Acting Game Ranger was to kill warthogs as vermin under the allegation that they were carriers of rinderpest. There was no rinderpest around and I liked and admired warthogs very much. But warthogs were very good to eat and, from the limited curve of his tusks, this was a young boar. So I slapped on Mthuka's leg for him to stop the car and I dropped out and ran to where I had a good clean shot at the boar trotting broadside. I shot, swinging well ahead of him, but I did not swing far enough. He rolled over as the bullet whocked, then regained his feet and went into the brush at a gallop. I shot and threw mud behind him and saw the red patch high up on his rump from the first shot as he went into the bush.

Since he was wounded it was necessary to follow him and kill him. Because he was classified as vermin and I was classified as the Acting Game Ranger it was permissible to use the motor vehicle to attempt to intercept him. Mthuka was turning the car when I got back to it and Ngui handed me my share of what was left of our second bottle of Tusker. While we intercepted, dodging branches, being slapped across the face and smashing through the greenery I was thinking that I had shot with reluctance and that was why I had shot behind. It was as good an alibi as I had for the moment but I knew it was possibly true.

We broke out, vine strewed and branch whipped, into the open and I saw the boar ahead, tail up, right buttock red blotched breaking for the next patch of bush. I hit the ground, fired, and threw behind him twice. We then circled widely and could not find him nor his tracks. We all worked it out on foot and the warthog had not come out of the very large patch of thick bush he had gone into.

"Hapana," Charo said.

"Hapana," the other two agreed.

So we drove back to where I had shot at him the last two times and found the plowed, dirt-thrown slits the bullets had made. There was no blood spoor that any of the four of us could find. There were tracks into the thick bush and I said to Ngui, "We'll go in."

I thought that we would find his hole and that would be the end of my responsibility. He could not have more than a small flesh wound as I had shot with solids. We knew where he lived and if he were really wounded I would come back and kill him tomorrow.

So we went into the bush and had gone in fifty feet or so with tracks and no blood when something on the right made the whirring purring noise of a rising quail. Ngui handed me the .577, we shuffling the two guns like cardsharpers. What wind there was I could feel on my forehead and it was in our favor so I knew the rhino must have heard us rather than smelled us. I had orders to shoot no rhino in this area and that self-defense shooting would be very dimly viewed.

I looked at Ngui and he grinned. Just then we heard another whirring purr much louder and closer and to the left. I could still feel the wind on my forehead and on my cheeks. The wind was all right. Ngui looked down at the pig tracks which looked very small indeed and grinned again. I motioned backwards with the fingers of my right hand detaching two of them from the sweated grip of the big gun. We did not retreat backwards with our weapons poised and ready. We were not covering anybody and there were no motion pictures. There would be no camera to register what happened if the shooting started as there is on fighter planes. I thought about this and about the dimly viewed acceptance of self-defense and the British love of interrogation and having everyone up before the Headmaster and I thought that Ngui and I would not go up before the Headmaster nor even before the Headmistress as a prominent police official was then referred to. We retreated stepping carefully and lifting branches for each other and I was happy that from pouring a little gin into it and the slimy cushion the blood made my right boot no longer squeaked.

We got out and went back to the car and I asked Mthuka to turn it around. We were then headed in the proper direction and had a good piece of clear ground to cross and the security of our tracks. I took one of the three spears we carried in the back of the car and went to the edge of the bush and started to talk in what we had learned of rhino talk in the last four months to the rhino. He did not answer the first part and then he did very angrily. I had moved into invective.

"Faru tú. Cobarde hijo de puta. Faru tú! Tú Faru! Ciego y malo y sin-vergüenza."

Then straight Faru talk trilling the tongue and the lips too so it sounded like a covey of birds rising. Then raising and lowering the decibels until he came out angry in a real charge.

"Should I take him with the spear?"

"Hapana," everybody shouted and I caught onto the car and Ngui pulled me aboard. The rhino that came was a big male with a fair rather thick horn and a funny looking lip and small pig eyes. He had a good gallop and I watched his eyes and studied the horn that rose and fell with his gallop. But we drew away from him and he quit and turned off to his right when we smashed into the bush trail.

When he was well behind and we were on the main track we stopped to clean the windshield of vines and creepers and opened a bottle of beer. I took a small drink from the Jinny flask because we were now not far from home and would be going through the lovely park-like country with the big trees and the islands of thick brush. It was almost noon and very hot and we did not know it but all our luck lay ahead of us.

We rode along through the park country and all of us watched every likely tree. The leopard we were hunting was a trouble leopard that I had been asked to kill by the people of the shamba where he had killed seven-teen goats and I was hunting him for the Game Department so it was per-missible to use the car in his pursuit as it was permissible to use it for the pursuit of the warthog who was classified as vermin. The leopard, once vermin and now Royal Game, had never heard of his promotion and re-classification or he would never have killed the seventeen goats that made him a criminal and put him back in the category where he started. Seven-teen goats were too many goats to kill in one night when one goat was all he could eat. Then too eight of the goats had belonged to Debba's family.

As we rode and watched hunting with our new policy of regarding the leopard as a target of opportunity I thought about Debba and about a poem I had written and never published that said my heart was a target of opportunity. In my stupidity I had made a thing in imitation of the outward actions of my African brothers that my heart was not involved with the shamba and that hers was not either. But I knew now at noon that we were all involved just as the leopard was when he made his angry, wild, and desperate mistake. We were hunting toward the shamba now instead of toward camp and I looked at Mthuka's beautiful carved face with the strange long upper lip and the arrow cut on the cheeks that I envied him and I saw that he was driving not on any track where we had left our mark but only taking the best direction to hunt the trees. I loved Mthuka very much because he was my good brother as Ngui was my bad brother. Mthuka, too, being Keiti's son was in permanent rebellion against Keiti as I was. Keiti was the law on both a tribal basis and a religious basis. None of us outsiders had accepted the religion but the tribal law and customs were as rigid as the traffic code and as much pleasure to break on an open road, a road where you could harm no one except yourself and whoever chose to ride with you.

I had been thinking about this when we came into a very beautiful glade and on our left there was a tall tree with one of its high branches extending on a straight parallel line to the left and another, more shaded branch extending on a straight line to the right. It was a green tree and its top was heavily foliaged.

"There's an ideal tree for leopard," I said to Ngui.

"Ndio," he said very quietly. "And there is a leopard in that tree."

Mthuka had seen us look and though he could not hear us and could not see the leopard from his side he stopped the car. I got out of the car with the old Springfield I had been carrying across my lap and when I was firmly planted on my feet I saw the leopard stretched long and heavy on the high right limb of the tree. His long spotted length was dappled by the shadows of the leaves that moved in the wind. He was sixty feet up in an ideal place to be on this lovely day and he had made a greater mistake than when he killed the sixteen unnecessary goats.

I raised the rifle breathing in once and letting it out and shot very carefully for the point where his neck bulged behind his ear. It was high and an absolute miss and he flattened, long and heavy along the branch as I shucked the cartridge case out and shot for his shoulder. There was a heavy thunk and he fell in a half circle. His tail was up, his head was up, his back down. His body was curved like a new moon as he fell and he hit the ground with a heavy thump.

Ngui and Mthuka were whacking me on the back and Charo was shaking hands. Pop's gunboy was shaking hands and crying because the fall of the leopard had been an emotional thing. He was also giving me the secret

Wakamba handgrip again and again. I was reloading with my free hand and Ngui in excitement had the .577 instead of the shotgun when we advanced carefully to view the body of the seventeen goat-killing, scourge of my father-in-law, already national magazine photographed in color with a camera larger than I had ever seen long before his demise and thus conscience clearing leopard. The body of the leopard was not there.

There was a depression in the ground where he had hit and the blood spoor, bright and in chunks, led toward a thick island of bush to the left of the tree. It was as thick as the roots of a mangrove swamp and no one was giving me any secret Wakamba handgrips now.

"Gentlemen," I said in Spanish. "The situation has radically changed." It had indeed. I knew the drill now having learned it from Pop but every wounded leopard in thick bush is a new wounded leopard. No two will ever act the same except that they will always come and they will come for keeps. That was why I had shot for the base of the head and neck first. But it was too late for postmortems on missed shots now.

The first problem was Charo. He had been mauled by leopards three times and was an old man, nobody knew how old, but certainly old enough to be my father. He was as excited as a hunting dog to go in.

"You keep the fucking hell out of this and get up on top of the car."

"Hapana, Bwana," he said.

"Ndio too bloody ndio," I said.

"Ndio," he said not saying, "Ndio, Bwana" which with us was an insult.

Ngui had been loading the Winchester 12-gauge pump with SSG which is buckshot in English. We had never shot anything with SSG and I did not want any jams so I tripped the ejector and filled it with No. 8 birdshot cartridges fresh out of the box and filled my pockets with the rest of the cartridges. At close range a charge of fine shot from a full-choked shotgun is as solid as a ball and I remembered seeing the effect on a human body with the small hole blue-black around the edge on the back of the leather jacket and all the load inside the chest.

"Kwenda," I said to Ngui and we started off on the blood spoor, me with the shotgun covering Ngui who tracked, and Pop's gunbearer back in the car with the .577. Charo had not gotten onto the roof but sat in the rear seat of the car with the best one of the three spears. Ngui and I were on foot and following the blood spoor.

Out of a clot of blood he picked up a sharp bone fragment and passed it to me. It was a piece of shoulder blade and I put it in my mouth. There is no explanation of that. I did it without thinking. But it linked us closer to the leopard and I bit on it and tasted the new blood, which tasted about like my own, and knew that the leopard had not just lost his balance. Ngui and I followed the blood spoor until it went into the mangrove root patch of bush. The leaves of this bush were very green and shiny and the trail of the leopard, which had been made with bounds of irregular length went into it and there was blood low on the leaves, shoulder-high where he had crouched as he went in.

Ngui shrugged his shoulders and shook his head. We were both very serious Wakamba now and there was no white man to speak softly and knowingly from his great knowledge, nor any white man to give violent orders astonished at the stupidity of his "boys" and cursing them on like reluctant hounds. There was only one wounded leopard with terrible odds against him who had been shot from the high branch of a tree, suffered a fall no human being could survive and taken his stand in a place where, if he retained his lovely and unbelievable cat vitality he could maim or grievously injure any human being who came in after him. I wished he had never killed the goats and that I had never signed any contracts to kill and be photographed for any national circulation magazines and I bit with satisfaction on the piece of shoulder bone and waved up the car. The sharp end of the splintered bone had cut the inside of my cheek and I could taste the familiarity of my own blood now mixed with the blood of the leopard.

The car came up slowly and quietly and none of us spoke. Ngui pointed where the leopard had gone in and everyone saw it and then we circled the island of bush in the car very slowly and carefully with Ngui and me sitting forward on the fender. There were no outgoing tracks and no blood spoor and we knew the leopard had decided to make his fight, if he were not already dead, wherever he lay.

It was high noon and very hot in the sun and the small island of tight bush looked as dangerous as anything that I remember. Of course it was not truly dangerous as though there was an armed man there. But if it had been an armed man we would have behaved differently and the man would have been killed or surrendered. In my experience of men if the leopard had been a man he would have broken his back when he fell shot through the shoulder and, if he were like most armed men that I have known, he would have surrendered when we surprised him in the tree. No one truly fears an armed man unless the man is crazy. A trained marksman who has gone crazy is the most dangerous animal there is. We did not have that problem. We only had a wounded leopard who had once killed seventeen goats for fun or irritation or dislike of goats and could be considered moderately crazy. The patch of tight bush, green and shining and dark below where the roots were intertwined, looked dangerous enough for this day.

Pop had always told me to let them stiffen up and smoke at least one pipe before going in and I remembered this. It was no great help now because I did not smoke and I would not take a drink under the circumstances. So I was only deliberate in telling Mthuka to get on the other side of the island of bush with the car and I gave him and Charo both spears. If the leopard broke out they were to start the car, which we would hear, and sound the Klaxon which we would most certainly hear. I told them to talk in the car and make any noise they wished. Up to this point it had all been as solemn as a serious wedding. But it was a rough blood wedding and when we heard the car stop her engine on the far side of the piece of bush I said to Ngui and Pop's gunbearer Mwengi, "Kwenda na chui."

I do not speak Swahili or Kiswahili nor any form of that bastard slave traders', ivory raiders' improvised language correctly but what I said meant, with no possibility of misunderstanding, "We go to the leopard."

CHAPTER 28

It was not very easy to go to the leopard. Ngui had the Springfield .30-06 and he had the good eyes. Pop's gunbearer had the .577 which would knock him, the gunbearer, on his ass if he shot it and he had as good eyes as Ngui. I had the old, well-loved, once burnt up, three times restocked, worn smooth old Winchester Model 12 pump gun that was faster than a snake and was, from thirty-five years of us being together, almost as close a friend and companion with secrets shared and triumphs and disasters not revealed as the other friend a man has all his life. I was not conscious of this other friend's presence as, at these times certain parts of one's body diminish, and I had noticed that the Masai who are justifiably proud of how they are built and are inclined to be boastful and showy about it are in no way exceptionally well constructed at the moment the lion is ringed by the spearmen. Ngui and I had joked about this and now as we got down on the ground to start the crawl I slapped myself very gently with the palm of my hand and said, "Tú?"

"Hapana," he whispered and we both laughed and started the close search. We covered the enlaced and crossed roots of the thicket from the blood spoor entry to the left or west end where we could see the car around the corner but we could not see the leopard. Then we went back crawling along and looking into the darkness of the roots until we reached the other end. We had not seen the leopard and we crawled back to where the blood was still fresh on the dark green leaves. Pop's gunbearer was standing up behind us with the big gun ready and I, sitting down now, started to shoot loads of number eight shot into the cross tangled roots traversing from left to right. At the fifth shot the leopard roared hugely. The roar came from well into the thick bush and a little to the left of the blood on the leaves.

"Can you see him?" I asked Ngui.

"Hapana."

I reloaded the long magazine tube and shot twice fast toward where I had heard the roar. The leopard roared again and then coughed twice.

"Piga tu," I said to Ngui and he shot toward where the roar had come from.

The leopard roared again and Ngui said, "Piga tu."

I shot twice at the roar and Pop's gunbearer said, "I can see him."

We stood up and Ngui could see him but I could not. "Piga tu," I told him.

He said, "Hapana tu. Kwenda na chui."

So we went in again but this time Ngui knew where we were going. We could only go in a yard or so but there was a rise in the ground the roots grew out of. Ngui was directing me by tapping my legs on one side or the other as we crawled. Then I saw the leopard's ear and the small spots on the top of the bulge of his neck and his shoulder. I shot where his neck joined his shoulder and shot again and there was no roar and we crawled back out and I reloaded and we three went around the west end of the island of brush to where the car was on the far side.

"Kufa," Charo said. "Mzuri kubwa sana."

"Kufa," Mthuka said. They could both see the leopard but I could not. They got out of the car and we all moved in and I told Charo to keep back with his spear. But he said, "No. He's dead, Bwana. I saw him die."

I covered Ngui with the shotgun while he cut his way in with a panga slamming at the roots and brush as though they were our enemy or all our enemies and then he and Pop's gunbearer hauled the leopard out and we swung him up into the back of the car. He was a good leopard, no bigger than Mayito's, but we had hunted him well and cheerfully and like brothers with no White Hunters nor Game Rangers and no Game Scouts and he was a Wakamba leopard condemned for useless killing on an illegal Wakamba shamba and we were all Wakamba and all thirsty except poor Charo who could not drink because he was a Moslem. He was thirsty too and he would drink Coca-Cola when we got to camp.

He was the only one who examined the leopard closely because he had been mauled twice by leopards and he had shown me where the charge of shot at close range had entered almost alongside the first bullet wound in the shoulder. I knew it must have as I knew the roots and the bank had deflected the other shots, but I was only happy and proud of us all and how we had been all day and happy that we would get to camp and to the shade and to cold beer.

We came into camp with the Klaxon of the car going and everyone turned out and Keiti was happy and I think he was proud. We all got out of the car and Charo was the only one who stayed to look at the leopard. Keiti stayed with Charo and the skinner took charge of the leopard. We took no photographs of him. Keiti had asked me, "Piga picha?" and I said, "Piga shit."

Ngui and Pop's gunbearer brought the guns to the tent and laid them on Miss Mary's bed and I carried the cameras and hung them up. I told Msembi to put the table out under the tree and bring chairs and to bring all the cold beer and to bring Pepsi-Cola or Coca-Cola for Charo. I told Ngui not to bother about cleaning the guns now but to go and get Mthuka; that we would drink formal beer.

Mwindi said that I should take a bath. He would have the water in no time. I said that I would bathe in the wash basin and to please find me my clean shirt.

"You should take big bath," he said.

"I'll take big bath later. I'm too hot."

"How you get all the blood? From chui?"

This was ironic but carefully concealed.

"From tree branches."

"You wash off good with blue soap and I put on the red stuff."

We always used Mercurochrome or Mentholatum instead of iodine if we could get them although some Africans preferred iodine since it hurt and so was considered a stronger medicine. I washed and scrubbed the scratches open and clean and Mwindi painted them carefully.

"What you do to the feet?"

"Hunt barefoot. Why you let shoes squeak?"

"Not squeak anymore."

"Squeak too bloody much today."

"Never squeak anymore."

I put on my clean clothes and I knew Mthuka, Ngui, Pop's gunbearer, and Charo were putting on their clean clothes.

"Did chui come?"

"No."

"Why everybody make so happy then?"

"Very funny shauri. Very funny hunt all morning."

"You make too many scratches. Every day new bad scratches. Now you kill the feet. Memsahib no like it. She tell me take care of you."

"I scrub the feet again you put more red stuff on."

"Why you want to be African?"

"I'm going to be Kamba."

"Maybe," said Mwindi.

"Fuck maybe."

"Here come your friends."

"Brothers."

"Brothers maybe. Charo not your brother."

"Charo my good friend."

"Yes," Mwindi said sadly handing me a pair of slippers that he knew were a little tight and watching to see how much they hurt when I put them on. "Charo good friend. Have plenty bad luck."

"How?"

"Every way. And is a lucky man."

"Thank you for the painting," I said and went out to join the others who were standing at the table with Msembi in his green robe and green skullcap standing ready with the beer in the faded green canvas bucket. The clouds were very high in the sky and the sky was the highest sky in the world and I looked back over the tent and could see the mountain high and white above the trees.

"Gentlemen," I said and bowed and we all sat down in the chairs of the bwanas and Msembi poured the four tall beers and the Coca-Cola of Charo. Charo was the oldest so I ceded to him and Msembi poured the Coca-Cola first. Charo had changed his turban to one slightly less gray and he wore a blue coat with brass buttons fastened together at the throat with a blanket pin I had given him twenty years before and a natty pair of well repaired shorts.

When the drinks had been poured I stood up and proposed the toast, "To the Queen." We all drank and then I said, "To Mr. Chui, gentlemen. He is Royal Game." We drank again with propriety and protocol but with enthusiasm. Msembi refilled the glasses this time starting with me and ending with Charo. He had great respect for the elders but it was hard to respect the carbonated beverage against Tusker beer.

"A noi," I said bowing to Ngui who had learned his Italian in the captured brothels of Addis Ababa and from the hurriedly discarded mistresses of an army in flight. I added, "Gli Wakamba now and forever and in the Happy Hunting Grounds."

We drank it off to the bottom of the glasses and Msembi refilled.

The next toast was a little rough but with the tendency of the times and the need to give our new religion some form of actional program which could later be channeled toward the highest and noblest ends I proposed, "Na nu'uaa."

We drank this solemnly although I noticed reservations in Charo and when we sat down I said, "Na jihad tu," trying to win the Moslem vote. But it is a hard vote to win and we all knew he was with us only in the formal beer drinking and the brotherhood and could never be with us in the new religion or the politics.

We all sat down and I could see that Mthuka was sad the formal toasts were over. We now all relaxed and Ngui said, "Papa, show me the feet." I kicked the slippers off and Ngui took the feet and raised them up like a blacksmith shoeing a horse and everyone looked at them and laughed. Mthuka said that all the black spots were thorns that he would get out. Then I said to Ngui , "Piga tu," and he answered, "Piga tu. Piga." Then they all started to talk in Kamba and it was so fast and funny and I could not follow. Then we drank some more beer and Charo rose and asked to be excused saying that his thirst was satisfied and he left us in peace.

Msembi came to the table and poured again and said the beer was now kwisha and I said this was the hell of a kind of management and that we would saddle up and leave at once for Loitokitok for more beer. We would take some cold meat to eat on the way up and a few tins of kipper snacks. Mthuka said, "Kwenda na shamba." So we agreed to go to the shamba and pick up a few bottles of beer if they had any to hold the group until we could reach another brewing shamba or Loitokitok. Ngui said I should pick up my fiancée and the widow and that he and Mthuka both were OK with the third Masai shamba up the road. Pop's gunbearer said he was OK and would be the protector of the widow. We wanted to take Msembi but we were four and the widow and my fiancée made six and we did not know what Masai we would run into. There were always plenty of Masai in Loitokitok.

I went over to the tent and Mwindi had the tin trunk open and my old Hong Kong tweed jacket out with the money buttoned in the flapped-down inner pockets.

"How much money you want?" he asked.

"Four hundred shilingi."

"Plenty money," he said. "What you do? Buy a wife?"

"Buy beer, posho maybe, medicine for shamba, Christmas presents, buy new spear, fill up car with petrol, buy whiskey for mtoto of police, buy kippah snacks—"

He laughed at the kippah snacks. "Take five hundred," he said. "You want hard shilingi too?"

Hard shilingi were kept in a leather pouch. He counted me out thirty and asked, "You wear good coat?"

The coat he liked me to wear best was a sort of hacking coat which had also come from Hong Kong.

"No. Wear leather coat. Take leather zip-up."

"Take woolie too. Cold come down from mountain."

"Dress me as you wish," I said. "But put the boots on very easy."

He had clean-washed cotton socks and I put them on and he worked the feet into the boots and left them open without pulling up the zippers at the sides. Ngui came into the tent. He was wearing his clean shorts and a new sport shirt that I had never seen. I told him that we would only take the .30-06 and he said he had ammo. He wiped the big gun clean and put it under the cot. It had not been fired and the Springfield had been shooting with non-corrosive primers and could be cleaned at night.

"Pistol," he said severely and I poked my right leg through the loop at the end of the holster and he buckled the big belt around my waist.

"Jinny flask," Mwindi said and handed the heavy Spanish leather shell panier to Ngui.

"Money?" Ngui asked.

"Hapana," I said. "Money kwisha."

"Too much money," Mwindi said. He had the key with which he had locked the tin trunk where he kept the money.

We went out to the car. Keiti was still benevolent and I asked him formally what was needed for the outfit. He said to bring a sack of posho if there was any of the good kind that came on the stage from Kajiado. He looked sad when we left and his head hung a little forward and to one side although he was smiling the slit smile.

I felt sad and wrong that I had not asked him if he wanted to go and then we were on the road to the shamba. It was a well-worn road by now and it would be worn more before this is over, I thought.

Mthuka had no finery except a clean shirt with a checked pattern and his washed trousers with the patches. Pop's gunbearer had a yellow sport shirt with no figured pattern and it went very well with Ngui's which was muleta-colored red. I was sorry that I was dressed so conservatively but since I had shaved my head the day before after the plane had left and then forgotten all about it I felt that I must have a certain baroque appearance if I removed my cap. When shaved, or even clipped closely enough, my head, unfortunately, has much the appearance of some plastic history of a very lost tribe. It is in no way as spectacular as the Great Rift Valley but there are historical features of terrain which could interest both archeologist and anthropologist. I did not know how Debba would take it but I had an old fishing cap on with a long slanted visor and I was not worried about nor concerned with my appearance when we drove into the shamba and stopped in the shade of the big tree.

Mthuka, I found later, had sent Nguili, the young boy who wanted be a hunter but was working as second mess attendant, ahead to warn the widow and my fiancée that we would be coming by to take them to Loitokitok to buy the dresses for the Birthday of the Baby Jesus. This boy was still a nanake in Kamba and so could not drink beer legally but he had made the trip very fast to show that he could run and he was sweating happily against the trunk of the big tree and trying not to breathe hard.

I got out of the car to stretch my legs and to thank the nanake.

"You run better than a Masai," I said.

"I am Kamba," he said trying hard to breathe without strain and I could imagine how the pennies tasted in his mouth.

"Do you want to go up the mountain?"

"Yes. But it would not be proper and I have my duty."

Just then the Informer joined us. He was wearing the paisley and he walked with great dignity balanced on his heels.

"Good afternoon, brother," he said and I saw Ngui turn away and spit at the word brother.

"Good afternoon, Informer," I said. "How is your health?"

"Better," said the Informer. "Can I go with you up the mountain?"

"You cannot."

"I can serve as interpreter."

"I have two interpreters on the mountain."

The child of the widow came up and bumped his head hard against my belly. I kissed the top of his head and he put his hand in mine and stood up very straight.

"Informer," I said. "I cannot ask beer from my father-in-law. Please bring us beer."

"I will see what beer there is."

If you liked shamba beer it was all right, tasting like home brew in Arkansas in the time of Prohibition. There was a man who was a shoemaker and who had fought very well in the First World War who brewed a very similar beer that we used to drink in the front parlor of his house. My fiancée and the widow came out and my fiancée got into the car and sat beside Mthuka. She kept her eyes down except for short triumphant looks at the other women of the village and wore a dress that had been washed too many times and a very beautiful trade goods scarf over her head. The widow seated herself between Ngui and Pop's gunbearer. We sent the Informer for six more bottles of beer but there were only four in the village. I gave these four bottles to my father-in-law. Debba looked at no one but sat very straight with her breasts pointing at the same angle as her chin.

Mthuka started the car and we were off leaving the village, all people who were jealous or disapproved, many children, the goats, the nursing mothers, the chickens, the dogs, and my father-in-law.

"¿Qué tal, tú?" I asked Debba.

"En la puta gloria."

This was the second phrase that she liked best in Spanish. It is a strange phrase and no two people would translate it alike.

"Did the chui hurt you?"

"No. There was nothing."

"Was he big?"

"Not very."

"Did he roar?"

"Many times."

"Did he not hurt anyone?"

"No one. Not even you."

She was pressing the carved leather pistol holster hard against her thigh and then she placed her left hand where she wanted it to be.

"Mimi bili chui," she said. Neither of us were Swahili scholars but I remembered the two leopards of England and someone must have known about leopards a long time ago.

"Bwana," Ngui said and his voice had the same harshness that came from love or anger or tenderness.

"Wakamba, tu," I said. He laughed and broke the rough bad thing.

"We have three bottles of Tuskah that Msembi stole for us."

"Thank you. When we make the big rise we'll turn off and eat the kippah snack."

"Good cold meat," Ngui said.

"Mzuri," I said.

There is no homosexuality among Wakamba people. In the old days homosexuals after the trial of kingole, which Mwindi had explained to me meant when you gathered together formally to kill a man, were condemned, tied in the river or any water hole for a few days to make them more tender, and then killed and eaten. This would be a sad fate for many playwrights, I thought. But, on the other hand and if you have another hand, you are lucky in Africa it was considered very bad luck to eat any part of a homosexual even though he had been tenderized in the Athi in a clean and nearly clear pool and according to some of my older friends a homosexual tasted worse than a waterbuck and could bring out sores on any part of the body but especially in the groin or in the armpits. Intercourse with animals was also punishable by death although it was not regarded as so fouling a practice as homosexuality and M'Cola who was Ngui's father, since I had proved mathematically that I could not be, had told me that a man who had rogered his sheep or his goats was as tasty as a wildebeest. Keiti and Mwindi would not eat wildebeest but that was a part of anthropology that I had not yet penetrated. And thinking of these facts and confidences and caring greatly for Debba who was a straight Wakamba girl replete with modesty and true basic insolence Mthuka stopped the car under a tree where we could see the great gap and break in the country and the small tin roofed shine of Loitokitok against the blue of the forest on the mountain which rose white sloped and square topped to give us our religion and our long and lasting hope while behind was all our country spread out as though we were in the aircraft but without the movement, the stress, and the expense.

"Jambo, tú," I said to Debba and she said, "La puta gloria."

We let her and the widow, who had been very happy between Ngui and Pop's gunbearer in the red and yellow shirts and with the black arms and the delicate legs, open the tins of kipper snacks and the two tins of false salmon from Holland. They could not open them properly and one key was broken but Mthuka used pliers to bend the tin back exposing the false smoked salmon that was Holland's glory in Africa and we all ate, exchanging knives, and drinking from the same bottles. Debba wiped the neck of the bottle and its lips the first time she drank using her headcloth but I told her that one man's chancre was everyman's chancre and after that we drank without ceremony. The beer was warmer than it was cool but at 8,000 feet and with the country we looked back over and the places we could see now as though we were eagles it was lovely beer and we finished it with the cold meat. We kept the bottles to trade in and piled the tins together, removing the keys, and left them under a heather bush close to the trunk of the tree.

There were no Game Scouts along so there were no people who had sold their Wakamba heritage to denounce their brothers' worship of Miss Mary and the hangman or the puppies of the police so that we were free in a way and we looked back at the country where no white woman had ever been, including Miss Mary, unless it counted when we had taken her, unwillingly but with the excitement of children onto the deck where she had never belonged nor known how its penalties equalized its small glories.

So we looked back at our country and at the Chyulu Hills which were as blue and strange as ever and we were all happy that Miss Mary had never been there and then we went back into the car and I said to Debba, stupidly, "You will be an intelligent wife," and she, intelligently, took hold of my place and of the well-loved holster and said, "I am as good a wife now as I will ever be."

I kissed her on the crinkly head and we went on up the beautiful road that swung strangely and curved up the mountain. The tin roofed town was still glistening in the sun and as we came closer we could see the

337

eucalyptus trees and the formal road that, heavily shaded and with Britannic might, ran up to the small fort and jail and the rest houses where the people who participate in the administration of British justice and paperwork come to take their rest when they are too poor to return to their home country. We were not going up to disturb their rest even though it meant missing the sight of the rock gardens and the guided, tumbling stream that, much later, became the river that we knew too well.

It had been a long hunt for Miss Mary's lion and all except fanatics, converts, and true believers in Miss Mary had been tired of it for a long time. Charo, who was none of these, had said to me, "*Shoot* the lion when she shoots and get it over with." I had shaken my head because I was not a believer but a follower and had made the pilgrimage to Compostela and it had been worth it. But Charo shook his head in disgust. He was a Moslem and there were no Moslems with us today. We needed no one to cut the throats of anything and we were all looking for our new religion which had its first station of whatever cross there was to be outside of Benji's General Store. This station was a gas pump and it was inside the store that Debba and the widow would select the cloth to make their dresses for the Birthday of the Baby Jesus.

It was not proper for me to go in with her although I loved the different cloths and the smells of the place and the Masai that we knew, the mwanamke, eager and unbuying with their cuckolded husbands up the street drinking Golden Jeep sherry from South Africa with a spear in one hand and the bottle of Golden Jeep in the other. They were cuckolded standing on one leg or on two and I knew where they would be and walked down the right side of the narrow tree-shaded street that was still wider than our wing tips as everyone who lived on it or walked it knew and I walked hurt footed and, I hoped, not insolent nor pistol proud down to the Masai drinking place where I said, "Supa," and shook a few cold hands and went out without drinking and, eight paces to the right, into Mr. Singh's. Mr. Singh and I embraced and Mrs. Singh and I shook hands and then I kissed her hand, which always pleased her since she was a Turkana and I had learned to kiss hands quite well and it was like a voyage to Paris which she had never heard of but would have ornamented on the clearest day Paris ever had. Then I sent for the interpreter who entered and removed his mission shoes and handed them to one of Mr. Singh's many boys, always clean turbaned and maliciously polite.

"How are you, Singh?" I asked with the interpreter.

"Not bad. Here. Doing business."

"And beautiful Madame Singh?"

"Four months until the baby."

"Felicidades," I said and kissed Madame Singh's hand again using the style of Alvarito Caro then Marqués de Villamayor, a town we had once entered but been forced out of.

"All young Singhs are well, I hope?"

"All are well except the third boy who has a cut on the hand from the sawmill."

"You want me to look at it?"

"They treated him at the mission. With sulfa."

"Excellent for children. But it destroys the kidneys of old men like you and me."

Mrs. Singh laughed her honest Turkana laugh and Mr. Singh said, "I hope your memsahib is well. That your children are well and all the aircraft are well."

The interpreter said, in good condition, in the reference to aircraft and I asked him not to be pedantic.

"The Memsahib, Miss Mary, is in Nairobi. She has gone in the aircraft and will return with the aircraft. All of my children are well. God permitting. All aircraft are well."

"We have heard the news," Mr. Singh said. "The lion and the leopard."

"Anyone can kill a lion and a leopard."

"But the lion was from Miss Mary."

"Naturally," I said, pride rising in me of beautifully sculptured, compact, irascible, and lovely Miss Mary with the head like an Egyptian coin, the breasts from Rubens, and the heart from Bemidji or Walker or Thief River Falls, any town where it was 45 below zero in the winter. It was a climate to make warm hearts that also could be cold. "With Miss Mary there is no problem with a lion."

"But it was a difficult lion. Many have suffered from this lion."

"The Great Singh strangled them with either hand," I said. "Miss Mary was using a 6.5 Mannlicher."

"That is a small gun for such a lion," said Mr. Singh and I knew then he had done his military service. So I waited for him to lead.

He was too smart to lead and Madame Singh said, "And the leopard?"

"Any man should be able to kill a leopard before breakfast."

"You will eat something?"

"With Madame's permission."

"Please eat," she said. "It is nothing."

"We will go in the back room. You have drunk nothing."

"We can drink together now if you wish."

The interpreter came into the back room and Mr. Singh brought a bottle of White Heather and a jug of water. The interpreter took off his shoes to show me his feet.

"I have only worn the shoes when we were in sight of the informers of religion," he explained. "I have never spoken of the Baby Jesus except with contempt. I have not said my morning prayers nor my evening prayers."

"What else?"

"Nothing."

"You rank as a negative convert," I said. He pushed his head hard against my belly as the widow's son did.

"Think of the mountain and of the happy hunting grounds. We may need the Baby Jesus. Never speak of him with disrespect. What tribe are you?"

"The same as you."

"No. What are you written as?"

"Masai-Chagga. We are the border."

"There have been good men from the borders."

"Yes, sir."

"Never say 'sir' in our religion or our tribe."

"No."

"How were you when you were circumcised?"

"Not the best but good."

"Why did you become a Christian?"

"Through ignorance."

"You could be worse."

"I would never be a Moslem," he said and started to add "sir" but I checked him.

"It is a long strange road and maybe you had better throw the shoes away. I will give you a good old pair and you can mould them to your feet."

"Thank you. Can I fly in the aircraft?"

"Of course. But it is not for children nor mission boys."

Then I would have said I am sorry but there is no such word in Swahili nor in Kamba and it is a just way of conducting a language since you are warned not to make errors.

The interpreter asked me about the scratches and I said that they were from thorn trees and explained to him and Mr. Singh that we had gone out early in the morning to check on the buffalo herds and later had encountered a rhino. I had been scratched while in the car. I was always scratched, I said, and Mr. Singh nodded and showed the interpreter where his thumb had been cut by the saw in September. It was an impressive cut and I remembered when it had happened.

"But you also fought with a leopard today," the interpreter said.

"There was no fight. It was a medium-sized leopard who had killed seventeen goats at the Kamba shamba. He died without making a fight."

"Everyone said you had fought him with your hands and killed him with the pistol."

"Everyone is a liar. We killed the leopard first with a rifle and then with a shotgun."

"But a shotgun is for birds."

Mr. Singh laughed at this and I wondered some more about him.

"You are a very good mission boy," I said to the interpreter. "But shotguns are not always for birds."

"But in principle. That is why you say gun instead of rifle."

"And what would a fucking babu say?" I asked Mr. Singh in English.

"A babu would be in a tree," Mr. Singh said, speaking English for the first time.

"I am very fond of you, Mr. Singh," I said. "And I respect your great ancestor."

"I respect all of your great ancestors although you have not named them."

"They were nothing."

"I shall hear of them at the proper time," Mr. Singh said. "Should we drink? The woman, the Turkana, brings more food."

The interpreter now was avid for knowledge and the scent of it was breast high and he was half Chagga and had a low but strong chest.

"In the library at the mission there is a book which says the great Carl Akeley killed a leopard with his bare hands. Can I believe that?"

"If you like."

"I ask truly as a boy who wishes to know."

"It was before my time. Many men have asked the same question."

"But I need to know the truth."

"There is very little of it in books. But the great Carl Akeley was a great man."

You could not break him away from the scent of knowledge since I had sought it all my life and had to be content with facts, coordinates, and statements vouchsafed in drunkenness or taken under duress. This boy, who had removed his shoes and rubbed his feet on the wooden floor of Mr. Singh's back parlor and was so intent on knowledge that he did not know that Mr. Singh and I were embarrassed by his public foot-hardening, moved in, as unshod as a hunting dog, from plane geometry to something far beyond calculus.

"Can you justify a European taking an African as his mistress?"

"We don't justify. That is the function of the judiciary. Steps are taken by the police."

"Please do not quibble," he said. "Excuse me, sir."

"'Sir' is a nicer word than 'bwana.' At one time it had a certain meaning."

"Can you then condone, sir, such a relationship?"

"If the girl loves the man and there is no coercion to me it is not a sin if adequate provision is made for the issue per stirpes and not per capita."

This came like an unexpected block and I was as pleased as Mr. Singh that I could throw it with no change of pace. He fell back on the basics that he had been crammed on.

"It is a sin in the eyes of God."

"Do you carry him with you and what type of drops do you use to insure his clearest vision?"

"Please do not make fun of me, sir. I left everything behind me when I entered your service."

"I have no service. We are the last free individuals in a country slightly larger than Connecticut and we believe in a very abused slogan."

"May I hear the slogan?"

"Slogans are a bore, mission boy."

"Can I not hear the slogan?"

"Life, liberty, and the pursuit of happiness," then to take the curse off having offered a slogan and because Mr. Singh was becoming solemn and ready to re-enlist I said, "Harden your feet well as you are doing, keep your bowels open, and remember that there is some corner of a foreign field that shall be forever England."

He could not quit which might have been his Chagga blood or might have been the Masai stain and he said, "But you are an officer of the Crown."

"Technically and temporarily. What do you want? The Queen's shilling?"

"I would like to take it, sir."

It was a little bit rough to do, but knowledge is rougher and more poorly compensated. I took the hard shilingi out of my pocket and put it in the boy's hand. Our Queen looked very beautiful and shining in silver and I said, "Now you are an informer, no that is wrong, because I saw Mr. Singh had been hurt by the dirty word. Now you are commissioned as a temporary interpreter for the Game Department and will be remunerated at the stipend of seventy shillings per month as long as I hold the tenure of acting temporary Game Ranger. On the cessation of my tenure your appointment shall cease and you will receive a gratuity of seventy shillings from the date of ceasing of tenure. This gratuity will be paid from my own private funds and you hereby avow that you have no claims of any sort nor any possible future claims against the Game Department nor any other etc. And may God have mercy on your soul. The gratuity shall be made in a single payment. Are there any questions?"

"No, sir."

"What is your name, young man?"

"Nathaniel."

"You will be known in the Game Department as Peter."

"It is an honorable name, sir."

"No one asked for your comments and your duties are strictly confined to accurate and complete interpretation when as and if you are called on. Your contact will be with Arap Meina who will give you any further instructions. Do you wish to draw any advance?"

"No, sir."

"Then you might go now and toughen your feet in the hills behind town."

"Are you angry with me, sir?"

"Not at all. But when you grow up you may discover that the Socratic method of acquiring knowledge is overrated and if you ask people no questions they will tell you no lies."

"Good day, Mister Singh," the former convert said donning his shoes in case there was a spy from the mission about. "Good day, sir."

Mr. Singh nodded and I said, "Good day."

When the young man had gone out of the back door and Mr. Singh had drifted toward the door almost absent-mindedly and then returned to pour another drink of White Heather and pass me the water in the cooling jug he settled himself comfortably and said, "Another bloody babu."

"But not a shit."

"No," Mr. Singh said. "But you waste your time on him."

"Why did we never speak English together before?"

"From respect," Mr. Singh said.

"Did the original Singh, your ancestor, speak English?"

"I would not know," Mr. Singh said. "That was before my time."

"What was your rank, Mr. Singh?"

"Do you wish my serial number as well?"

"I'm sorry," I said. "And it is your whiskey. But you put up with unknown tongue for a long time."

"It was a pleasure," Mr. Singh said. "I learned much unknown tongue."

"What do you know, Mr. Singh?"

"Strictly nothing," Mr. Singh said, "except that loose wallah is waiting for you outside."

"Which loose wallah?"

"Loose wallah number one."

"My true friend?"

"One of your numerous brothers. One of your people is cohabiting with his wife if that is of any interest."

"Not in the slightest," I said and Mr. Singh was pleased.

We touched glasses and finished the good drink and I went out into the forward part of the store where a Masai, heavily built, over-ochered and over thirty-two years old and still wearing his morani headdress that dripped down between his eyes was supporting himself on an unblooded spear while he drank a bottle of Tusker.

"How are you, Simeon?" I asked noting he had not taken care of his toenails and that this was not the first bottle he had faced by the light perspiration on his upper lip and that he was sweating across the shoulders and under the arms.

"How are you, sir?"

"Very well."

"We have noted that Memsahib killed the destructive lion."

"Very kind of you," I said. "Please tell the elders that I came into town to report it at my first free moment."

"Congratulations on your chui, sir."

"The chui was rather a chickenshit show. Nothing was involved."

"You did not kill him with the pistol nor strangle him?"

"I might kill you with the pistol on one of your bright days or hang you but the chui was killed with a shotgun."

"Such as you use for shooting kanga and kwali."

"Exactly."

"It is very extraordinary."

"You are a little extraordinary yourself," I said. "Is the spear loaded?"

"As all Masai spears are."

"You know where you can stick it."

"I do not understand your meaning."

I explained my meaning and felt Mr. Singh moving into second leopard's position and Mrs. Singh, a good Turkana, was taking a short-bladed spear from behind the counter.

Before we left the back parlor I had unhooked the top of the holster and Mr. Simeon was in what the French refer to as a state of manifeste inférior-ité unless he wished to make a play in which case with the steel-butted spear with the long blade erect, as he would seldom be, he was invincible.

"Give Mr. Simeon some bubble gum," I said to Madame Singh thinking that we had better bring it on or get it over with. I dropped my right hand low and sloped the thigh up a little and Mrs. Singh extended the carton which contained the bubble gum. She did this with politeness. It was all a little too rough and it was not the ideal comedy of manners but we had been vouchsafed a chance to judge Simeon since September so I said, "Why don't you make a play now, Simeon, instead of taking the bubble gum? Does your wife chew bubble gum when so and so takes her?"

But he did not take the bubble gum nor did he make a play and I turned my back and waited to feel it in the kidneys and walked over to the wooden bar and notion counter. I could feel that I was sweating pretty badly and I was pleased to see that Mr. Singh was sweating really well at the line of his turban. He was also sweating on his cheeks above his beard.

"Mr. Singh," I said. "We must build up a better class of trade in this duka."

I still did not know whether Mr. Simeon might try a throw from the door as he was undecided; his great error.

"It is difficult," Mr. Singh said. "The trade is divided in too many ways."

CHAPTER 29

Mr. Singh and I went into the back room and he handed me the White Heather and I poured for us both. The Scottish courage with plain water added never had tasted better.

"Pity you don't drink, Mr. Singh."

"I have always missed it greatly," Mr. Singh said. "May I be permitted an observation?"

"More than permitted."

"I do not think all our recent performance was entirely necessary."

"How right you are. Would you care to offer a critique? It would be welcome."

"I believe the reference to this misconduct of the wife imperiled both of your flanks."

"And my rear."

"We have only small amusements in Loitokitok. May I thank you for the diversion? I had him covered."

"Oh?"

"I have a license for it," he said. "Or someone has. No one wants to be hanged these days."

He shrugged one shoulder slightly and it appeared in his left hand like a conjuring trick. It was an old Webley .455.

"Admirable. Let's see it go back."

It went back as fast as it came out.

"The old elastic cord," Mr. Singh said. "The only trick is that the strength and degree of expansion of the cord should maintain an exact ratio to the weight and balance of the weapon."

"It is wholly admirable."

Mr. Singh handed me the bottle and I poured two very small drinks and we each added water.

"If you like I would be very happy to enter your service as an unpaid volunteer," Mr. Singh said. "At present I am informing for three government services none of whom coordinate their information nor have any proper liaison."

"Things are not always exactly as they seem and it is an Empire which has been functioning for a long time."

"Do you admire the way it functions now?"

"I am a foreigner and a guest and I do not criticize."

"Would you like me to inform for you?"

"With carbons furnished of all other information delivered."

"There are no carbons of oral information unless you have a tape recorder. Do you have a tape recorder?"

"Not with me."

"You could hang half Loitokitok with four tape recorders."

"I have no desire to hang half Loitokitok."

"Neither do I. And who would buy at the duka?"

"Mr. Singh, if we did things properly we would perpetrate an economic disaster."

"Instead of the type of disaster we have now," Mr. Singh said. "Are you going to pick up that son of a bitch Simeon when you draw the net on Christmas?"

"I'm sorry, Mr. Singh. For the first time I do not understand you."

"Sahib," he said.

"Bwana Singh."

The Turkana woman looked in the door. She had heard our voices change.

"Simeon will be the interpreter at the big ngoma on the day of the Birthday of the Baby Jesus. The Masai are a friendly nation, not simply a tribe. Simeon is well educated and we are all proud of him. No tribe stands higher in the estimation of the British raj than the Masai. Remember their war service and their generosity."

"May I come by and hear the speech?" Mr. Singh asked. "As a Sikh it would be good for me. I heard the shorter speech today."

"I hope to give you the same hospitality that you have extended to me. Although we are under canvas at the moment."

"Under canvas," said Mr. Singh. "Under canvas."

"Now I must go up to where we left the car."

"I will walk with you if you don't mind. Three paces to the rear and on your left."

"Please don't trouble yourself."

"It is no trouble."

I said goodbye to Mrs. Singh and told her we would be by with the car to pick up three cases of Tusker and a case of Coca-Cola and walked out into the lovely main and only street of Loitokitok.

Towns with only one street make the same feeling as a small boat, a narrow channel, the headwaters of a river, or the trail up over a pass. Sometimes Loitokitok, after the swamp and the different broken countries and the desert and the forbidden Chyulu Hills, seemed an important capital and on other days it seemed like the rue Royale. Today it was straight Loitokitok with overtones of Cody, Wyoming, or Sheridan, Wyoming, in the old days. I kept as good a watch for Simeon as though we were hunting but, with Mr. Singh at my back, it was a relaxed and pleasant walk which we both enjoyed and in front of Benji's with the gas pump, the wide steps like a Western general store, and the many Masai standing around the hunting car I stopped by the car and told Mwengi I would stay with the rifle while he went to shop or drink. He said no that he would rather stay with the rifle. So I went up the steps and into the crowded store. Debba and the widow were there still looking at cloth. Mthuka was helping them and turning down pattern after pattern. I hated shopping and the rejection of materials and I went to the far end of the long L-shaped counter and began to buy medicines and soaps. When these were stacked into a box I began to buy tinned goods, mostly kipper snacks, sardines, silts, tinned shrimp, and various types of false salmon along with a number of tins of local tinned meat which were intended as a gift for my father-in-law and then I bought two tins each of every type of fish exported from South Africa including one variety labeled simply FISH. Then I bought half a dozen tins of Cape spiny lobster and, remembering we were short of Sloan's Liniment, bought a bottle of that and one half a dozen cakes of Lifebuoy soap. By this time there were a crowd of Masai watching this purchasing. Debba looked down once and smiled proudly. She and the widow could still not make up their minds and there were not more than a half a dozen rolls of cloth to be inspected.

Mthuka came down the counter and told me the car had been filled up and that he had found the good posho that Keiti wanted. I gave him a hundred shilling note and told him to pay for the girls' purchases.

"Tell them to buy two dresses," I said. "One for the shamba and one for the Birthday of the Baby Jesus."

Mthuka knew that no woman needed two new dresses. She needed her old one and the new one. But he went down and told the girls in Kamba and Debba and the widow looked down, all impudence replaced by a shining reverence as though I had just invented electricity and the lights had gone on over all of Africa. I did not meet their look but continued purchasing, now moving into the field of hard candies, bottled, and the various types of chocolate bars both nutted and plain.

By this time I did not know how the money was standing up but we did have the gas in the car and the posho and I told the relative of the owner who was serving behind the counter to load everything and box it carefully and I would return to pick it up with the bill. This gave Debba and the widow more time to select and I would drive the hunting car down to Mr. Singh's and pick up the bottled products.

Ngui was at Mr. Singh's. He had found the dye powder we wanted to dye my shirts and hunting vests Masai color and he and I drank a bottle of Tusker and took one out to Mwengi in the car. Mwengi had the duty but next time it would be different.

In the presence of Ngui Mr. Singh and I again conversed in unknown tongue and non-flying pigeon Swahili.

Ngui asked me in Kamba how I would like to bang Mrs. Singh and I was delighted to see that either Mr. Singh was a very great actor or that he had not had the time or opportunity to learn Kamba.

"Kwisha maru," I said to Ngui which seemed sound double talk.

"Buona notte," he said and we clinked bottles.

"Piga tu."

"Piga tu."

"Piga chui, tu," Ngui explained just a little beerily I thought to Mr. Singh who bowed in congratulations and indicated that these three bottles were on the house.

"Never," I said in Hungarian, "Nem, nem, soha."

Mr. Singh said something in unknown tongue and I made signs that he give me the bill which he proceeded to write out and I said to Ngui, in Spanish, "Vamanos. Ya es tarde."

"Avanti Savoia," he said. "Na nu'uaa."

"You *are* a bastard," I said.

"Hapana," he said. "Blood brother."

So we loaded up with the help of Mr. Singh and several of his sons. It was understandable that the interpreter could not help since no mission boy could be seen carrying a case of beer. But he looked so sad and he was so obviously troubled by the words na nu'uaa that I asked him to carry the case of Coca-Cola.

"May I ride with you when you drive?"

"Why not?"

"I could have stayed and watched the rifle."

"You don't start on your first day watching the rifle."

"I am sorry. I meant only that I could have relieved your Wakamba brother."

"How do you know he is my brother?"

"You addressed him as brother."

"He's my brother."

"I have much to learn."

"Never let it get you down," I said, laying the car alongside of Benji's front steps where the Masai who wanted to ride down the mountain were waiting.

"Fuck 'em all," said Ngui. This was the only English phrase he knew or at least the only one he used, since for some time English had been considered the language of the hangman, government officials, civil servants, and bwanas in general. It was a beautiful language but it was becoming a dead language in Africa and it was tolerated but not approved. Since Ngui, who was my brother, had used it I used it in return and said, "The long and the short and the tall."

He looked out at the importuning Masai that had he been born in the older times which were still within the span of my life, he would have enjoyed dining on and said in Kamba, "All tall."

"Interpreter," I said and corrected to say, "Peter, will you be so good as to go into the duka and tell my brother Mthuka that we are ready to load?"

"How will I know your brother?"

"He is Kamba tu."

Ngui did not approve of the interpreter nor of his shoes and he was already moving with the compact insolence of an unarmed Kamba through the spear-carrying Masai who had gathered hopeful of a ride, their positive Wassermans not flying like banners from the spear shafts. I sat at the wheel and passed the time of day with Simeon's wife who stood tall, mud-bronze, and truly beautiful beside the car knowing, proudly, and with her beautiful face alight as though she had been chosen by God or some great beauty contest that she would ride. She would ride all right and had been ridden and we had a secret name for her as they have secret names for every person in that country. Her name was "For Kamba Only," which, within its harmony, contained a triple joke of counterpoint regarding segregation and the airport of Nairobi.

Finally everyone came out and the purchases were loaded. I stepped out to let Mthuka take the wheel and to let Debba and the widow in and to pay the bill. I made the bill with ten shillings to spare and I could see Mwindi's face when I came home with no money. He was not only the Secretary of the Treasury but also my self-appointed conscience.

"How many Masai can we take?" I asked Mthuka.

"Kamba Only and six others."

"Too many."

"Four others."

So we loaded with Ngui and Mwengi choosing and Debba very excited and stiffly proud and unlooking and I watched for Simeon but did not see him anywhere. We were three in the front seat and five in the back with Kamba Only and the widow riding with Ngui and Mwengi and four second favorites seated on the sacks of posho and the purchases in the rear. We might have taken two more but there were two bad places in the road where the Masai always became seasick.

We came down the hill which was the term we used for the lower slope of the big mountain and Ngui was opening the beer bottles which are as important in Wakamba life as any other sacrament. I asked Debba how she was. It had been a long and, in some ways, a hard day, and with the shopping and the change of altitude and the curves she had more than a full right to feel any way she was. The plain was laid out before us now and all the features of the terrain and she took hold of the carved holster of the pistol and said, "En la puta gloria."

"Yo también," I said and asked Mthuka for snuff. He passed it to me and I passed it to Debba who passed it back to me, not taking any. It was a very good snuff, not as powerful as that of Arap Meina but enough snuff to let you know you had snuff when you tucked it under your upper lip. Debba could not take snuff but she passed the box, in her pride and in our descent of the hill, to the widow. It was excellent Kajiado snuff and the widow took it and passed it back to Debba who gave it to me and I returned it to Mthuka.

"You don't take snuff?" I asked Debba. I knew the answer and it was stupid to ask and the first undelighting thing that we had done all day.

"I cannot take snuff," she said. "I am unmarried to you and I cannot take snuff."

There was nothing to say about this so we did not say anything and she put her hand back on the holster which she truly loved, it having been carved better in Denver than anyone had ever been carved or tattooed, by Heiser and Company in a beautiful flowered design which had been worn smooth with saddle soap and lightened and destroyed by sweat, still faintly encrusted from the morning of this day and she said, "I have all of you in the pistol."

And I said something very rude. Between Kamba there is always impudence by the woman carried into insolence and far past it if there is no love. Love is a terrible thing that you would not wish on your neighbor and, as in all countries, it is a moveable feast. Fidelity does not exist nor ever is implied except at the first marriage. Fidelity by the husband that is. This was the first marriage and I had little to offer except what I had. This was little but not unimportant and neither of us lived with any doubts at all.

CHAPTER 30

It turned out to be rather a quiet evening. In the tent Debba did not wish to bathe and neither did the widow. They were afraid of both Mwindi, who had to bring the hot water, and they were afraid of the large green canvas tub on its six legs. This was understandable and understood.

We had dropped some people off at the Masai manyattas and we were past the bravado stage and things, in the dark and in a definite place, were a little bit rough and there was no repeal nor any thought of any. I had told the widow to leave but since I was protecting her I did not know whether, under Kamba law, she had the right to be there. Any rights she had under Kamba law I was prepared to grant her and she was a very nice and delicate woman with good manners.

The Informer had turned up during the period of unquietness and both Debba and I had seen him steal the bottle of lion fat. It was in an empty bottle of the Grand MacNish and both Debba and I knew that it had been adulterated with eland fat by Ngui before he and I had decided to be brothers. It was like 86-proof whiskey instead of one hundred-proof and we came awake to see him steal it and she laughed very happily, she always laughed happily and said, "Chui tu." And I said, "No hay remedio."

"La puta gloria," she said. We did not have a great vocabulary and were not great conversationalists and had no need for an interpreter except on Kamba law and we went to sleep for one or two minutes with the widow, fiercely, on guard. She had seen the Informer steal the off-shape bottle with the too white lion fat that we all knew well and it had been her cough which had called our attention.

At this time I called Msembi, the good rough boy who served as mess steward and was a hunting, not a crop raising Kamba, but was not a skilled hunter and was reduced, since the war, to servant status. We were all servants since I served the government, through the Game Department, and I also served Miss Mary and a magazine named *Look*. My service to Miss

Mary had been terminated, temporarily, with the death of her lion. My service to *Look* had been terminated, temporarily, I had hoped permanently, with the death of the leopard on the noon of that day. I was wrong, of course. But neither Msembi nor I minded serving in the least and neither of us had served our God nor our King too well to be stuffy about it.

The only laws are tribal laws and I was a mzee which means an elder as well as still having the status of a warrior. It is difficult to be both and the older mzees resent the irregularity of the position. You should give up something, or anything that was necessary, and not try to hold everything. I had learned this lesson in a place called the Schnee Eifel where it had been necessary to move from an offensive to a defensive position. You give up what you have won at great cost as though it had not cost a dime and you become eminently defensible. It is hard to do and many times you should be shot for doing it, but you should be shot quicker if you did not make the adjustment.

So I had told Msembi that he would serve dinner in one half of an hour in the mess tent and that plates would be laid for Debba, the widow, and myself. He was completely delighted and full of Kamba energy and malice and went off to give the order. Unfortunately that was not how it turned out. Debba was brave and la puta gloria is a better place than most people ever reach or attain. The widow knew it was a rough order and she knew that no one ever took Africa in a day nor on any given night. But that was the way it was going to be.

Keiti killed it in the name of his loyalty to the bwanas, to the tribe, and to the Moslem religion. He had the courage and the good taste not to delegate to anyone his order and he knocked on the tent pole and asked if we might speak. I might have said no, but I am a disciplined boy. Not with twelve of the best as Pop disciplined but with the implacable discipline of all of our lives.

He said, "You have no right to take the young girl violently." (In this he was wrong. There had never been any violence ever.) "This could make great trouble."

"All right," I said. "You speak for all the mzees?"

"I am the eldest."

"Then tell your son who is older than I am to bring the hunting car."

"He is not here," Keiti said and we knew about that and his lack of authority over his children and why Mthuka was not a Moslem but it was too complicated for me.

"I will drive the car," I said. "It is not a very difficult thing."

"Please take the young girl home to her family. I will go with you if you like."

"I will take the young girl, the widow, and the Informer."

Mwindi was standing, in his green robe and cap, beside Keiti now since it was torture for Keiti to speak English.

Msembi had no business there but he loved Debba as we all did. She was feigning sleep and she was the wife that we would all wish to purchase, all of us knowing we would never own anything that we had bought.

Msembi had been a soldier and the two heavy elders knew this and were not unconscious of their treason when they became Moslems and, since everyone becomes an elder eventually, he threw quick against their complaisance and with the true African litigational sense, using titles, which had been abolished, and his own knowledge of Kamba law, "Our Bwana can keep the widow since she has a son and he protects her officially."

Keiti nodded and Mwindi nodded.

Putting an end to it and feeling too bad about Debba who in her sense of glory had eaten the meal and slept the night as we were not permitted to sleep but as we slept so many times without the judgment of the splendid elders who had attained their rank uniquely, no that was not just, by seniority, I said, to the interior of the tent, "No hay remedio. Kwenda na shamba."

This was the beginning of the end of the day in my life which offered the most chances of happiness.

CHAPTER 31

Having accepted the decision of the elders and driven Debba, the widow, and the Informer home to the shamba where I left her with the things that I had bought for her I returned to camp. The things that I had bought made a difference and they did both have the cloth for their dresses. I would not speak to my father-in-law and gave him no explanations and we all acted as though we were returning, a little late perhaps, from a purchasing expedition. I had seen the bulge of the Grand MacNish bottle containing the adulterated lion fat wrapped in the Informer's paisley shawl but that meant nothing. We had better lion fat than that and would have better if we wished and there is no minor satisfaction comparable to have anyone, from a writer on up, and up is a long way, steal from you and think that they have not been detected. With writers you must never let them know since it might break their hearts if they had them and some have them and who should judge another man's cardiac performance unless you are in competition? With the Informer it was another matter, involving, as it did, his degree of loyalty which was already in dispute. Keiti hated the Informer, with considerable cause, since he had served under Keiti in the old days and they had many old unresolved things dating from when the Informer had served as a lorry driver and offended Keiti with his, then, youthful insolence and with his treasonable frankness about the great nobleman who was, by other accounts than his, a backward man. Keiti had loved Pop ever since he had taken service under him and with the Kamba hatred of homosexuality he could not tolerate a Masai lorry driver impugning a white man and especially one of such renown and when the bad boys painted the lips of the statue that had been erected to this man with lipstick, as they did each night in Nairobi, Keiti would not look at it when he rode past. Charo, who was a more devout Moslem than Keiti, would look at it and laugh the way we all did. But when Keiti had taken the Queen's shilling he had taken it for always. He was a true Victorian and the rest of us who had been Edwardians and then Georgians and now were frankly and completely Elizabethans within our capacity to serve and our tribal loyalties, had little in common with Keiti's Victorianism. On this night I felt so bad that I did not wish to be personal nor think about any personal things and especially not to be unjust with someone that I admired and respected. But I knew Keiti was more shocked that Debba and the widow and I should eat together at the table in the mess tent than he was worried about Kamba law because he was a grown man with five wives of his own and a beautiful young wife and who was he to administer our morals or lack of them?

Driving along in the night, trying not to be bitter, and thinking of Debba and our arbitrary deprivation of formal happiness which could have been overlooked by anyone regardless of their seniority I thought of turning off to the left and going down that red road to the other shamba where I would find two of our group and not Lot's nor Potiphar's, but Simeon's wife and see if we could parlay yaws into true love. But that was not the thing to do either so I drove home and parked the car and sat in the mess tent and read Simenon. Msembi felt terrible about it but he and I were not conversationalists either.

He made one very gallant suggestion that he would go with our lorry driver and bring the widow. I said hapana to that and read some more Simenon.

Msembi kept feeling worse all the time and had no Simenon to read and his next suggestion was that he and I should go with the car and get the girl. He said it was a Kamba custom and there was nothing to be paid but a fine. Besides he said the shamba was illegal; no one was qualified to bring us to trial and I had made my father-in-law many presents as well as having killed a leopard for him on this same day.

I thought this over and decided against it. Some time before I had paid the tribal price to sleep in the bed of my mother-in-law which is a rough thing to do. How was Keiti to know this? He was supposed to know everything but the outfit we had built up was very taut and just possibly rougher than he knew. I was not sure about this since I respected and admired him so especially since Magadi. He had tracked there when he had no need to and with both his snakes out above his cheekbones and under his turban until I was beat and Ngui was having difficulty. He had done this tracking in a heat of 105 degrees Fahrenheit in the shade on the good thermometer in camp and the only shade we had was when I, beat, would take a break under a small tree, taking the shade as a great gift, breathing deeply and trying to compute how many miles we were from campi, that fabulous place with the wonderful shade of the fig trees and the rippling stream and the water bags sweating cool.

Keiti had whipped us on that day with no ostentation and I did not respect him without cause. But tonight I still was not sure why he had intervened. They always do it for your own good. But I knew one thing; Msembi and I should not go back as rummies do and resume the exercise.

Africans are not supposed to ever feel bad about anything. This is an invention of the whites who are temporarily occupying the country. Africans are said not to feel pain because they do not cry out; that is, some of them do not. Yet not showing pain when it is received was a tribal thing and a great luxury. While we in America had television, motion pictures, and expensive wives always with soft hands, grease on their faces at night, and the natural, not the ranch, mink coat somewhere under refrigeration with a ticket like a pawnbroker's to get it out, the African, of the better tribes, had the luxury of not showing pain. We, Noi, as Ngui called us had never known true hardship except in war which is a boring, nomadic life with the occasional compensations of combat and the pleasure of looting given as a bone is thrown to a dog by a master who cares nothing for him. We, Noi, who at this moment were Msembi and myself, had known what it was to sack a town and we both knew, although the subject was never to be talked about but only shared secretly, what the mechanics and the procedure were to implement the Bible phrase they put the men to the sword and carried the women into captivity. This was no longer done but anyone who had done it was a brother. Good brothers are difficult to find but you can encounter a bad brother in any town.

The Informer was my brother as he continually stated. But I had not chosen him. In the thing which we had now, which was not a safari and where "Bwana" was very close to a direct insult, Msembi and I were good brothers and on this night, without mentioning it, we both remembered that the slave raiders who had come up the different routes from the sea were all Moslems and I knew that was why Mthuka with the slashed arrow on each cheek would never, nor could ever have been converted to the fashionable religion his father, Keiti, and dear honest Charo and Mwindi, the honest and skillful snob, had been received into. So I sat there and we had a sharing of our sorrow. Nguili came in once, humble as a nanyake should come, but wishing to weigh in with his sorrow if it was permissible. It was not permissible and I slapped him on his green frocked ass, lovingly, and said, "Morgen ist auch noch ein Tag." This is an old German phrase which is the opposite of "No hay remedio," which is a true and beautiful phrase but which I felt guilty for having implanted as though I had the guilt of a defeatist or a collaborationist. I translated it carefully into Kamba with the help of Msembi and then feeling the guilt of a phrase-utterer I asked Ngui if he would find my spears because I was going out to hunt when the moon rose.

It was more than a little bit theatrical; but so is Hamlet. We were all deeply moved. Possibly I was the most moved of the three of us because, having made the old mistake of not watching my mouth, I now had to hunt with the spear and the backing up spears and with no dog. But I remembered that I had the pistol and it felt very good and I loved the pistol and its non-slapping firmly swung and secured weight and went back to reading Simenon. The lamp had a new mantle and was working well and the moon would be up in around ten minutes. It was not a long time to wait and I knew that Ngui would be oiling the spears. He did not know how to hone them but Charo, who had not gone to Loitokitok, and who loved the spears and what they stood for and against, would have cared for them as he cared for the guns. But any spear should be checked and oiled before you carry it out to kill with.

I don't remember when spear hunting first started. I know we started to learn a little about spears at the first camp in Salengai when I used to go bird shooting with a group of young Masai morani that were the best Masai we had met and were young men who were not spoiled nor corrupted in any way. We had met them one evening in the thick country where there was an island between two branches of the dry sand river below Salengai. They were returning from some ceremony they had been holding in the center of the island. It had involved the eating of meat and was a seasonal observance and they were as cheerful and rough after the solemnity as a good football team that has just attended mass.

I was alone and an intruder in their country and I could not speak Masai and they, feeling boisterous, acted a little as though they were a war party. But they had never seen a shotgun nor a bird killed in flight and I shot two kwali that rose whirring from where we were standing looking each other over and, at the thump of the birds in the brush, they were completely delighted. They found them and brought them in and stroked and admired them and from then on we hunted together. We were rather a large group to hunt with anything but a shotgun but they saw roosted guinea fowl that I would never have seen; the big bird hunched tight down onto the high limb and when they made me see it the gun would speak, suddenly, and there would be the heavy flopping of the bird through the branches and then the final thump. If another bird flew aroused by the shot and showing clearly over our heads against the last clearness of the sky suddenly collapsed and thumped down, once hitting one of the morani as he fell, then we all embraced.

There were rhino in that country and I tried to explain this and that we should be careful but they thought I wanted to shoot a rhino which was very impractical with the shotgun but they showed what they would do with the spears and I suppose that was when the spear business really started. I was worried about the drill for rhino on a combined operation of shotgun and Masai spears on him but I figured that if one did come the best thing to do would be to try to get him in the eyes or make sure of one eye and then to hope for the best. I was sure I could get an eye if I waited him out but then I reflected that a rhino could barely see anyway and that his nose would still be functioning but I thought I could get the second shot into the nose if I could keep my legs still and that I certainly must do that before my new friends and business associates so we hunted very lightheartedly.

This was evidently a time when morani of this age class had no duties except to be in the woods so we hunted together whenever I had time and I started to try to learn Masai and, respectfully, how to use the spear and our small group of guinea slayers and potential rhino confronters was known as the Honest Ernies. Ngui and I were neither friends nor brothers then and I wanted to hunt alone both for pleasure and prestige and I was well on the way to being a traitor, if I had been a Kamba then, or, at least, a collaborationist when the Honest Ernies had to leave. I never knew what it was about except that it was a tribal thing connected with the same ceremony that had brought us so happily in contact in the forest. It could have been my fault but each Honest Ernie left with shotgun shells for ear plugs and a penny which had been held between the forefinger and the thumb of the right hand and shot out of that position with a .22 pistol bullet. That was the only tradition that the unit had and we had never fought a rhino nor killed anything larger than a guinea fowl. I had learned very little about the spear and perhaps twelve words of Masai but it had been no time lost in one's life.

Now the moon was up over the shoulder of the mountain and I wished that I had a good big dog and that I had not declared to do something that would make me a better man than Keiti. But I had and so I checked the spears and put on my soft moccasins and thanked Nguili and left the mess tent. There were two men on guard with the rifles and the ammo and a lantern on the tree outside the tent and I left these lights behind and left the moon over my right shoulder and started off on the long walk.

The spear haft felt good and heavy and it was taped with surgical tape so that your hand would not slip if it was sweaty. Often, using the spear, you sweat heavily under your armpits and on your forearms and the sweat runs down the haft. The grass stubble felt good under my feet and then I felt the smoothness of the motor tire track that led to the airstrip we had made and the other track we called the Great North Road. This was the first night I had gone out alone with the spear and I wished I had one of the old Honest Ernies or the big dog. With the German shepherd dog you could always tell if there was something in the next clump of bush because he fell back at once and walked with his muzzle against the back of your knee. But being properly scared as I was when out with the spear at night is a luxury that you have to pay for and like the best luxuries it is worth it most of the time. Mary, G.C., and I had shared many luxuries and some had been potentially expensive but, so far, all had been worth the price. It was the stupidities of daily life with its unflagging erosion that was not worth what it cost, I thought, and I checked in my mind the various bushes and dead trees that had cobra holes and hoped that I would not step on any of them if they were out hunting. We always joked about the cobra being Tony's grandfather and therefore not a dangerous thing and I had never seen one do anything but run. But G.C. had one of the spitting variety launch venom onto the windshield of his Land Rover and Tony's father had been blinded by one.

In camp I had heard two hyenas but they were quiet now. I heard a lion up by the Old Manyatta and resolved to keep away from the Old Manyatta. I did not have enough courage to go up there anyway and that was also rhino country. Ahead, on the plain, I could see something asleep in the moonlight. It was a wildebeest and I worked away from him or her; it turned out to be him; and then got back onto the trail again.

There were many night birds and plover and I saw bat-eared foxes and leaping hares but their eyes did not shine as they did when we cruised with the Land Rover since I had no light and the moon made no reflection. The moon was well up now and gave a good light and I went along the trail happy to be out in the night not caring if any beast presented himself. All the nonsense about Keiti and the girl and the widow and our lost banquet and night in bed seemed of no importance and I looked back and could just not see the lights of camp but could see the mountain high and square-topped and wonder white in the moonlight and I hoped I would not run onto anything to kill. I could always have killed the wildebeest, maybe; but if I did I would have to dress him out and then stay with the carcass so the hyenas did not get him or else rouse the camp and get the truck and be a show-off and I remembered that only six of us would eat wildebeest and that I wanted some good meat for when Miss Mary came back.

So I walked along in the moonlight hearing the small animals move and the birds cry when they rose from the dust of the trail and thought about Miss Mary and what she would be doing in Nairobi and how she would look with her new haircut and whether she would get it or not and the way she was built and how there was almost no difference between the way she was built and the way Debba was built and that I would have Miss Mary back by two o'clock the next day. No; the day after we were on that day today, and that it was a damned good thing all the way around. By this time I was nearly up to where she had killed her lion and I could hear a leopard hunting in the edge of the big swamp to the left. I thought of going on up to the salt flats but I knew if I did I would be tempted by some animal so I turned around and started on the worn trail back to camp looking at the mountain and not hunting at all.

CHAPTER 32

In the morning Mwindi brought tea and I thanked him, drank it outside the tent by the remnants of the fire thinking and remembering while I drank it, and then dressed and went out to see Keiti. He was up early as old men are and I asked him first, formally, if the posho that we had brought from Loitokitok was good. He said it was. Then I thanked him for the action he had taken as an elder and told him that I would approach the father of the girl Debba formally. He smiled very happily. Then I told him that if I had a child from the girl Debba he would have a choice of a career as a soldier, a doctor, or a lawyer or that he could go for his upbringing to the Kingdom of Mayito. If he wished to stay with me as a son and not have to make a career he could be my true son and we would hunt together. Keiti was very happy about this and we were friends again.

There is no word for "sorry" in Africa and we did not try to find one. Both of us were sorry. Keiti asked me if I had killed anything with the spear, being sure that I had, and I told him, "Nothing." I could have killed a wildebeest but I left him asleep and merely walked around the country. He asked me if I had heard the lion and I answered that I heard him up by the old manyatta but had not gone near him. He said there had been a leopard that had come by up the river and I said that I had heard him.

We were formal and friendly and he said that he would like to go out with me one night with the spears. I was very touched by this and knew that he would be a better man than I was. So I asked him if everything was correct and in order in the camp and he said that the camp was in perfect order but that some of the young men had come in late after celebrating the leopard.

We left it at that and he thanked me for the Coca-Cola. We both laughed and I said I would need the hunting car in an hour. I walked back to the mess tent to think things out and have breakfast. There were several air-mail editions of the *London Times* and one of the *Daily Telegraph* that I had not read and I abandoned thinking things out, since there was only one answer, and took up the pleasure of reading of the great world beginning with the "Court Circular" and finally ending with the usual column that the *Telegraph* devoted to the doings of Senator McCarthy. I had taken about as many remarks about the Senator and his two assistants as I could swallow from Europeans and not being anti-Semitic I had never given my opinion on the two assistants except perhaps a dozen times when I had attempted to explain how such things worked from the old example of the smart one and the rich one. In the last shipment of books we had received two books on the Senator and G.C. and I had tried to understand him and the problem that he presented. Pop had refused to read the books after a quick look through them and had dismissed the problem saying, "No ——— like that can exist for long." He had been slightly more pungent about the Senator and then dismissed both the problem and the Senator. Miss Mary had refused to read about the Senator and would not have him discussed in her presence. She put it quite clearly by saying, "There are enough disgusting things in life without me having to read about that Senator whatever his name is."

But G.C. and I continued to be fascinated by the Senator and especially his two assistants and their antics and on this morning I read the *Daily Telegraph* with true appreciation. It was an excellent paper anyway and I had been attempting to follow racing in it. But there is no true stimulus in following racing, except as a mental exercise, when there was no bookmaker in Loitokitok and the paper arrived, sometimes, a week or a month after the horses had gone to the post. From what I had learned of Mr. Singh the day before I was sure it would have been possible for him to get a bet down. But our communications were too tenuous.

So I ate an excellent breakfast served by Nguili who started to serve with sadness and then, seeing that I was not depressed, rose to his true Kamba cheerfulness and his wish to be a warrior who was daunted by nothing. He wanted to know about the spearing and I told him it was sin novedad, and taught him how to pronounce it. It was not as lovely a phrase to him as no hay remedio was to Debba but it is not so poetical and the feeling of drama or of catharsis is lacking.

"Listen, Sin Novedad," I told him, in this way giving him a name which is necessary in Africa as it is in Spain, "you can go with us on the routine patrol today."

"Mzuri," he said. "Asanta sana, Bwana."

"No fucking bwanas," I said.

He was worried by this but repeated dutifully, "Hapana frucky bwanas."

This was rough for him but in the well of hatred we drew our daily water from it was less than enough to moisten the bottom of a bucket.

"Hapana frucky bwanas," he repeated.

"Many bwanas very good," I explained. "Bwana Pop is my father."

"I am young," he said. "You will have to explain much."

"We go together in the car. The others will explain."

"Ndio, Bwana," he said and I knew that there were difficulties in founding any movement or religion and resumed reading the "Court Circular."

It was at this moment that the Informer appeared, paisley shawled, pork-pie hat in hand, his eroded face expressing sorrow and dignity.

"A chair for our devoted Informer," I said to Nguili inspired by the "Court Circular." Nguili looked at the Informer with straight, clean, young Kamba hatred.

"Any news from London?" I asked the Informer.

"Nothing, brother. I come from the shamba. There is a very large pack of wild dogs."

"Very good of you to tell me," I said. "Will you have a kipper? I suppose you have them surrounded."

"No," he said. "They are moving to the right of the road coming from the shamba. There are more than thirty in the pack."

"Tell Mthuka to have the car prepared and ask Ngui to come here," I said to Nguili.

"Informer," I said, "are you sure these are actual wild dogs and not spots that you are seeing before your eyes? All your snakes are out and your eyes are baggy."

"Have I ever lied to you, brother?"

"No. I don't believe so. Some of the information has been a little cold and some was common knowledge."

"Brother, the life of an informer is difficult and you and I are from the same circumcision. Can an informer inform every day?"

"Probably not."

"I am glad that you agree."

"I don't agree too bloody far."

"Brother, your fiancée is desperate."

"How?"

"Last night the widow passed the entire night persuading her not to do away with herself. This is the truth from your brother and trusted informer."

Ngui came in looking much the worse for wear and I told him to put the shotgun, the small rifle, and the big rifle in the car. I told Nguili to change his clothes and fill the Jinny flask and bring six bottles of beer and a selection of the new provisions. I told Nguili to tell Keiti that he was off duty and that he would be hunting with us.

Through the flap of the open end of the mess tent I watched Charo and Ngui carry out the guns and the Informer said, "Brother, could I have a small one? It was a difficult night."

"Pour any size," I said. "There is the glass and the bottle. You ought to know the labels."

"I know them too well."

He poured himself a gigantic gin and put bitters in it and said, "To your good health, brother."

"I would not have any if I drank that in the morning."

"I too had better standards before I was ruined by the bwanas."

"A man is only ruined by himself. And bottles were made to help him."

"I am far from ruined," the Informer said, and remembering how the shamba was organized and his seventy shillings a month I was not the man to doubt him.

"Finish your kipper, brother, and we will look for the wild dogs."

The Informer finished his kipper with one lift of the fork and we were off.

All of us were the worse for wear but we found the wild dogs quite easily and, since they were classed as vermin and no one had promoted them to the status of Royal Game, I, being the Acting Game Ranger, shot three of the pack from the car and missed two. I was short on ammo for the .30-06 and did not want to waste any more since it was our meat gun as well as the all-purpose gun. Nguili had never seen a dead wild dog so we stopped and examined one and I told him to take the spear and slip it into him. The dog had huge ears, was multicolored with orange and black splotches, was thoroughly dead and very mangy with open patches along the flanks and on his butt and withers and Nguili approached him very cautiously and gave him the spear so gently that Ngui became angry and took the spear and jammed the steel-shod butt end of it through the carcass and then left the spear imbedded in the ground and quivering. He was talking to Nguili in Kamba and it was so fast and rough that I could not follow it at all. It was a tribal thing and not my business.

The shots at the pack, except for two, the first, when they were confident had been the type of shot that writers on Africa describe as at "flitting shapes." I did not want to drive the pack out of the area and I had no ammo to spare for the flitting shape type of shooting so Mthuka and Charo and I waited while Ngui showed Nguili how to clean both ends of a spear properly on a dead animal, wiping it shining and clean and avoiding the scabby or mangy areas and then we got back into the car. Ngui was always bad tempered in the early morning when Mthuka and I were most cheerful and I asked him, "Didn't you fuck well last night?"

"Better than you," he answered.

"Any goat fucked better than I did last night," I said. Even Charo laughed although he was with the elders and for some reason that we did not know in spite of his incomparable and always beautiful bravery had the fear of death with him carried as Napoleon's soldiers were said to have carried a Maréchal's baton in their musettes. This was probably rhetoric or journalism, but Charo, being fearless, did carry the fear of death with him and he had tried to convert me so that I would be saved, as he was, ever since I had known him. He knew all about the new religion and nobody made secrets in front of him but he hoped, in some way, that we might all be saved.

Now that we had found the wild dogs I wanted to get rid of the Informer. Everyone hated him but me and I looked at Mthuka, deaf as a post, with the blue cut arrow on his high cheek and, since we communicated with our eyes and with our hands he knew, instantly, and said, "Kwenda na shamba."

"I did produce the wild dogs as promised," the Informer said and he was very hurt because he knew we were off to hunt.

"It was very good but the wild dogs are finished for the moment."

"Brother, we have no meat."

"You'll get meat."

So we went to the shamba which was unlovely in the early morning and dropped the Informer. I asked him to ascertain if there were any complaints or depredations by animals or any irregularities and he spoke to several people and returned to say that everything was in order. I did not speak to my father-in-law since we were a hunting party and he was not and never would be a hunter. Debba was holding one of her sister's children and standing under the sacred tree with the children and the chickens and the goats.

"Jambo, tú," I said and she turned her head away and did not answer. Then she turned her head halfway back and smiled. We were all dead faced and we drove away on the old trail to the north.

It was good to be rid of the Informer and I was happy to know no one was desperate at the shamba or, at least, any more desperate than we all were always. In Africa you live in a state of happy carefree despair and perhaps what the Informer had meant to say was the girl had despair during the night. That would have been normal since I had experienced it myself. But among all of us only the Informer had remorse. He carried remorse with him as a man might carry a baboon on his shoulder. Remorse is a splendid name for a racehorse but it is a poor lifetime companion for a man. I had a truly lovely grandmother with a face like an angel if angels were eagles and she used to twirl a Tibetan prayer wheel which one of her sons had brought her after a visit to the Dalai Lama along with a bolt of red cloth and a quantity of extremely unsavory butter and some very fine tea and she had told me, after writing an excuse for my absence from high school and caring for me for six days when I had picked up a concussion acquired when boxing under another name than my own since nobody, then, would pay to see a boy named Hemingway fight, "Ern, promise me to do what you truly want to do. Do it always. I am an old woman now and I have always tried to be a good wife to your grandfather and as you know he can be a difficult man. But I want you to remember, Ern. Can you remember now, Ern?"

"Yes, Grandmother. I can remember everything except six rounds."

"They don't matter," she said. "Remember this now. The only things in life that I regret are the things that I did not do."

"Thank you very much, Grandmother. I'll try to remember."

I lay in bed with the ice pack still on my scrotum and the immense pain that not many people know and the strange ringing in the head if you even moved it and I remembered hearing people, paying customers, say, "Put that fucking cocksucker away. Put him away. What do you let him stay for, you bum? Throw the right, you yellow cocksucker. Throw it. For Christ sake throw it." Nobody knew it was broken and that now it was the size of an ordinary cantaloupe. But everyone knew how to talk and held their opinions and now I was trying to remember, exactly, what my grandmother said and then she said, "Don't try to think too hard, Ern. I know everything will be all right."

So I loved my grandmother more than anyone in the world and more than I could love anyone ever again and she said, "Let me take your good hand and you go to sleep."

So on this day, leaving the shamba and heading north on the trail the cattle used, herded by the small boys one of whom was my godson, and not always herded too well, our duty, mine, as acting temporary Game Ranger was to find and kill the warthog who had been wounded, slightly, the day before. This we had little heart for since all of us had been wounded much worse than the warthog and had recovered. But it was the law and since the British have a fetish in regard to the animal which has even been grazed by a bullet being put out of its misery, which is often nonexistent as any man who has been grazed by a bullet knows. The heat of the bullet cauterizes the small wound and the pain is much less if the bullet had not hit nerve nor broken bone and is in what the Spanish call el blando which is any part of the meat where there is no organ, nerve, or bone. Personally I would rather be wounded in the blando any day with a small caliber weapon than go to the dentist. But we had to remember that the warthog had neither sulfa nor penicillin or even iodine and it was our duty to find him and kill him. This we accomplished before ten o'clock and we dropped the tailgate of the hunting car and lifted his sad body with the unbelievable ugly, comic, genial face and the tusks he wore like the upturned mustaches of an old hussar into the back of the car. The wound had only grazed him and he had rolled in mud to close it and there were no maggots nor infection and I knew that was the last warthog I would ever kill, Acting Game Ranger or not.

The warthog, I thought, had a much better right to be in Africa than I did and as for his carrying rinderpest and having to be exterminated, there was no rinderpest at the time so how could he carry it? If there was any we would probably carry it ourselves on our shoes and with our tires. If you live in Masai country long enough you grow very tired of protecting cattle that overgraze the country and are never dipped for ticks and, often, only are a walking symbol of wealth.

What we wanted was an eland with his sweet breath and meat better than any cattle ever grown. We wanted an eland with his striped gray sides and his killing trot and his ability to leap his thousand pounds of good meat like an antelope and his kind beautiful eyes and curving horns and his meat, nyama, that would make us all strong again so we would have the strength that we had all misspent so thoroughly. We hunted all morning but we could not find one. Pof is the Kamba word for eland but there were no pof that we could find. They were all far over by the Chyulu Hills and finally I shot a zebra stallion for his hide and for basic camp meat. He was very handsome standing in the brown lava rocks with the mountain behind him and the bullet took him under the left ear making him so completely dead that Charo would not halal him. Ngui wanted me to slip the spear into him at the sticking place to bleed him and to show Nguili how to use the spear. I think what he wanted was for me to practice too. I went into the bad walking crouch weaving with the spear and then put it in hard. The blood pumped out as I withdrew and wiped the spear carefully across the rump. The zebra could not have been deader but the flesh was still jumping and crawling under the hide and we all thought Charo had been a little stuffy about refusing to make it legal meat but then neither he nor any of the other Moslems ate zebra anyway unless we were really bad off for meat as on the Great Ruaha. Zebra are strange in that the animal is truly dead but the body remains alive the same way that turtles' bodies do. No one has ever killed a loggerhead turtle's body by cutting the turtle's head off and in Key West they used to have a saying that the meat jumped in your belly all night even after it was cooked. Green turtles are very different, but their bodies do not die easily either.

Now we had this zebra and there was no shade but we skinned him out, Ngui, Charo, and I all skinning, spitting on our knives and passing the stone back and forth. We were not skinning competitively but there was a certain amount of showing off of minor skills and tricks and we all gave orders to Nguili. Then with the skin off but the carcass still resting on it we butchered cleanly me trying to translate into Kamba, "Haven't cut a gut in forty years," and then, with Mthuka, we carried the quarters to the car and Ngui rolled the hide up neatly.

Not being short of meat we left the tripe for the birds who had arrived and were shuffling and squatting around in their best attitudes of Royal Game.

In the charnel house we now had the pig and four quarters of zebra and we drove to a very shallow water hole that was used by both elephant and rhino and stopping the car we all squatted or knelt by the shallow depression with the imprints in the mud of those who had visited that night or morning and washed our arms and hands. The water was a little foul in odor and after we were finished I had Ngui pour some of the water from the water bag over my hands and wrists. Then we drove to a place where there was good shade under a wide acacia tree and I opened a tin of kipper snacks and one of false Dutch smoked salmon and we drank beer. It had been nothing as a morning but everyone was happy and rested now and I explained about the Happy Hunting Grounds.

In the religion, when we died, all of us who had been good men and good brothers would go direct to the Happy Hunting Grounds. Pof there were as common as Tommy on the plains. We would each have our own small shamba with good water the year around the way it was here at Kimana. Our wives would work the shambas and the religion would give each man five fertile wives, all Wakamba and all young and beautiful and with hard hands. There would be no taxes of any kind and no government. Only the religion. We would all be elders and would make the laws and enforce them ourselves. There would be no Game Department. I was the Game Department and we would hunt as we wished and take care of the game according to the laws of the religion. No white man could ever come into the Happy Hunting Grounds and there would be no D.C.s nor missionaries nor settlers. The climate was so healthy no one would ever be sick. We would all be pilots and have our own planes and petrol would be furnished by the religion. We would have a posho mill and make our own posho. We would have free sugar from the religion to make beer.

Ngui asked where I would get whiskey, gin, and Tusker beer and I said everyone in the Happy Hunting Grounds would have a card on which he could draw free anything that was good for him from the duka of the religion. If the other members of the religion met with him and he and they agreed that he drank too much his ration would be limited.

Charo asked what was the name of this our religion and I told Ngui to answer him. I said that I was not allowed to mention the name of the religion before a Moslem and I also knew but did not tell him that I was sure he would give the name and details of the religion to Keiti and Mwindi.

"Let us retreat for a moment," I said to Ngui so we got out and went over to the far side of the tree and each drank beer from the same bottle and consulted. Then we went back to the car and got in and I said, "You may tell him, Ngui."

"It is the Holy War Meat Eaters and Beer Drinkers Happy Hunting Ground and Mountain religion," Ngui told him. Charo was impressed by this title since the first word was "jihad."

"Who is your prophet?"

"I am the prophet," I said modestly to keep Ngui out of trouble.

"Are there members of other tribes than the Wakamba?"

"There are members of the Northern Cheyenne, a few Sioux, a few Blackfeet, and one or two Crows."

"Do you accept other tribes beside the Wakamba?"

"Not as yet."

"Hapana Kikuyu," Ngui said.

"Hapana," I backed him up.

"Arap Meina?"

I looked at Ngui and he shrugged his shoulders. Nguili acted like a boy who had wandered into a consistory of bishops. Mthuka had his face as rigid as he must have kept it at his circumcision ceremony.

"He's in the candidate's book," I told Charo in English. He did not understand and Mthuka said, "Kwenda na shamba." He and I each took a drink from his bottle of beer. This was shocking but impressive to Charo although he had seen it many times before.

I said, "Aideba endobera oldyani," which in Masai is what we told the women with the yaws since it means that "one has made medicine." But I was using it in the religious sense.

"Iaw illigaidulet," Ngui said. This was a result of his anthropological studies in the Masai beer-making manyatta and meant, "Bring more bottles."

"Ershal kennangoriok," which can be translated as "stupid woman."

Charo had not been studying Masai at the same school we attended and since he was an elder we did not wish ever to be offensive. Mthuka was unable to keep from laughing when we went into our beer-manyatta Masai so I broke it off and said, "Kwenda," and we drove on the old cattle trail through the thick trees to the clearing with the big sacred tree, the red earth, and the huts of my father-in-law's shamba. Debba was not there and I thought she must have gone into the mealie patch to do some work so we put a quarter of zebra on my father-in-law's doorstep and I caught a chicken, a young cockerel, and put his head under his wing and rocked him back and forth until he was asleep and then laid him on top of the piece of meat where he slept peacefully. Then we drove off toward camp.

It had been a quiet but a good morning and we had been happy after the zebra. There had been no eland but we were all thinking about the Happy Hunting Grounds and in that place you would never be out of sight of eland.

There are difficulties in founding a religion unless you choose to be pompous or infallible. It is best to be both of these to make the religion successful and we were prepared to assume the obligation with other tribes. But no Kamba has either of these qualities and as a founding member and number one apostle Ngui raised a question.

"Who runs the duka in the Happy Hunting Grounds?"

"That has not been revealed to me."

"If Indian runs the duka Happy Hunting Grounds kwisha."

Kwisha is a very terminating word and I respected my fellow founder for his long view into eternity.

The question required an immediate answer and I said, "American Indian runs the duka. American Indian is without ambition."

This was the Word but it had been improvised and I was open to correction. Ngui thought it over and said, "Let good Kamba woman manage the duka."

This was something that had never yet happened in the history of Africa nor of the world and I was amazed and pleased at Ngui's liberal views or, at least, liberal strategy.

"OK," I said. "You know the woman?"

"My mother," said Ngui. "Or Debba when she is old."

"May she never be old."

"All women are old quickly."

I could not agree to this but I said, "Agreed. Your mother" (and I remembered her when neither of us was old) "runs the duka. We will not need Debba for a long time."

"Who knows?" said Ngui.

So we came into camp and swung down out of the hunting car and I asked Charo and Ngui to clean all of the weapons carefully. It was a high, dry country but the presence of the mountain and the strange winds that came from her when there was new snow made unnoticed dampness which was not good for precision weapons.

At the mess tent Msembi, a member of our religion, asked me what I would like to drink. I did not feel like drinking after having talked about the religion and I told him, "Nothing." He was worried and asked me if I would like snuff. I said that I would and when he brought it I put it under my armpit, as a prophet should, and started to read *The Times Literary Supplement*.

CHAPTER 33

It was not to be a completely quiet day nor one devoted to reading and contemplation as I had hoped. Arap Meina came to the open flap of the mess tent and saluted smartly and said, "Bwana, there are small problems."

"Of what type?"

"Nothing grave."

In what amounted to the reception room in the area beyond the cooking fires where there were several large trees there were the leading men from two Masai manyattas. They were not chiefs since a chief is a man who has taken money or a cheap medal from the British and is a bought man. They were simply the heads of their villages which were separated by more than fifteen miles and they both had lion trouble. I sat in the chair outside the tent with my mzee stick and tried to make intelligent and dignified grunts when I understood or did not understand and Mwindi and Meina interpreted. None of us were Masai scholars but these were good serious men and the troubles were obviously legitimate. One man had four long grooves across a shoulder that looked as though they had been made by a hay rake and the other at some time had lost an eye and had an atrocious old wound that started a little above the line of his scalp and came down, over the lost eye, almost to the point of his jaw.

The Masai love to talk and to argue but neither of these men was a talker and I told them and those who had come with them and stood saying nothing that we would attend to the problem. To do this I had to speak to Mwindi who then spoke to Arap Meina who then spoke to our clients. I leaned on my mzee stick which has a silver shilling pounded out and flattened into the head of it and grunted in the purest Masai which sounds a little like Marlene Dietrich when she is expressing sexual pleasure, understanding, or affection. The sounds vary. But they are deep and have a rising inflection.

We all shook hands and then Mwindi who loved to announce the worst possible news said in English, "Bwana, there are two ladies with bubu."

Bubu is any form of venereal disease but also includes yaws about which the authorities do not agree. Yaws certainly have a spirochete much like that of syphilis but opinion is divided as to how one acquires them. People are supposed to be able to acquire the old rale from a drinking glass or from sitting injudiciously on the seat of a public toilet or from kissing a stranger. In my limited experience I have never known anyone so unfortunate in their acquisition.

Yaws, by now, I knew almost as well as I knew my brother. That is to say that I had much contact with them without ever being able to appreciate them at their true worth.

The two Masai ladies were both quite beautiful and this reinforced me in my theory that, in Africa, the more beautiful you are the more yaws you got. Msembi loved the practice of medicine and produced all the yaws remedies without being prompted. I made a general cleaning and threw the result into the still alive ashes of the fire. After that I painted the edge of the lesion with violet gentian for psychologic effect. Violet gentian, hitherto unused in the areas we worked in, has a wonderful effect on the morale of the patient and it inspires the physician and the spectators with its lovely purple color tingeing into gold. I made a practice, usually, of making a small dot with it on the forehead of the husband.

After this, to take no chances, I would sprinkle the lesion, sometimes having to hold my breath to work with it, with sulfathiazole and then smear it with Aureomycin and apply a dressing. Always I would give oral penicillin and, if the yaws did not clear up, after the daily cure I would administer as massive doses of penicillin as we could afford. Afterwards I took the snuff out from under my armpit and put half of it behind the ear of each patient. Msembi loved this part of the treatment but I asked him to bring a bowl of water and the good truly blue Neko two percent soap so that I might wash my hands after shaking hands with each patient. Their hands were always lovely and cold and once you take a Masai woman's hand, even in the presence of her husband, she does not wish to give your hand up ever. This could be tribal or it could be personal to a yaws doctor. It was one of the few things I could not ask Ngui as we had no vocabulary to handle it. In return for the services performed a Masai might bring you a few mealies. But this would be exceptional.

The next patient was no inspiration even to an amateur physician. He was a prematurely old man if you could judge from the teeth and the genitals. He breathed with difficulty and his temperature was 104. His tongue was white and furry and there were white pockets and caves in his throat when I depressed his tongue. When I touched his liver, lightly, the pain was almost unbearable. He said he had great pain in his head, in his belly, in his chest and he had not been able to evacuate for a long time. He did not know how long. If he had been an animal it would have been better to shoot him. Since he was a brother in Africa I gave him Atabrine for the fever, in case it was malaria, a mild cathartic, aspirin to take for the pain if it continued, and we boiled the syringe and laid him flat on the ground and gave him one million and a half units of penicillin in the tired, sunken, black cheek of his left buttocks. It was a waste of penicillin. We all knew it. But if you go for broke that is the way you go and we all felt ourselves to be so fortunate in the religion that we were trying to be kind to all those outside of it and who should hoard penicillin when he is headed, self-propelled, for the Happy Hunting Grounds?

Mwindi, who had entered into the spirit of it all and was wearing his green robe and green skull cap and thought that we were all non-Islamic bums but also Kamba bums said, "Bwana, there is another Masai with bubu."

"Bring him here."

He was a nice boy, still a warrior, and proud but shy from his defect. It was the classical. The chancre was hard and it was not new and after feeling it I added up the penicillin we had left in my mind and remembered that no man should ever panic and that we had an aircraft that could bring more and I told the boy to sit down and we boiled the syringe and the needle again, although what he could get from them that was worse than he had I did not know, and Msembi wiped off the buttocks area with cotton and alcohol, this time hard and flat as a man's ass should be, and I made the puncture and watched the tiny oily ooze that was that mark of my inefficiency and the wastage of that which now was like the Host, and through Mwindi and Arap Meina I told the boy, upright now and with his spear, when he should come back and that he should come six times and then take a note to the hospital that I would give him. We did not shake hands because he was younger than me. But we smiled and he was proud of having had the needle.

Mthuka, who had no business there, had wandered by to watch the practice of medicine and in the hope that I would undertake some form of surgery since I did surgery out of a book which Ngui held and which had fascinating colored pictures some of which folded over and could be opened so that you saw the organs of both the front and the rear of the body at the same time. Surgery everyone loved but there had been no surgery today and Mthuka came up, long and loose and deaf and scarred beautifully to please a girl a long time ago and said, wearing his checked shirt and his hat that had once belonged to Tommy Shevlin, "Kwenda na shamba."

"Kwenda," I said and to Ngui, "Two guns. You and me and Mthuka."

"Hapana halal?"

"OK. Bring Charo."

"Mzuri," Ngui said since it would have been insulting to kill a good piece of meat and not have it legally butchered for the Moslem elders. I had to make my peace with Keiti too. I should have made it at first light but since I had not, the only proper time to make it was in the evening when the fire was lit. Charo would have told him all about the religion by now and he would have time to think that over and know that he faced a serious thing. Keiti knew only too well that we were all bad boys but now that we had the backing of a serious religion, and I had explained that this religion in its origin was as old if not older than the mountain although I was not sure on this point, Keiti would take it seriously. I think we could have converted Charo which would have been a terrible thing to do since he had the comfort of his own faith which was much better organized than ours, but we were not proselytizing and we had made a great stride when Charo took the religion seriously.

Miss Mary hated what she knew of the religion, which was very little, and I am not sure that in our group everyone desired that she be a member. If she was a member by tribal right it was all right and she would be obeyed and respected as such. But on an elective entrance I am not positive she would have made it. With her own group, of course, headed by all the Game Scouts and led by the magnificent, well starched, erect and handsome Chungo she would have been elected to be the Queen of Heaven. But in our religion there was not going to be any Game Department and while we planned to abolish both flogging and capital punishment against anyone except our enemies and there was to be no slavery except by those we had taken prisoner personally and cannibalism was completely and absolutely abolished except for those who chose to practice it, Miss Mary might not have received the same number of votes that she would certainly have had from her own people.

So we drove to the shamba and I sent Ngui to get Debba and with her sitting beside me, one hand holding the carved holster of the pistol, we drove off, Debba receiving any salutes from children or old people as though she were taking the salute from any regiment of which she might have been Honorary Colonel. At this time she was patterning her public behavior after the photographs in illustrated weeklies I had given her and she had selected the dignity and grace of the better royalty as though she were going over the bolts of cloth in the duka. I never asked her who she was patterning her public behavior on but it had been a year of well-photographed pageantry and she had much to choose from. I had tried to teach her the lift of the wrist and undulation of the fingers with which the Princess Aspasia of Greece would greet me across the smoke-filled clamor of Harry's Bar in Venice but we had no Harry's Bar in Loitokitok; or at least there had been none established at that point.

So now she was receiving salutes and I was maintaining a rigid amiability while we went off on the road that curved up the slope of the mountain to where I hoped to kill a beast sufficiently large, fat, and succulent to make everyone happy. We hunted diligently and lay until almost dark on an old blanket on the high side of a hill waiting for a beast to feed out onto the open hillside. But no beast fed out and when it was time to go home I killed a Tommy ram which was all we really needed. I lined up on him and with us both sitting down had her put her finger on the trigger ahead of mine and while I tracked him with the sight I felt the pressure of her finger and her head against mine and could feel her trying not to breathe. Then I said, "Piga," and her finger tightened on mine tightened on the trigger only a tiny cheating shade faster and the ram, whose tail had been switching as he fed, was dead with his four legs oddly rigid toward the sky and Charo was running out to him in his ragged shorts and old blue blazer and his dingy turban to cut his throat and make him legal.

"Piga mzuri," Ngui said to Debba and she turned to him and tried for her royal manner and couldn't make it and started to cry and said, "Asanta sana."

We sat there and she cried and then stopped it clean and well. We watched Charo do his business and the hunting car come down from behind the brow of the hill and drive to the beast and Mthuka get out and lower the tailgate and he and Charo, very small at the distance and the big car small too, stoop and lift and swing the carcass up into the back of the car. Then the car came up the hill toward us, larger every moment as it came. There had been a moment when I had wished to pace the distance of the shot. But it would have been a chicken thing to do and a man should be able to shoot at all distances giving the proper allowance for shooting downhill.

Debba looked at him as though it was the first antelope she had ever seen and put her finger in the hole where the solid had passed through the very top of both shoulders and I told her not to get dirty with the blood on the floor. The floor had strips of iron on it to lift the meat above the heat of the car and let the air circulate and although well washed always it was a sort of charnel house.

Debba left her beast and we drove downhill with her sitting between Mthuka and me and we both knew she was in a strange state but she did not talk at all and only held tight onto my arm and held tight to the carved holster. At the shamba she became regal but her heart was not in it and Ngui butchered out the ram and threw the tripe and the lungs to the dogs and opened the stomach and cleaned it and put the heart, kidneys, and liver in the stomach sack and handed it to a child to take into Debba's house. My father-in-law was there and I nodded to him. He took the white, wet sack with its red and purple content and went inside the house which was really quite a beautiful building with its conical roof and red walls.

I got out of the car and helped Debba down.

"Jambo tu," I said and she said nothing and went into the house.

It was dark by now and when we got to camp the fire was burning and my chair and the table with the drinks had been set out. Mwindi had bath water ready and I took a bath, soaping carefully, and then dressed in pajamas, mosquito boots, and a heavy bathrobe and came out to the fire. Keiti was waiting.

"Jambo, Bwana," he said.

"Jambo, Mr. Keiti," I said. "We killed a small Tommy. Charo will have told you he is OK."

He smiled and I knew we were friends again. He had the nicest, cleanest smile of anyone I ever knew.

"Sit down, Keiti," I said.

"No."

"I am very grateful for what you did last night. You acted correctly and exactly as you should. I have seen the father of the girl for some time and have made the necessary visits and presents. There was no way you should know this. The father is worthless."

"I know. Women rule that shamba."

"If I have a son by the girl he will be educated properly and may choose to be a soldier, a doctor, or a lawyer. This is exact. If he wishes to be a hunter he can remain with me as my son. Is this clear?"

"It is very clear," Keiti said.

"If I have a daughter I will give her a dowry or she may come to live with me as my daughter. Is that clear?"

"It is clear. Better, maybe, stay with the mother."

"I will do everything according to Kamba law and custom. But I cannot marry the girl and take her home because of stupid laws."

"One of your brothers can marry her," Keiti said.

"I know."

The case was now closed and we were the same good friends as always.

"I would like to come some night and hunt with the spear," Keiti said.

"I am only learning," I said. "I am very stupid and it is difficult without a dog."

"Nobody knows the night. Not me. Not you. Nobody."

"I want to learn it."

"You will. But be careful."

"I will."

"No one knows the night except in a tree or in some safe place. The night belongs to the animals."

Keiti was too delicate to speak about the religion but I saw the look in his eye of one who has been led up to the top of a high hill and seen the temptations of the world spread out before him and it reminded me that we must not corrupt Charo. I could see that we were winning now and that I could have had Debba and the widow for dinner now with a written menu and place cards. So, winning, I crowded just a little for the extra point.

"Of course, in our religion, everything is possible."

"Yes. Charo told me about your religion."

"It is very small but very old."

"Yes," Keiti said.

"Well, good night then," I said. "If everything is in order."

"Everything is in order," Keiti said and I said good night again and he bowed again and I envied Pop that Keiti was his man. But, I thought, you are starting to get your own men and while Ngui can never compare with Keiti in many ways yet he is rougher and more fun and times have changed.

CHAPTER 34

In the night I lay and listened to the noises of the night and tried to understand them all. What Keiti had said was very true; no one knew the night. But I was going to learn it if I could alone and on foot. But I was going to learn it and I did not want to share it with anyone. Sharing is for money and you do not share a woman nor would I share the night. I could not go to sleep and I would not take a sleeping pill because I wanted to hear the night and I had not decided yet whether I would go out at moonrise. I knew that I did not have enough experience with the spear to hunt alone and not get into trouble and that it was both my duty and my great and lovely pleasure to be in camp when Miss Mary should return. It was also my duty and my wonderful pleasure to be with Debba but I was sure that she would sleep well at least until the moon rose and that after the moon rose we all paid for whatever happiness or sorrow we had bought. Africans, according to a popular and convenient British concept, are supposed neither to suffer pain nor to be capable of love. The low class Britisher that rules in Africa suffers so visibly and audibly that he commands little respect. The Bible-punching Dutchmen and their wives fear the African and his superiority so that they have barred all contact with him, or her, mostly her because no man who was not a Bible-puncher would give preference to the white wife who is a common scold. The Protestant wife is taught to be a scold and all she has to offer against an African is her skin which will not take the sun and either efficiency, Bible-punching, and unswerving and always bleated loyalty; or disloyalty, an easily tanned skin and, usually, an addiction to gin. Gin is to the good wife, I thought, what the whorehouse is to the good husband. So I lay in the cot with the old shotgun rigidly comfortable by my side and the pistol that was my best friend and severest critic of any defect of reflexes or of decision lying comfortably between my legs in the carved holster that Debba had polished so many times with her hard hands and thought how lucky I was to know

Miss Mary and have her do me the great honor of being married to me and to know Miss Debba the Queen of the Ngomas. But then you remembered that more than half of your life had been spent, at night, which should be the best time, with women who could not come enough or who could come too easily and who were always stubbing out cigarette butts and commencing their sentences with the word "Darling."

This is a word a man can stand to hear only so many times in his life and the stubbed out cigarette butt has an evil smell so I thought about this which was not inspiring nor life bringing nor educational and I listened to the night, which was a normal night, promising and lovely as a whore; but not for me because I had not slept for too long and so, listening, I went to sleep.

So far I have never slept alone nor without rewarding or destructive dreams. They are difficult to recall sometimes if one is awakened by the sound of small-arms fire or by the telephone or by an irascible wife; but usually the dreams are worth what they cost you and on this night I dreamed that I was in an inn, or gasthaus rather, in the province of Vaud in Switzerland. The wife I had loved first and best and who was the mother of my oldest son was with me and we were sleeping close together to keep warm and because that was the best way to sleep if both people love each other and it is a cold night. There was a wisteria tree, or vine, that grew up the face of the hotel and over an arbor and the horse chestnut trees in bloom were like waxen candelabras. We were going to fish the Rhône canal and the day before the dream we had fished the Stockalper. Both streams were milky with snow water and it was the early spring. My first and best wife was sleeping soundly, as always, and I could smell every scent of her body and the chestnut trees as well and she was warm in my arms and her head was under my chin and we were sleeping as close, and as trusting, as kittens sleep. I had bad dreams then as a residue or inheritance from a badly organized war and sleep, or his brother death, were all that interested me at night. That was, of course, after we had slept together. But there was no problem, then, about knowing the night because we had known the night too well. But tonight, in the dream, I slept happily with my true love in my arms and her head firmly under my chin and when I woke I wondered about how many true loves to which you were faithful, until you were unfaithful, a man could have and I thought about the strange strictures of morality in different countries and who it was that could make a sin a sin. Now that we had the religion it was easy. Ngui, Mthuka, and I could decide what was a sin and what was not.

Ngui had five wives, which we knew was true, and twenty head of cattle which we all doubted. I had only one legal wife due to American law but everyone remembered and respected Miss Pauline who had been in Africa long ago and was much admired and beloved especially by Keiti and Mwindi and I knew that they believed she was my dark Indian wife and that Miss Mary was my fair Indian wife. They were all sure that Miss Pauline must be looking after the shamba at home while I had brought Miss Mary to this country and I never told them that Miss Pauline was dead because it would have saddened everyone. Nor did we tell them of another wife they would not have liked who had been reclassified so that she did not hold that rank or category. It was generally presumed even by the most conservative and skeptical of the elders that if Ngui had five wives I must have at least twelve due to the difference between our fortunes.

It was generally understood that I was married to Miss Marlene who, through photographs I had received and letters, was supposed to be working for me in a small amusement shamba I owned called Las Vegas. They all knew Miss Marlene as the author of "Lili Marlene" and many people thought that she was Lili Marlene and we had all heard her many hundreds of times singing a song called "Johnny" on the old crank up phonograph when "Rhapsody in Blue" was a new tune and Miss Marlene, then, sang about "muts aroun the phlegm." This tune had always moved everyone deeply and when I was gloomy or dispirited in those days on rare occasions, being far from my amusement shamba, Molo, who was Ngui's half brother would ask, "Muts arouna flem?" and I would say to put her on and he would crank the portable phonograph and we would all be happy hearing the beautiful, deep, off-key voice of my beautiful nonexistent wife singing in my amusement shamba which she ran so well and faithfully.

This is the material from which legends are built and the fact that one of my wives was supposed to be Lili Marlene was no deterrent to the religion. I had taught Debba to say, "Vamanos a Las Vegas," and she loved the sound of it almost as much as "No hay remedio." But she was always afraid of Miss Marlene although she had a large picture of her wearing what looked to me like nothing on the wall above her bed along with an advertisement for the washing machine and garbage disposal units and the two-inch steaks and cuts of ham and the paintings of the mammoth, the little four-toed horse, and the saber-toothed tiger that she had cut from *Life* magazine. These were the great wonders of her new world and the only one she feared was Miss Marlene.

Because I was awake now and I was not sure that I would ever sleep again I thought about Debba and Miss Marlene and Miss Mary and another girl that I knew and, at that time, loved very much. She was a rangy-built American girl running to shoulders and with the usual American pneumatic bliss that is so admired by those who do not know a small, hard, well-formed breast is better. But this girl had good Negro legs and was very loving although always complaining about something. She was pleasant enough to think about at night though when you could not sleep and I listened to the night and thought about her a little and the cabin and Key West and the Lodge and the different gambling places we used to frequent and the sharp cold mornings of the hunts we had made together with the wind rushing by in the dark and the taste of the air of the mountains and the smell of sage back in the days when she cared for hunting other things than money. No man is ever really alone and the supposed dark hours of the soul when it is always three o'clock in the morning are a man's best hours if he is not an alcoholic nor afraid of the night and what the day will bring. I was as afraid as the next man in my time and maybe more so. But with the years fear had come to be regarded as a form of stupidity to be classed with overdrafts, acquiring a venereal disease, or eating candies. Fear is a child's vice and while I loved to feel it approach, as one does with any vice, it was not for grown men and the only thing to be afraid of was the presence of true and imminent danger in a form that you should be aware of and not be a fool if you were responsible for others. This was the mechanical fear that made your scalp prickle at real danger suddenly and when you lost that reaction it was time to get into some other line of work.

So I thought of Miss Mary and how brave she had been in the ninety-six days she had pursued her lion, not tall enough to see him properly ever, doing a new thing with imperfect knowledge and unsuitable tools, driving us all with her will so we would all be up an hour before daylight and sick of lions, especially at Magadi, and Charo, loyal and faithful to Miss Mary but an old man and tired of lions had said to me, "Bwana, kill the lion and get it over with. No woman ever kills a lion."

Instead we had kept on forever and Miss Mary had killed her lion as Pop had wished, for his last hunt and with his love for Miss Mary, and then, the hunt having taken a bad turn, she had doubted all of us. I remembered standing where the lion should come and moving to try to draw the lion's charge and then I thought the hell with lions and remembered Debba killing her first beast and her pride and her sorrow. Then I remembered that I must give her the hide and the horns. I had given her the empty cartridge case. She did not have her ears pierced yet but the widow was probably wearing it. She was some kin to Debba and she reminded me of a sister-in-law I once had except that the sister-in-law, then, was beautiful. But she and the widow had the same quality of a tree that has not flourished and has begun to dry in the sap although both of them were wonderful company and made fine jokes. Nearly all Wakamba make excellent jokes and a man never needs to be depressed because his copy of *Punch* is overdue at the New Stanley bookstall or at Woolworth's.

Lying in bed and remembering I thought that I liked the widow better than I did my former sister-in-law because she never had headaches although, with the not completely ordered life we led, she was most certainly entitled to them. The Informer, being of an alien tribe, was not a proper protector for her but he worked at it according to his standards, which were not high. I did not like to think of the widow with her sullen but suddenly brightly lighting face in bed with the Informer even if he had removed his paisley shawl and his pork-pie hat. My imagination was not great enough to picture the Informer when he was a Masai moran before his corruption by the great backward noble lord and the bwanas but I had taken his word, which had been true about the wild dogs, and much as I doubted his word, with cause, if you take it on a specific point you have taken it. It was a difficult word to take but I had taken worse ones from people who were, legally, entitled to much more respect. Lying in bed it was a pleasure to remember great and respected liars and some of their more formidable lies. Ford Madox Ford was perhaps the greatest liar I had known in civil life and I recalled him, if not with affection, with esteem. When I had first heard him lying astoundingly and unmistakably in Ezra Pound's old studio in the rue Notre Dame des Champs at a late hour in the evening I had been shocked and, puritanically, offended. Here was a man old enough to be my father and a self-confessed master of English prose who lied so badly that I was embarrassed. After Ford had left with his wife of the moment, whom he was unable to marry since he had never been properly divorced, I asked Ezra if the strange man with the wheezing breath which was less pleasant to be near than the breath of a hyena and the ill-fitting teeth and the pompous manner of the early and unsuccessful models of the armored tracked vehicles always lied so much to men who were familiar with the subject on which he was discoursing.

Ezra, who is a good and kind man and only ruthless in print, said, "Hem, you must try to understand. Ford only lies when he is very tired. It is a way of relaxing."

Ezra was then trying to educate me, a process he later abandoned as hopeless, and I was teaching him to box. This also was a project I was forced to abandon and he took up playing the bassoon instead. Of the two arts, boxing, in the time before television, is probably the more difficult to master and the apprenticeship is certainly more arduous. I could not stand to hear Ezra play the bassoon and thought of trying to interest him in the bass viola or the tuba, two not too complex instruments which I felt he might dominate, but no one had enough money to purchase either one of those large instruments in those days so I took to going to the studio a little less and Ezra and I played tennis each afternoon instead.

This was a sport at which neither of us was intolerably efficient and we played in a court to which you paid a fee each time you played which was situated exactly opposite the place where the guillotine is set up for those morning performances the French still love so much, and the pavement was sometimes newly washed as, carrying an extra coat which for me was the lining of an old Burberry, we would ring for the concierge at the iron gate that led into the courts.

At this time I could not afford tennis nor could I afford almost any other thing except work which we are born to afford and the supplying of food and lodging to my wife and child. Ezra, who was not a rich man either and had at one time lived in London on a budget which included one duck egg daily, since he had read somewhere that they were seventy percent more nourishing than hens' eggs, and I enjoyed the luxury of our tennis greatly and played with what was our conception of savage elegance. Ezra wore flannels. Ezra played better than I did, which is as it should be in tennis if you are to have pleasure. At that time, and up to a few years ago, I had a mysterious service called the pig ball. This landed flat and dead but with speed and did not bounce at all. You can only serve a certain amount of pig balls since it is the slice which is stroked heavily on top with a very violent but caressing motion which is extremely destructive to the ligaments of the right shoulder. There are many pitches which you can throw which are extremely difficult to hit but you cannot throw them too often and that, and the fact that people still consume alcohol, accounts for many relief pitchers being relief pitchers rather than starting pitchers.

So I thought about this and about Hughie Casey, now a suicide, and Kirby Higby, now an evangelist, and the fun we used to have together nights in Havana and afternoons pigeon shooting with Augie Galan, Curt Davis, Larry French, and Billy Herman. They were all splendid shots except Higby who never came to shoot since he was reserving himself entirely for night life. He loved to pick fights in gambling places and in nightclubs. But once the fight was picked, he would call out, "Come on, Ernie. You take him." So I had come to occupy much the same position in Higby's fighting life as Hughie Casey held in his pitching life on the Brooklyn Dodgers.

Those were the last carefree months for many years. I could not bring myself, as a writer and an individual, that after the Spanish war and then China I should have to start the whole destructive process of war all over again. I knew, though, I had been fortunate to have had the time to write one book. Now I stopped thinking about this and about Havana, although you could never be lonely thinking about Havana, and I started to think about the Spanish Civil War. You could never be lonely thinking about that either and although we usually tried not to think about a war when it was over it is always impossible not to think or remember sometimes.

So I remembered a British correspondent, one of several correspondents for whom I was responsible to the Spanish government. An offensive was being organized and these correspondents could only be given passes to visit the front if I accompanied them. They did not know this and I did not tell them. This correspondent, whose newspaper owned a car, loved to drive at an exaggerated speed and it meant nothing to him if he ran over dogs. The first dog he ran over was sleeping quietly in the dusty street of a small village and I had him stop the car and when the car was stopped I got out and went back to see what could be done for the dog. The correspondent remained in the motor car. There was nothing to be done for the dog as the tire had gone over his back and broken his back and his kidneys. The dog was in great pain and the boy who owned him was desperate.

"Matalo," he said. "Por Dios, matalo."

I put the kind small muzzle of the .22 caliber pistol close against the back of the dog's head and when his front legs jerked forward and blood came from his eyes, the boy said, "¡Ay, mi perro!"

I gave him a twenty-five peseta note and went back and got in the car with the correspondent. He had not looked back but he said, "Did you hear a shot in that village?"

"No, I don't think so."

He killed two more dogs that day and one I am sure was intentional. I saw it quite clearly and saw him make the swerve toward the animal. I resolved the next time I took him out that I would take him someplace where he would be killed surely and I had a try at it on the way home. But nothing came of it.

This was not the sort or variety of remembering that would put me to sleep so I thought of places and of odd and funny things.

I thought how I had persistently exposed the dog-killing correspondent to the most excellent chances of being killed and how, braver each day, and with his character unchanged he had come to regard me as a talisman of safety. Several times after he had killed dogs or, worse, wounded them I had thought of shooting him myself at the base of the spine with the .22 using the hollow-point bullet. But there was always someone else in the car and then, too, there was too much abuse of the pistol in Spain and I was officially and personally against it. So I remembered waiting for him to be killed in action whereby he might possibly do some good to our side. But instead he flourished and I think finally came to believe that there was no danger, for him, in war at all.

This was not much to think about so I gave up the Spanish Civil War temporarily as a thinking ground and rolled on my right side to go to sleep. In a little while I was asleep and then I was awake and Mwindi was there with the tea.

It was a new day and the lantern was still lit, yellow in the first dawn against the tree trunk, and something would be happening today and I woke happy as always.

"Put out all clean clothes," Mwindi said. "Memsahib come in ndege."

I dressed in the all clean clothes and drank the tea and said, "Mwindi you know of course nothing happened here the other night."

"Nothing happen. Ndio."

"Nothing. Absolutely nothing."

"How you break bed then?"

CHAPTER 35

It was a beautiful day for flying and the mountain was very close. I sat against the tree and watched the birds and the grazing game. Ngui came over for orders and I told him he and Charo should clean and oil all the weapons and sharpen and oil the spears. Keiti and Mwindi were removing the broken bed and taking it to Bwana Mouse's empty tent. I got up to go over there. It was not badly broken; one cross leg in the center had a long greenstick fracture and one of the main poles that held the canvas was broken. It was easily reparable and I said I would get some wood and have it sawed to measure and finished at Mr. Singh's.

Keiti, who was very cheerful that Miss Mary was arriving, said we would use Bwana Mouse's cot which was identical and I went back to my chair and the bird identification book and more tea. I felt like someone who had dressed for the party too early on this morning that felt like spring in a high alpine plateau and as I went over to the mess tent for breakfast I wondered what the day would bring. The first thing it brought was the Informer.

"Good morning, brother," the Informer said. "How is your good health?"

"Never better, brother. What is new?"

"May I come in?"

"Of course. Have you had breakfast?"

"Hours before. I breakfasted on the mountain."

"Why?"

"The widow was so difficult that I left her to wander alone in the night as you do, brother."

I knew this was a lie and I said, "You mean you walked to the road and caught a ride up to Loitokitok with one of Benji's boys in the lorry."

"Something like that, brother."

"Go on."

"Brother, there are desperate things afoot."

"Pour yourself your pleasure and tell me."

"It is set for Christmas Eve and Christmas Day. Brother, I believe it is a massacre."

I wanted to say, "By them or by us?" but I controlled myself.

"Tell me more," I said looking at the Informer's proud, brown, guilt-lined face as he raised a shot glass of Canadian gin with a glow of bitters in it to his gray-red lips.

"Why don't you drink Gordon's? You'll live longer."

"I know my place, brother."

"And your place is in my heart," I said quoting the late Fats Waller. Tears came into the Informer's eyes.

"So this St. Bartholomew's Eve is for Christmas Eve," I said. "Has no one any respect for the Baby Jesus?"

"It is a massacre."

"Women and children too?"

"No one said so."

"Who said what?"

"There was talk at Benji's. There was much talk at the Masai stores and at the Tea Room. There was talk at all the clandestine drinking places."

"Are the Masai to be put to death?"

"No. The Masai will all be here for your ngoma for the Baby Jesus."

"Is the ngoma popular?" I said to change the subject and to show that news of impending massacres meant nothing to me a man who had been through the Zulu War and whose ancestors had done away with George Armstrong Custer on the Little Big Horn. No man who went to Mecca not being a Moslem as another man might go to Brighton or Atlantic City should be moved by rumors of massacres especially if he knew them, through his own mimeographed copy of the orders, to be false.

"The ngoma is the talk of the mountain," the Informer said. "Except for the massacre."

"What did Mr. Singh say?"

"He was rude to me."

"Is he participating in the massacre?"

"He is probably one of the ringleaders."

The Informer unwrapped a package he had in his shawl. It was a bottle of White Heather whiskey in a carton.

"A gift from Mr. Singh," he said. "I advise you to examine it carefully before drinking, brother. I have never heard the name."

"Too bad, brother. It may be a new name, but it is good whiskey. New brands of whiskey are always good at the start."

"I have information for you on Mr. Singh. He has undoubtedly performed military service."

"It is hard to believe."

"I am sure of it. No one could have cursed me as Mr. Singh did who had not served the raj."

"Do you think Mr. Singh and Mrs. Singh are subversives?"

"I will make inquiries."

"The gen has been a little shadowy today, Informer."

"Brother, it was a difficult night. The coldheartedness of the widow. My wanderings on the mountain."

"Take another drink, brother. You sound like *Wuthering Heights*."

"Was that a battle, brother?"

"In a way."

"You must tell me about it someday."

"Remind me. Now I want you to spend the night in Loitokitok, sober, and bring me some information that is not bullshit. Go to Brown's Hotel and sleep there. No. Sleep on the porch. Where did you sleep last night?"

"On the floor of the Tea Room under the billiard table."

"Drunk or sober?"

"Drunk, brother."

"If I give you money to sleep in a bed tonight where did you get this money?"

"Memsahib gave it to me for rare plants and flowers I brought for her on her return from Nairobi."

"All right. Go and bring some rare plants and flowers."

"Brother, I do not know much about rare plants and flowers."

"Get some empty tins from the kitchen and bring me some bhang and a poison-arrow shrub. And any beautiful plants you see."

"I will do it, brother. How much will my expense fund be?"

"Twenty shillings."

"I will bring back presents for everyone and the absolute solemn truth."

Ngui came to say the guns and the spears were ready but would I put the Sten gun together. The Sten gun was the old Winchester Model 12 pump gun and the threading of the aged barrel and receiver together was a mystery. They all believed it was an automatic weapon since it could be fired faster than any automatic shotgun and it was a mzee among shotguns since M'Cola had told Ngui about it when Ngui was a mtoto, and Charo too revered it and they would never assemble it for fear of cross threading. It takes twenty thousand cartridges to break in a pump gun so that it handles quicker than your eye can follow and this gun had shot

391

around two hundred thousand cartridges. Both Charo and Ngui had seen five guineas dead in the air from it, in the soft clean evening air against the high trees above the sand riverbed when the great flock had been turned and properly flushed back in the country of the Honest Ernies. It was regarded as a straight witchcraft gun and it was never used unless we needed meat badly or for backing up or going in as for the leopard. It was a goose, guinea, and leopard gun and a back-up gun on lion.

As I put it together and handed it to Charo who put it in its clipped lamb's wool cover I said, "You like the old gun?"

Ngui looked up as though I had gone out of my head.

"Mzuri," Charo said. "Mzuri sana."

Ngui grunted. It was about as sensible a question to him as if I had asked a Father at one of the missions if he cared about Our Lord.

"How's the bed?" I asked Mwindi.

"Good," he said. "No difference. You tell Abdullah he can take tins?"

"I go tell Keiti it's all right."

I knew Keiti and the Informer had trouble many years ago and I should have gone out and picked out the tins for him myself.

"Put the three rifles and the Purdey in the car," I told Ngui. The Purdey was not a Purdey but a straight-stocked long-barreled Scott live-pigeon full choke in both barrels that I had bought from a lot of shotguns a dealer had brought down from Udine to the Kechlers' villa in Codroipo. The Scott and a very beautiful twenty-eight inch barrel over-and-under Merkel had fitted me and I had shot them both for many years. Ngui and Charo called the Scott the Purdey and so the Purdey it was. It was a lovely shooting gun whoever made it.

Out at the commissary Keiti had kept a list of what the Informer had taken. I told him what they were for and Keiti was not in a bad mood. I gathered that he had insulted the Informer copiously and had not been insulted back.

"What do you need for meat?" I asked.

"Are you sending any meat with the ndege?"

"Maybe a piece."

"We could use meat then."

"Tell me, Keiti, how does a dry cow impala look?"

"She is at the head of the does and she is darker."

"How much darker?"

"Only a little darker. You will know."

"I never studied the does as I should."

"Charo will know. I will tell him."

"Does Ngui know?"

"You and he can learn. What time does the ndege come?"

"Not before noon."

Mary would certainly wait for the bank to open so that she could get the mail. It was a good day for flying and there was no sign of anything building up and I did not think Willie would be in any hurry about getting out. I knew there was not time to get Debba and take her out hunting and get her back to the shamba. The hurrying would not be dignified either and it could be interpreted to seem that the ndege commanded me rather than that I commanded the ndege. It would mean to Charo and Keiti and Mwindi that I was not a serious man and it might harm the religion.

So we set off for the airstrip to see the sock was not entangled with the pole and to run a few lengths of the strip where the white flowering weeds had grown higher and we chased the storks off the airstrip and left them worming dartingly and diligently in an adjoining stretch of meadow. I had once had a jackrabbit come through a windshield late at night between Big Horn and Sheridan, Wyoming, and had seen a gooney bird hit the Plexiglas on a Boeing Clipper takeoff at Wake and I made a mental note to come back and keep the strip clear before Willie and Miss Mary came in.

In the meantime we went for the closest impala herd I knew of, the herd that ranged the edge of the forest to the west along the river that ran northwest into the big swamp. We left the car and Charo and I went ahead and Ngui followed with the trouble gun. Charo only had his knife to make the meat fit for Moslem consumption. We moved very quietly and with no wind in the tall yellow-barked trees we were among the impala almost as soon as we had left the plain and entered the forest. An impala barked and they commenced to stream past us red fawn coated with the big gentle eyes and the forward pointed ears. The one who barked had seen something but these had not. They were moving as they moved so many times each day and in the night from the leopard or their fear of him or of the cheetah in the open. Charo watched them all pass until a big doe came, only faintly darker than the rest but with the same reddish fawn cast. He touched my arm and I whistled a small whistle that you cannot hear, the whistle that you make to attract lizards. She turned her lovely head to look and stood still and I shot her through the neck just below the ear. As she fell the forest exploded into impala, leaping as though there were no law of gravity as one leaps sometimes in dreams and when we pulled her out into the open so the car could come and we could load her in there were two big bucks standing in the meadow that had not known what to do when the panic started.

We drove back to camp by the airstrip and ran some new storks off it and then unloaded the dry doe. She was very fat for an impala and Charo said she must have been dry two years. I did not understand this but there were so many things I did not understand in Africa I let it alone.

"Keep the heart and the kidneys and a piece of the stew meat for the widow," I told Ngui. "Put it in a piece of cheesecloth in the tree."

I had looked at the hide and the darkness was barely perceptible.

"Can you tell a dry impala cow now?" I asked Ngui.

"Hapana."

"Hapana me too."

"I can tell a dry pof cow."

"Me too."

We were both so hungry for eland meat it was like a vice.

"Maybe we can get pof in the Chyulus."

"Maybe."

I put a couple of cool bottles of beer in the hunting car and Ngui, Mthuka, and I drove out to the airstrip with Arap Meina in the back. Meina would mount guard over the plane and he was smart and very sharp in his uniform and his .303 with the sling was freshly polished and oiled. We made a run around the meadow to put the birds to flight and then retired to the shade of a big tree where Mthuka killed the engine and we all sat back and were comfortable. Charo had come along at the last minute because he was Miss Mary's gunbearer and it was only proper that he should meet her.

It was past noon and I opened one of the quarts of Tusker and Mthuka and Ngui and I drank from it. Arap Meina was under discipline for a recent drunkenness but he knew I would give him some later.

I told Ngui and Mthuka I had a dream last night that we should pray to the sun as it rose and again, to the sun, as it set.

Ngui said he would not kneel down like a camel driver or a Christian even for the religion.

"You don't have to kneel down. You turn and look at the sun and pray."

"What do we pray in the dream?"

"To live bravely, to die bravely, and to go directly to the Happy Hunting Grounds."

"We are brave already," Ngui said. "Why do we have to pray about it?"

"Pray for anything you like if it is for the good of us all."

"I pray for beer, for pof, and for a new wife with hard hands. You can share the wife."

"That's a good prayer. What do you pray for, Mthuka?"

"We keep this car."

"Anything else?"

"Beer. You not get killed. Rain good in Machakos. Happy Hunting Grounds."

"What you pray for?" Ngui asked me.

"Africa for Africans. Kwisha Mau Mau. Kwisha all sickness. Rain good everywhere. Happy Hunting Grounds."

"Pray every day think of different things," Ngui said.

"Pray to have fun," Mthuka offered.

"Pray sleep with wife of Mr. Singh."

"Must pray good."

"Take wife of Mr. Singh to Happy Hunting Grounds."

"Too many people want to be in religion," Ngui said. "How many people we take?"

"We start with a squad. Maybe make a section, maybe a company."

"Company very big for Happy Hunting Grounds."

"I think so too."

"You command Happy Hunting Grounds. We make a council but you command. No Great Spirit. No Gitchi Manitou. Hapana King. Hapana Queen's Road. Hapana HE. Hapana D.C. Hapana Baby Jesus. Hapana Police. Hapana Black Watch. Hapana Game Department."

"Hapana," I said.

"Hapana," Mthuka said.

I passed the bottle of beer to Arap Meina.

"Are you a religious man, Meina?"

"Very," said Meina.

"Do you drink?"

"Only beer, wine, and gin. I can also drink whiskey and all clear or colored alcohols."

"Are you ever drunk, Meina?"

"You should know, my father."

"What religions have you held?"

"I am now a Moslem." Charo leaned back and closed his eyes.

"What were you before?"

"Lumbwa," Meina said. Mthuka's shoulders were shaking. "I have never been a Christian," Meina said with dignity.

"We speak too much of religion and I am still the Bwana Game and we celebrate the Birthday of the Baby Jesus in four days." I looked at the watch on my wrist.

"Let us clear the field of birds and drink the beer before the plane comes."

"The plane is coming now," Mthuka said. He started the motor and I passed him the beer and he drank a third of what was left. Ngui drank a third and I drank half of a third and passed what was left back to Meina. We were already putting up storks at full speed at the approaches and seeing them after the running rush straighten their legs as though they were pulling up their undercarriages and commencing their reluctant flight.

We saw the plane come over blue and silvery and spindle-legged and buzz the camp and then we were barreling down along the side of the clearing and she was opposite us, with the big flaps down, passing us to land without a bounce and circling now, her nose now high and arrogant, throwing dust in the knee-deep white flowers.

Miss Mary was on the near side now and she came out in a great small rush. I held her tight and kissed her and then she shook hands with everyone, Charo first.

"Morning, Papa," Willie said. "Let me have Ngui to pass some of this out. She's a bit laden."

"You must have bought all Nairobi," I said to Mary.

"All I could afford. They wouldn't sell the Muthaiga Club."

"She bought the New Stanley and Torr's," Willie said. "So we're always sure of a room, Papa."

"What else did you buy?"

"She wanted to buy me a Comet," Willie said. "You can pick up quite good bargains in them now, you know."

"I bought G.C. three air hostesses."

"Got them cheap too. But I'm afraid they won't dress out more than about seven stone even the big Scandinavian."

"Papa doesn't want to eat them."

"I was thinking of his followers."

"We could set them up as white goddesses."

"Hapana white goddesses," Miss Mary said.

"How do you get more in an aircraft than a 3/4-ton truck on a safari body will hold?"

"Tricky little beasts these Cessnas. No one's ever really explored their capabilities."

"I brought a lovely present for your fiancée," Mary said. "It's a Flexible Flyer and you and she can go up to the top of Kibo and coast down together."

"She's getting on toward empty unless you plan to give Papa the engine and let him build one for himself along his own ideas."

"Arap Meina's going to look after her. Let's go."

We drove to camp with Miss Mary and me sitting close together in front. Willie was talking with Ngui and Charo. At camp Mary wanted the stuff unloaded into Bwana Mouse's empty tent and I was to stay away and not watch it. I had been told not to watch anything in detail at the aircraft either and I had not watched. There was a big bundle of letters, papers, and magazines and some cables and I had taken them into the mess tent and Willie and I were drinking a beer.

"Good trip?"

"Not lumpy. The ground doesn't really heat up any more with these cold nights. Mary saw her elephants at Salengai and a very big pack of wild dogs."

Miss Mary came in. She had received all the official visits and was beaming. She was well beloved, well received, and people had been formal about it. She loved the designation Memsahib.

"I didn't know Mousie's bed was broken."

"Is it?"

"And I haven't said a thing about the leopard. Let me kiss you. G.C. launched your cable about him."

"They've got their leopard. They don't have to worry. Nobody has to worry. Not even the leopard."

"Tell me about him."

"No. Sometime when we are coming home I'll show you the place."

"Can I see any mail you're finished with?"

"Open it all."

"What's the matter with you? Aren't you glad to have me back? I was having a wonderful time in Nairobi or at least I was going out every night and everyone was nice to me."

"We'll all practice up and be nice to you and pretty soon it will be just like Nairobi."

"Please be good, Papa. This is what I love. I only went to Nairobi to be cured and to buy presents for Christmas and I know you wanted me to have fun."

"Good. And now you're back. Give me a hold hard and a good anti-Nairobi kiss."

She was slim and shiny in her khakis and hard inside them and she smelled very good and her hair was silver gold cropped close and I rejoined the white or European race as easily as a mercenary or Henry IV saying Paris was worth a mass.

Willie was happy to see the rejoining and he said, "Papa, any news beside the chui?"

"Nothing."

"No troubles?"

"The road, at night, is a scandal."

"It seems to me they rely a little too much on the desert as being impassable."

"Have you enough gas so we can take a look around the property?"

"Oh yes. I came away full and I have an extra tin or two at G.C.'s."

"We'll take a look around after lunch."

"Aren't you hungry, Willie?" Miss Mary said. "I'm terribly hungry. Papa, please open some mail. I'll make you a Campari."

The charm of mail in Africa is greatly overrated. The papers and the news magazines fill a depraved hunger but mail, except from Berenson, was rarely worth the reading. Marlene was either in the depths or so triumphant that you could imagine her marching at the head of her troops under the arch at the Étoile and later, in her tenderness, removing her casque to shed a few tears at the Invalides. It was a bad lighting for her there but if she had taken the country she could have the lighting changed and I thought of her and Maurice Chevalier and Noel Coward singing a trio of "See What the Boys in the Back Room Will Have," and the dead of Austerlitz, Tilsit, Wagram, and Moskva coming out in the uniforms they had been buried in, if they had not been stripped, to join in the chorus. The other girl I wrote to irregularly had ceaseless troubles. Troubles ran out of her ears like butterflies out of the ears of a dead in a Breughel picture. They came out of her nose too that always reddened perceptibly under enough rich troubles and I slit her letter and handed it to Willie to read.

"No, Papa. No. But if the other one sent any pictures I'd be happy to see them."

"She sent some; all diaphanous."

Miss Mary was reading the giant, handsome, bold writing of the girl who specialized in sorrows, injustices, and complaints. Any complaint, in that handwriting, became a casus belli, and I thought that the simple account of the breaking of an old-fashioned toilet chain would have the cartographic roar and rumble of the carrying away of the Aswan dam.

"Is she very unhappy?" I asked Miss Mary. "Has her life been thwarted or frustrated? Have they had to move from one coast to another coast? Have former wives' children been dumped on her?"

"I wish she'd mention me," Miss Mary said. "You'd think it would only be polite to mention me since I'm married to you."

"She didn't even mention you when you were bucking for Boot Hill in Casper. I used to bring you and the oxygen tent up on the phone."

"It's funny she never mentions me. It doesn't please you, does it?"

"Not at all. I suggest it to her and she remembers a couple of times. Then it's the same as ever."

"Well, she is a nice girl and good company and she does know how to dress and buy jewelry. You never buy me any jewelry."

"If you make your own money and pay your taxes you can go to Africa or buy jewelry."

"I'd rather have both," Miss Mary said.

"Bravo, Miss Mary," Willie said. "What type of jewelry is it he refuses to buy?"

"Any good sound jewels."

"Diamonds are what she really wants."

"I know a chap knows all about diamonds," Willie said. "In the end they're cheaper than aircraft too."

"I don't believe you have as much fun with them."

"In the end though they say the safety factor is higher."

"I just want them to have them," Miss Mary said. "Everyone has them except me. That's not fair. Is it, Willie?"

"No," he said. "Perhaps we ought to have lunch, Miss Mary, and Papa and I get our time in. I can call Kimberley for you when I get back to Nairobi."

"I must write that nice girl and try to get her out here. All she needs is one personal boy to look after her. We could meet her in Nairobi and fly her in."

"We could charter a DC-3 for her baggage and her jewels."

"Land a Dakota anywhere," Willie said. "We might lengthen the strip just as a gesture."

"I'll start carrying it across the road tomorrow."

"Make it homey to have more aircraft about. No chance of getting the diaphanous one out and have her sing at nights in front of the fire? 'Get along, little doggies.' Songs like that?"

"We might have gotten her out when she was broke," I said. "I don't think there's much chance now that she's in the money again."

"Don't despair, Papa," Willie said. "We could run her up some whacking great gaming place to where she could sing and in no time get the lumber down off the mountain. You could pay her by check. They soak the airmail stamps off at the Post Office and it takes over three months for the check to bounce. Meantime she's probably eaten by savage beasts or men even. Keeps singing that one about 'See what the boys in the back room desire' and one day they stampede up onto that great planked stage, call it the Kibo Palladium, and whack her to bits and into the pot she goes. They desire her you see."

"Here's lunch," Miss Mary said. "We couldn't do that to Miss Marlene."

"Make her immortal," Willie said. "Every great artist wishes to be immortal. Gotten it myself since I've been around with you chaps. G.C.'s caught it bad. Wants to be immortal every day."

We were eating impala tenderloin, broiled, with browned potatoes and fresh mealies from the shamba. There was Major Grey's Chutney and tomato catsup and we were drinking fresh cool Bulwer's Dry Cyder Mary had brought.

"We could make her immortal as the Florence Nightingale of Dry Gulch," Willie said.

"Florence Nightingale wasn't a singer," Mary said. "She was a nurse in the Boer War."

"The Peninsular War," I corrected.

"I always keep getting her mixed up with Alfred Lord Tennyson and General William Booth."

"They were a great pair," Willie said. "Those two and W. G. Grace. But you'll find, Miss Mary, that Florence Nightingale will be remembered as a singer. Too many great poets have written about the nightingale. You read them at school. Miss Marlene will be remembered as the Angel of Dead Men's Gulch. What is a gulch, Papa?"

"It's a steep draw. The lower part is like a donga. On the higher part there's a khud on each side."

"A feature of terrain," Willie said happily. "I'd always thought it was an impromptu movement of the stomach."

"Give Willie some more meat."

"Just a little," said Willie. "Then we must get up and play at pitch-and-toss with our well hung mortalities."

"Some dry gulch on a foreign field shall be forever England."

"You see, Miss Mary? I'm from somewhere and Papa's some sort of renegade Wakamba from the great Staked Plain and the aircraft is American but we transmute the Dry Gulch into England."

"You transmute yourselves back here and leave the Dry Gulch alone," Mary said. "Are you taking Ngui?"

"Nope."

"He'll be hurt."

"He got a little out of line about the Baby Jesus. Do him good to see Willie and me off alone."

"He'll be sad."

"Yep."

"Why do you have to talk like Coops?"

"I don't know rightly, Ma'am."

"They had him walking up and down that street in Nairobi but we went to the Travellers Club instead. Dear sweet Coops."

"You saddled up, Willie?"

"Yep."

"Reckon we'll be driftin', Ma'am."

"Drift," Miss Mary said. "Aren't you going to read the cables?"

"Nope."

"I'll read them."

"That's good of you, Ma'am."

CHAPTER 36

When we were airborne Willie said to me, "How's the show going, Papa?"

"They know something's on at Loitokitok but they don't know what. They ought to bag a lot."

"Where do you want to go?"

The green meadows and parklands were below and the yellow-barked trees and the dark green of the swamp were on our right.

"Let's turn about ninety left and have a look at those two roads that come down off the mountain."

"Good."

"They'll be the escape route after they've pulled the trap."

"How's this for altitude?"

"Take her up a little. I don't want to count the pebbles."

"I thought if we just dragged the contours nobody would see us and then we'd fly down a few gulches to make you feel at home."

We worked up the shoulder of the mountain and I studied the road so that I would know it in the dark. There were three places on it that I would not have cared to be jumped at if I were blocking nor intercepted. They were foolproof to trap you both ways.

"Interesting road," said Willie.

"Very."

"Don't think we better go much further up," Willie said.

"Right."

"Hold tight in these gulches."

"Holding."

From a field of dark lava boulders that seemed to stretch out before us like a Doré, Dali, Chirico, *National Geographic* illustration he dropped the aircraft into a small but nasty canyon.

"This a gulch, Papa?"

"Yep."

"I know another gulch better than this."

"Let's get out of this one and try the new one."

"This is better than the new one but this one has more snakes in it than any gulch I've ever known. This is where snakes really live it up. Is 'live it up' correct, Papa?"

"It was anyway. How'd you get to know this gulch?"

"Tell you sometime."

"Let's skip the next gulch and recce the other road."

"Next gulch might come in handy some time. It's got water."

"Good water?"

"Spring comes up in one end, looks like a little trout brook. Disappears in the lava at the shallow end."

"Snakes?"

"Not so many."

"Who uses it?"

"Nobody. Only aircraft can get in. Shallow end's impossible for klip-springers."

"Where is it from here?"

"Hold tight."

"Holding."

This time it was bad. I could see the clear lovely water as we were fighting in our climb against the black wall and the white scattered skeleton of an elephant with both tusks still in the sockets of the huge skull lay by the stream. One tusk was broken but they both were huge. We cleared the wall and leveled off over the lava boulders.

"Flying can be fun," Willie said. "Did you know, Papa, more executives are taking it up all the time?"

"The hell with you."

"That was a real gulch, wasn't it, Papa?"

"That was a box canyon."

"Whole thing's hopeless. I could hunt for a true gulch."

"Let me learn this road first," I said. It had appeared, tree lined, before us. We flew it at tree level and I asked Willie where the trees came from.

"Must be one of the mysteries of Africa," Willie said happily.

There were lorry tracks on the road in patches where it had been rained on. But we saw no traffic.

"Care to land on the road and take rubbings of those tires?"

"No."

"Not much initiative today," Willie said. "Not the trusting type."

"How would you take rubbings of those tires?"

"Like old brasses," Willie said. "Read about it in books. Serious chaps always off on their bicycles taking rubbings of old brasses. Thought you'd be keen for it."

"Do you know many gulches on the mountainside?"

"Quite a few, Papa. Should we work out a few more?"

"Any special ones near here?"

"Not too near. Just the usual gulch around here. There's one rather wizard one but we'd have to cross high up in back of camp to get to it. Has ice caves right out in the black lava desert. Very holy place."

"Have you been in?"

"No. Chap told me about it and I located it all right. Chap went to Zanzibar to die. Very odd chap. Plenty of money. Already dead but still moving around. Used to say he had the largest spleen in the world and a liver the size of a pickled walnut. Where do you want to go now?"

"Let's go across the desert to the Chyulus."

"Very unusual chap," said Willie, climbing a little. "Used to produce a pickled walnut to show the size of his liver. Then eat the pickled walnut. Said any given pickled walnut could do him in. Would eat the walnut and say, 'Ha' and ask for a gin and it."

"What's that ahead?"

"Masai with donkeys."

"Good. Swing wide of them."

"Toward the oryx?"

I hadn't seen the oryx but I saw them now, plum colored as the donkeys and with their straight horns at all angles as they fed and looked about. They were on a large patch of bright green deep grass a cloud burst must have made and the calves were nearly out of sight in the lake of tall grass.

"There are some big heads, aren't there, Papa?"

"Very big."

"We'll give them a miss," Willie said. "Wouldn't want any beast to break a leg."

We moved over to the right toward the blue black of the folds of the Chyulus and even our shadow never came near the oryx.

"Did you see the lion?" Willie asked.

"No."

"He was on my side under a tree."

"By himself?"

"Yes. Well, this chap decided he did not want to die in Zanzibar. Too sticky he said and too many mangoes. So he decided to die in Nairobi. I suggested Arusha but he said too many Greeks. He took to his bed finally and the house doctor cut off his ration of pickled walnuts and he was gone in less than a week."

"Pity," I said.

"I'd flown him both ways to Zanzibar and he told me where this ice gully was and gave me the coordinates."

"Why didn't you go down and look it over?"

"He said he didn't want to be flying around it. Didn't want anyone to see a plane around it."

"What did he have stored there, pickled walnuts?"

"Ivory," Willie said. "I was sure the story would get more interesting, Papa. Seems he was the chap killed all the elephants off the mountain. Didn't make any deals with the Game Department. Didn't make any deals with anybody. Very early-days type."

"The porters must have known where it was."

"Killed the porters."

"Rugged type."

"Very," Willie said. "Rather on the downgrade physically when I first started to fly him about. Loved aircraft. Loved to fly this time of day. Want to go over and see your other flank? It's crawling with troops."

"Let them crawl."

"They're going to close on the railway anytime. Most important junction point. Probably alive with the Mickeys. Might see a pitched battle, Papa. Troops closing in from both sides. No boundaries except the railways. Imagine they'll really fight for the marshalling yards."

"You mean that water tower and switching point?"

"Call it what you like," Willie said. "Don't want to hear the rattle of small-arms fire and the crump of the mountain guns?"

"Let's fly over the shamba and go home."

"Strange lack of interest," Willie said. "Close to apathy."

We had come out of the hills and were crossing the eastern edge of the great swamp. I could see the eland on the hard ground of the prairie and all the streams that kept us from getting at them from the camp. Then it was Lion Hill, high and red with the jaunty palm parasols and then the straight run, by air, to the shamba.

"Do you think he told other people, Willie?"

"No. I haven't told any other people either."

"It changes things a little. Were the porters Kamba?"

"No. Chagga."

"Can you climb? Know about it?"

405

"I know about it but I can't do it."

"We can't find it while I'm with the Game Department. I'd have to turn it in."

I thought about it and we came down over Miss Mary's gerenuk desert and over the heavy bush to the shamba. We came down and I saw Debba and waved and we went up and I said, "Let's swing around once and then go home."

"Plenty of time, Papa."

"Was this character yellow colored?"

"Sort of a dark canary color toward the last."

"Tall?"

"Around your height."

"Old?"

"Very old, Papa."

"Why did he stash the ivory there?"

"Didn't like the price. Never split with anybody. Never agreed with the price. Had sidelines."

"Sure he's dead?"

"Guarantee it, Papa."

"Let's go home," I said. So we came over the camp and landed on the strip and drove to camp.

"What did you see?" Miss Mary asked us.

"Nothing much, honey. We looked at a couple of empty roads that came down from the mountain where they lumber off that big timber and Willie showed me some gulches. One was sort of like Malad Canyon."

"Didn't you see any game?"

"Up north and around the Chyulus and the great swamp."

"There's a couple of cables you should answer. Do you have time, Willie?"

"Plenty of time, Miss Mary."

"Answer these two," Miss Mary said. So I answered them.

"When are you coming back, Willie?"

"We agreed on Boxing Day, didn't we, Papa? I'll try to be here by ten to show the bloke around his domain."

I sent for the saddle of meat for Willie and Mary went to our tent for her letters. We rode out and Willie took off. Everyone's face shone at the angle he pulled her into and then when he was a distant silver speck we went on our way home.

Mary was loving and lovely and Ngui was feeling bad because I had not taken him. It would soon be evening and there would be *Time* and the British airmail papers for the bright reading light and the fire and a tall drink. Too much had happened today. Probably too much had happened in the last few days. Or maybe it was too little.

The hell with it, I thought. I have complicated my life too much and the complications are extending. Now I'll read whichever *Time* Miss Mary doesn't want and I have her back and I will enjoy the fire and we'll enjoy our drink and the dinner afterwards. Mwindi was fixing her bath in the canvas tub and mine was the second bath. I thought that I would wash everything away and soak it out with the bathi and when the canvas tub had been emptied and washed out and filled again with former petrol tins of hot water from the fire I lay back in the water and soaked and soaped with the Lifebuoy soap.

I rubbed dry with my towel and put on pajamas and my old mosquito boots from China and a bathrobe. It was the first time since Mary had been gone that I had taken a hot bath. The British took one every night when it was possible. But I preferred to scrub every morning in the washbowl when I dressed, again when we came in from hunting, and in the evening.

Pop hated this as the bathi ritual was one of the few surviving rites of the old safari. So when he was with us I made a point of taking the hot bathi. But in the other kind of washing yourself clean you found the ticks you'd picked up in the day and had either Mwindi or Ngui remove those that you could not reach. In the old days when I had hunted alone with M'Cola we had burrowing chiggers that dug into the tocs under the toenails and every night we would sit down in the lantern flare and he would remove mine and I would remove his. No bathi would have taken these out, but we had no bathi.

I was thinking about the old days and how hard we used to hunt or, rather, how simply. In those days when you sent for an aircraft it meant you were insufferably rich and could not be bored by any part of Africa where it was at all difficult to travel or it meant that you were dying.

"How are you really, honey, after your bathi and did you have a good time?"

"I'm well and fine. The doctor gave me the same stuff I was taking and some bismuth. People were very nice to me. But I missed you all the time."

"You look wonderful," I said. "How did you get such a fine Wakamba haircut?"

"I cut it square at the sides some more this afternoon," she said. "Do you like it?"

"It's beautiful."

"It's just a good Wakamba haircut. A little long maybe. But you shaved yours."

"Just clipped. Don't you remember everybody was going to have theirs clipped or shaved?"

"Is it popular, yours?"

"It means something I haven't figured out. Then of course there are the holes and dents."

"I'm going to photograph them."

"Tell me about Nairobi."

"The first night I ran into a very nice man and he took me to the Travellers Club and it wasn't so bad and he brought me home to the hotel."

"What was he like?"

"I don't remember him terribly well but he was quite nice."

"What about the second night?"

"I went out with Alec and his girl and we went someplace that was terribly crowded. You had to be dressed and Alec wasn't dressed. I don't remember if we stayed there or went somewhere else."

"Sounds wonderful. Just like Kimana."

"What were you doing?"

"Nothing. I went out to a few places with Ngui and Charo and Keiti. I think we went to a church supper of some kind. What did you do the third night?"

"Honey, I don't remember really. Oh yes. Alec and his girl and G.C. and I went somewhere. Alec was difficult. We went a couple of other places and they took me home."

"Same type of life we've been having here. Only Keiti was difficult instead of Alec."

"What was he difficult about?"

"It escapes me," I said. "Which of those *Time*s would you rather read?"

"I've looked at one. Does it make any difference to you?"

"No."

"You haven't said you loved me or were glad to have me back."

"I love you and I'm glad to have you back."

"That's good and I'm so glad to be home."

"Anything else happen in Nairobi?"

"I got that nice man who took me out to take me to the Coryndon Museum. But I think he was bored."

"What did you eat at the grill?"

"There was fine fish from the big lakes. In filets but like bass or walleyed pike. They didn't tell what fish. Just called it samaki. There was really good fresh smoked salmon that they flew in and there were oysters I think but I can't remember."

"Did you have the Greek dry wine?"

"Lots of it. Alec didn't like it. He was in Greece and Crete I think with that friend of yours in the R.A.F. He doesn't like him either."

"Was Alec very difficult?"

"Only about small things."

"Let's not be difficult about anything."

"Let's not. Can I make you another drink?"

"Thank you very much. Keiti's here. What do you want?"

"I'll take Campari with just a little gin."

I told Keiti what we wanted and he brought it very happily and made the miracle of the siphon splashing into the glass with the red drink under the bright white light.

"Did you go hunting, Keiti?" Mary asked him.

"Ndio, Memsahib."

"What did you shoot?"

"Everything," Keiti said. "We killed everything."

"Did bwana hunt with the spear?"

Keiti looked at me stone faced. I shook my head.

"He shot with the rifle."

"I don't like the spear," Mary said.

"Ndio, Memsahib."

"See that all spears are oiled," I said.

"Ndio, Bwana."

He went back to the mess tent and Miss Mary said, "Why do you try to mix him all up for?"

"He's not mixed up. He loves the spear like everybody else."

"Did you have a big spear hunt while I was away?"

"No. I hunted one night by myself."

"You'll kill yourself doing that."

"No. I don't think so."

"It's probably just a substitute for what you and G.C. do."

"No. It's not, honey. I don't go anywhere that I don't know perfectly in daylight and I don't look for trouble."

"What do you have to do it for?"

"I want to find out things."

"I like it when you're home in bed. Let's go to bed right after supper."

"Good."

"You promise you won't go out tonight?"

"I promise."

So after the supper I sat and read the *Time* air edition while Mary wrote in her diary and then she walked on the new cut path with her searchlight to the latrine tent and I turned off the gas light and put the lantern on the tree and undressed folding my things carefully and laying them on the trunk at the foot of the bed and got into my bed folding the mosquito bar back under the mattress.

It was early in the night but I was tired and sleepy.

After a while Miss Mary came into the bed and I put the other Africa away somewhere and we made our own Africa again. It was another Africa from where I had been and at first I felt the old splitting up my chest and then I accepted it and did not think at all and felt only what I felt and Mary felt lovely in bed. We made love and then made love again and then after we had made love once more, quiet and dark and unspeaking and unthinking and there like a shower of meteors on a cold night we went to sleep. Maybe there was a shower of meteors. It was cold enough and clear enough.

Sometime in the night Mary left the bed for her bed and I said, "Good night, blessed."

She said, "Don't wake up. Stay sound asleep."

CHAPTER 37

I woke when it was getting light and put on a sweater and mosquito boots over my pajamas and buckled my bathrobe around with the pistol belt and went out to where Msembi was building up the fire to read the papers and drink the pot of tea Mwindi had brought. First I put all the papers in order and then started to read the oldest ones first. The horses would just be finishing at Auteuil and Enghien now but there were no French racing results in these British airmail editions.

While I was reading the news a white-headed crow flew in and lit not far behind the mess tent. He was a very bad luck bird according to Kamba belief and it was my duty to kill him as soon as I saw him and especially before breakfast. But I did not want to wake Miss Mary by a shot so early in the morning. So I kept an eye on the crow who was investigating some refuse or other.

I wanted to read, even if it had to be about the Mau Mau by our special correspondent, or about the then junior Senator from Wisconsin, or the things we had that winter to read about but the white-headed crow made me nervous. I remembered the bad luck we had experienced each time we had one in camp. I could try him with the pistol but if I missed him it would make the luck that much worse and I knew how much feathers there were and how little crow so finally I went into the tent and got the old pump gun out from my bed and eased over to behind the mess tent. When I came around the corner of the mess tent the crow saw me and flew and I dropped him beak down.

The shot did not wake Miss Mary and everybody seemed very pleased about the crow and Ngui cut off his head with his panga. But nobody touched him and they left him there and the early breeze off the mountains blew his feathers and I went back to the airmail papers. I wished that I knew about British football of which there was a great spate of results but it was too late to learn.

I started to sort out the duties. There were the two widely separated Masai manyattas that had lion trouble. I could not get the hunting car to within ten miles of either one so I decided to send Arap Meina with the truck and a detail of boulder lifters and stone rollers to see how far he could get in and scout the lion situation out and see how much work the Masai were prepared to do so that we could get a Land Rover or a truck in. That would be two days scouting for him on the two projects and I could not afford to have the truck away too many hours of the day.

I expected the Informer in and I hoped he would show up so I could deal with him before Mary should wake and come over for breakfast. The cold night had made me very hungry and I decided I would eat and then have coffee with her while she had breakfast. As Keiti brought in the breakfast the Informer appeared under the fly of the tent.

"May I come in, brother?" he asked.

"Come in, brother. How is the mountain?"

"Very cold, brother."

"Did you come down with the early lorry?"

"Yes, brother."

"How is the massacre developing?"

"I have news for you. No whites are to be killed. It is a slaughter of the Mau Mau. That may be of course a trick."

"Where did you hear this?"

"All over the town."

"Have the Kikuyu who work in the forest heard it?"

"How can I know, brother? Most of what I heard I heard at Brown's. It was a working day and there was no one in from the cuttings."

"Did you see Mr. Singh?"

"Yes. He was rude to me again but he asked me to bring you this."

It was another bottle of White Heather.

"Beware of him, brother. He is trying to buy your favor."

"Stupid chap," I said. "So you think there is no danger for the women and children?"

"From what I heard there is none."

"Good," I said. "Doing away with them on Christmas Day was repugnant to me."

"For me too, brother. I dreaded this massacre."

"Are you sure of your information?"

"I only know what I heard. Brother, may I have a drink?"

"Of course."

"I have most of the rare herbs and plants."

412

"Good. I have a present for you when you bring them all. Take another small drink and I must eat this sandwich while it is hot. Have you eaten?"

"Yes, brother."

The sandwich of fried egg with a slice of raw onion and catsup was very good. The Informer looked hungry and I urged him to go and get something to eat at the cook fire but he said, "They do not like me there."

"I'll get something for you here."

"They would like that less."

"I'll order one of these sandwiches and you can take it with you on your botany expedition."

I knew that if Miss Mary came out and found me eating breakfast with the Informer it would not make her happy.

"Have you enough eggs?" the Informer asked.

"Plenty."

I ordered the sandwich and the Informer had a small drink. "For my stomach," he said, "and so I can know the plants faster."

"Don't get too fast on the plants, brother. I don't want you confusing the deadly nightshade with cannabis indica."

"What does the deadly nightshade look like?"

"You'll recognize it all right by the taste. It tastes like the spitting cobra."

"Will it kill me if I handle it?"

"I don't think so."

"I have quite a big arrow-poison tree and four sorts of bhang."

"Who is your preceptor?"

"I take the old arrow-poison maker. He was in some trouble and he came here many years ago. You know him. You have given him medicine for his back."

I knew him well and no medicine was going to cure his back where he had been beaten to death but had recovered. Sloan's Liniment made his back feel better though on mornings when the cold came off the snow on the mountain when it had rained, cold, on the plateau and there was no sun all day. The old horse liniment warmed him inside where no fire could reach and I had cared for him many times but never asked him who had beaten him. They were old wounds and he must have been beaten until both kidneys had been broken.

"Who beat him?"

"Game Scouts and police."

"Kamba Game Scouts?"

"I never asked him. Do you wish to know?"

"No," I said. "Here is the sandwich." I wrapped it in *The Economist*. "Read this at lunch," I said. "It's invaluable if you have any long-term investment problems or if you want the true gen on the U.S. economic position. There are even little jokes in it if you are an economist."

"Are you sure you are through with it?"

"Quite. It's straightened me out completely."

He left, saluting smartly, his onion and fried egg sandwich wrapped in *The Economist* tucked under his left arm like a dispatch case.

"Remember we don't want the best. We want the impossible."

"Yes, brother," he said. "The impossible."

Well, I thought, that's a good start for the morning at the foot of the mountain. So I went to see if Miss Mary was awake and she was up and dressed, fresh and shining and putting drops in her eyes.

"How are you, darling? How did you sleep?"

"Wonderfully," I said. "And you?"

"Until just this minute. I went right back to sleep when Mwindi brought the tea."

I held her in my arms feeling her fresh early morning shirt and her lovely build. Picasso had called her my Pocket Rubens once and she was a Pocket Rubens now but trained down to 112 pounds and she had never had a Rubens face and now I felt her clean, freshly washedness that enclosed the Pocket Rubens and whispered something to her.

"Oh yes and you?"

"Yes."

"Isn't it wonderful to be here alone with our own mountain and our lovely country and nothing to spoil it?"

"Yes. Come on and get your breakfast."

She had a proper breakfast with impala liver broiled with bacon and a half of papaya from town with lemon to squeeze on it and two cups of coffee. I drank a cup of coffee with tinned milk but no sugar and would have taken another cup but I did not know what we were going to do and I did not want coffee sloshing in my stomach whatever we did.

"Did you miss me?"

"Oh yes."

"I missed you terribly but there were so many things to do. There wasn't any time at all really."

"Did you see Pop?"

"No. He didn't come into town and I didn't have any time nor any transport to get out there."

"Did you see G.C.?"

"I told you he was in one evening."

414

"I remember now. You dined at the New Stanley grill and went out somewhere and Alec was difficult."

"Yes. G.C. said for you to use your own judgment but adhere strictly to the scheme as outlined. He made me memorize it."

"Is that all?"

"That's all. I memorized it. He's invited Wilson Blake down for Christmas. They get in the night before. He says for you to be prepared to like Wilson Blake."

"Did he make you memorize that?"

"No. It was just a remark. I asked him if it was an order and he said no that it was a hopeful suggestion."

"I'm open to suggestion. How was G.C.?"

"He wasn't difficult in the same way Alec was. But he's tired. He says he misses us and he's very outspoken with people."

"How?"

"I think fools are beginning to annoy him and he's rude to them."

"Poor G.C.," I said.

"You're both quite a bad influence on each other."

"Maybe," I said. "Maybe not."

"Well, I think you're a bad influence on him."

"Didn't we go into this once or twice before?"

"Not this morning," Miss Mary said. "Certainly not recently. Did you write anything while I was away?"

"Very little."

"Didn't you write any letters?"

"No. Oh yes. I wrote G.C. once."

"What did you do with all your time?"

"Small tasks and routine duties. I made a trip to Loitokitok after we killed the unfortunate leopard."

"Well, this morning we are going to get the real Christmas tree and that will be something accomplished."

"Good," I said. "We'll have to get one we can bring back in the hunting car. I've sent away the truck."

"We're going to get that one that I picked out."

"Good. Did you find out what sort of tree it is?"

"No. But I'll find it in the tree book."

"Good. Let's go and get it."

"I'll need a little time first after the coffee."

We started out, finally, to get the tree. Keiti was with us and we had shovels, pangas, sacking for the roots of the tree, large guns and small guns in the rack across the back of the front seat and I had told Ngui to bring four bottles of beer for us and two of Coca-Cola for the Moslems. We were clearly out to accomplish and except for the nature of the tree, which would make an elephant drunk for two days if he ever ate it, we were out to accomplish something so fine and so blameless that I might write about it for some religious publication.

We were all on our good behavior and we noted tracks without commenting on them. We read the record of what had crossed the road that night and I watched sand grouse flighting in long wavering wisps to the water beyond the salt flats and Ngui watched them too. But we did not comment. We were hunters but this morning we were working for the Forestry Department of Our Lord the Baby Jesus.

Actually we were working for Miss Mary so we felt no great shifting in our allegiance. We were all mercenaries and it was clearly understood that Miss Mary was not a missionary. She was not even under Christian orders; she did not have to go to church as other memsahibs did and this business of the tree was her shauri as the lion had been.

We went into the deep green and yellow trunked forest by our old road that had become overgrown with grass and weeds since we had been over it last. Coming out in the glade where the silvery leafed trees grew, Ngui and I made a circle, he one way and I the other, to check if the rhino and her calf were in the bush. We found nothing but some impala and I found the track of a very big leopard. He had been hunting along the edge of the swamp. I measured the pugmarks with my hand and we went back to join the tree diggers.

We decided that only so many could dig at a time and since Keiti and Miss Mary were both issuing orders we went over to the edge of the big trees and sat down and Ngui offered me his snuff box. We both took snuff and watched the forestry experts at their work. They were all working very hard except Keiti and Miss Mary. It looked to us as though the tree would never fit into the back of the hunting car but when they finally had it dug out it was obvious it would and that it was time for us to go over and help with the loading. The tree was very spiky and not easy to load but we all got it in finally. Sacks wet down with water were placed over the roots and it was lashed in about half its length projecting from the rear of the car.

"We can't go back the same way we came," Miss Mary said. "It will break the tree in those turns."

"We'll go by a new way."

"Can the car get through?"

"Sure."

Along this way through the forest we hit the tracks of four elephants and there was fresh dung. But the tracks went to the south of us. They were good-sized bulls.

I had been carrying the big gun between my knees because Ngui and Mthuka and I had all seen these tracks where they crossed the north road on our way in. They might have crossed over from the stream that ran into the Chyulu swamp.

"All clear now to campi," I said to Miss Mary.

"That's good," she said. "Now we'll get the tree up in good shape."

At camp Ngui and Mthuka and I hung back and let volunteers and enthusiasts dig the hole for the tree. Mthuka drove the car over out of the shade when the hole was dug and the tree was unloaded and planted and looked very pretty and gay in front of the tent.

"Isn't it lovely?" Miss Mary said and I agreed that it was.

"Thank you for bringing us home such a nice way and for not worrying anybody about the elephants."

"They wouldn't stop there. They have to go south to have good cover and feed. They wouldn't have bothered us."

"You and Ngui were smart about them."

"They are those bulls we saw from the aircraft. They were smart. We weren't smart."

"Where will they go now?"

"They might feed a while in the forest by the upper marsh. Then they'll cross the road at night and get up into that country toward Amboseli that the elephant use."

"I must go and see they finish properly."

"I'm going up the road."

"Your fiancée is over under the tree with her chaperone."

"I know. She brought us some mealies. I'm going to give her a ride home."

"Wouldn't she like to come and see the tree?"

"I don't think she would understand."

"Stay at the shamba for lunch if you like."

"I haven't been asked," I said.

"Then you'll be back for lunch?"

"Before."

CHAPTER 38

Mthuka drove the car over to the Waiting Tree and told Debba and the widow to get in. The widow's little boy bumped his head against my stomach and I patted it. He got into the back seat with Debba and his mother but I stepped down and had Debba come and sit in the front seat. She had been a brave girl to come to the camp, bringing the mealies and to stay at the Waiting Tree until we had come in and I did not want her to ride back to the shamba in any but her usual place. But Miss Mary being so nice about the shamba had put us all on our honor or as though we had given our parole.

"Did you see the tree?" I asked Debba. She giggled. She knew what sort of a tree it was.

"Maiz muy bueno," she said.

"Como tú."

"No hay remedio," she said politely.

"How's the meat?"

"Terminado."

This word too she had learned very early but it was a single word and sad and had nothing of the splendor of "No hay remedio," and she had cut it, sometimes, to the length of a Kamba word and would say, "No termi. No termi. Hapana termi."

"We will go and shoot again."

"Ndio." She sat up very straight as we drove past the outer huts and stopped under the big tree. I got down to see if the Informer had any botanical specimens ready to transport but could locate nothing. He probably has them in the herbarium, I thought. When I came back Debba was gone and Ngui and I got in the car and Mthuka asked where we were going.

"Na campi," I said. Then thought and added, "By the big road."

We might see one of the troops of baboons by the big road. I had not done any proper vermin control lately and I thought I should get a little ahead of the vermin before G.C. came. Then too I might possibly run into Arap Meina. But thinking it over I knew it was too early for that. We drove across the stream that fed the swamp at the sandy ford and seeing no baboons turned around where the southwest road cut in and turned back toward camp.

It was still early for lunch and so we stopped in the shade of one of the very tall trees and opened a quart of beer and a tin of kipper snacks. I had corrupted Ngui into eating the false black heavily salted caviar we could buy tinned in the Indian dukas and he and I had both gotten to be minor addicts of it. Mthuka would not eat it but he loved kipper snacks and Norwegian sprats. We always drank the oil from the empty tins. The sprats and snacks were good and ceremonious food but Ngui and I knew how the false salted caviar made the beer even more wonderful than it was.

Today we were in suspense, suspended between our new African Africa that we had dreamed and invented and the old Africa and the return of Miss Mary. Soon there would be the return of whatever Game Scouts G.C. brought and the presence of the great Wilson Blake who could enunciate policy and move us or throw us out or close an area or see that someone got six months as easily as we could take a piece of meat to the shamba.

No one of us was very cheerful but we were relaxed and not unhappy. We would kill an eland to have for Christmas Day and I was going to try to see that Wilson Blake had a good time. G.C. had asked that I try to like him and I would try. When I had met him I had not liked him but that had probably been my fault. I had tried to like him but probably I had not tried hard enough. Perhaps I was getting too old to like people when I tried. Pop never tried to like them at all. He was civil or moderately civil and then observed them through his blue, slightly bloodshot and hooded eyes without seeming to see them. He was watching for them to make a mistake.

Sitting in the car under the tall tree on the hillside I decided to do something special to show my liking and appreciation for Wilson Blake. There was not much in Loitokitok he would care for and I could not picture him as truly happy at a party given for him in one of the illegal Masai drinking shambas nor in the back of Mr. Singh's. I had grave doubts if he and Mr. Singh would get on too well. I knew what I would do. It was absolutely an ideal present. We would charter Willie to fly Mr. Blake over the Chyulus and all of his domain that he had never seen. I could not think of a finer nor more useful present and I began to like Mr. Blake and to give him almost Most-Favored-Nation status. I would not go along but would stay modestly and industriously at home photographing my botanical specimens perhaps or identifying finches while G.C. and Willie and Miss Mary and Mr. Blake worked out the country.

"Kwenda na campi," I told Mthuka and Ngui opened another bottle of beer so that we would be drinking while we crossed the stream at the ford. This was a very lucky thing to do and we all had a drink from the bottle while we watched the small fish in the pool above the long ripple of the ford. There were good catfish in the stream but we were too lazy to fish.

Miss Mary was waiting under the shade of the double fly of the mess tent. The back of the tent was up and the wind blew new and cool from the mountain.

"Weren't you quite a while at the shamba?"

"No. We drove up the big road a way and waited for baboons."

"Were there any?"

"Not today."

"Did you shoot many while I was away?"

"No. None I think."

"What did you do mostly?"

"Hunted and scouted the buff."

"Where are they now? I feel out of everything. It's as though I had been away a year."

"They are probably back in the forest south of where we got the tree today. But I didn't see their tracks this morning."

"Where could they be?"

"They might have been up at the upper end of the swamp. There's fine feed there now."

"Are you going to kill the huge old bull?"

"I don't know now. I've seen him quite close a couple of times and everybody is so fond of him. He hasn't been run out of the herd and the herd protects him. I don't want to kill him."

"How close have you been to them?"

"Once pretty close. Once very close."

"How did you get so many scratches? You're scratched all over. Some of them are bad."

"They're not bad. Mwindi put Mercurochrome on all of them."

"He said your feet were bad and that I should look after them. Are they bad?"

"Not now. They're fine."

"Mwindi says too much new religion. You go barefoot too much. He says Charo is frightened that you are all crazy."

"Charo isn't frightened of that. Maybe he's frightened of the new religion."

"I'd be frightened of it if I didn't know it was a joke."

"It's not a joke."

420

"Mwindi says that you have declared a holy war."

"Mwindi is mixed up. He's just an all-mixed-up elderly Moslem. Ask him what religion the people were who first raided the Kamba from the coast. No don't ask him anything. Did he tell you all this himself?"

"I asked him how things had been and he was full of the subject."

"Tell him there is no holy war. He's truly mixed up on that, I promise you."

"And you're not going to hang anybody?"

"Nobody."

"Good. And your feet are really all right?"

"Fine. They're perfect."

"I hate it when you have pussy things under Band-Aids."

"They were washed carefully and touched with Merthiolate and then I put bismuth-formic-iodide powder on them. You know the tin. And clean socks. I've dressed them once since and they were fine."

"Mwindi's worried about you hunting barefoot and going out nights."

"Mwindi's an old woman. I took my boots off once because they squeaked and the reason they squeaked was his fault for not dubbing them properly. He's too bloody righteous."

"It's easy to call someone righteous when they're looking after your own good."

"Leave it at that."

"Well why is it that you take so many precautions and sometimes you don't take any at all?"

"Because sometimes they signal possibility of bad peoples and then you hear they're somewhere else. I always take what precautions we need."

"But when you go out by yourself nights."

"Someone sits up with you and the guns and there are always the lights. You're always guarded."

"But why do you go out?"

"I have to go out."

"But why?"

"Because the time is getting short. How do I know when we can get back? How do I know we'll ever get back?"

"I worry about you."

"You're usually sound asleep when I go out and sound asleep when I come back."

"I'm not always. Sometimes I touch the cot and you're not there."

"Well I can't go now until there's a moon and the moon gets up very late now."

"Do you really want to go so much?"

"Yes, truly, honey. And I always have somebody keep guard over you."

"Why don't you take somebody with you?"

"It isn't any good with anybody with you."

"It's just another craziness. But you don't drink before you do it, do you?"

"No and I wash clean and put on lion fat."

"Thanks for putting it on after you get out of bed. Isn't the water cold in the night?"

"Everything is so cold you don't notice it."

"Let me make you a drink now. What will you have? A gimlet?"

"A gimlet would be fine. That or a Campari."

"I'll make us each a gimlet. Do you know what I want for Christmas?"

"I wish I did."

"I don't know whether I should tell you. Maybe it's too expensive."

"Not if we have the money."

"I want to go and really see something of Africa. We'll be going home and we haven't seen anything. I want to see the Belgian Congo."

"I don't."

"You don't have any ambition. You'd just as soon stay in one place."

"Have you ever been in a better place?"

"No. But there's everything we haven't seen."

"I'd rather live in a place and have an actual part in the life of it than just see new strange things."

"But I want to see the Belgian Congo. Why can't I see something I've heard about all my life when we are so close to it?"

"We're not that close."

"We can fly. We can make the whole trip flying."

"Look, honey. We've been from one end of Tanganyika to the other. You've been to the Bohora flats and down the Great Ruaha."

"I suppose that was fun."

"It was educational. You've been to Mbeya and to the Southern Highlands. You've lived in the hills and hunted on the plain and you've lived here at the foot of the mountain and in the bottom of the Rift Valley beyond Magadi and hunted nearly down to Natron."

"But I haven't been to the Belgian Congo."

"No. Is that what you really want for Christmas?"

"Yes. If it's not too expensive. Do you think we could go to Abyssinia too?"

"Maybe."

"We don't have to go right after Christmas. You take your time."

"Thanks," I said.

"You haven't touched your drink."

"Sorry."

"It isn't any fun if you give someone a present and you're not happy about it."

I took a sip of the pleasant unsweetened lime drink and thought how much I loved it where we were.

"You don't mind if I bring the mountain along, do you?"

"They have wonderful mountains there. That's where the Mountains of the Moon are."

"I've read about them and I saw a picture of them in *Life* magazine."

"In the African number."

"That's right. In the African number."

"When did you first think about this trip?"

"Before I went to Nairobi. You'll have fun flying with Willie. You always do."

"We'll gen the trip out with Willie. He's coming here day after Christmas."

"We don't have to go until you want to. You stay until you're finished here."

I knocked on wood and drank the rest of the drink.

"What did you plan to do this afternoon and evening?"

"I thought I'd take a siesta and catch up on my diary. Then we could go out together in the evening."

"Good," I said. "I have some things to attend to."

CHAPTER 39

Arap Meina was out at the lines getting something to eat. He stood to attention and I told him to finish and then come over to the mess tent. The lorry was in and had gone out for wood. Keiti was sending it for water as soon as it came in. He said with these two lion trips we would have to send the lorry up to Loitokitok for petrol or I could go up and bring a drum down in the hunting car. This seemed the most practical as we would fill the tank on the hunting car too and could bring posho and Christmas supplies.

Arap Meina came in and I asked him about the setup at the first manyatta. He said there was a lioness and a lion, which seemed strange this time of year, and that they had killed five head of stock in the last half moon and the lioness had clawed a man the last time they had come over the thorn boma but the man was all right. Arap Meina had wanted to bring him in for me to treat his wounds but the wounds had not infected and Arap Meina had sifted them full of sulfathiazole. Two Masai claimed to have wounded the lioness the last time the lions had raided and three men had claimed to have wounded the lion. The lions had not returned. Arap Meina had gone out with the Masai, who he said were high-grade fighting Masai and not bubble gum Masai, and they had shown him old dried blood on several stones. He had tracked until they ran out of blood in stony brush country. They left it that the Masai would let us know as soon as the lions came back. He himself thought that the lions had drifted to another easier country and he thought it was possible one of them might have died although the Masai had said they had seen no birds.

They had made the road passable to within an hour's walk of the manyatta and the Masai said they would fix it all the way if we had to go in.

They were very good Masai, he said, and they had fought the lion at night without any stuff to make them brave. He was sure both lions were wounded. But he could not say how badly since the blood was old and had lost its color.

There is no one hunting in the area I thought and I cannot get a report in to G.C. before I see him so I will have the Informer spread the word about the lions. They should work down hill, or across it, but we will hear of them unless they go toward Amboseli. I'd make the report to G.C. and it was up to him to deal with that end of it.

"Tomorrow you check the other manyatta," I told Meina.

"I could have followed them if there had not been rain squalls at different parts of the mountain. Where the manyatta was it had not rained. But two miles away everything was washed clean. So I did not come back for you."

"Do you think they will come back to that manyatta?"

"No," Meina shook his head.

"Do you think they are the same ones that attacked the other manyatta?"

"No."

"I will go to Loitokitok for petrol this afternoon."

"Perhaps I could hear something there."

"Yes."

I went over to the tent and found Miss Mary awake reading with the back of the tent propped up.

"Honey, we need to go into Loitokitok. Would you like to go?"

"I don't know. I was just getting sleepy. Why do we have to go?"

"Arap Meina came in with some news of some lions that have been making trouble and I have to get petrol for the lorry. You know, what we used to call gas for the truck."

"Well it is petrol and it is a lorry out here. I'll wake up and clean up and come along. Do you have plenty of shilingi?"

"Mwindi will get them."

We started off on the road through the open park country that led to the road that went up the mountain and saw the two beautiful Tommy rams that always grazed close to camp. They were full brothers I think and they were nearly always together and they looked up at us as they passed. Then they dropped their heads with their black curved horns that looked almost as big as Grant's horns and their tails flipped steadily as they fed. I was always afraid the cheetahs would kill one of them and we called them the Brothers.

Mary sat in the back seat with Charo and Arap Meina. Keiti was in the back on a box. They were all pleased to see the Brothers and how tame we had made them with the hunting car and the lorry. I worried about their tameness and I thought we would have to scare them before we left. But we did not have to be worrying about leaving yet, not for a month anyway.

Then I began to worry; had Mary said three weeks from now or three weeks after the first of the year? I would hold out for three weeks after the first of the year. There was plenty of work to do after Christmas and there would be work all the time. I knew I was in the best place I had ever been having a fine if complicated life and learning something every day and to go flying all over Africa when I could fly over our own country was the last thing I wished to do. But maybe we could work out something.

In the meantime we were climbing the road up the mountain in different light than I had ever seen before and the desert to the west of the Chyulus was a dark rose color with dust pillars traveling across it and the Chyulus were darker than I had ever seen them.

"Rain," Ngui said.

"When?"

He shrugged his shoulders. He did not know this piece of country any better than I did as we had entered it together but the terrible clarity of the atmosphere could always mean there was rain coming.

"Rain?" I asked Charo.

"Ndio," he said.

"Going to rain, Miss Mary?" I asked.

"I hope not before we get down the mountain."

"It's a matter of a couple of days," I said. "Did you ever see such a strange clear light?"

"Never so close to the mountain. It's been just as clear but never so harsh."

"Do you want to shoot any color?"

"I don't think we could get anything. The desert looks like the Grand Canyon."

"I don't think so."

"I mean the color. There aren't any features to show from here."

"All right," I said. I would like to have painted the desert and the plain and Lion Hill and the Chyulus. But I could not paint. A long time ago I had learned not to suggest pictures to a photographer.

We were up now to where Debba and I had waited for the game to feed out that afternoon. But I had also learned not to think about Debba when I was with Miss Mary and I applied this bit of learning and started wondering about the rain. All the fall rains had been local this year and we had received a couple of heavy ones. I did not think we were going to get any more heavy rain as it was getting late now. But we would see tomorrow.

Soon the tin roofs of Loitokitok were in sight.

"Why did you get so funny about the rain?" Miss Mary asked.

"I didn't know I was funny."

"You were."

"I must have been thinking."

426

"No. It was something different."

"We're almost into Loitokitok. One bad turn, a quick rise and we're in the heart of the city."

"I hate this road when it rains. It's really dangerous."

"Honey, it's not going to rain today and probably not tomorrow. And you'll be back in camp."

"Can we get started back in time so I can hunt on the way home?"

"Absolutely."

In front of the big duka I told Charo to stay with the rifles. Mthuka, Ngui, Keiti, and one of the duka boys could load the big petrol drum and I told Mthuka to check on the posho and carry out Miss Mary's shopping. The duka was very full of Masai and everyone was busy and you had to go behind the counters and find your own things on the shelves.

I had been told to keep away from Loitokitok but this visit for petrol and supplies and Arap Meina's news of the lions made our visit completely normal and necessary and I was sure G.C. would have approved of it. I wouldn't see the police boy but I would stop in for a drink with Mr. Singh and to buy some beer and Coca-Cola for camp since I always did that. I told Arap Meina to go over to the Masai stores and tell what news he had and pick up any news there was and to do the same at the other Masai hangouts.

At Mr. Singh's there were several Masai elders that I knew and I greeted them all and made my compliments to Mrs. Singh. Mr. Singh and I conversed in my phrase-book Swahili.

Meina came in to say that a lioness had been found dead and almost entirely eaten by hyenas and birds by a boy herding cattle out of a manyatta four hours across the mountain from where he had tracked the two lions on the cold trail this morning.

"Which way across the mountain?"

"This way."

"Give the word on the lion."

I hoped that she had been dead before the hyenas hit her but I thought it was a very long way for her to have gone if she were wounded badly enough to die.

"Come and have a drink," Mr. Singh said and we went into the back room and sat at the table under the colored calendar of the Singh of Singhs.

"Did you wound her?" he asked.

"No. The Masai four days ago."

"Are you very busy?"

"Quite."

"How was the White Heather? Did that son of a pig bring it to you?"

"Yes. It was very good."

"This is the same."

"Do you think we should talk English?"

"Sure. I have the two younger boys out there. The big boy is in back. Your good health."

"To your own."

We drank and Mr. Singh said, "Is there anything you would like to know?"

"Yes. Where do you get the White Heather?"

"They are introducing it and I get it at a considerable discount. I am supposed to give it to my important clients as a Christmas gift. Also to all government officials who will accept a Christmas gift. So far none has refused."

"I accept it with great pleasure."

"What would you like to know?"

"Anything new."

"In spite of all the talk the operation seems headed toward complete success. If you keep up this lion business you may have good hunting afterwards."

"You keep off the roads when you shouldn't be on them."

"Right."

One of the younger boys came in and spoke with his father.

"Your Christian Game Scout is outside."

"Bring him in."

He came in and made a salute of dubious precision. Mr. Singh excused himself and left the whiskey and water on the table. I poured myself a very small whiskey and put water in it.

"How are you, Peter?" I asked in English.

"Look, sir." He removed a shoe and held the foot up for inspection. It was clean, the toenails were cut straight across, and the sole of the foot was beginning to harden. I pressed it carefully with my thumb and then examined the other foot.

"Who showed you how to cut your toenails?"

"A Kikuyu who had been an askari. He was in the last war."

I nodded.

"Are there many Kikuyu about who have been askaris?"

"Quite a number in the timber camps of the forest."

"Can you speak Kikuyu?"

"I can speak it a little and I understand more."

"It is an interesting language."

"Do you speak it, sir?"

"No," I said. "Unfortunately."

"I have my spear," the boy said. "It is well oiled and it is hidden."

"You must toughen up the feet more," I said. "I want them as tough as buffalo hide."

"Will we hunt buffalo?"

"When it is necessary."

"I have never even seen a buffalo."

"You will."

"Will we hunt the male lion who is wounded?"

"You heard that?"

"Just now."

"We will hunt him. I don't know whether you will be ready by then."

"If you have no commands for me I will go out now and work at toughening my feet."

"Let us talk for a moment first."

"I had the feeling when we spoke last that you considered me a man for talking and not a man of action."

"I want you to talk now, Peter, with the people you know. I want you to tell of the lions that we are hunting and that there are two more we go to hunt tomorrow. I want Loitokitok to know we do our work diligently."

"Everyone knows it, sir."

"Now I want you to go to the big duka where the hunting car is and to tell my wife Lady Miss Mary that we are ready to leave when she is. Assist her in any way you can."

"Yes, sir."

"You may go, Peter. No, don't go quite yet. I wish you to interpret for me now with Mr. Singh and anyone else I wish to speak with."

"Yes, sir."

We went out into the front room where there was a strong smell of old men and Golden Jeep sherry that had been drunk and sweated into dirty leather. The young men, the warriors, were in the Golden Jeep place next door. The old men were waiting for me to buy them a beer.

I asked the interpreter to ask Mr. Singh to please serve a bottle of beer to these gentlemen. There were four and he opened one bottle for the four of them.

I was brusque but cheerful as befitting a man whose mind was taken up by lions and I asked the interpreter to ask Mr. Singh how much Tusker he could let us have. He said only one case and half a case of Coca-Cola but there was more coming from Kajiado. He would order what we wanted for the Christmas ngoma and hold it for us.

The old men who had been deprived of their dignity by their early session with the Golden Jeep told me through the interpreter that they were sad I would not drink with them.

I asked Mr. Singh in Swahili for another bottle for them and for one for myself. Then I toasted them, handed back my bottle to Mr. Singh after a single long swallow from it and asked Peter to go up to the duka and deliver my message.

Arap Meina came in and asked if he might have a bottle of wine. I told him not while we were hunting lions and he agreed. But he had put in a hard day and refused many drinks I knew and I asked him to come into the back room and poured us each a very small glass of White Heather.

"Go on to the end of town and hear what you hear. When the car comes I will call you."

"I will not drink at all."

"If they offer you beer drink a little beer."

"No. With this in my stomach I am well."

We went outside and I was impatient for I wanted Mary to have her hunt if she wanted it and there was nothing for us to do in Loitokitok now. I had decided I would go to the other lion manyatta with Arap Meina the next day. We would use less gas in the hunting car and this time we might find the lion or his trail. It would be sloppy to send Meina twice alone.

Outside in Mr. Singh's the elders needed a bottle of beer badly and I bought it and drank a symbolic gulp from my own bottle.

Peter came in to say the car would be down immediately and I sent him to look for Arap Meina. The car came down the road with the drum roped and three Masai women in the back. Miss Mary was talking happily to Charo. Ngui came in to get the cases with Keiti. I handed my bottle of beer to them and between them they drained it. Keiti's eyes shone with absolute delight as he drank beer. Ngui drank it like a racing driver quenching his thirst at a pit stop. He saved half for Keiti.

Ngui took a bottle out for Mthuka and me to share and opened up a Coca-Cola for Charo.

Arap Meina came up with Peter and climbed into the back with the Masai women. They all had boxes to sit on. Ngui sat in front with me and Mary sat with Charo and Keiti behind the gun rack. I said goodbye to Peter and we started up the road to turn to the west into the sunlight.

"Did you get everything you wanted, honey?"

"There's really nothing to buy. But I found a few things we needed."

I thought of the last time I had been there shopping but there was no use thinking about that and Miss Mary had been in Nairobi then and that is a better shopping town than Loitokitok. But then I had never shopped in Macy's either and I had just begun to learn to shop in Loitokitok and I liked it because it was like the general store and post office in Cooke City, Montana.

They did not have the cardboard boxes of obsolete calibers that the old timers bought two to four cartridges from each season in the late fall when they wanted to get their winter meat. They sold spears instead. But it was a home feeling place to buy things and almost everything on the shelves and in the bins you could have found a use for if you lived around there.

But today was the end of another day and tomorrow would be a new one and there were no people walking on my grave yet, no one that I could see looking into the sun or ahead over the country. Looking at the country spread ahead and below us and trying to see all that I had seen from the air and fit it into place I knew approximately where the gulch was that Willie had told me about and I knew that was one problem that I did not have. As long as I had anything to do with the Game Department or owed them any allegiance that gulch was the same as if I had never heard of it. There was no moral problem nor any problem of any kind. I was not obliged to report it because I did not know about it and no information had come to me from any paid informer.

It was probably all gone anyway. Maybe the man with the jaundiced skin had made it up as a story. I could have asked Keiti about him as Keiti's memory would go back to that early time. But if I asked about him at all I became implicated in it and Keiti would undoubtedly tell Pop. It was nothing to be implicated in. I would like to have told Mary about it because it was a good story and it was more ivory than I had ever heard of. But I knew I should not tell her nor anyone. I had suggested once to G.C. that I believed ivory was moving out of the country to the coast and Zanzibar and that I believed Arap Meina knew something about it. G.C. had corrected me and said I did not know what I was talking about and that he would back Meina's honesty with his life and his career. This was before I had grown so fond of Arap Meina and I had not distrusted his honesty nor imputed anything against it. I had only said he might know or have suspicions. Now I, in turn, had reached a point where I did not know because I avoided knowing but where I had suspicions.

The British are justly proud of the probity of their officials and of their police. But there had been changes in late years in the quality of both in East Africa and when we had gone down into Tanganyika after leaving the mountain for the first time the scandal of a District officer who had been arrested with quite a number of large tusks of illegal ivory under his bed had been a fresh scandal. Illegal killing of elephants was a very bad scandal both in Tanganyika and Kenya and when I had first run into the arrow-shaft factory operating within a stone's throw of the Game Ranger's tent and the lines of the Game Scouts in the Magadi country I had been very innocent and inexperienced about many things having to do with game and ivory. Now I was trying to be less ignorant and was certainly more experienced but I was trying to keep clear of things I had been told, officially, did not exist. If Meina was pure so was I. Neither Ngui nor I was pure I know, but we would not lead each other into temptation on anything to do with ivory.

Thinking about this and watching the country as we came down the mountain I had forgotten that Mthuka would be thirsty and as I opened the bottle of beer and wiped its neck and lips, Miss Mary asked, very justly, "Aren't wives ever thirsty?"

"I'm sorry, honey. Ngui can get you a full bottle if you like."

"No. I want just one drink of that."

I passed it to her and she drank what she wished and passed it to me.

"I'll give this to Mthuka and split one with you."

"No," she said. "I've had all I want."

Even the secret thinking about the gulch had made something come between us that you could feel.

"I'm sorry that I was thoughtless."

"You *are* quite a lot lately."

"I've been thinking about a lot of stupid things."

"You haven't opened your mouth since we left Loitokitok."

"I'm sorry."

I thought how nice it was that there were no African words for "I'm sorry" then I thought I better not think that or it would come between us and I took a drink of the beer to purify it from Miss Mary and wiped the neck and the lip of the bottle with my good clean handkerchief and handed it to Mthuka.

Charo didn't approve of any of this and would have liked to see us drink properly with glasses. But we were drinking as we drank and I did not want to think anything that would make a thing between Charo and me either.

"I think I will have another swallow of beer," Miss Mary said. I told Ngui to open a bottle for her. I would share it with her and Mthuka could pass his to Ngui and Keiti when he had quenched his thirst. I had not said any of this aloud.

"I don't know why you have to be so complicated about the beer," Mary said.

"I'll bring cups for us the next time."

"Don't try to make it more complicated. I don't want a cup if I drink with you."

"It's just tribal," I said. "I'm truly not trying to make things any more complicated than they are."

"Why did you have to wipe the bottle so carefully after I drank and then wipe it after you drank before you passed it on?"

"Tribal."

"But why different today?"

"Phases of the moon."

"You get too tribal for your own good."

"Very possibly."

"You believe all this?"

"No. I just practice it."

"You don't know enough about it to practice it."

"I learn a little every day."

"I'm tired of it."

"All right. Keep your eyes open for the piece of meat you're going to kill."

"Everybody's watching."

"Excuse me, Miss Mary. I'll watch now too."

"Don't you want some of this beer you opened so extravagantly?"

"If you don't want it."

"I don't want it."

I did not want it myself either but I was not going to think any thoughts at all but just watch for game. It was no place to see game now. But soon we would be going through the country where Debba and I had hunted that afternoon and it was getting toward the time of day when game would have fed out. There was no room in the back of the car for any good-sized animal unless we off-loaded the Masai women and it was quite a way still to the side track that led to their manyatta. For several reasons I would have preferred to find a beast for food later on but I did not think about the reasons because I did not want them to come between Mary and me.

As we came down a long slope Mary saw a big kongoni about six hundred yards away standing tall and yellow at the lower crest of the slope. No one had seen it until she pointed it out and then everyone saw it at once. We stopped the car and she and Charo got out to make their stalk. The kongoni was feeding away from them and the wind would not carry their scent to the animal as it was blowing high across the slope. There were no bad animals around here and we stayed back with the vehicle so we would not harm their approach.

433

We watched Charo leading from one piece of cover to another and Mary following him crouched down as he was. The kongoni was out of sight now but we watched Charo freeze and Mary come up beside him and raise her rifle. Then there was the sound of the shot and the heavy plunk of the bullet and Charo ran forward out of sight with Mary following him.

Mthuka drove the car cross country through the bracken and the flowers until we came to Mary and Charo and the dead kongoni. The kongoni or hartebeest is not a handsome animal in life nor in death but this was an old male, very fat and in perfect condition, and his long sad face, his glazing eyes, and his cut throat did not make him unattractive to the meat eaters. The Masai women were very excited and very impressed by Miss Mary and kept touching her in wonderment and unbelief.

"I saw him first," Mary said. "The first time I ever saw anything first. I saw him before you and Mthuka and you were in front. I saw him before Ngui and Keiti and Charo."

"You saw him before Arap Meina," I said.

"He doesn't count because he was looking at the Masai women. Charo and I stalked him by ourselves and when he looked back toward us I shot him exactly where I wanted to."

"Low down in the left shoulder and hit the heart."

"That's where I shot for."

"Piga mzuri," Charo said. "Mzuri mzuri sana."

"We'll put him in the back. The women can ride up front."

"He isn't handsome," Mary said. "But I'd rather shoot something that isn't beautiful for meat."

"He's wonderful and you're wonderful."

"Well we needed meat and I saw the best kind of meat we could get and fat and the biggest next to eland and I saw him myself and just Charo and I stalked him and I shot him myself. Now will you love me and not go off alone by yourself in your head?"

"You ride up in front now. We won't be shooting any more."

"Can I have some of my beer? I'm thirsty from stalking."

"You can have all of your beer."

"No. You take some too to celebrate me seeing him first and we being friends again."

"We were always friends."

"You went a long way away for a friend and a brother. I'm your small brother too. The one that kills the meat."

We had a happy ride home and when the Masai women got out they shook hands with Miss Mary and stroked her bush jacket and touched her old hat she'd bought such a long time ago in Sultan Hamud.

"It's a shame they didn't see me make the shot," she said. "Aren't they beautiful?"

"Yes. But you wash your hands good with the blue soap when we get home. Two of them are my patients."

"But can you get it from shaking hands?"

"I don't know enough about yaws yet. But you use the blue soap."

"Africa is so wonderful. But there's always something."

"Something or something awful," I quoted.

"Well we haven't had anything awful."

"No and because we're bringing in the old kongoni whole the people who like tripe can have it and all the delicacies and nothing of him is wasted."

"I don't think of him as old. He was just in the very prime of life."

"When you saw him before six other men. How did you do it?"

"I don't know."

I thought I knew but I did not want thoughts like that and we rode happily into camp where the fire was already lit and I could see our chairs set out by it. I stayed behind to talk with Ngui and Arap Meina about our early start in the morning and to see the butchering. When we were alone Ngui tossed me a .30-06 one hundred and eighty grain solid. It looked weathered and I remembered I had seen him pick up something from the heather. He did not say anything and I put the cartridge in my pocket.

He and Keiti opened up the old kongoni buck and we looked at the clean layer of white fat.

"He could be the brother of the other," Ngui said. I said nothing and they went on butchering.

CHAPTER 40

Sitting by the fire with our drinks, wearing bathrobes over the pajamas, and with mosquito boots on we talked about people and problems and there was nothing that had come between us now. I explained the whole lion problem or, rather, the small part of the problem that I was responsible for and told Mary that I would go at daylight, that it was just a routine thing and probably a hundred to one we would not run onto the lion or lions. She could come if she wanted to, but it would just be a tiring job of tracking and if she wanted to catch up on her diary or had any letters to do she could sleep late. We might be back for lunch or we might not and if she stayed in camp please not to wait lunch for me.

She said she had many things to do and already had good pictures of a manyatta. So we had a pleasant supper and went to bed early. I had bad dreams in the night and I was awake and dressed before Mwindi brought the tea. Once in the night my dreams had been so bad that I had reached over and touched Mary but she was sleeping well and did not wake. She was still sleeping sweetly and well when I took the guns out from under the cot and handed them to Ngui and Keiti and we were off.

It was impossible to get close to this manyatta with the hunting car and we had a long walk to find that the lions had not returned and no more stock had been lost. This was a happy but dull solution of the problem and the chief elder of the manyatta promised that they would clear away boulders so that we could get the car up if they had to send for us again.

Ngui was gloomy but I thought it was just the early morning. Finally when we were back at the car he asked me if I had dreamed last night. I told him I had and he asked me if it was good or bad. I said bad.

"Was it about the Happy Hunting Grounds?"

"No."

He grunted. We were all a little shaken that Miss Mary had seen the kongoni and no one else had seen it at the exact place of the other hunt.

Also it had not looked like the place of the other hunt and I had never seen the big tree at all. But Ngui had picked up one of my solids. Solids were scarce and very valuable and were your protection when you were out with the light rifle. Neither Ngui nor I made a practice of dropping them around the country. But worst of all was Miss Mary seeing the kongoni when none of us had seen it. Ngui, Keiti, Mthuka, and I were all worried. Arap Meina did not know what any of it was about but because we were worried he was worried.

Riding home I figured where the big tree must have been and why we had not seen it. It had been behind and below us. That was all right. I could have spilled a solid out of the cloth cartridge holder I had sewn low on each side of the zipper chamois leather vest that I wore against the sudden cold wind or put on when I had been sweating from running or climbing. One of the spaces where they had sewed it at the duka was too tight and I remembered pushing a solid in and out to loosen it. I showed the vest to Ngui and he cheered up a little and said, "Maybe."

But it was a pretty shaky thing when you added it all up and nobody liked it. I would eat the kongoni because Miss Mary was going to eat it and I must share with her but it seemed better if the others did not. There was no use taking chances and there was more game than the country could carry.

So I killed a wildebeest and we left a quarter of it on my father-in-law's doorstep. Debba was not there.

We came into camp at lunchtime and I went over to wash up.

Miss Mary called to me from the mess tent where she was writing and I told her the lions had not been back and that she had missed nothing.

When I came over to the tent and kissed her good morning she said, "Weren't they unloading something from the car?"

"Wildebeest," I said.

"Did you need him?"

"Yes," I said. We left it at that but nothing came between us.

"I'm glad you're home," she said.

"Glad to be home."

"Did you sleep well, honey?"

"Awful."

"Why didn't you wake me up?"

"I touched you but you were sleeping so soft and sweetly that I couldn't wake you."

"If it's anything bad you wake me or just come into bed."

"All right."

"Your brother the Informer has been around with a collection of poisonous and noxious plants and shrubs."

437

"They were supposed to be a surprise."

"We don't have to have them here in the tent, do we?"

"No. We can put them anywhere."

"Let's not just put them anywhere. Couldn't we have a special poisonous plant area?"

"Sure."

"He's brought every kind except a plant that eats little birds. He says he's still seeking that. He has it almost located. He and another very venomous looking man."

"Old Scar Tissue," I said.

"I didn't get his name. The Informer introduced him as a big poison-arrow manufacturer. I think they had a bird-eating plant but it tried to eat one of your father-in-law's chickens and it choked. When did you buy that rooster, by the way?"

"I don't remember really."

"He's not part of the religion is he?"

"I hope not. You haven't heard him crowing thrice have you?"

"That's the smallest he crows."

"Keiti seems very fond of him."

"Everyone's fond of him. I bought him as a surprise to make a chicken dinner. Now he's so popular I wouldn't want to touch a feather of him."

"I think it's quite nice for you to have your poisonous plants and shrubs collection if we find a good place to keep them.

"It's as close as I'll ever come to botany. I missed it at school."

"I'm not against everything crazy or wild that you do. I just don't want anything to happen to you. And the religion does confuse me."

"It confuses me a little. But it has a sound scientific as well as spiritual base."

"What's the scientific base?"

"Overcoming protein deficiency."

"And the spiritual?"

"Eternal life enjoyed in happiness and things the way they were at their best. Also free beer."

"It sounds like quite a good religion. Can I make you a free gimlet or a Campari to enjoy in happiness?

"I'd love one."

"Lunch should be here right away."

In the afternoon we went out on a ride around the country and found by their tracks that the buffalo were back in the forest by the swamp. They had come in early in the morning and the trail was wide and deep-cut like a cattle trail but cold now and the dung beetles were working rolling up the balls of buffalo sign. The buff had headed into the forest where the glades and the openings were full of fresh new heavy grass.

I had always liked to see the dung beetles work and since I had learned that they were the sacred scarabs of Egypt, in a slightly modified form, I thought we might find some place for them in the religion. Now they were working very hard and it was getting late for the dung of that day. Watching them I thought of the words for a dung beetle hymn.

Ngui and Mthuka were watching me because they knew I was in a moment of profound thought. Ngui went for Miss Mary's cameras in case she should want to take any pictures of the dung beetles but she did not care to and said, "Papa, when you get tired of watching the dung beetles do you think we might get on and see something else?"

"Surely, Miss Mary. If you are interested we can find a rhino and there are two lionesses and a lion around."

"How do you know?"

"Several people heard the lions last night and the rhino crossed the buffalo trail back there."

"It's too late for good color."

"Never mind. Maybe we can just watch them."

"They're more inspiring than dung beetles."

"I'm not seeking inspiration. I'm seeking knowledge."

"It's lucky you have such a wide open field."

"Yes."

I told Mthuka to try and find the rhino. He had regular habits and now that he was on the move we knew about where we might find him.

The rhino was not far from where he should have been but, as Miss Mary had said, it was too late to photograph well in color with the speed of film that was then available. He had been to a water hole in gray-white clay and in the green of the brush and against the dark black lava rocks he looked a ghostly white.

We left him undisturbed but magnificently and stupidly alert after his tick birds had left him and swung wide downwind of him to come out, finally, onto the salt flats that stretched toward the edge of the marsh. There would be very little moon that night and the lions would be hunting and I wondered how it would be for the game knowing the night was coming on. The game had no security ever but on these nights the least of all and I thought how it was on a dark night like tonight the great python would come out from the swamp to the edge of the flats to lie coiled and waiting. Ngui and I had followed his track once into the swamp and it was like following the single track of an oversize lorry tire. Sometimes he sunk so that it was like a deep rut. We found the tracks of the two lionesses on the flat and then along the trail. One was very large and we expected to see them lying up but did not. The lion, I thought, was probably over by the old abandoned Masai manyatta and he might be the lion that had been raiding the Masai we had visited that morning. But that was conjecture and no evidence to kill him on. Tonight I would listen to them hunt and tomorrow if we saw them I would be able to identify them again. G.C. had said, originally, we might have to take four or perhaps six lion out of the area. We had taken three and the Masai had killed a fourth and wounded another.

"I don't want to go over too close to the swamp so we won't give our wind to the buff and maybe they will feed out in the open tomorrow," I told Mary and she agreed. So we started back toward home on foot and Ngui and I read the sign on the flats as we walked.

"We'll get out early, honey," I said to Mary, "and there is a better than fair chance we'll find the buff in the open."

"We'll go to bed early and make love and listen to the night."

"Wonderful."

The night started off wonderfully. We were in bed and it was quite cold and I lay curled against the tent side of the cot and it was lovely under the sheet and the blankets. No one has any size in bed; you are all the same size and dimensions are perfect when you love each other and we lay and felt the blankets against the cold and our own warmth that came slowly and we whispered quietly and then listened when the first hyena broke into the sudden flamenco singing noise as though he were blasting into a loudspeaker in the night. He was close to the tent and then there was another one behind the lines, and I knew the drying meat and the offal out beyond the lines had brought them.

Mary could imitate them and she did it very softly under the blankets.

"You'll have them in the tent," I said.

Then we heard the lion roar off to the north toward the old manyatta and after we had heard him we heard the coughing grunts of the lionesses and we knew they were hunting. We thought we could hear the two lionesses and then we heard another lion roar a long way away.

"I wish we did not have to ever leave Africa," Mary said.

"I'd like never to leave here."

"Bed?"

"We'd have to leave bed in the daytime. No. This camp."

"I love it too."

"Then why do we have to go?"

"Maybe there will be more wonderful places. Don't you want to see the most wonderful places before you die?"

"No."

"Well we're here now. Let's not think of going away."

"Good."

The hyena slipped into night song again and took it far up past where it was possible then broke it sharp off three times.

Mary imitated him and we laughed and the cot seemed a fine big bed and we were comfortable and at home in it. Afterwards she said, "When I'm asleep just straighten out good and take your rightful share of the bed and I'll get into mine."

"I'll tuck you in."

"No, you stay asleep. I can tuck myself in asleep."

"Let's go to sleep now."

"Good. But don't let me stay and you be cramped."

"I won't be."

"Good night, my dearest sweet."

"Good night, dear lovely."

As we went to sleep we could hear the closer lion making deep heavy grunts and far away the other lion roaring and we held each other hard and gently and went to sleep.

I was asleep when Mary went to her bed and I did not wake until the lion roared quite close to camp. He seemed to shake the guy ropes of the tent and his heavy coughing was very close. He must have been out beyond the lines but he sounded, when he woke me, as though he were going through the camp. Then he roared again and I knew how far away he was. He must be just at the edge of the track that ran down to the landing strip. I listened as he moved away and then I went back to sleep.

In the gray time before daylight as I sat by the fire with my tea I asked Mwindi if the lion had waked him.

"I thought he was going to eat up the camp," Mwindi said. "He even wake Mthuka."

That must have been with the roar that seemed to vibrate the tent ropes. I went out as soon as it was light through the wet grass and found his pugmarks on the airstrip trail. Keiti and Ngui had both come out too and we all laughed when we saw where he had dug and braced himself to roar.

Back at the tent in the cold misty light I found Mary awake drinking her tea in bed.

"Did you hear the lion in the night?"

"Of course. Before you went to sleep."

"No. I mean afterwards."

"No."

"He felt very strongly about something."

441

"I feel very strongly about breakfast. Do you think this mist will last?"

"No. The sun will burn it off."

"We can get a good early start and maybe find the buff and get good pictures of tracks."

"I wish we had a picture of that python track."

"Maybe we can find one."

"I think he ate enough to hold him for a month. I imagined him coming out last night. But I don't think he'll be out. How did you sleep, honey?"

"I must have slept pretty well not to have heard the lion. I don't even remember getting in my bed."

"I don't remember it either."

We had breakfast and loaded all the photographic equipment and the necessary rifles and the usual supplies in the hunting car. The people who make only motion or still pictures of African animals often speak contemptuously of those who hunt as butchers, if not worse, and they do not mention the number of animals that have to be killed by the white hunter to protect them when they have gotten into trouble nor the rhino they let charge their specially protected truck until he broke his neck finally. No, they never use rifles and they go unarmed and despise those who carry rifles and all who kill but they employ men to protect them and in the National Parks they will let a rhino kill himself pitifully, goaded into charging again and again to make a non-killing picture with no cruelty in it.

We needed our rifles for many purposes. I had not planned to shoot anything. But you could not tell. You could not tell what would happen on any day when you started out in the country there at the foot of the mountain, nor any night, I thought. I was looking forward to the moon when I could go out at night again.

We stopped the car just outside of camp and I showed Mary the big lion's tracks and where he had held onto the earth when he had roared. We followed him on foot for a way and she was excited at how he had liked to walk in the trail we had made. He followed the trail well up past the landing strip and then turned off to the east. The sun was well up now and I thought we might work to the east of him and with the sun behind us we might see him then. We could always see if we might be able to get up to him to take pictures.

We were back in the car and there was much game now, zebra and wildebeest and many Grant's gazelle. We were not trailing the lion but only trying to keep to the eastward of where he might have gone. Twice there were clumps of vultures in trees but there was no kill. They were only drying their wings in the sun after the cold wet mist.

Then Mary saw something that none of us saw and put her hand on Mthuka's shoulder for him to stop. None of us had seen it but there it was, a heavyset oryx bull in the herd of zebra and wildebeest. With the glasses I could see his gray plum-colored flanks and his thickset shoulders and the dark mask on his face and the black stripes that ran down from his eyes and his straight heavy based horns grooved round like black ivory that slanted up and back from his head. He dropped his head and fed.

Mary and Charo were out of the car and had started their stalk along the edge of the bush keeping into the sun from the feeding game. There was no wind. I watched Mary work to within good range. Then she and Charo were out of sight behind some bush and there was the noise of the shot and then the sound of the bullet striking. When the sound of the bullet came the oryx stiffened on his legs and his head came up and his horns swept back. He seemed to shake and tremble and then he went over on his side and I remember seeing his unshod hooves kicking.

We all came up as the wildebeest and the zebra galloped off. I was very proud of Mary for the way she had seen the oryx and proud of how she had shot. It was a fine old bull and my pride was nothing to hers.

"I saw him and I shot him exactly where you told me. Maybe not exactly but perfectly where I wanted to shoot him."

I could not remember having said a word about where to shoot him and was quite sure any advice had come from Charo or, rather, that Charo had just said, "Shoot," when they had stalked as close as they could. But Mary was truly happy about getting her oryx. She was happy and pleased and excited and proud and many oryx photos were taken and everyone was happy except the oryx. Finally we loaded him into the car to take back to the camp and there more oryx pictures were taken. Unfortunately I did not think of posing Miss Mary and the oryx with Kilimanjaro and his brother Mawenzi as a background but we obtained all the other combinations.

It was rather miraculous for the oryx to have been there, far from his range, and for Mary to have seen him and have shot him. But it was good magic instead of bad magic and Charo had made him legal Mohammedan meat. Now, I thought, maybe she will get her gerenuk too and then we shall all be truly happy for the rest of our lives. A gerenuk, though, is not as impressive in death as an oryx. An oryx, like a statesman, can look almost as good dead as he does alive if you remember to put a stitch or a piece of wire through his lips so his tongue does not hang out.

I knew that I should not joke to myself but should keep on the simple, high plane of the death of the oryx. So I stopped any possible jokes at their source. It was a little like stopping bat-eared fox earths and not really healthy nor conducive to anything so after I washed up I went into the mess tent to have a private drink with myself and get onto the high plane of oryx death happiness if it was achievable.

The gimlet was as good as always and I drank it slowly. There was a large shadow outside the tent topped in silhouette against the canvas by a porkpie hat.

"Come in, brother," I said. "We are celebrating a truly remarkable shot made by the Memsahib versus a splendid oryx."

"A very sturdy head," the Informer said. "I have just congratulated the Memsahib."

"What are you drinking?"

"Anything," he said. "Were you happy with the plants?"

"I've never been happier," I said making his Canadian gin and bitters and omitting the Rose's lime juice which was low.

"Your lady did not seem pleased with them."

"She'll grow to love them. She likes Charles Addams' drawings. She's sure to learn to appreciate those plants."

"There is six months for possessing some of them. Do you think I should keep them at the shamba?"

"No. I take responsibility for them."

"Brother, is there anyone you wish killed?"

"Not at the moment."

"May I have another excellent Canadian gin?"

"As long as I don't see it."

"Are you worried about something, brother?"

"Nothing. How is everything at the shamba?"

"Everything is good but it was very cold this morning with the mist. Brother, do you have an old sweater?"

"My old and new sweaters are worn by everyone in camp. Maybe I will have an old sweater after the Birthday of the Baby Jesus."

"Could you buy me some sort of cardigan in Loitokitok against future wages?"

"What do you hear from Loitokitok?"

"All is quiet awaiting the great operation."

"Who did you hear this from?"

"A lorry driver I met last evening. He brought me a small quantity of snuff and this letter for you."

"That's the hell of a way to deliver a letter," I said.

"I agree. I should have come with it in the night but I was afraid of the dark."

"I have to go now, brother," I said.

"Can I take back some meat?"

"No. I'll bring some later. Then you'll have no trouble with Keiti."

"Papa, aren't you coming?" Miss Mary's voice called. "It's getting late and we'll have no time."

Her voice always sounded forced and harsh when she raised it to shout although when she spoke or sang low it was soft and beautiful.

"I am disappointed at the lateness of the letter."

"When I came, leaving the shamba in the mist before there was sun, you were gone."

"I'll see you at the shamba," I said and went out to the car where Miss Mary was already seated.

"What were you doing? Drinking with that informer?"

"Yes," I said. "A gin and lime juice. I started it by myself and finished it with him."

"Don't you think it's a little early to drink in the morning?"

"Not this morning."

"We haven't much of it left."

"Which? The gin, the lime juice, or the morning?"

"The morning."

"We haven't much of the lime juice left either."

"And I like gimlets so."

"It's all yours. There's plenty of other things."

"I like Campari too."

"The Campari's yours too. If I want a drink I'll have whiskey."

"Whiskey bores me so. It tastes like brown sugar and water."

"That's too bad," I said and remembered the old days and how you looked forward to the one beyond all price.

445

CHARACTERS

Following the lead of Patrick Hemingway's abridged edition *True at First Light,* as an aid to readers we append a list of characters with brief descriptions. When Ernest Hemingway changed names in the writing of the manuscript, we regularized and used the names he later settled on and presumably intended to make consistent. For instance, he began by naming the professional hunting guide Wilson Harris; then, perhaps remembering that he had used that name (hyphenated) for the Englishman who joined Jake Barnes and Bill Gorton trout fishing in *The Sun Also Rises,* he switched to Philip Percival, the actual name of Hemingway's guide for his 1933–34 and 1953–54 East African safaris.

The narrator, Ernest Hemingway, is nicknamed *Pop, Papa, Big Kitten,* and *General.* Hemingway was designated Honorary Game Warden by the Kenya Game Department.

Arap Meina (sometimes humorously called *Arab Minor*) is a scout for the Kenya Game Department under G.C.'s command.

Wilson Blake is a government administrator, the "D.C." or District Commissioner.

Charo is a mzee (respected elder) and Mary's devoted gunbearer.

Chungo is an African game scout in G.C.'s command; he is much admired by Miss Mary.

Debba is the young Wakamba woman with a strong mutual attraction to Papa, who sometimes refers to her facetiously as his *fianceé.*

Harry Dunn (not the young policeman Harry) is a senior police officer of the district in Kenya in which the Hemingways hunt and are camped.

G.C., or *Gin Crazed,* is the name Hemingway bestowed on the game warden of the district containing the Hemingways' safari camp. G.C. was based on Denis Zaphiro, a Londoner, a veteran of World War II in Africa, and a good friend of the Hemingways, whom he visited in Cuba in 1957. He is sometimes referred to as *Bwana Game* and sometimes as *Duke*.

Harry is a young and inexperienced policeman.

The Informer (as he is titled), *Reginald*, is a manipulative Masai police agent.

Keiti is the headman of Philip Percival's safari crew. "He loved his master and his master loved him."

Mahdi is the title of the Islamic messiah.

Mary, or *Miss Mary* or *the Memsahib*, is the narrator's wife and based on Mary Hemingway. *Kittner*, from *Kitten*, is Papa's pet name for her.

Mayito Menocal, cited but never present, is a Cuban friend of the Hemingways and was with them on the first part of the safari that began in September 1953.

Molo, a safari servant, is Ngui's half-brother and the son of M'Cola, Hemingway's gunbearer and blood brother from the 1933–34 safari.

Bwana Mouse refers to Ernest's son Patrick Hemingway, who worked in East Africa in game management and as a hunting guide for twenty years.

Mthuka is Papa's driver and boon companion and Keiti's son. Sometimes he is referred to as deaf, but at other times not.

Mwindi is Keiti's assistant in charge of the domestic safari servants.

Ngui is Papa's gunbearer, tracker, boon companion, and son of *M'Cola*, who had become a good friend of Hemingway's during his 1933–34 safari (as in *Green Hills of Africa*).

Nguili is a safari mess servant.

Philip Percival, or *Mr. P.* or *Pop*, is "the white hunter" who leaves the safari camp to return to his Kenyan farm and other duties.

Simeon is a Masai who hangs around the Singh duka in Loitokitok where Hemingway confronts him. His Masai wife has a "secret" name, "For Kamba Only," because of her preference for Kamba men.

Mr. and Mrs. Singh are the proprietors of a general store in Loitokitok, the town closest to the safari camp and where the Hemingways bought supplies. Mr. Singh is a Sikh from India and his wife is a Turkana from Africa.

Tony is an able African game ranger in G.C.'s command. He is Masai and a former sergeant in the British army.

The *widow* is the sister of Debba and in a relationship with Reginald the Informer.

Willie is a bush pilot of a Cessna flying out of Nairobi. He is much admired by Ernest and Mary for his character and flying skills.

GLOSSARY

Unless otherwise noted, the following words are Swahili, a Bantu language with many Arabic borrowings and widely used as a lingua franca in Central and East Africa. It varies somewhat from region to region in its grammar and orthography, depending on time as well as place.

Words borrowed from English by Swahili but more or less recognizable (e.g., *campi* for "camp," *motocah* for "motorcar") may be understood in context.

adesso (adv.; Italian) now

anake, wmanake (n.) young men

asante (v., pron.) thank you

askari (n.) soldier, policeman

Ay, mi perro (Spanish) Oh, my dog.

bili (for *mbili*) (adj.) two, twice

bini (n.) binoculars

boma (n.) a village enclosure

bongo (n.) African antelope of mountain forests

bubo, bubu (n.) venereal disease

bunduki (n.) gun

buona notte (adj., noun; Italian) good night

bwana (n.) gentleman, sir

chai (n.) tea

chakula (n.) food

chini (adv.) down

chui (n.) leopard

chutta (adj.) alcoholic

cotoletta milanese (n.; Italian) cutlet Milan style

dawa (n.) medicine

dekko (n.; British slang from Hindi) look, peep

dudus (n.) large bugs

duka (n.) store

duma (n.) cheetah

dume (n.) male animal

faru (n.) rhinoceros

fiche (n.; French) voucher or similar document

fisi (n.) hyena

frontón (n.; Spanish) main wall of a jai alai court

gen (n.; British slang) general information

448

halal (v.) to kill animals according to Moslem law

hapa (adv.) here

hapana (adv.) no

hiko (pron.) this

hodi (interj.) hello

jambo (interj.) hello, goodbye, how are you?

jihad (n.; Arabic) Moslem holy war

juu (adv.) above, up

kanga (n.) guinea fowl

kidogo (adj.) small, little

kingole (n.; Kamba) gathering for an execution

kubwa (adj.) big, large, powerful

kufa (v.) die

kuru (n.) waterbuck

kwali (n.) the francolin, a game bird

kwenda (v.) go

kwisha (v., adj.) finished, over

lete, leti, leta (v.) bring or serve

locataire (n.; French) tenant, lodger

mafuta (n.) cooking oil

mama (n.) married woman, mother

manamuki (adj.) pregnant

manyatta (n.) kraal or corral

mara (n., adv.) time, occasion; suddenly

mbongolo (n.; Kamba) magic spell

mganga (v.) heal or cure; (n.) true or good witch doctor

mimi (pron.) I, me

mingi (adj.) many, much

moja (adj.) one

molto grazie (adj., n.; Italian) many thanks

moran, morani (n.; Masai) young warrior

mshale (n.) arrows

mtu (n.) human being, person

mwanamke (n.) woman

mzee (n.) elder tribesman

mzuri (adj.) good

na (prep.) and, with, by

na nu'uaa (clause; Kamba) And, rejoice, but you are dead.

n'anyake, nanake (n.; Kamba) a young lion or man

ndege (n.) bird or airplane

ndio (adv.) yes

ngoma (n.) a dance party

No hay remedio (clause; Spanish) There is no remedy.

noi (pron.; Italian) we

nyama (n.) meat

nyani (n.) baboon

pala (n.) sable antelope or short for impala

panga (n.) machete

piga (v.) hit, shoot

pof (n.; Kamba) eland

pofu (n.) eland

poli poli (adv.) slowly

pombe (n.) home-brewed beer

posho (n.) cornmeal, an East African staple

pukka (n.; Anglo-Indian) genuine, superior

recce (n.; British) short for "reconnaissance"

risasi (n.) bullet(s)

saba (n.) seven

sahib (n.; Hindi) master, sir

samaki (n.) fish

sana (adv., adj.) very

sanlich (n.) sandwich

shaitani (adj.) possessed magically

shamba (n.) farm

shauri (n.) duty, problem, affair

shilingi (n.) shillings; Kenya's currency

simba (n.) lion

sin novedad (phrase; Spanish) as usual

supa (n.; Masai) greetings

Sus amigos estuvo un poco ingrieto (clause; Spanish) Your friends are a little worried.

tembo (n.) elephant

toto, mtoto (n.) child, children

tu (adj., adv.) just, only

tú (pron.; Spanish) you

wallah (n.; Anglo-Indian) person in a particular occupation

watu (n.) the people

woi (n.) wizard, witchcraft

TEXTUAL NOTES

Chapter 2, p. 23

In the left margin is a vertical autograph note: "Throw out or re-write all this EH." The note apparently refers to the writing from the second sentence of the second paragraph to the beginning of the sixth paragraph, but the theme of childhood innocence sometimes extending into maturity begins in the first paragraph and continues through the entire sixth paragraph of the chapter. Regardless of the reference of Hemingway's marginalia, the paragraphs introduce a theme continued in the book.

Chapter 7, p. 69

Here and later Hemingway wrote, "There is no word for sorry in Swahili." But some Swahili-English sources indicate otherwise, citing *ku-sikitika* for "be sorry" and *samahani!* for "sorry!" As noted in our glossary, Swahili is very much a living language, and Hemingway's own Swahili-English dictionary, referred to later, is unidentified by title or author. It well may be that words for "sorry," like many others, were subsequently borrowed or coined.

Chapter 7, p. 72

Here is an interesting problem better presented than arbitrarily ignored. Following the sentence "Debba walked away until we were out of any light and then raised her face to be kissed," the succeeding eleven sentences were marked with a vigorous X. But by whom and why? No other marginalium is present, and the mark is not characteristic of other authorial editing. (But see Chapter 11, p. 97.) Furthermore, the omission of these sentences creates an odd transition. Instead of receiving the kiss, Debba says, "Kwenda na shamba." Here are the linking sentences:

I kissed her and it was like kissing a rock or the fold of a hill. She was hard, steady and certain, and then she did something that was very Wakamba and said, "I will be a good wife. Truly."

"Go home now," I said. "There are many problems."

"I will go home," she said. "I am your youngest and smallest wife."

"Eat well," I said. "And get much bigger."

"How can I get bigger? I am the same size as Memsahib Mary."

Chapter 9, p. 88

Hemingway added a parenthetical note to himself (after "cheese cloth"), "check for British term." Perhaps "muslin" was the generic term used by the British that he had in mind.

Chapter 9, pp. 90, 109

Assuming that Hemingway intended the setting of his narrative to coincide with the late August 1953 to early March 1954 time of his East African sojourn, writing that "Tenzing the Sherpa carried that talented New Zealand beekeeper to the top of [Mount Everest] last year" is in error. Edmund Hillary and Tenzing Norkay reached the summit of Mount Everest on May 29, 1953, and at this point in the narrative the Hemingways are anticipating Christmas 1953. The error may lie in Hemingway's possible confusion of the years of the setting (1953–54) with the years of his writing of the book (1955–56).

Chapter 11, pp. 96, 102

Twice in this chapter lines of dialogue—"What about so-and-so?" and "Why are you not at so-and-so?"—are uncharacteristically vague, as if Hemingway wanted to continue his writing progress before returning to look up or otherwise determine the person(s) and place(s). But no marginalium supports this possibility.

Chapter 11, p. 97

Again, as in Chapter 7, p. 72, a decisive X was drawn through a paragraph with no further marginalia. But the paragraph preceding the one beginning "There were all the technical problems" is clearly written and apropos of the context:

Late in the night by the fire it was not hard to stay awake because there were many things to think about. The shotgun across my lap was one of my oldest friends and a wood fire was an older friend and comforter than any that I knew. They took away my worry and I thought of technical problems and then about what Mary had said about our never being able to know the animals. This was true of course. We could only observe them and learn their habits and customs. But we could know the people. Maybe not. But maybe yes too. I had never sought out nor tried to know anyone in Africa nor any place else I hoped.

Chapter 11, p. 105
Here the manuscript has extra spacing before the noun "roller," suggesting the author's intention to return in the process of revision to provide the specific name. (Rollers are a large family of colorful birds, three of which are common in East Africa.)

Chapter 12, p. 111
In the left margin midway between "Then watching Miss Mary" and "I wondered what a six-week rain would be to her," Hemingway wrote "re-do entire sentence."

Chapter 13, p. 123
In the margin a vertical line with the note "fix" designates the passage beginning "She put her head against my chest" and ending "and nobody looked back."

Chapter 14, p. 138
Hemingway did not provide a verb in the sentence beginning "We on up the track." Since elsewhere he used "drive" in similar idioms, "drove," among other possibilities, seems a reasonable choice.

Chapter 15, p. 152
Between the paragraphs beginning "We reached and passed" and "Then, to the right of the track," Hemingway typed a note to himself in parentheses: "re-write Put in the feel of the rifle and always cleaning the rear aperture with a tooth-pick."

Chapter 15, p. 158
After "Nguili had come and gone and I read," Hemingway parenthetically noted to himself "insert," presumably of specific tactical instructions. In lieu of arbitrarily constructing some, we echo the phrase "to our role" three paragraphs above.

Chapter 15, p. 169
After "the abandonment of a British Protectorate," Hemingway added a parenthetical "check status of Sudan." The Sudan had been ruled by an

Anglo-Egyptian condominium from 1899 to 1955 (presumably including the years of G.C.'s military service). Ethiopia was never a British protectorate, strictly speaking, but the British had fought the Italian occupiers of Ethiopia beginning in 1941 and ending when the Italians withdrew and surrendered all claims to it. The references in this paragraph are to Ethiopia, not Sudan.

Chapter 16, p. 184

After G.C. says "I'm the contemplative type and I was only contemplating," Hemingway inserted a parenthetical note to himself: "Put in about what happened to man who tried to do it with fires at night."

Chapter 17, p. 194

At the end of the paragraph beginning "We waited by the hunting car," Hemingway added the parenthetical "re-do."

Chapter 17, p. 205

In the margin by the sentence beginning "He found life quite hard," Hemingway parenthetically noted "fix," possibly because of the rhythm of the sentence.

Chapter 18, p. 209

After "flight-weary B-17" Hemingway left a two-inch space with a marginal note: "Fill in Glen [?] and Wade [?] in bomb bay, the wireless operator, hysterics, seeing P's school, N. Y." At the end of the first week of March 1945, Hemingway flew from Paris and London to New York. "P's school" refers to son Patrick who then accompanied Hemingway to Key West and then, with son Gregory, to Cuba.

Chapter 18, p. 212

Beginning in the margin from near "The lion made a bound" to "I fired again," Hemingway wrote "Improve the shooting/make lion clearer and sharper," but he made no such revisions here as he did elsewhere in this chapter.

Chapter 18, p. 217

In the margin by the paragraph beginning "We came into camp," Hemingway wrote "Put in the banging of the pots and pans and the dance at the game scouts' camp afterwards."

Chapter 19, p. 224

After "It was a good new book called" Hemingway left a blank, presumably to fill in later. This passage in *True at First Light* does not provide the title but does, after "new book," insert "by Praed and Grant." A check of those names led to the title *African Handbook of Birds* published in 1952.

Chapter 19, p. 225

In the sentence beginning "I went out again with the bird book and identified," Hemingway left spaces after "the," "the," and "and the," presumably to add names of three birds. Again, *True at First Light*, edited by Patrick Hemingway, a long-time resident in and student of East Africa, helpfully provided shrike, starling, and bee-eater, common East African birds.

Chapter 21, p. 265

Frequently Hemingway made revisions by first deleting and then writing or typing in the desired changes, sometimes stylistic, sometimes substantive. Another study of the manuscript may include omissions that are decipherable. Here is an example of an interesting one. After "her own discovering" and before "It is stupid" this passage was X'd out:

> I had known a girl for a long time who cared nothing for anything that I cared for. She had simulated that she had cared for a long time many things . . .

Chapter 26, p. 312

At the end of the sentence beginning "It [ivory] had many other strange and satisfying things," Hemingway wrote "fix" parenthetically. One might understand "for it" to follow the last word "committed."

Chapter 26, p. 315

Between "so many countries" and a new paragraph beginning "I knew this Christmas," Hemingway parenthetically added a note to himself: "For later. All of us killers who have killed so many times and with pleasure and denied it thrice."

Chapter 29, pp. 350, 351

Here is a notable instance of how a seemingly minor editorial change can produce confusion and lose a good joke. As Hemingway is preparing for the return drive to his camp, he reveals that a promiscuous woman has a "secret" name, "For Kamba Only," meaning she has no favors to give other tribesmen. Because of her popularity, she may have a seat in the safari vehicle. In *True at First Light* this passage describing "Simeon's wife" was omitted, but immediately following the shortened form of her secret name, "Kamba Only," twice became "Kamba only," muddling both the arithmetic and tribal identity of the riders.

Here, too, is one of a number of instances in which Mthuka, the driver, often referred to as "quite deaf," carries on a seemingly ordinary conversation with Hemingway.

Chapter 32, p. 364

Here Hemingway edits Pop's "No —— like that can exist for long." Although he had argued with Scribner's not to censor vulgar words from his manuscripts, he here censors his admired mentor.

Chapter 34, p. 383

The phrases "muts aroun the phlegm" and "Muts arouna flem" are the misunderstood pronunciations of Marlene Dietrich's "moths around a flame" (words from the song "Falling in Love Again").

Chapter 38, p. 422

Hemingway had apparently intended to add a further place name or names to the sentence "You've been to Mbeya and to the Southern Highlands and —— —— —— —— twice."

Chapter 40, p. 445

Without any explanatory note, the last sentence of the manuscript ends with the preposition "in," which we deleted to give some sense of closure. Nor have we found indications elsewhere that Hemingway had finished the book in spite of Michael Reynolds noting "1956 April EH finishes the African book" (*Hemingway: An Annotated Chronology*). Yet in Reynolds's *Hemingway: The Final Years* he wrote, "On February 10 [1956], Hemingway packed up the 856-page typescript of his African novel to devote himself totally to the film project" of *The Old Man and the Sea* (294), repeating the February 10 date in his *Chronology* (366). See also Hemingway's "A Situation Report" in *Look*, September 4, 1956, reprinted in *By-Line: Ernest Hemingway*, for his own statement that the book was unfinished but that he would return "to work tomorrow on the long book" (472).

As noted in the introduction to this volume, Hemingway often inserted marginal notes of the dates of his writing, and the last date in this chapter is February 27.

arious

mericans so rich and old that and convinced of their importance and

ower that/reigning princes ~~~~~~~~~ seem like well mannered
            they made
chool boys and many people who had hoped to come to/Africa During the
                                                      East all of
heir lives and who devoted themselves diligently to killing the

ecessary beasts that represented , in big game hunting , so many acade

egrees . These were the easiest people to handle . They were sensible

nd reasonable and devoted themselves to enjoying and savouring

very minute , hour and day of their expensive pleasure . When they were

ot too rich they tipped well , they studied Swahili , and they made a po

f learning the names of those who served them instead of shouting , "Boy

he head man's name was Masaku and no one who called him by it knew that

as a very noble name in Wakamba . Masaku knew it and he also knew he had

o noble lineage but that at his unknown age he could track and hun

s well as any except the talented bad boys who would almost certainly

ome to no good end . That is he knew he could do this
until the time when he would precipitate another

    Things were not too simple in this safari although it is
very happy outfit , because things had changed very much in East Africa .
                              I respected him as I had never respected
he white hunter had been a close friend of mine for many years . the
                                                             however
rusted me which was xx more than I deserved x by It was something

o try to be merit(Y) He had taught me by putting me on my own and

orrecting me when I made mistakes . When I made a mistake he would expl

t . Then if I did not make the same mistake again he would trust me

a little more . He was a very complicated man compounded of absolute

courage , all the good human weaknesses and a strangely subtle and

very critical understanding of people . He was completely dedicated to

his family and his home and he loved much more to live away from them .

He loved his home and his wife and his children . But he was nomadic .

When he was finally leaving us because it was necessary for him
                                            twenty thousand acre
to be at his xx farm , which is what they call a cattle ranch in Kenya , h

told me in the morning before daylight , " Pop I won't say anything
                                      trusted
about the Memsahib . I've ~~~~~~~ her to you for a long time now .